THE WORLD ALMANAC®

FOR KIDS

2012

WORLD ALMANAC® BOOKS
An Imprint of Infobase Learning

THE WORLD ALMANAC®

FOR KIDS

2012

Project Management: Robert Famighetti
New Content: RJF PUBLISHING

Contributors: Emily Dolbear, Matthew Friedlander, Richard Hantula, Lisa M. Herrington, Amanda Hudson, William A. McGeveran
Photo Research: Edward A. Thomas
Index Editor: Nan Badgett

Design: BILL SMITH GROUP
Chief Creative Officer: Brian Kobberger
Project Manager: Carol Thompson
Design: Brock Waldron, Tamara English, Mike Gibson
Production: Rob Duverger, Kim Spiegel, Mie Tsuchida

INFOBASE LEARNING
Editorial Director: Laurie E. Likoff
Senior Editor: Sarah Janssen
Project Editor: Edward A. Thomas

World Almanac® Books
An imprint of Infobase Learning
132 West 31st Street
New York NY 10001

Hardcover
ISBN-13: 978-1-60057-152-7
ISBN-10: 1-60057-152-2

Paperback
ISBN-13: 978-1-60057-153-4
ISBN-10: 1-60057-153-0

For Library of Congress cataloging information, please contact the publisher.

The World Almanac® for Kids is available at special discounts when purchased in bulk quantities for businesses, associations, institutions, or sales promotions. Please call our Special Sales Department in New York at (800) 322-8755.

You can find The World Almanac® for Kids online at www.worldalmanac.com

Book printed and bound by RR Donnelley, Crawfordsville, IN
Date printed: July 2011
Printed in the United States of America

RRD BSG 10 9 8 7 6 5 4 3 2 1

CONTENTS

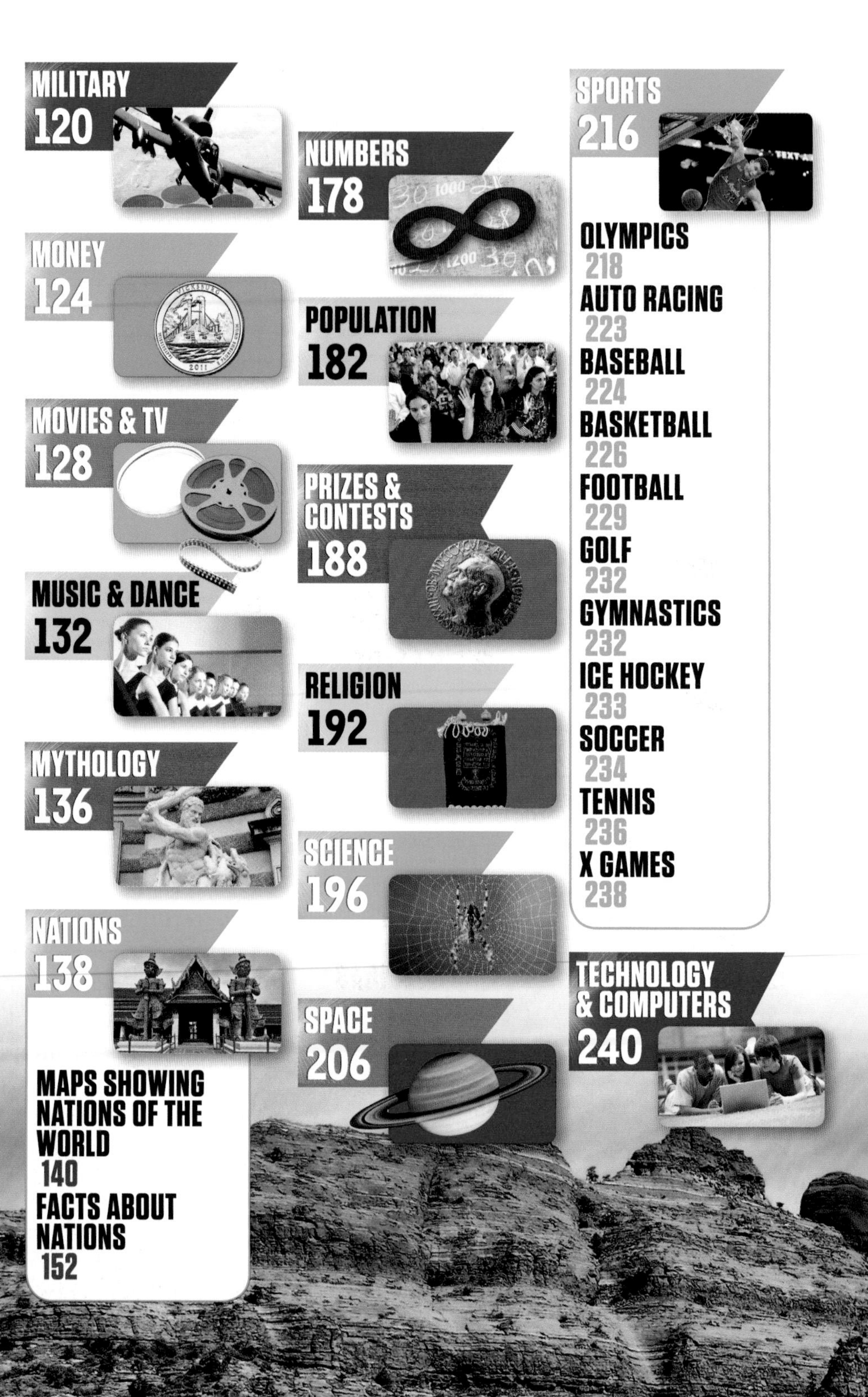

FACES & PLACES IN THE NEWS

PROTESTS IN EGYPT

Day after day, tens of thousands of Egyptians gathered in Cairo in early 2011 to demand changes in the government. In February, President Hosni Mubarak resigned.

QUAKE IN JAPAN

On March 11, 2011, a powerful earthquake followed by a giant sea wave struck Japan's northeast coast. Thousands were killed.

ROYAL WEDDING On April 29, 2011, Prince William, who is second in line to become king of England, was married to Kate Middleton, as the world looked on.

BIN LADEN CAUGHT In a daring raid in Pakistan, May 1, 2011, U.S. forces killed Osama bin Laden, mastermind of the September 11, 2001, terrorist attacks on the U.S. At the White House, President Barack Obama and key aides waited for word of the raid's success.

IN THE NEWS

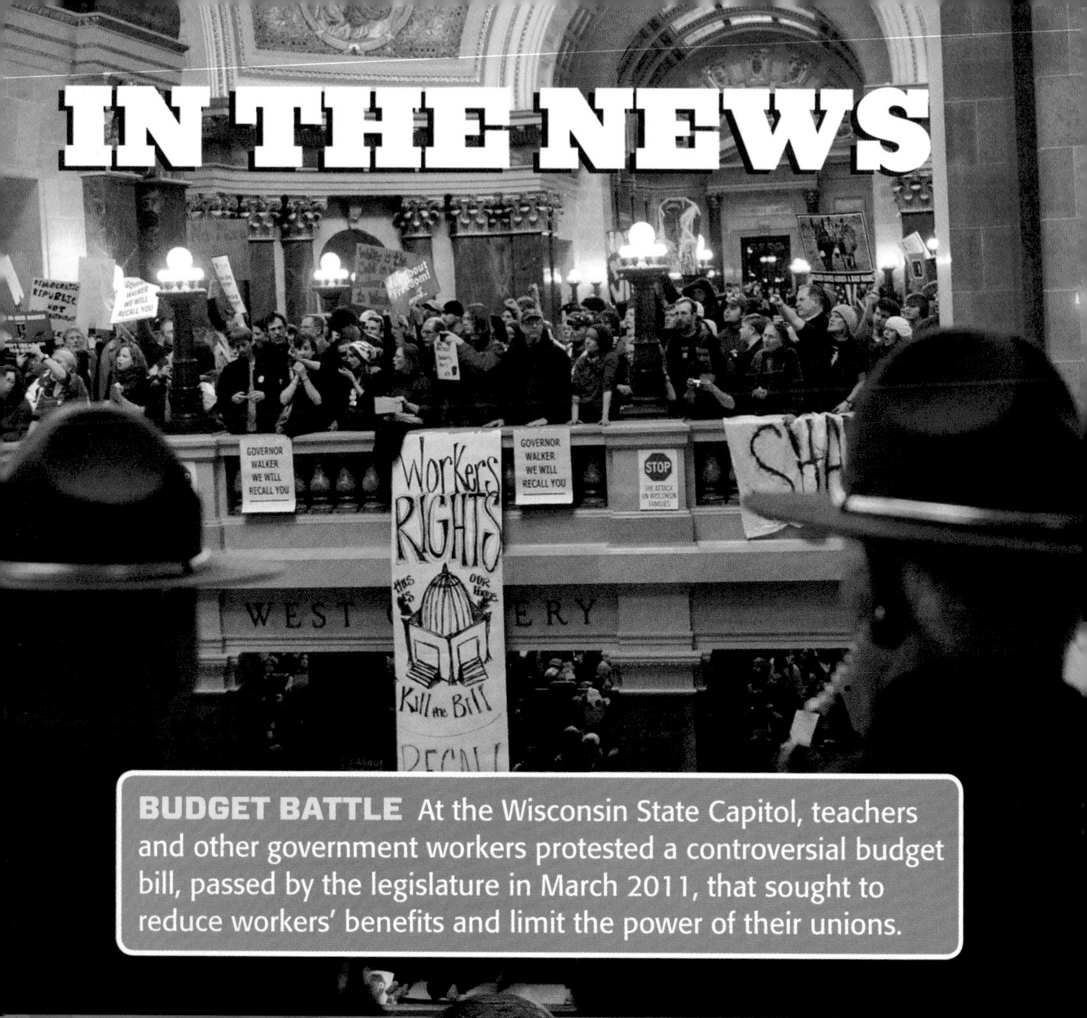

BUDGET BATTLE At the Wisconsin State Capitol, teachers and other government workers protested a controversial budget bill, passed by the legislature in March 2011, that sought to reduce workers' benefits and limit the power of their unions.

NEW LEADER Republicans won a majority in the U.S. House of Representatives in the November 2010 elections, and Ohio's John Boehner took over the gavel as Speaker of the House in January 2011.

REMEMBERING THE CIVIL WAR On April 14, 1861, Union soldiers surrendered at Fort Sumter, South Carolina, and the Civil War began. The event was reenacted in the same place on April 14, 2011, 150 years later.

TORNADO TRAGEDY Many buildings were destroyed when a powerful tornado tore through Joplin, Missouri, May 22, 2011, killing more than 150 people.

TELEVISION

***IDOL* WINNER** Scotty McCreery (left) beat out runner-up Lauren Alaina in the tenth season of *American Idol*.

***FAMILY* FUN** Viewers tuned in for laughs with the Dunphys and Pritchetts on *Modern Family*.

NEW DIRECTIONS The second season of *Glee* was filled with more singing, dancing, and special guest stars—and also tackled important issues such as bullying.

DARK *DIARIES*
Mysterious events took place in the town of Mystic Falls on *The Vampire Diaries*.

MOVIES

FINAL CHAPTER Viewers said goodbye to the kids from Hogwarts in the series' final film, *Harry Potter and the Deathly Hallows: Part 2*.

GREEN GUY Ryan Reynolds took on the starring role in *Green Lantern*.

WIMPY SEQUEL *Diary of a Wimpy Kid: Rodrick Rules* was a successful follow-up to the first movie in the series, *Diary of a Wimpy Kid.* Both films were based on popular books.

COLORFUL CHAMELEON Johnny Depp was the voice of a courageous chameleon in *Rango.*

MOVIES

STAR-CROSSED GNOMES
James McAvoy and Emily Blunt did the talking for garden gnomes in *Gnomeo and Juliet*.

SURFER GIRL
The inspirational *Soul Surfer* was based on the true story of Bethany Hamilton, who lost her arm in a shark attack.

LOVE STORY Jennifer Aniston and Adam Sandler charmed audiences in the romantic comedy *Just Go With It*.

SPARROW RETURNS Johnny Depp and Penelope Cruz starred in *Pirates of the Caribbean: On Stranger Tides*, the fourth movie in the blockbuster series.

MUSIC

GAGA FOR GAGA Lady Gaga took home three Grammy awards in 2011 and continued to make headlines for her outrageous fashions.

TEENAGE DREAM Katy Perry sang in sold-out venues all over the world on her *California Dreams* tour.

BIEBER MANIA For Justin Bieber, 2011 was another big year. *My World 2.0* continued to top the charts, and crowds flocked to his 3-D concert movie *Justin Bieber: Never Say Never.*

LADIES FIRST The group Lady Antebellum had another big hit with their song "Just a Kiss," which they performed on *American Idol.*

SPORTS

JOLLY RODGERS Quarterback Aaron Rodgers threw three touchdown passes in the Green Bay Packers' 31–25 victory in Super Bowl XLV.

NUMBER 3,000 With a home run July 9, 2011, New York Yankee veteran Derek Jeter became the 28th player in MLB history to get 3,000 career hits.

SHOOTING STAR Texas A&M junior Danielle Adams scored 30 points in her team's 76–70 victory in the 2011 NCAA women's college basketball title game.

ULTIMATE GOALIE In June 2011, the Boston Bruins won their first Stanley Cup in 39 years. Bruins goaltender Tim Thomas was the MVP of the playoffs.

SPORTS

CAM-TASTIC! Auburn quarterback Cam Newton was named the 2010 Heisman Trophy winner and helped his team win the BCS National Championship Game for the NCAA college football title.

KIM POSSIBLE After ending a two-year retirement in 2009, Belgium's Kim Clijsters had won three Grand Slam tennis titles by early 2011—the 2009 and 2010 U.S. Opens and the 2011 Australian Open.

HIGH FIVE Jimmie Johnson set a record in 2010 when he won his fifth straight NASCAR Sprint Cup championship.

MARVELOUS MAVS The Dallas Mavericks, led by Dirk Nowitzki (left) and Jason Kidd (center), defeated the Miami Heat in June 2011 to capture their first-ever NBA title.

ANIMALS

What is the smallest bird in the world? → page 26

Furry or scaly, creepy or crawly, schoolbus-sized or microscopic—animals can often surprise us. Here are some facts about the Animal Kingdom.

WEIRD ANIMAL FACTS

KOMODO DRAGON

The Komodo dragon is an endangered species, found only on a few Indonesian islands. It is the heaviest living species of lizard. Komodo dragons can weigh more than 300 pounds. They eat other animals as large as deer, wild pigs, and even buffalo. They are cold blooded and do not have enough energy to chase prey for long periods of time, but they don't need to. A dragon's bite contains deadly bacteria and venom. If an animal is not killed after a Komodo dragon attacks it, the dragon will follow it at a leisurely pace until the animal gets weak and dies.

INTERSPECIES FRIENDSHIPS

Scientists are not sure why, but animals from two different species will sometimes form a close bond. Animal shelters have seen orphaned kittens nursed by mother dogs. A baby hippo was "adopted" by a giant tortoise at a zoo in Kenya. Sometimes bonds even develop between animals who would normally have a predator-prey relationship in the wild, such as a cat and a bird.

LIFE ON EARTH

This time line shows how life developed on Earth. The earliest life forms are at the top of the chart. The most recent are at the bottom. All dates are years before the present.

Precambrian

4.6 billion

Formation of Earth

3.8 billion to 542 million

First evidence of life on Earth. All life is in water. Early single-celled bacteria and achaea appear, followed by multi-celled organisms, including early animals.

Paleozoic

542 to 443 million

Animals with shells (called trilobites) and some mollusks form. Primitive fish and corals develop. Evidence of the first primitive land plants.

443 to 417 million

Coral reefs form. Other animals, such as the first known freshwater fish, develop. Relatives of spiders and centipedes develop.

417 to 354 million

The first trees and forests appear. The first land-living vertebrates, amphibians, and wingless insects appear. Many new sea creatures also appear.

354 to 290 million

Reptiles develop. Much of the land is covered by swamps.

290 to 248 million

A mass extinction wipes out 95% of all marine life.

Mesozoic

248 to 206 million

In the Triassic period, marine life develops again. Reptiles also move into the water. Reptiles begin to dominate the land areas. Dinosaurs and mammals develop.

206 to 144 million

The Jurassic is dominated by giant dinosaurs. In the late Jurassic, birds evolve.

144 to 65 million

In the Cretaceous period, new dinosaurs appear. Many insect groups, modern mammal and bird groups also develop. A global extinction of most dinosaurs occurs at the end of this period.

Cenozoic

65 to 1.8 million

Ancestors of modern-day horses, zebras, rhinos, sheep, goats, camels, pigs, cows, deer, giraffes, elephants, cats, dogs, and primates begin to develop.

1.8 million to 10,000

Large mammals like mammoths, saber-toothed cats, and giant ground sloths develop. Modern human beings evolve.

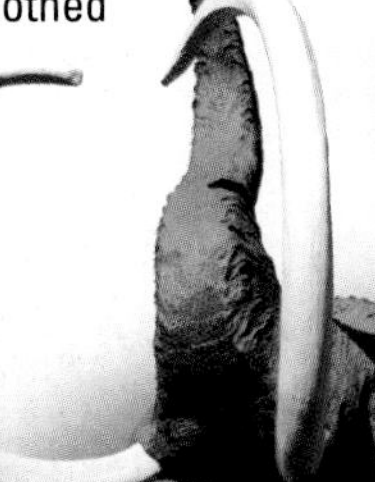

10,000 to Present

Human civilization develops.

ANIMAL KINGDOM

The world has so many animals that scientists looked for a way to organize them into groups. A Swedish scientist named Carolus Linnaeus (1707–1778) worked out a system for classifying both animals and plants. We still use it today.

The Animal Kingdom is separated into two large groups—animals with backbones, called **vertebrates**, and animals without backbones, called **invertebrates**.

These large groups are divided into smaller groups called **phyla**. And phyla are divided into even smaller groups called **classes**. The animals in each group are classified together when their bodies are similar in certain ways.

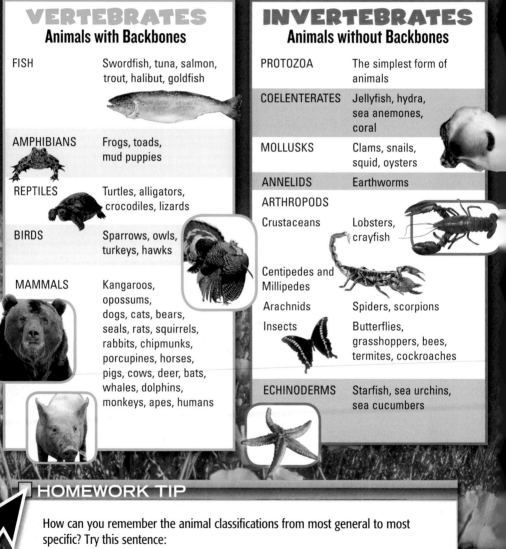

VERTEBRATES
Animals with Backbones

FISH	Swordfish, tuna, salmon, trout, halibut, goldfish
AMPHIBIANS	Frogs, toads, mud puppies
REPTILES	Turtles, alligators, crocodiles, lizards
BIRDS	Sparrows, owls, turkeys, hawks
MAMMALS	Kangaroos, opossums, dogs, cats, bears, seals, rats, squirrels, rabbits, chipmunks, porcupines, horses, pigs, cows, deer, bats, whales, dolphins, monkeys, apes, humans

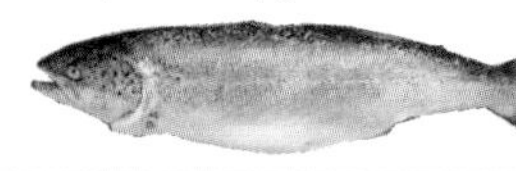

INVERTEBRATES
Animals without Backbones

PROTOZOA	The simplest form of animals
COELENTERATES	Jellyfish, hydra, sea anemones, coral
MOLLUSKS	Clams, snails, squid, oysters
ANNELIDS	Earthworms
ARTHROPODS	
Crustaceans	Lobsters, crayfish
Centipedes and Millipedes	
Arachnids	Spiders, scorpions
Insects	Butterflies, grasshoppers, bees, termites, cockroaches
ECHINODERMS	Starfish, sea urchins, sea cucumbers

HOMEWORK TIP

How can you remember the animal classifications from most general to most specific? Try this sentence:

King **P**hilip **C**ame **O**ver **F**rom **G**reat **S**pain.

K = Kingdom; **P** = Phylum; **C** = Class; **O** = Order; **F** = Family; **G** = Genus; **S** = Species

PARASITES AMONG US

A PARASITE is an organism that usually lives on or in another organism, called a **host**. Parasites usually feed off their host. It's gross to think about, but parasites are everywhere! A common example of a parasite is a flea that feeds on the blood of a pet dog or cat. But there are many other types of common parasites. Here are some examples.

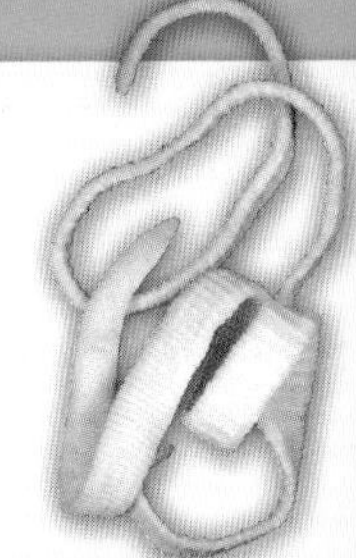

TAPEWORMS live inside animals and people. They usually live in the intestines, because they find their way into a host by being eaten—when food that is raw or that has not been cooked properly is consumed. Tapeworms are flat, like tape, and have hooks or suckers on their heads that allow them to latch on to the slimy surface of the intestines. They absorb digested food, which can deprive the host of nourishment.

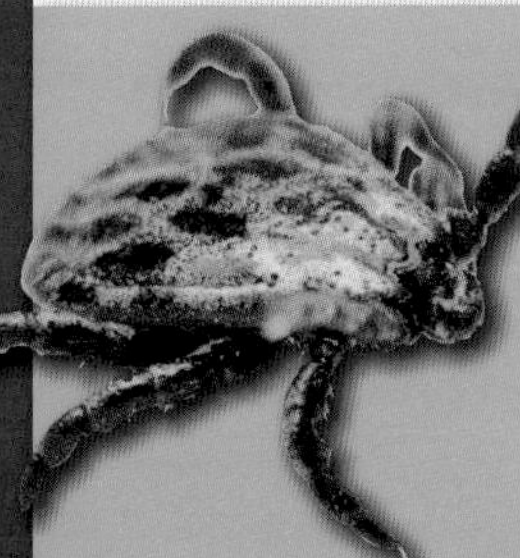

TICKS are external parasites. This means that they latch on to the outside of a host, rather than living inside the host like a tapeworm. They are often found in tall grasses and shrubs, and they can latch on to a host as it walks by. Ticks attach themselves by digging their heads into the host's skin. Then they fill with blood as they feed. Ticks can be very dangerous to humans and pets, since some types of ticks carry diseases, such as Lyme disease.

Parasites Q&A

Are all parasites harmful? No. According to one estimate, the average American carries about two pounds of parasites in his or her body. Most of these parasites do not cause problems. Scientists are starting to learn that some may even be helpful.

How can harmful parasites be avoided? To avoid many types of internal parasites, make sure that food is washed and cooked properly. Wash all fruits and vegetables before eating, and wash your hands after handling raw meat. Parasites thrive in water—never drink from ponds or lakes, and change your pet's water often.

Are all parasites visible to the naked eye? No. Many can be seen only under a microscope. Dirty water is filled with these types of parasites.

did you Know?

The illness trichinosis is caused by a type of parasite called a roundworm. The roundworm usually lives in pigs and certain other types of animals. People may become infected if they eat pork or game meats that have not been fully cooked. Most people with trichinosis have digestive system problems and flu-like symptoms. In very severe cases, though, trichinosis can be fatal.

BIGGEST, SMALLEST, FASTEST

IN THE WORLD

WORLD'S BIGGEST ANIMALS

Marine mammal: Blue whale (100 feet long, 200 tons)

Heaviest land mammal: African bush elephant (12 feet high, 4–7 tons)
Tallest land mammal: Giraffe (18 feet tall)

Reptile: Saltwater crocodile (20–23 feet long, 1,150 pounds)

Heaviest snake: Green anaconda (16–30 feet, 550 pounds)
Longest snake: Reticulated python (26–32 feet long)

Fish: Whale shark (40–60 feet long, 10–20 tons)

Bird: Ostrich (9 feet tall, 345 pounds)

Insect: Stick insect (15 inches long)

WORLD'S FASTEST ANIMALS

Marine mammal: Killer whale and Dall's porpoise (35 miles per hour)

Land mammal: Cheetah (70 miles per hour)

Fish: Sailfish (68 miles per hour, leaping)

Bird: Peregrine falcon (200 miles per hour)

Insect: Dragonfly (35 miles per hour)

Snake: Black mamba (14 miles per hour)

WORLD'S SMALLEST ANIMALS

Mammal: Bumblebee bat (1.1–1.3 inches)

Fish: *Paedocypris progenetica* or stout infantfish (0.31–0.33 inches)

Bird: Bee hummingbird (1–2 inches)

Snake: Thread snake and brahminy blind snake (4.25 inches)

Lizard: Jaragua sphaero and Virgin Islands dwarf sphaero (0.63 inch)

Insect: Fairyfly (0.01 inch)

HOW FAST DO ANIMALS RUN?

This table shows how fast some animals can go on land. A snail can take more than 30 hours just to go 1 mile. But humans at their fastest are still slower than many animals. The human record for fastest speed for a recognized race distance is held by Usain Bolt, who set a new world record in 2009 in the 100-meter dash of 9.58 seconds, for an average speed of about 23 miles per hour.

ANIMAL	SPEED (miles per hour)
Cheetah	70
Pronghorn antelope	60
Elk	45
Ostrich	40
Rabbit	35
Giraffe	32
Grizzly bear	30
Elephant	25
Wild turkey	15
Crocodile	10
Tiger beetle	5.5
Snail	0.03

HOW LONG DO ANIMALS LIVE?

Most animals do not live as long as humans do. A monkey that's 14 years old is thought to be old, while a person at that age is still considered young. The average life spans of some animals in the wild are shown here. An average 10-year-old boy in the U.S. can expect to live to be about 75.

ANIMAL	AVERAGE LIFE SPAN	ANIMAL	AVERAGE LIFE SPAN
Galapagos tortoise	100+ years	Dog (domestic)	13 years
Blue whale	80 years	Camel (bactrian)	12 years
Alligator	50 years	Pig	10 years
Chimpanzee	50 years	Deer (white-tailed)	8 years
African elephant	35 years	Kangaroo	7 years
Bottlenose dolphin	30 years	Chipmunk	6 years
Horse	20 years	Guinea pig	4 years
Tiger	16 years	Mouse	3 years
Lobster	15 years	Opossum	1 year
Cat (domestic)	15 years	Worker bee	6 weeks
Tarantula	15 years	Adult housefly	1–3 weeks

BATS: FACT OR FICTION?

Many people are afraid of bats. These small flying mammals can look scary, and most kinds leave their homes only at night. But bats are useful to humans in many ways. They eat insects and help pollinate plants. Learn the facts about these unusual animals.

Fact or fiction? Bats are flying rodents.
Fiction. Like rodents, bats are mammals, but bats and rodents are not closely related to each other. Recent evidence has shown that bats are more closely related to primates (the group of animals that includes monkeys, apes, and humans).

Fact or fiction? Bats carry rabies.
Fact. All bats do not carry the disease rabies, but a very small percentage of them do. Because the disease can be transferred to humans, scientists who study bats get shots before working with the animals. These shots make it easier to treat rabies.

Fact or fiction? Flying bats can get tangled in human hair.
Fiction. Many kinds of bats see very well in the dark, and many use echolocation to fly and hunt at night. This means the bats send out sounds that bounce off even tiny objects, such as insects, and create an echo that the bats can hear. The echo tells the bats where an object is located. It is easy for a bat to avoid a large object like a human. Also, most bats are afraid of people, and they would not go near one intentionally.

Fact or fiction? Vampire bats commonly drink human blood.
Fiction. Three types of bats are known as "vampire bats," but they almost never bite humans. These bats—common, white-winged, and hairy-legged vampire bats—almost always consume animal blood.

WHAT ARE GROUPS OF ANIMALS CALLED?

Here are some (often odd) names for animal groups:

BEARS: ***sleuth*** of bears
CATS: ***clowder*** of cats
CATTLE: ***drove*** of cattle
CROCODILES: ***bask*** of crocodiles
CROWS: ***murder*** of crows
FISH: ***school*** or ***shoal*** of fish
FLIES: ***swarm*** or ***cloud*** of flies
FOXES: ***skulk*** of foxes
GIRAFFES: ***tower*** of giraffes
HARES: ***down*** of hares
HAWKS: ***cast*** of hawks
HYENAS: ***cackle*** of hyenas
JELLYFISH: ***smack*** of jellyfish
KITTENS: ***kindle*** or ***kendle*** of kittens
LEOPARDS: ***leap*** of leopards
MONKEYS: ***troop*** of monkeys
MULES: ***span*** of mules
NIGHTINGALES: ***watch*** of nightingales
OWLS: ***parliament*** of owls
OYSTERS: ***bed*** of oysters
PEACOCKS: ***muster*** of peacocks
RAVENS: ***unkindness*** of ravens
SHARKS: ***shiver*** of sharks
SQUIRRELS: ***dray*** or ***scurry*** of squirrels
TURTLES: ***bale*** of turtles
WHALES: ***pod*** of whales

DOGS AT THE TOP

Here are the most popular dog breeds in the United States:

1. Labrador Retriever
2. German Shepherd Dog
3. Yorkshire Terrier
4. Beagle
5. Golden Retriever
6. Bulldog
7. Boxer
8. Dachshund
9. Poodle
10. Shih Tzu

Source: American Kennel Club, 2010

Labrador Retriever

PETS Q&A

Why do cats have scratchy tongues? Cat tongues are lined with tiny hooks called papillae. These hooks help a cat hold prey in place. They also help cats groom themselves. All types of cats, including tigers and lions, have papillae on their tongues.

True or false? Dalmatians are born without spots. True. Dalmatian puppies are pure white when they are born. Black or brown spots start to form when a puppy is about a week old.

What is a polydactyl cat? Polydactyl cats have extra toes on one or more paws. Cats with this inherited trait may have as many as seven toes on each paw. Usually, cats have five toes on each front paw and four toes on each hind paw.

WHICH PET IS RIGHT FOR YOU?

Freshwater fish (like goldfish), cats, and dogs—in that order—are the three most popular pets in the United States. If your family has decided to get a pet, how can you decide which type will be the best fit for you?

Freshwater fish are an excellent option if you live in a small space or if any family members suffer from allergies. Some people think that fish require very little work and care, but this is not necessarily the case. Fish do not need to be walked or taken on regular trips to a veterinarian, but responsible fish owners keep the bowl or tank very clean and research which types of fish can share a living space. Even a simple goldfish in a bowl can be a big commitment—a goldfish may live for 10 years!

Cats are very popular pets, and with good reason. They can be playful and affectionate, but they are independent in many ways. Most cats use a litter box indoors, and they keep clean by licking themselves. But cats must be taken to a veterinarian at least once a year, and cats with claws often tear furniture or clothing. Many people are allergic to cats, so it is important for all family members to spend time with a cat before bringing one home.

Dogs are well-known for being loyal and loving to their owners. But of all the popular pets, dogs require the most work. Puppies often take many months to be housebroken, or trained to relieve themselves only outside. Adult dogs need daily exercise, and many breeds require regular grooming. Dogs are often given to animal shelters by owners who are overwhelmed by the need to care for them. Once your family has decided to get a dog, animal shelters are a great place to start your search!

ENDANGERED

When a species becomes extinct, the variety of life on Earth is reduced. In the world today, many thousands of known species of animals and plants are in danger of becoming extinct. Humans have been able to save some endangered animals and are working to save more.

Some Endangered Animals

Manatee Sometimes called "sea cows," these large mammals move slowly and usually live in warm, shallow waters. They are easy targets for hunters and are often accidentally killed by motorboats. The largest manatee population is found along the coast and in the rivers of Florida.

Reasons for population decline:

- Fishing methods, including use of nets and hooks, that indirectly harm manatees
- Hunting by humans
- Pollution
- Injuries caused by boat propellers and hulls

Orangutan The shaggy orange orangutan is known for its intelligence and cheerful personality—orangutan means "person of the forest" in a Malayan dialect. Found only on the Southeast Asian islands of Sumatra and Borneo, these primates spend most of their time in trees. As their habitat has been lost to logging and development, their numbers have been drastically reduced.

Reasons for population decline:

- Habitat loss due to deforestation
- Low rate of reproduction
- Hunting by humans

Snow Leopard Snow leopards live in the mountains of Central Asia. They have thick, spotted fur to keep them warm and large feet that work like snowshoes. They have been hunted for their beautiful fur and for their organs, which are used to make medicine. There are only about 6,000 left in the wild.

Reasons for population decline:

- Hunting by humans
- Loss of habitat due to increased development

SPECIES

Success Stories

Siberian Tiger Also known as the Amur tiger, this powerful big cat was on the brink of extinction in 1940. At that time, perhaps only about 40 remained in the wild. Thanks to conservation efforts—including laws that made it illegal to hunt tigers in Russia—the tiger population began to grow. The animals are still endangered, but there are now an estimated 400 in the wild.

Bald Eagle The bald eagle is the national bird and symbol of the United States. In 1967, the bird was added to the U.S. government's endangered species list. A pesticide called DDT, used to kill insects, was preventing eagle eggs from developing and hatching properly. Strict laws were put into place, providing for harsh penalties for anyone who harmed the birds. In 1972, use of DDT was banned in the United States. The bald eagle population responded quickly. The bird is no longer considered an endangered species.

Extinct?

West African Black Rhino

The black rhinoceros is native to eastern and central Africa. In the 1960s, about 100,000 black rhinos could be found in the wild. Their numbers have now been drastically reduced. The animals are illegally hunted for their horns, which are used to make medicine. The West African black rhino, one of four black rhino subspecies, is now thought to be extinct. The other three subspecies are critically endangered.

ANIMALS WORD SCRAMBLE

Unscramble these words to find the names of endangered animals.

wnso epodalr	aaetnem
abkcl ohirn	rannuatgo
ieiaSrnb iergt	oodomK agrond

ANSWERS ON PAGES 334–336.

CREATURES OF THE DEEP

Though scientists have been studying underwater creatures for many years, they are always making new discoveries about life in the deepest parts of the ocean. The deep sea is the largest habitat on Earth, but it is a difficult one for humans to study. At depths below 3,300 feet, the water is extremely cold and pitch black. The pressure from the water above would crush humans and most other animals. But some creatures have adapted—often in surprising ways—and live comfortably in these deep waters. These creatures are divided into three groups.

Microorganisms make up the largest group of deep-sea life forms. Many of these organisms have just one cell, and they provide food for the other creatures. In some areas, they are so common that they group together in huge formations that look like rugs.

Invertebrates are creatures without backbones. Many types of worms, crabs, and sponges—all invertebrates—live on the deep-sea floor. They often live at hydrothermal vents. These vents shoot out water that is warmer than the rest of the deep sea and that is rich in minerals and other chemicals. The giant tube worm is one of the invertebrates that can be found at these vents. These worms can grow to as much as 5 feet long.

Fish are the only creatures with backbones found in the deep sea. These fish must be able to withstand the pressure at these depths. Because the water is so dark, many fish have features that produce light. They also digest their food very slowly, to help them survive in a place where food is scarce. Many of these fish, like the common fangtooth (see photo at top of page), have long teeth that help grab onto large prey. These teeth are not meant for chewing—the fish swallows its food whole.

Giant tube worms ▶

THE WORLD ALMANAC FOR KIDS

ON THE JOB: VETERINARIAN

Veterinarians are doctors who take care of animals. Some work mostly with small animals, such as dogs and cats, in vet clinics. Some specialize in one type of illness or work with large animals on farms or in zoos. Simon Alexander, a veterinarian who co-owns a clinic, agreed to talk to *The World Almanac for Kids* about his work.

What do you do in a typical day?

On Wednesday afternoons and Saturday mornings, I do my small animal work at the clinic. The rest of the time, I do ambulatory large animal work. That means I travel to see different animals. I'm in a rural area, so I'm usually traveling to farms. If I'm going to treat sick animals, I might see only eight or nine patients in a day. Most of the time, though, I see hundreds of them. I might check a hundred cows for pregnancy at one farm, then go to another farm to get hundreds of milk samples. We have to test the milk to make sure the cows are healthy.

What interests and strengths of yours make this job right for you?

I like people! Most people don't realize this, but that's one of the most important parts of this job. Animals can't tell you what hurts or how long it's been since they've eaten. The people who spend time with the animals have to give you those answers—and you have to know how to ask them the right questions.

What kind of education or training did you need to get in order to do your job?

I have a doctor of veterinary medicine degree from the University of Pennsylvania.

What do you like best about your job? What is most challenging?

I love helping people and their animals—that's pretty great. The most challenging parts of the job are the long hours and the finances. Vets generally make less money than people in other medical professions. But overall I love my job—the benefits outweigh the challenges.

ART

What kind of art does Claes Oldenburg create? → page 35

ART Q&A

IS ARTISTIC TALENT SOMETHING YOU ARE BORN WITH OR SOMETHING YOU CAN LEARN?

Learning to draw is a skill like writing or playing a sport. Some people are naturally more talented, but anyone can learn to draw. Even people with severe physical disabilities can make masterpieces.

HOW OLD IS ART?

Art goes back to our earliest records of human life. See the cave paintings on the next page for an example.

WHEN I SEE A PAINTING IN A MUSEUM, WHAT MIGHT I SAY ABOUT IT?

Look at the painting without thinking too hard about it. How does it make you feel? Happy, sad, confused, silly? Study the painting and try to discover the colors, shapes, and textures that create those feelings in you.

Look at the information card next to the work of art. Usually, it will tell you who painted it, when it was made, and what media (materials) were used. You can compare it to other works of art by the same artist, from the same time, or in the same medium.

WHAT IS ART?

The answer is up for debate. People who study this question are studying aesthetics (ess-THET-ics), which is a kind of philosophy. Usually art is something that an artist interprets for an audience. Art reveals something that you can see, that then makes you think and feel.

DIFFERENT KINDS OF ART

Throughout history, artists have painted pictures of nature (called landscapes), pictures of people (called portraits), and pictures of flowers in vases, food, and other objects (known as still lifes). Today many artists create pictures that do not look like anything in the real world. These are examples of abstract art.

Photography, too, is a form of art. Photos record both the commonplace and the exotic and help us look at events in new ways.

Sculpture is a three-dimensional form made from clay, stone, metal, or other material. Sculptures can be large, like the Statue of Liberty. Some are realistic. Others have no form you can recognize.

Artists work with many materials. Some artists today use computers and video screens to create their art.

ART ALL-STARS

These works of art helped change the way we see the world around us.

Lascaux (13,000–15,000 B.C.)

Lascaux is a cave in France. It contains some of the earliest known cave art. The cave was discovered in 1940 by four teenagers. The images found on the cave walls consist of handprints and animals such as bison, deer, horses, and cattle. It is believed that the paintings may have been part of a ritual to help make a successful hunt.

LEONARDO DA VINCI (1452–1519)
The Lady with the Ermine (1496)

Leonardo lived in Italy at a time of great creativity known as the Renaissance. Most famous as a painter, he was also a scientist, inventor, musician, and map-maker. His best-known painting is the *Mona Lisa*, but he did a number of other portraits of women that feature fascinating facial expressions and delicate lighting.

CLAUDE MONET (1840–1926)
White Nenuphars (1899)

The French painter Claude Monet was one of the leading artists who painted in the style known as Impressionism. The Impressionist painters did not try to achieve a sharp, realistic image. They were more interested in how light affects colors and shape. Monet settled in the tiny town of Giverny, near Paris, in 1883. There, he built a large Japanese garden, which he painted often. Many of these paintings show the water lilies called nenuphars.

CLAES OLDENBURG (1929–)
Spoonbridge and Cherry (1988)

The Swedish sculptor Claes Oldenburg spent most of his childhood in the United States and later became a U.S. citizen. He is most famous for his amusing large sculptures of everyday objects, such as a saw, a dropped ice cream cone, and a cherry on a spoon. His sculptures are usually displayed in public spaces.

COLOR WHEEL

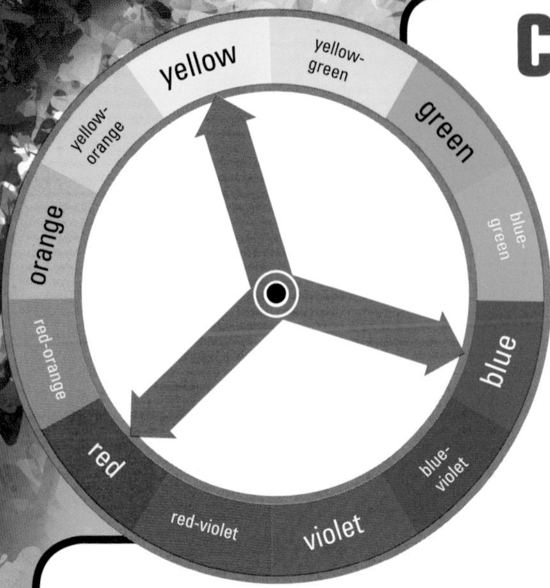

This color wheel shows how colors are related to each other.

Primary colors The most basic colors are **RED**, **YELLOW**, and **BLUE**. They're called primary because you can't get them by mixing any other colors. In fact, the other colors are made by mixing red, blue, or yellow. Arrows on this wheel show the primary colors.

Secondary colors **ORANGE**, **GREEN**, and **VIOLET** are the secondary colors. They are made by mixing two primary colors. You make orange by mixing yellow and red, or green by mixing yellow and blue. On the color wheel, **GREEN** appears between **BLUE** and **YELLOW**.

Tertiary colors When you mix a primary and a secondary color, you get a tertiary, or intermediate, color. **BLUE-GREEN** and **YELLOW-GREEN** are intermediate colors.

More Color Terms

VALUES The lightness or darkness of a color is its value.

Tints are light values made by mixing a color with white. **PINK** is a tint of **RED**.

Shades are dark values made by mixing a color with black. **MAROON** is a shade of **RED**.

COMPLEMENTARY COLORS

Contrasting colors that please the eye when used together are called complementary colors. These colors appear opposite each other on the wheel and don't have any colors in common. **RED** is a complement to **GREEN**, which is made by mixing **YELLOW** and **BLUE**.

COOL COLORS

Cool colors are mostly **GREEN**, **BLUE**, and **PURPLE**. They make you think of cool things like water and can even make you feel cooler.

WARM COLORS

Warm colors are mostly **RED**, **ORANGE**, and **YELLOW**. They suggest heat and can actually make you feel warmer.

ANALOGOUS COLORS

The colors next to each other on the wheel are from the same "family." **BLUE**, **BLUE-GREEN**, and **GREEN** all have **BLUE** in them and are analogous colors.

ON THE JOB: GRAPHIC DESIGNER

Graphic designers are the people who decide how things we see every day will look—books and magazines, websites, advertisements, and the packaging for items we buy. Tammy West, a graphic designer who has her own company, agreed to talk to *The World Almanac for Kids* about her work.

What do you do in a typical day?

I usually spend most of my day at the computer. To start a design, I may sketch out a few ideas and then move to the computer to create it for real. I'm also in contact with a lot of different individuals—editors, art directors, other designers, and company owners. A design can go through a number of revisions before a client approves it, so there is a lot of back and forth with each client. I have a lot of different projects at any one time, so the job never gets boring. It's great to finish something and move on to the next creation.

This book cover was designed by Tammy West.

What interests and strengths of yours make this job right for you?

Of course, creativity helps to make the job easier. You also need to be a good listener and to have the ability to execute other people's ideas. It's important to be able to multitask. I find myself working on one thing and having to switch to something else suddenly to accommodate a co-worker or meet an urgent deadline.

What kind of education or training did you need to get in order to do your job?

I have a four-year degree in graphic design and lots of continuing software training.

What do you like best about your job? What is most challenging?

The most rewarding thing about my job is creating things that people are proud of, whether it's a book, logo, brochure, or web design. Receiving compliments on your work is the best reward. The most challenging thing can be to execute someone else's idea. Everyone has different likes and dislikes, so trying to understand what each client is looking for can sometimes be a challenge.

BIRTHDAYS

What symbol represents a Leo? → page 42

Martin Luther King Jr.

January
Birthstone: Garnet

1 J.D. Salinger, author, 1919
2 Christy Turlington, model, 1969
3 Eli Manning, football player, 1981
4 Isaac Newton, physicist/ mathematician, 1643
5 Diane Keaton, actress, 1946
6 Early Wynn, baseball player, 1920
7 Nicolas Cage, actor, 1964
8 Stephen Hawking, physicist, 1942
9 Catherine (Kate Middleton), Duchess of Cambridge, 1982
10 George Foreman, boxer, 1948
11 Mary J. Blige, singer, 1971
12 Christiane Amanpour, journalist, 1958
13 Orlando Bloom, actor, 1977
14 Jason Bateman, actor, 1969
15 Rev. Martin Luther King Jr., civil rights leader, 1929
16 Sade, singer, 1959
17 Michelle Obama, first lady, 1964
18 Mark Messier, hockey player, 1961
19 Edgar Allan Poe, writer, 1809
20 Buzz Aldrin, astronaut, 1930
21 Jack Nicklaus, golfer, 1940
22 Sir Francis Bacon, philosopher, 1561
23 John Hancock, revolutionary leader, 1737
24 Mary Lou Retton, gymnast, 1968
25 Alicia Keys, singer, 1981
26 Paul Newman, actor, 1925
27 Hannah Teter, snowboarder, 1987
28 Jackson Pollock, artist, 1912
29 Greg Louganis, diver, 1960
30 Christian Bale, actor, 1974
31 Justin Timberlake, singer, 1981

February
Birthstone: Amethyst

1 Langston Hughes, poet, 1902
2 James Joyce, author, 1882
3 Elizabeth Blackwell, first woman physician in U.S., 1821
4 Clint Black, musician, 1962
5 Hank Aaron, baseball player, 1934
6 Babe Ruth, baseball player, 1895
7 Laura Ingalls Wilder, author, 1867
8 Jules Verne, author, 1828
9 Carole King, musician, 1942
10 Emma Roberts, actress, 1991
11 Taylor Lautner, actor, 1992
12 Abraham Lincoln, 16th president, 1809
13 Grant Wood, artist, 1891
14 Gregory Hines, dancer/actor, 1946
15 Matt Groening, cartoonist, 1954
16 John McEnroe, tennis player, 1959
17 Billie Joe Armstrong, musician, 1972
18 John Travolta, actor, 1954
19 Amy Tan, author, 1952
20 Gloria Vanderbilt, fashion designer, 1924
21 Ellen Page, actress, 1987
22 Edna St. Vincent Millay, poet, 1892
23 Dakota Fanning, actress, 1994
24 Steve Jobs, computer innovator, 1955
25 George Harrison, musician, 1943
26 Marshall Faulk, football player, 1973
27 John Steinbeck, author, 1902
28 Linus Pauling, scientist, 1901
29 Ja Rule, rapper, 1976

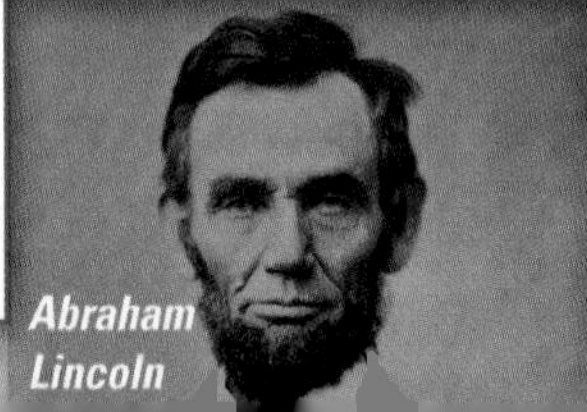
Abraham Lincoln

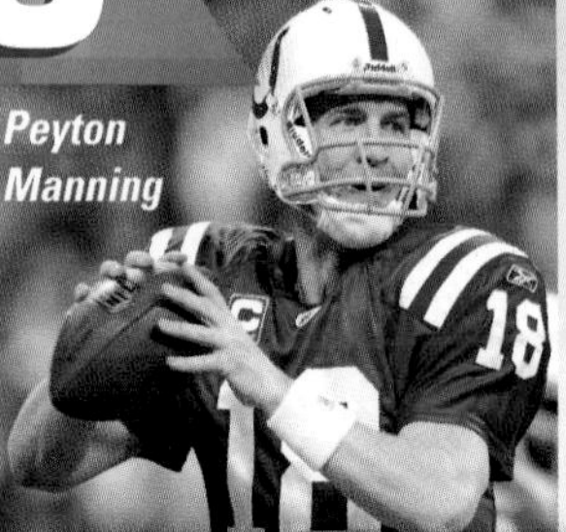
Peyton Manning

March
Birthstone: Aquamarine

1 Justin Bieber, singer, 1994
2 Dr. Seuss, author, 1904
3 Alexander Graham Bell, inventor, 1847
4 Landon Donovan, soccer player, 1982
5 Eva Mendes, actress, 1974
6 Shaquille O'Neal, basketball player, 1972
7 Jenna Fischer, actress, 1974
8 Kenneth Grahame, author, 1859
9 Bow Wow, actor/rapper, 1987
10 Carrie Underwood, singer, 1983
11 Benji and Joel Madden, musicians, 1979
12 James Taylor, musician, 1948
13 Emile Hirsch, actor, 1985
14 Albert Einstein, physicist/ Nobel laureate, 1879
15 Eva Longoria, actress, 1975
16 Flavor Flav, rapper, 1959
17 Mia Hamm, soccer player, 1972
18 Queen Latifah, rapper/ actress, 1970
19 Bruce Willis, actor, 1955
20 Spike Lee, filmmaker, 1957
21 Matthew Broderick, actor, 1962
22 Reese Witherspoon, actress, 1976
23 Keri Russell, actress, 1976
24 Peyton Manning, football player, 1976
25 Danica Patrick, racecar driver, 1982
26 Robert Frost, poet, 1874
27 Quentin Tarantino, director, 1963
28 Lady Gaga, singer, 1986
29 Cy Young, baseball player, 1867
30 Vincent Van Gogh, artist, 1853
31 Cesar Chavez, labor leader, 1927

April
Birthstone: Diamond

1 Phil Niekro, baseball player, 1939
2 Marvin Gaye, singer, 1939
3 Leona Lewis, singer, 1985
4 Robert Downey Jr., actor, 1965
5 Booker T. Washington, educator, 1856
6 Paul Rudd, actor, 1969
7 Billie Holiday, singer, 1915
8 Taylor Kitsch, actor, 1981
9 Kristen Stewart, actress, 1990
10 John Madden, sportscaster, 1936
11 Joss Stone, singer, 1987
12 Brooklyn Decker, model/actress, 1987
13 Thomas Jefferson, 3rd president, 1743
14 Abigail Breslin, actress, 1996
15 Emma Watson, actress, 1990
16 Jon Cryer, actor, 1965
17 Jennifer Garner, actress, 1972
18 America Ferrera, actress, 1984
19 Kate Hudson, actress, 1979
20 Luther Vandross, musician, 1951
21 Queen Elizabeth II, British monarch, 1926
22 Robert J. Oppenheimer, physicist, 1904
23 Dev Patel, actor, 1990
24 Kelly Clarkson, singer, 1982
25 Ella Fitzgerald, singer, 1917
26 Kevin James, actor, 1965
27 Samuel Morse, inventor, 1791
28 Harper Lee, author, 1926
29 Dale Earnhardt Sr., race car driver, 1951
30 Dianna Agron, actress, 1986

Tina Fey

May
Birthstone: Emerald

1 Tim McGraw, musician, 1967
2 Lily Allen, singer, 1985
3 Sugar Ray Robinson, boxer, 1921
4 Audrey Hepburn, actress, 1929
5 Adele, singer, 1988
6 Gabourey Sidibe, actress, 1983
7 Johannes Brahms, composer, 1833
8 Enrique Iglesias, singer, 1975
9 Billy Joel, musician, 1949
10 Bono, musician/activist, 1960
11 Salvador Dali, artist, 1904
12 Tony Hawk, skateboarder, 1968
13 Robert Pattinson, actor, 1986
14 Miranda Cosgrove, actress, 1993
15 Emmitt Smith, football player, 1969
16 Megan Fox, actress, 1986
17 Sugar Ray Leonard, boxer, 1956
18 Tina Fey, actress/comedian, 1970
19 Malcolm X, militant civil rights activist, 1925
20 Busta Rhymes, rapper, 1972
21 John Muir, naturalist, 1838
22 Ginnifer Goodwin, actress, 1978
23 Margaret Wise Brown, author, 1910
24 Tracy McGrady, basketball player, 1979
25 Mike Myers, actor, 1963
26 Sally Ride, astronaut, 1951
27 Chris Colfer, actor, 1990
28 Gladys Knight, singer, 1944
29 Andre Agassi, tennis champion, 1970
30 Cee Lo Green, singer, 1974
31 Walt Whitman, poet, 1819

June
Birthstone: Pearl

1 Morgan Freeman, actor, 1937
2 Freddy Adu, soccer player, 1989
3 Rafael Nadal, tennis player, 1986
4 Angelina Jolie, actress, 1975
5 Mark Wahlberg, actor, 1971
6 Cynthia Rylant, author, 1954
7 Michael Cera, actor, 1988
8 Kanye West, musician, 1977
9 Natalie Portman, actress, 1981
10 Maurice Sendak, author/illustrator, 1928
11 Shia LaBeouf, actor, 1986
12 Anne Frank, diary writer, 1929
13 William Butler Yeats, poet, 1865
14 Kevin McHale, actor, 1988
15 Neil Patrick Harris, actor, 1973
16 Tupac Shakur, rapper/actor, 1971
17 Venus Williams, tennis player, 1980
18 Sir Paul McCartney, musician, 1942
19 Zoe Saldana, actress, 1978
20 Grace Potter, musician, 1983
21 Prince William of Great Britain, Duke of Cambridge, 1982
22 Kurt Warner, football player, 1971
23 Bob Fosse, choreographer, 1927
24 Minka Kelly, actress, 1980
25 Sonia Sotomayor, U.S. Supreme Court justice, 1954
26 Derek Jeter, baseball player, 1974
27 Ed Westwick, actor, 1987
28 John Cusack, actor, 1966
29 William James Mayo, doctor, 1861
30 Michael Phelps, Olympic champion, 1985

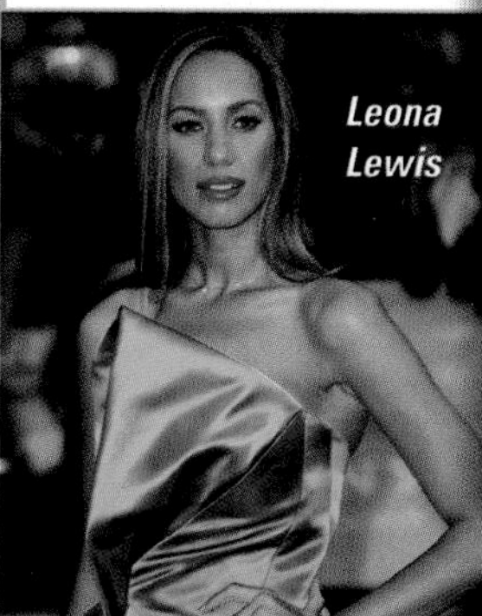

Leona Lewis

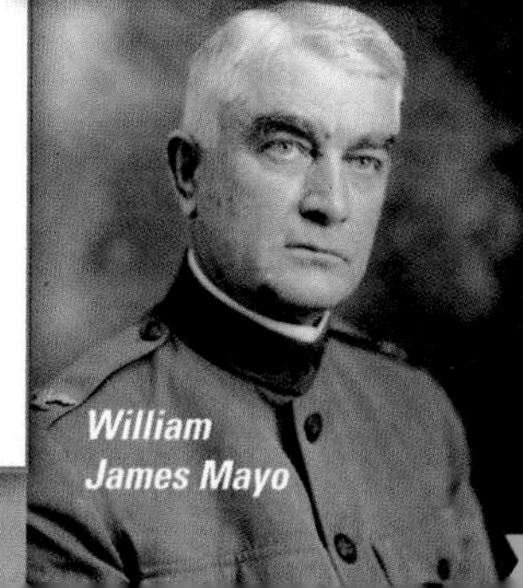

William James Mayo

Ashley Tisdale

July
Birthstone: Ruby

1 Missy Elliott, rapper, 1971
2 Ashley Tisdale, actress, 1986
3 Franz Kafka, author, 1883
4 Neil Simon, playwright, 1927
5 P. T. Barnum, showman/circus founder, 1810
6 George W. Bush, 43rd president, 1946
7 Michelle Kwan, figure skater, 1980
8 Jaden Smith, actor/rapper, 1988
9 Jack White, musician, 1975
10 Arthur Ashe, tennis player, 1943
11 E. B. White, author, 1899
12 Andrew Wyeth, painter, 1917
13 Harrison Ford, actor, 1942
14 Jane Lynch, actress, 1960
15 Rembrandt van Rijn, artist, 1606
16 Will Ferrell, actor, 1967
17 Donald Sutherland, actor, 1935
18 Kristen Bell, actress, 1980
19 Edgar Degas, artist, 1834
20 Carlos Santana, musician, 1947
21 Ernest Hemingway, author, 1899
22 Selena Gomez, actress/singer 1992
23 Daniel Radcliffe, actor, 1989
24 Jennifer Lopez, actress/singer, 1969
25 Walter Payton, football player, 1954
26 Sandra Bullock, actress, 1964
27 Alex Rodriguez, baseball player, 1975
28 Beatrix Potter, author, 1866
29 Allison Mack, actress, 1982
30 Laurence Fishburne, actor, 1961
31 J. K. Rowling, author, 1965

August
Birthstone: Peridot

1 Robert Cray, musician, 1953
2 Sam Worthington, actor, 1976
3 Tom Brady, football player, 1977
4 Barack Obama, 44th president, 1961
5 Neil Armstrong, astronaut, 1930
6 Andy Warhol, artist, 1928
7 Charlize Theron, actress, 1975
8 Dustin Hoffman, actor, 1937
9 Eric Bana, actor, 1968
10 Antonio Banderas, actor, 1960
11 Alyson Stoner, actress, 1983
12 Pete Sampras, tennis player, 1971
13 Alfred Hitchcock, filmmaker, 1899
14 Mila Kunis, actress, 1983
15 Jennifer Lawrence, actress, 1990
16 Steve Carell, actor, 1963
17 Robert De Niro, actor, 1943
18 Meriwether Lewis, explorer, 1774
19 Bill Clinton, 42nd president, 1946
20 Demi Lovato, actress/singer, 1992
21 Stephen Hillenburg, SpongeBob creator, 1961
22 Carl Yastrzemski, baseball player, 1939
23 Kobe Bryant, basketball player, 1978
24 Rupert Grint, actor, 1988
25 Tim Burton, director, 1958
26 Chris Pine, actor, 1980
27 Alexa Vega, actress, 1988
28 Jack Black, actor, 1969
29 Lea Michele, actress, 1986
30 Cameron Diaz, actress, 1972
31 Van Morrison, musician, 1945

Neil Armstrong

Ray Charles

September
Birthstone: Sapphire

1 Conway Twitty, country singer, 1933
2 Christa McAuliffe, teacher/astronaut, 1948
3 Shaun White, snowboarder, 1986
4 Beyoncé Knowles, singer/actress, 1981
5 Rose McGowan, actress, 1973
6 Roger Waters, musician, 1943
7 Evan Rachel Wood, actress, 1987
8 Latrell Sprewell, basketball player, 1970
9 Michelle Williams, actress, 1980
10 Colin Firth, actor, 1960
11 Ludacris, rapper, 1977
12 Jennifer Hudson, singer/actress, 1981
13 Roald Dahl, author, 1916
14 Tyler Perry, director, 1969
15 Prince Harry of Great Britain, 1984
16 David Copperfield, magician, 1956
17 Rasheed Wallace, basketball player, 1974
18 Lance Armstrong, cyclist, 1971
19 Jim Abbott, baseball player, 1967
20 Red Auerbach, basketball coach, 1917
21 Hiram Revels, first black U.S. senator, 1822
22 Andrea Bocelli, singer, 1958
23 Ray Charles, musician, 1930
24 Jim Henson, Muppet creator, 1936
25 Will Smith, actor/rapper, 1968
26 Serena Williams, tennis player, 1981
27 Lil Wayne, rapper, 1984
28 Gwyneth Paltrow, actress, 1972
29 Kevin Durant, basketball player, 1988
30 Elie Wiesel, author, 1928

October
Birthstone: Opal

1 William Boeing, founder of Boeing Company, 1881
2 Mohandas Gandhi, activist, 1869
3 Stevie Ray Vaughan, musician, 1954
4 Anne Rice, author, 1941
5 Jesse Eisenberg, actor, 1983
6 Olivia Thirlby, actress, 1986
7 Simon Cowell, television personality, 1959
8 Matt Damon, actor, 1970
9 John Lennon, musician, 1940
10 Maya Lin, sculptor and architect, 1960
11 Steve Young, football player, 1961
12 Hugh Jackman, actor, 1968
13 Sacha Baron Cohen, actor, 1971
14 Usher, singer, 1978
15 Elena Dementieva, tennis player, 1981
16 John Mayer, musician, 1977
17 Eminem, rapper/actor, 1972
18 Freida Pinto, actress, 1984
19 Ty Pennington, TV personality, 1965
20 Snoop Dogg, rapper/actor, 1971
21 Dizzy Gillespie, trumpet player, 1917
22 Ichiro Suzuki, baseball player, 1973
23 Ryan Reynolds, actor, 1976
24 Brian Vickers, racecar driver, 1983
25 Katy Perry, singer, 1984
26 Pat Sajak, game show host, 1947
27 Teddy Roosevelt, 26th president, 1858
28 Bill Gates, computer pioneer, 1955
29 Winona Ryder, actress, 1971
30 John Adams, 2nd president, 1735
31 Willow Smith, singer/actress, 2000

Willow Smith

Louisa May Alcott

November
Birthstone: Topaz

1 Coco Crisp, baseball player, 1979
2 James K. Polk, 11th president, 1795
3 John Barry, composer, 1933
4 Sean Combs (Diddy), producer/rapper, 1969
5 Johnny Damon, baseball player, 1973
6 Emma Stone, actress, 1988
7 Marie Curie, scientist/Nobel laureate, 1867
8 Bonnie Raitt, musician, 1949
9 Carl Sagan, scientist, 1934
10 Ellen Pompeo, actress, 1969
11 Leonardo DiCaprio, actor, 1974
12 Ryan Gosling, actor, 1980
13 Robert Louis Stevenson, author, 1850
14 Condoleezza Rice, American statesperson, 1954
15 Georgia O'Keefe, artist, 1887
16 Maggie Gyllenhaal, actress, 1977
17 Martin Scorsese, director, 1942
18 Owen Wilson, actor, 1968
19 Calvin Klein, fashion designer, 1942
20 Joe Biden, 47th vice president, 1942
21 Jena Malone, actress, 1984
22 Scarlett Johansson, actress, 1984
23 Miley Cyrus, singer/actress, 1992
24 Sarah Hyland, actress, 1990
25 Donovan McNabb, football player, 1976
26 Charles Schulz, cartoonist, 1912
27 Bill Nye, "The Science Guy," 1955
28 Jon Stewart, TV host, 1962
29 Louisa May Alcott, author, 1832
30 Mark Twain, author, 1835

December
Birthstone: Turquoise

1 Sarah Silverman, actress/comedienne, 1970
2 Monica Seles, tennis player, 1973
3 Amanda Seyfried, actress, 1985
4 Jay-Z, rapper, 1969
5 Walt Disney, cartoonist/filmmaker, 1901
6 Otto Graham, football player/coach, 1921
7 Larry Bird, basketball player/coach, 1956
8 AnnaSophia Robb, actress, 1993
9 Felicity Huffman, actress, 1962
10 Bobby Flay, chef, 1964
11 Mos Def, actor/rapper, 1973
12 Frank Sinatra, singer/actor, 1915
13 Taylor Swift, singer, 1989
14 Vanessa Hudgens, actress/singer, 1988
15 Adam Brody, actor, 1979
16 Jane Austen, author, 1775
17 Sean Patrick Thomas, actor, 1970
18 Brad Pitt, actor, 1963
19 Jake Gyllenhaal, actor, 1980
20 Rich Gannon, football player, 1965
21 Samuel L. Jackson, actor, 1948
22 Vanessa Paradis, singer/actress, 1972
23 Alge Crumpler, football player, 1977
24 Stephenie Meyer, author, 1973
25 Clara Barton, American Red Cross founder, 1821
26 Carlton Fisk, baseball player, 1947
27 Louis Pasteur, scientist, 1822
28 Denzel Washington, actor, 1954
29 Charles Goodyear, inventor, 1800
30 LeBron James, basketball player, 1984
31 Henri Matisse, artist, 1869

Clara Barton

What's Your Sign?

ASTROLOGY is a study of the positions of celestial bodies—such as the sun, moon, planets, and stars—that looks to find connections between these bodies and things that happen on Earth. Most scientists do not believe that there are connections, and astrology is often called a "pseudoscience" or "superstition." Still, many people enjoy learning about astrology and using it for entertainment.

THE ZODIAC is very important to people who follow astrology. The zodiac is a belt-shaped section of the sky that has been divided into twelve constellations. A constellation is a cluster of stars that can be seen from Earth. Astrologers give special meaning to these constellations. They believe that every person is influenced by one of these twelve constellations—or twelve signs—depending on his or her birthday. For example, a person born between July 23 and August 22 is a Leo. Leos are said to be confident and generous, but stubborn.

A HOROSCOPE is a prediction about a person's future based on his or her astrological sign. Daily or monthly horoscopes can be found in many newspapers and magazines, in print or online, and on other websites.

SIGNS OF THE ZODIAC

Here are the twelve signs of the zodiac, with the approximate date span for each one and the symbol commonly used to represent it.

Aries
March 21 – April 19
RAM

Taurus
April 20 – May 20
BULL

Gemini
May 21 – June 20
TWINS

Cancer
June 21 – July 22
CRAB

Leo
July 23 – August 22
LION

Virgo
August 23 – September 22
MAIDEN

Libra
September 23 – October 22
SCALES

Scorpio
October 23 – November 21
SCORPION

Sagittarius
November 22 – December 21
ARCHER

Capricorn
December 22 – January 19
GOAT

Aquarius
January 20 – February 18
WATER CARRIER

Pisces
February 19 – March 20
FISHES

Celebrity Crossword Puzzle

ıink you know a lot about celebrities? It's time to put that knowledge the test! Fill in the words that go with each clue. If you're stumped, e answers can all be found in *The World Almanac for Kids*. Look in ese chapters: **Birthdays, Faces & Places, Movies & TV,** and **Music Dance**. Good luck!

int: When the clue is about a person, the answer could be the person's ll name or just the person's last name.

ACROSS

2. Youngest Academy Awards host
4. *Hunger Games* actress
6. *Doo-Wops & Hooligans* singer
8. Mr. Popper actor
10. *I Am Number Four* author

DOWN

1. Comedy film starring Jennifer Aniston and Adam Sandler
3. Kristen Stewart's *Twilight* role
5. Dark Knight actor
7. Football player born in March
9. *Rango* star

ANSWERS ON PAGES 334–336.

BOOKS

Who wrote *The Hunger Games?* → page 46

BOOK AWARDS, 2011

Newbery Medal
For the author of the best children's book
2011 winner: ***Moon Over Manifest***, by Clare Vanderpool

Michael L. Printz Award
For excellence in literature written for young adults
2011 winner: ***Ship Breaker***, by Paolo Bacigalupi

Coretta Scott King Award
For artists and authors whose works encourage expression of the African American experience
2011 winners:
Author Award: ***One Crazy Summer***, by Rita Williams-Garcia
Illustrator Award: ***Dave the Potter: Artist, Poet, Slave***, illustrated by Bryan Collier

Caldecott Medal
For the artist of the best children's picture book
2011 winner: ***A Sick Day for Amos McGee***, illustrated by Erin E. Stead and written by Philip C. Stead

NEW BOOK SPOTLIGHT

***Turtle in Paradise*, by Jennifer L. Holm, takes place in 1935 during the Great Depression, a time of economic hardship for the country. Eleven-year-old Turtle is sent from New Jersey to live with relatives in Key West, Florida, whom she has never met. There, she discovers a whole new world and lost treasures found.**

Famous Children's Authors

Author	Try the Book
Kate DiCamillo (1964–) won the Newbery Medal for *The Tale of Despereaux.* She was inspired to write it after a friend's son asked her to create an unlikely hero with exceptionally large ears. Besides her story about Despereaux the mouse, her other well-known titles include *Because of Winn-Dixie* and *The Tiger Rising.*	***The Magician's Elephant***
 **Stephenie Meyer** (1973–) is the author of the world-famous Twilight vampire-romance series. Her novels have sold more than 100 million copies and been translated into 37 languages. In June 2003, a dream sparked the idea for the series. Three months later, she finished writing *Twilight,* her first novel in the saga. It was published in 2005.	***Twilight*** (the first book in the Twilight series)
Christopher Paolini (1983–) began writing *Eragon* when he was 15. He read many fantasy and science fiction books and wanted to see if he could write one himself. By the time he was 20, *Eragon* was a bestseller. His younger sister Angela inspired the character of "Angela the herbalist" in his books. 	***Eragon*** (the first book in the Inheritance series)
Gary Paulsen (1939–) worked a variety of jobs—including as an engineer, construction worker, and truck driver—before realizing he wanted to be a writer. His dedication to writing has led him to produce more than 175 books for children and adults. In addition to writing, Paulsen trains dogs for the Iditarod sled race in Alaska.	**The Brian Saga: *Hatchet, The River, Brian's Winter,* and *Brian's Return***
 **J.K. Rowling** (1965–), whose initials stand for Joanne Kathleen, is the British author of the world-famous Harry Potter series. The idea for Harry Potter came to her suddenly during a train trip. She spent the next five years making an outline of the story and writing it out before *Harry Potter and the Sorcerer's Stone* was published.	***Harry Potter and the Sorcerer's Stone*** (the first book in the Harry Potter series)
E.B. White (1899–1985), born Elwyn Brooks White, is the author of the beloved children's classics *Stuart Little, The Trumpet of the Swan,* and *Charlotte's Web.* White worked as a reporter, essayist, and magazine writer. *Stuart Little,* his first children's book, was published in 1945. White, who lived on a farm in Maine, said the animals there inspired many of the characters in his stories.	***The Trumpet of the Swan***

COOL READS

Calling all bookworms! There are two main types of literature: **fiction** and **nonfiction**. Fiction is a made-up story. Nonfiction, on the other hand, is a true story. Within these two groups are different types of stories called **genres** (ZHAN-ruhs). Check out these recommended reads from various genres.

Fiction

Mysteries and Thrillers

These suspense-filled tales follow a secret that needs to be uncovered or a crime that needs to be solved.

Try These ***The House With a Clock in Its Walls,*** **by John Bellairs;** ***The Westing Game,*** **by Ellen Raskin**

Adventure, Fantasy, and Science Fiction

These stories transport you to imaginary worlds filled with unusual characters and magical creatures.

Try These ***The Hunger Games,*** **by Suzanne Collins;** ***The Lightning Thief,*** **by Rick Riordan;** ***A Wrinkle in Time,*** **by Madeleine L'Engle**

Realistic Fiction

Do you enjoy reading stories that you can relate to? This genre is about real-life situations that kids and teens deal with every day.

Try These ***Hoot,*** **by Carl Hiaasen;** ***Tales of a Fourth Grade Nothing,*** **by Judy Blume**

Historical Fiction

Authors of this genre put a new twist on history. They take exciting historical events or periods and place intriguing fictional characters smack in the middle of them.

Try These ***The Day of the Pelican,*** **by Katherine Paterson;** ***Esperanza Rising,*** **by Pam Muñoz Ryan**

Myths and Legends

These made-up stories go way back. Many tell of how things in nature came to be.

Try These ***Amazing Greek Myths of Wonder and Blunders,*** **by Mike Townsend;** ***The Girl Who Helped Thunder and Other Native American Folktales,*** **by James Bruchac and Joseph Bruchac**

Graphic Novels, Comics, and Manga

These types of books convey their stories with drawings and text.

Try These ***Gettysburg: The Graphic Novel,*** **by C. M. Butzer;** ***Diary of a Wimpy Kid,*** **by Jeff Kinney**

Nonfiction

Biographies, Autobiographies, and Memoirs

Do you like reading about the details of a real person's life? Then get up-close and personal with this genre!

Try These ***Amelia Earhart (DK Biography),*** **by Tanya Lee Stone;** ***Justin Bieber: First Step 2 Forever: My Story,*** **by Justin Bieber**

History

Books in this genre can be about an event, an era, a country, or even a war.

Try These ***All Stations! Distress!: April 15, 1912, The Day the*** **Titanic** ***Sank,*** **by Don Brown;** ***Moonshot: The Flight of*** **Apollo 11, by Brian Floca**

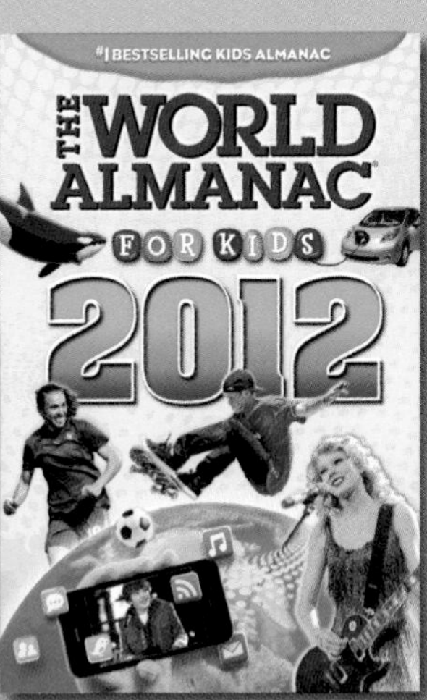

Reference

Reference books provide reliable facts and sources of information. Almanacs, atlases, dictionaries, and encyclopedias are examples of reference books.

Try This ***The World Almanac for Kids***

ALL ABOUT . . . BOOKS

If a Roman emperor wanted to read a book, he had to unroll it. Books were written on long scrolls that were unrolled as people read. Around A.D. 100 the codex was invented. It was made up of a stack of pages stitched together at the side and protected by a cover. The codex was easier to carry around, to store, and to search through. Books on paper that we read today look something like a codex.

In the Middle Ages books were made by monks who copied them by hand onto prepared animal skins called parchment. The monks often decorated the pages with beautiful color illustrations called illuminations. Books were scarce and very expensive, and few people who were not priests or monks could read.

A big change came with the inventions of paper and printing in China. Paper came into Europe through the Muslim world and was common by the 14th century. Johann Gutenberg of Germany perfected printing in the 1450s. Once books no longer had to be copied by hand and could be printed on paper, they became less expensive and reading became more common.

At first, books were still not easy to make and not cheap. Each letter was on a separate piece of type, and a typesetter had to put each letter into place individually. Once all the letters for the page were in place, they were covered with ink and printed, one page at a time, by hand on a press. By the 19th century, however, steam-powered presses could print out hundreds of pages at a time. Another invention was the linotype machine, which stamped out individual letters and set them up much faster than a typesetter could. Now books had become truly affordable, and the skill of reading was something that everyone was expected to learn. Today, with the use of computers, books can be easily transferred into electronic files and read as e-books.

WHO AM I?

The year 2012 marks the 200th anniversary of my birth. I was born in 1812 in Portsmouth, England. When my father was put in prison because he could not pay back money he owed, I went to work in a factory. I wrote about that harsh experience in my book *David Copperfield.* My first book, a collection of stories called *Sketches by Boz,* was published in 1836. I quickly became a successful writer and some of my most famous books include *Oliver Twist* (1838), *A Tale of Two Cities* (1859), and *Great Expectations* (1861). My books often focused on the poor and how badly they were treated. One of my classic tales, *A Christmas Carol,* was published in 1843. It tells of a cold-hearted miser who sees the error of his ways after a visit from three ghosts on Christmas Eve. I died in 1870, but my works remain hugely popular today.

Answer: Charles Dickens

E-Books and E-Readers

More and more people today are reading books in electronic form—known as e-books. According to the Association of American Publishers, e-book sales grew 164 percent from 2009 to 2010, to a total of $441 million in sales in 2010. Some well-known e-book readers include the Kindle, the Sony Reader, and the Nook.

E-readers allow users to download books, magazines, newspapers, and other material wirelessly from the Internet. They have a number of interactive features. You can control screen brightness, type size, and other aspects of how each page looks. On some devices, you turn a page using a page button. On others, you run your finger across the screen.

Some e-readers have a keyboard, which allows you to add comments to the page as you read. Others have a touch screen keyboard. Some allow website access and some let you download books as audio files. Those devices will even read the book aloud to you!

Tablets for Reading and More

Tablets are a line of computers that allow you to read books and also access the Internet, play music, e-mail, watch videos, and download apps with the touch of your finger. Thin and light, a tablet is like a laptop computer, e-reader, and smartphone combined. One of the most popular is Apple's iPad. In March 2011, the iPad2 was released. The iPad 2 is faster and thinner than the original version. It also has two cameras for taking pictures and video chatting. According to Apple, 19.5 million iPads were sold from the launch of the original version in April 2010 through March 2011.

BUILDINGS

What was the purpose of the El Castillo pyramid at Chichén-Itzá? → page 53

TALLEST BUILDINGS IN THE WORLD

Here are the world's tallest buildings, with the year each was completed. Heights listed here don't include antennas or other outside structures.

Burj Khalifa (Khalifa Tower)
Dubai, United Arab Emirates (2010)
Height: 162 stories, 2,717 feet

Taipei 101
Taipei, Taiwan (2004)
Height: 101 stories, 1,667 feet

World Financial Center
Shanghai, China (2008)
Height: 101 stories, 1,614 feet

International Commerce Center
Hong Kong, China (2010)
Height: 108 stories, 1,588 feet

Petronas Towers 1 & 2
Kuala Lumpur, Malaysia (1998)
Height: each building is 88 stories, 1,483 feet

Greenland Financial Center
Nanjing, China (2009)
Height: 66 stories, 1,476 feet

★ Burj Khalifa

The Burj Khalifa (Khalifa Tower), which was officially opened on January 4, 2010, is the world's tallest building. A slender shaft built of aluminum-covered round sections set on top of one another, the building has an observation deck on the 124th floor, as well as 24,348 windows. It houses apartments, corporate offices, restaurants, a fitness center, and a luxury hotel. The building can hold up to 35,000 people. Outside the tower is a large park. The tower holds many world records besides its height. For example, it has the world's highest mosque (on the 158th floor) and the world's highest swimming pool (on the 76th floor).

WORLD'S TALLEST WHEN BUILT

Great Pyramid of Giza, Egypt
Built c. 2250 B.C. Height: 480 feet

Washington Monument, Washington, D.C. Built 1848–84. Height: 555 feet

Eiffel Tower, Paris, France
Built 1887–89. Height: 984 feet

Chrysler Building, New York, NY
Built 1930. Height: 1,046 feet

Empire State Building, New York, NY
Built 1931. Height: 1,250 feet

did you Know?

The tallest building in the United States is the Willis Tower, in Chicago, Illinois. Originally called the Sears Tower, it stands 1,450 feet tall and has 110 stories. However, when it is completed in 2013, the new One World Trade Center building in New York, being built on the site of the 9/11 attacks, will stand 1,776 feet tall (recalling the year of American independence).

A Short History of Tall Buildings

Throughout history, tall buildings have been symbols of power, wealth, and personal importance. Think about how impressed we are by the ancient Pyramids in Egypt, and then imagine how much more impressive they must have seemed to ancient people, who weren't used to seeing such enormous structures. But, in addition to trying to impress other people, the makers of tall buildings had to figure out how to support them and keep them from collapsing from their own weight. One answer was to have a huge, thick base that could support the weight above. The base of the Washington Monument, for example, has walls that are 15 feet thick!

By the 1880s, three **key factors in the evolution of tall buildings** were in place:

1. A NEED FOR SPACE Crowded cities had less space for building, and land got expensive. To create more space, buildings had to go up instead of out.

2. BETTER STEEL PRODUCTION Mass-producing steel meant more of it was available for construction. Long vertical **columns** and horizontal girders could be joined to form a strong cube-like grid that was lighter than a similar one made of stone or brick. Weight was also directed down the columns to a solid **foundation**, usually underground, instead of to walls.

3. THE ELEVATOR Tall buildings need elevators! The first elevator, powered by steam, was installed in a New York store in 1857. Electric elevators came along in 1880.

As buildings got taller, a new problem sprang up—**wind**. Too much movement could damage buildings or make the people inside uncomfortable. Some tall buildings, like New York's Citicorp Center, actually have a counter-weight near the top. A computer controls a 400-ton weight, moving it back and forth to lessen the building's sway.

In California and Japan, **earthquakes** are a big problem, and special techniques are needed to make tall buildings safer from quakes.

IT'S NOT ALL ABOUT... TALL!

When it comes to buildings, the tall ones grab people's attention. But many other buildings are interesting and fun to look at. Here are a few really cool buildings.

GUGGENHEIM MUSEUM, Bilbao, Spain

This stunning building, which houses a collection of modern art, was designed by the Canadian-American architect Frank Gehry. Its exterior is composed of many curved titanium panels that look as if they have been piled up at random. Since Bilbao is a port, the building was given a shape resembling that of a ship. The museum, which opened in 1997, received more than one million visitors in 2010. It has attracted tourists to Bilbao from all over the world.

COMMUNITY BOOKSHELF, Kansas City, Missouri

The "wall of books" decorates the exterior of the parking garage for the Kansas City Library. It was designed by a local architecture firm. Each "book" measures about 9 feet wide and 25 feet high. The titles were chosen by the city's residents and include books of local interest, as well as classics such as Mark Twain's *The Adventures of Huckleberry Finn.*

NATIONAL AQUATICS CENTER, Beijing, China

The "Water Cube" was built for the 2008 Olympic Games swimming and diving competitions. It's made to look natural and random, like soap bubbles or plant cells. The walls and roof are made of thousands of steel polygons fitted with inflated Teflon (plastic) bubbles. The bubbles capture solar energy to heat the pools. Each bubble has skin as thin as a pen tip but can hold the weight of a car. Since 2010, the building has been used as a water park, featuring water rides and slides.

30 ST. MARY AXE, London, England

The unusual office tower in the financial center of London opened in 2004. It was carefully designed to be energy efficient and uses sunlight to heat the interior during the winter. The building's unique shape has earned it the nickname "the Gherkin" (a gherkin is a kind of pickle). It has appeared in a number of films, including *Harry Potter and the Half-Blood Prince.*

HISTORICAL WONDERS

TREASURY

Petra, Jordan; **1st century B.C.**

Petra is an ancient city located in modern Jordan. It is famous for its buildings cut into the local red rock. The city was ruled by the Egyptians, the Romans, and others throughout its long history. The Treasury building is the most magnificent building at the site. Despite its name, historians think it was actually either a royal tomb or a temple.

DOME OF THE ROCK

Jerusalem, Israel; **687**

The Dome of the Rock is the oldest Islamic monument still standing. A shrine, it was built over a rock sacred to both Muslims and Jews. Its 25-meter dome is covered with gold. Because the structure is considered the center of the Earth for the Arabs who built it, there are exits leading north, east, south, and west.

EL CASTILLO PYRAMID

Chichén-Itzá, Mexico; **800–1200**

El Castillo is the greatest pyramid at Chichén-Itzá, a center of Mayan civilization. Historians believe that the pyramid served as a calendar. It has 91 steps on each of its four sides. If you count the step onto the platform at the top, the total number of steps is 365, the number of days in a year. The base of the northern side of the pyramid is decorated with huge plumed serpents.

FORBIDDEN CITY

Beijing, China; **1406–1420**

This was the exclusive home for emperors of the Ming and Qing dynasties for 492 years. The palace grounds are the world's largest (178 acres). It was "forbidden" because people could not enter without the emperor's permission. The palace itself contains thousands of wooden chambers and great halls that cover 37 acres. Every roof is yellow, the color of Chinese royalty.

BRIDGES

There are four main bridge designs: beam, arch, truss, and suspension or cable-stayed.

BEAM

The beam bridge is the most basic kind. A log across a stream is a simple style of beam bridge. Highway bridges are often beam bridges. The span of a beam bridge, or the length of the bridge without any support under it, needs to be fairly short. Long beam bridges need many supporting poles, called piers.

ARCH

You can easily recognize an arch bridge, because it has arches holding it up from the bottom. The columns that support the arches are called abutments. Arch bridges were invented by the ancient Greeks.

TRUSS

The truss bridge uses mainly steel beams, connected in triangles to increase strength and span greater distances.

SUSPENSION

On suspension bridges, the roadway hangs from smaller cables attached to a pair of huge cables running over two massive towers. The ends of the giant cables are anchored firmly into solid rock or huge concrete blocks at each end of the bridge. The weight of the roadway is transferred through the cables to the anchors. On a cable-stayed bridge, the cables are attached directly from the towers (pylons) to the deck.

Building Quiz

Can you match each building in the left column with a description in the right column?

Guggenheim Museum	Tallest building in the world
30 St. Mary Axe	Ancient pyramid that served as a calendar
Burj Khalifa	Building that looks like a pickle
El Castillo	Building shaped like a ship

ANSWERS ON PAGES 334–336.

PARTS OF A SUSPENSION BRIDGE

Anchorage Main cables are attached here, adding strength and stability
Deck Surface of the bridge
Main cable Primary load-bearing cables, secured by anchorages
Pier Supports for pylons
Pylon Tower supports that hold up cables and decks
Suspender cable Vertical cables that hold up the deck

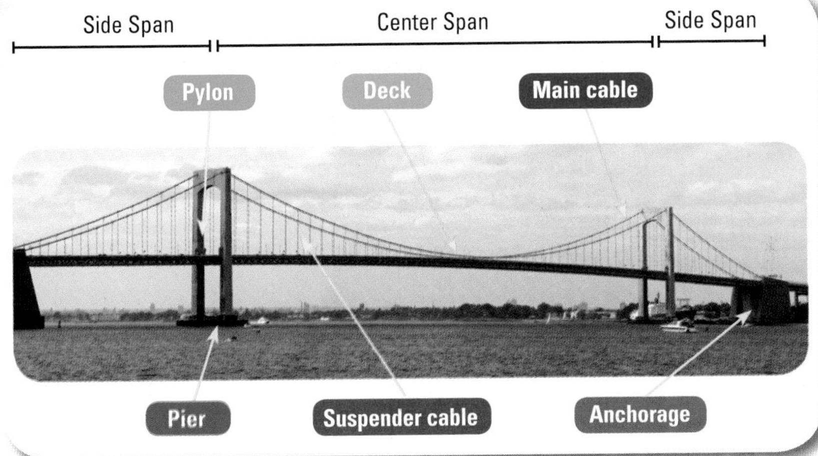

DAM FACTS

Dams are built to control the flow of rivers. They can provide water for drinking or farming, prevent flooding, and create electricity. The first dams were embankment dams built thousands of years ago out of walls of rocks and dirt to prevent flooding or to make lakes called reservoirs for irrigation. Today, most dams are made of concrete. "Hydroelectric" dams are used to generate electricity by channeling the force of rivers and waterfalls into tunnels in the dam to move enormous machines called turbines.

Hoover Dam in Nevada

CALENDAR

When is Memorial Day? → page 59

CALENDAR BASICS

Holidays and calendars go hand in hand. Using a calendar, you can see what day of the week it is and look for the next special day. Calendars divide time into days, weeks, months, and years. According to our calendar, also known as the Gregorian calendar, a year is the time it takes for one revolution of Earth around the Sun: 365¼ days. To make things easier, every four years we add an extra day, February 29, in "leap years," such as 2012.

THE NAMES OF THE MONTHS

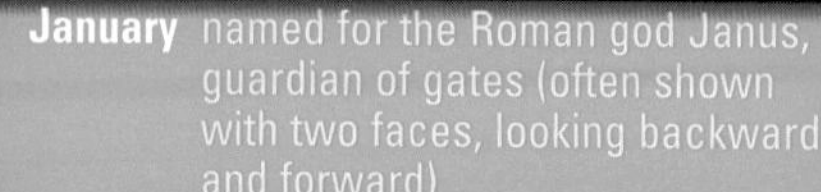

January	named for the Roman god Janus, guardian of gates (often shown with two faces, looking backward and forward)
February	named for Februalia, a Roman time of sacrifice
March	named for Mars, the Roman god of war (the end of winter meant fighting could begin again)
April	"aperire," Latin for "to open," as in flower buds
May	named for Maia, the goddess of plant growth
June	"Junius," the Latin word for the goddess Juno
July	named after the Roman ruler Julius Caesar
August	named for Augustus, the first Roman emperor
September	"septem," Latin for seven (the Roman year began in March)
October	"octo," the Latin word for eight
November	"novem," the Latin word for nine
December	"decem," the Latin word for ten

Other Calendars

The **Gregorian calendar** is used by the United States and much of the rest of the world. But some nations and religions use other calendars.

Islamic Calendar The Islamic calendar is used by Muslim people around the world. Twelve lunar months, each beginning with the new Moon, make up the year. The year is 354 days long (355 days in leap years). Al-Hijra/Muharram (Islamic New Year) in Islamic year 1434 starts at moon crescent on November 14, 2012.

Jewish Calendar The Jewish calendar has months of 29 and 30 days, and its years are either 12 or 13 months long. It is a lunar-solar calendar, which means its months are lunar, but its years adjust to the movement of Earth around the Sun. It is the official calendar in Israel and is used as a religious calendar by Jewish people worldwide. Rosh Hashanah (New Year) in the year 5773 begins at sundown on September 16, 2012, on the Gregorian calendar.

Chinese Calendar The Chinese calendar is a lunar-solar calendar that runs on a 60-year cycle. Within the cycle, years are given one of twelve animal designations: Rat, Ox, Tiger, Rabbit, Dragon, Snake, Horse, Sheep, Monkey, Rooster, Dog, and Pig. On January 23, 2012, the Year of the Dragon starts.

HOLIDAY HIGHLIGHTS

Each month brings new chances to celebrate famous people, historic events, and special occasions. On federal holidays, U.S. government offices are closed as are many schools and businesses. There are also other holidays that might not mean a day off from school, but they are still enthusiastically celebrated. Holidays marked with an asterisk (*) are federal holidays.

JANUARY 2012

January is National Oatmeal Month and National Skating Month. Learn how to ice skate—for free—at events at participating ice rinks nationwide. Grab a bowl of oatmeal beforehand for a nutritious way to stay warm from the inside out.

*** January 1: New Year's Day**
Until the year 1753, New Year's Day was celebrated on March 25 every year. When the Gregorian calendar was adopted in 1582, the date was switched to January 1.

*** January 16: Martin Luther King Jr. Day**
Martin Luther King Jr. Day takes place on the third Monday in January. The holiday honors the famous civil rights leader who was born on January 15, 1929.

January 23: Chinese New Year
The year 4710 begins on January 23 according to China's traditional lunar-solar calendar. The celebration lasts for 15 days, ending with the Lantern Festival.

FEBRUARY 2012

February is Black History Month and American Heart Month. Learn about the contributions of some important African Americans who changed history. See if your school is sponsoring a "Jump Rope for Heart" event.

February 2: Groundhog Day
On February 2, thousands of people gather in the small town of Punxsutawney, Pennsylvania, to see if Punxsutawney Phil will see his shadow. According to legend, if the famous groundhog sees his shadow, winter will last six more weeks. If he doesn't, spring will come early.

February 14: Valentine's Day
Valentine's Day is mostly a way to celebrate those you care about—people have been exchanging Valentine cards with loved ones since the 1500s.

*** February 20: Presidents' Day**
Observed on the third Monday in February, Presidents' Day honors George Washington and Abraham Lincoln. Both presidents were born in February. George Washington was born on February 22, 1732, and Abraham Lincoln was born on February 12, 1809.

MARCH 2012

March is Women's History Month. From science to sports, discover some of history's leading ladies. March is also National Nutrition Month. It is a good time to learn how to eat well and stay fit all year long.

March 17: St. Patrick's Day

This day celebrates the patron saint of Ireland. Many people, especially those with Irish heritage, consider St. Patrick's Day a time to remember their ancestors and eat traditional Irish foods.

March 20: First Day of Spring

Today marks the first day of spring in the Northern Hemisphere. Also known as the Vernal Equinox, the first day of spring is observed when the center of the Sun appears directly above the Earth's equator.

APRIL 2012

April is National Humor Month and National Poetry Month. Be sure to laugh at any pranks on April Fools' Day, then try telling a new joke every day during the month. Visit the library for books of poetry (try *Where the Sidewalk Ends*, by Shel Silverstein), then try writing some of your own.

April 1: April Fools' Day

People have been celebrating April Fools' Day with pranks and gags for more than 400 years. Have fun tricking your family or friends, but make sure that none of your pranks are cruel or harmful.

April 22: Earth Day

First celebrated in the United States in 1970, Earth Day is an occasion for people to take action and care for our environment. Today, more than one billion people around the globe commemorate Earth Day. Some will plant trees or clean up local parks and waterways. Others will make a commitment to recycle. For more information on how you can make a difference, visit ***www.earthday.org***.

MAY 2012

May is National Bike Month. Give up that car. Ride and bike instead. Biking is good for the environment. It's also a fun way to stay fit. Before you jump on your bike, be sure to wear a helmet to stay safe.

May 5: Cinco de Mayo
Mexicans remember May 5, 1862, when Mexico defeated the French army in the Battle of the Puebla.

May 13: Mother's Day
Since 1914, Mother's Day has been celebrated on the second Sunday of May. Each year, more than 155 million cards are bought and given to moms across the United States. And that doesn't even include the special homemade cards that moms receive!

*** May 28: Memorial Day**
Originally celebrated in honor of members of the military who died during the Civil War, Memorial Day now honors all men and women who have died while serving in the U.S. military. It falls on the last Monday in May.

JUNE 2012

June is Great Outdoors Month. Be sure to get outside and get active at special events, from National Boating and Fishing Week to the Great American Backyard Campout, to celebrate the Great Outdoors.

June 14: Flag Day
Celebrated on June 14, this day remembers the adoption of the first version of the Stars and Stripes by the Continental Congress in 1777. Flag Day is not an official federal holiday, but many communities hold celebrations to honor the American flag.

June 17: Father's Day
This day that celebrates fathers falls on the third Sunday in June.

June 19: Juneteenth
Juneteenth, also known as Emancipation Day, celebrates a military order on June 19, 1865, that formally completed the freeing of the slaves. People all over the country—especially in Texas, where it is a state holiday—spend Juneteenth celebrating freedom.

June 20: First Day of Summer
The first day of summer in the Northern Hemisphere is observed on the Summer Solstice, when the Sun rises and sets the farthest north on the horizon and daylight hours are longest.

JULY 2012

July is Cell Phone Courtesy Month. This month reminds the more than 233 million cell phone users in the United States to be more aware of how cell phone use in public places affects other people.

July 1: Canada Day

Canada Day (called Dominion Day until 1982) celebrates the creation of the Dominion of Canada on July 1, 1867. Like the Fourth of July in the United States, Canada Day is celebrated with parades and fireworks.

*** July 4: Independence Day**

Commonly known as the Fourth of July, this federal holiday marks the anniversary of the signing of the Declaration of Independence on July 4, 1776. Americans celebrate with picnics, parades, barbecues, and fireworks.

July 14: Bastille Day

This holiday commemorates the beginning of the French Revolution by the storming of the Bastille, an event that eventually led to the formation of modern France.

AUGUST 2012

August is American Adventures Month and Happiness Happens Month. Celebrate vacations in North, South, and Central America, by going on one of your own or remembering a fun vacation you've taken in the past. Happiness Happens Month encourages people to appreciate happiness.

August 5: Friendship Day

Celebrated on the first Sunday in August, this special day honors friendship.

August 26: Women's Equality Day

This holiday remembers the day that the 19th Amendment to the U.S. Constitution was ratified to grant women the right to vote.

SEPTEMBER 2012

September is Library Card Sign-Up Month and Hispanic Heritage Month (September 15–October 15). If you don't already have a library card, now is the time to get one. And take advantage of the library to learn about the 500-year-old roots of Hispanic culture in the Americas.

* September 3: Labor Day

A federal holiday that takes place on the first Monday in September, Labor Day celebrates workers with a day off in their honor. Labor Day has its roots in the late 19th-century labor movement, when workers began to organize to demand shorter hours and fairer pay. It was made a federal holiday in 1894.

September 9: National Grandparents Day

Celebrated on the Sunday after Labor Day, Grandparents Day honors grandparents and the knowledge they pass on.

September 17: Constitution or Citizenship Day

Constitution Day celebrates the rights and responsibilities of U.S. citizens. It takes place on September 17, the date the U.S. Constitution was signed in 1787.

September 22: First Day of Autumn

Today is the first day of autumn, or fall, in the Northern Hemisphere. Also known as the Autumnal Equinox, the first day of fall occurs when the center of the Sun appears directly above the Earth's equator.

OCTOBER 2012

October is National Dental Hygiene Month and National Popcorn Poppin' Month. When you snack on popcorn this month, experiment by adding your own flavors or spices to the wholesome treat. If you get a kernel stuck in your teeth (or just eat too much Halloween candy!), brush and floss extra carefully.

* October 8: Columbus Day

Celebrated on the second Monday in October, Columbus Day marks Christopher Columbus's landing on an island in the Bahamas, then thought of as the New World, in 1492.

October 31: Halloween

Halloween always falls on the last day of October. A holiday similar to Halloween has been celebrated since at least the seventh century. Today, global customs vary as much as costumes do, but trick-or-treating remains the most common way to celebrate in the United States.

NOVEMBER 2012

November is National American Indian Heritage Month. Learn about Native Americans and their roles in American history.

November 6: Election Day

The first Tuesday after the first Monday in November, Election Day is a mandatory holiday in some states.

*** November 11: Veterans Day**

On this special day, Americans honor U.S. veterans—men and women who have served in the armed forces. Veterans Day originally marked the "eleventh hour of the eleventh day of the eleventh month" in 1918. This is when World War I battles came to an end according to the conditions of an armistice (an agreement to stop fighting) signed earlier that morning.

*** November 22: Thanksgiving**

Every year on the fourth Thursday in November, Americans take the day to honor the people, events, and things in their lives for which they are thankful. Tradition calls for a big meal, shared with friends and family, along with watching the televised Thanksgiving Day parade and football.

DECEMBER 2012

December is National Drunk and Drugged Driving Prevention Month. Impaired driving causes an injury every two minutes and a death every half hour. Contribute something to raise awareness of the danger of drunk and drugged driving this month.

December 21: First Day of Winter

The first day of winter, in the Northern Hemisphere, is observed on the Winter Solstice, when the Sun rises and sets the farthest south on the horizon and daylight hours are shortest. Get outside for your favorite winter activity. Don't worry if the days seem short—they'll be getting longer from this day on leading up to summer.

December 31: New Year's Eve

This day isn't technically a holiday, but you'll still find a lot of people celebrating the end of one year and the beginning of the next. Get a head start on making your New Year's resolutions before you go to bed.

MORE DAYS TO CELEBRATE

Mark your calendar! Here are some exciting and unusual days you don't want to miss:

January 17: Kid Inventors' Day
What do water skis, earmuffs, and the Popsicle have in common? They were all invented by kids! Celebrate young minds on the birthday of Ben Franklin, who invented the first swim fins at age 12.

February 5: Super Bowl XLVI
The year's biggest game is the grand finale of the NFL season. Super Bowl XLV in 2011 averaged 111 million viewers, making it the most-watched American TV program of all time.

March 3: National Anthem Day
O say, can you see... "The Star-Spangled Banner," written by Francis Scott Key during the War of 1812, officially became the U.S. national anthem on March 3, 1931.

April 27: National Arbor Day
Give a tree a hug today. Arbor Day, observed each year on the last Friday in April, encourages people to plant and care for trees. For ideas on how to celebrate, visit ***www.arborday.org.***

May 5: Kentucky Derby
Known as "The Most Exciting Two Minutes in Sports," the Kentucky Derby is held each year on the first Saturday in May at Churchill Downs in Louisville, Kentucky.

June 27: Sunglasses Day
Rain or shine, sport your stylish shades because there is a big reason to celebrate this day. Sunglasses protect our eyes from the Sun's harmful untraviolet rays.

July 15: National Ice Cream Day
Let's all scream for ice cream! Also known as "Sundae Sunday," National Ice Cream Day celebrates America's popular dessert on the third Sunday in July.

August 19: National Aviation Day
Up, up, and away! The Wright brothers (Wilbur and Orville) made history in 1903 with the first self-powered flights in a heavier-than-air aircraft. In recognition of flight, people celebrate National Aviation Day on Orville's birthday.

September 16: Mayflower Day
Destination: America! This day commemorates the anniversary of the *Mayflower's* departure from Plymouth, England, in 1620 with 102 passengers and a small crew.

October 16: Dictionary Day
Calling all wordsmiths! Learn a new word today in honor of the birthday of Noah Webster, the father of the American dictionary.

November 7: International Tongue Twister Day
Peter Piper picked a peck of pickled peppers. Can you say that three times fast? Celebrate this day by practicing some of your favorite tongue twisters.

December 15: Bill of Rights Day
The first ten amendments to the U.S. Constitution are called the Bill of Rights. This day commemorates the date in 1791 when they were officially added to the Constitution.

What is a Ponzi scheme? → page 65

FORENSICS:

USING SCIENCE TO SOLVE CRIMES

Any use of scientific procedures to help resolve legal issues can be called **forensics**. But the word is often used to refer specifically to the scientific analysis of evidence in order to solve a crime.

Checking a crime scene

Fingerprints: Some forensic methods have been used for a long time. One example is gathering fingerprints at a crime scene in order to compare them with prints of known individuals on file. Technological advances have made this method more effective and simpler to use. Certain chemicals can expose a fingerprint to view, and modern computer networks make it easier to build and access large collections of fingerprints.

Guns: With many guns, when a bullet goes through the gun barrel, it picks up markings that are distinctive for the gun. Comparing these markings with those on file from known guns can identify the gun that fired the bullet.

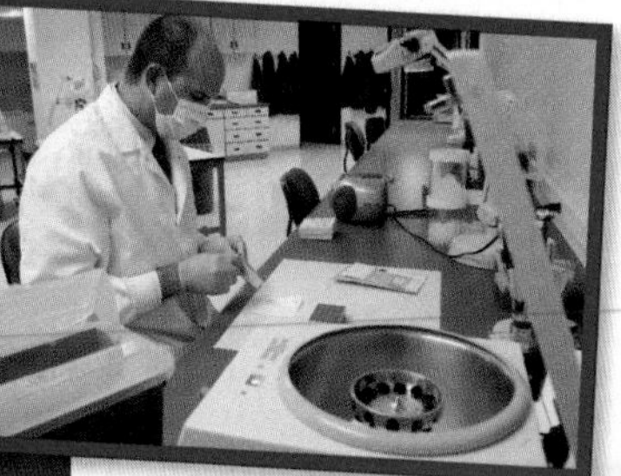

DNA lab work

DNA: DNA, or genetic, evidence can be very helpful in identifying individuals. Except in identical twins, every person's DNA is unique. Investigators often gather it from sources such as blood, saliva, and skin.

Chemistry: Many chemistry techniques are valuable aids in solving crimes. For example, an investigator may apply a chemical such as luminol at a crime scene to make hidden bloodstains visible. Well-equipped crime labs use sophisticated techniques to learn the makeup of unknown substances found at a crime scene.

did you Know?

*Crime investigators sometimes call on the help of various experts. The **toxicologist**, for instance, specializes in drugs and poisons. The **pathologist** deals with the changes disease and injury can make in the body. A **forensic anthropologist** can analyze human remains such as bones. A **forensic dentist** can match teeth patterns with dental records. **Forensic entomologists**, experts in insects, can use their knowledge of the life cycles of bugs that feed on corpses to help identify the time of death.*

Thieves and Swindlers

SOME NOTORIOUS NONVIOLENT CRIMES

Nonviolent crimes cause no physical harm to any person. Still, they may do major damage to an individual, a group, or an entire country. Many notorious crimes involve **fraud**, or deceiving people in order to get money from them. Others involve theft—of valuable objects or valuable information.

Ponzi Fraud Scheme

In 1920, Charles Ponzi gained quick fame by promising people a big profit fast if they gave him their cash to invest. He claimed earnings as high as 50 percent in just 45 days. He didn't actually do any investing. He simply used cash from new clients to pay off old ones who wanted their money. Many chose not to withdraw their money, in hopes of amassing still more riches. In just eight months, before his fraud was exposed, Ponzi took in an estimated $15 million. To this day, this type of swindle is known as a Ponzi scheme.

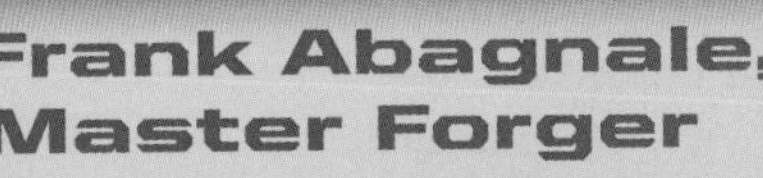

Frank Abagnale, Master Forger

At the age of 16, Frank W. Abagnale Jr. began a five-year career in fraud. He cashed $2.5 million in forged checks in more than two dozen countries, including the U.S. Along the way, he assumed many fake identities, including airline pilot, lawyer, college teacher, and doctor. After his 1969 capture, he spent a few years in French, Swedish, and U.S. prisons. He then became a successful security consultant. His exploits were the basis for a 2011 Broadway musical and a 2002 movie, both called *Catch Me If You Can.*

Gardner Museum Theft

The largest art theft in history took place in 1990 at Boston's Isabella Stewart Gardner Museum. In the middle of the night, two men disguised as police entered the building, tied up two guards, and then walked through the building, taking more than a dozen works of art. The items, valued at an estimated $500 million, were still missing more than 20 years later.

Madoff Ponzi Scheme

The biggest Ponzi scheme ever was carried out by Bernard Madoff. A former head of the Nasdaq stock market, he was a financial expert and managed to keep his investment fraud going for a couple of decades before it collapsed. Overall, he took $65 billion from more than 1,300 victims. Many of them lost their life savings. In 2009, Madoff was sentenced to 150 years in prison.

How was Hawaii formed? → page 68

EARTHQUAKES

There are thousands of earthquakes each year. Most are small, but about 1 in 500 causes damage. Some quakes are incredibly powerful and destructive, such as the huge quake in Japan in March 2011 and the somewhat smaller quake that hit New Zealand the month before.

Damaged buildings in New Zealand

WHAT CAUSES EARTHQUAKES?

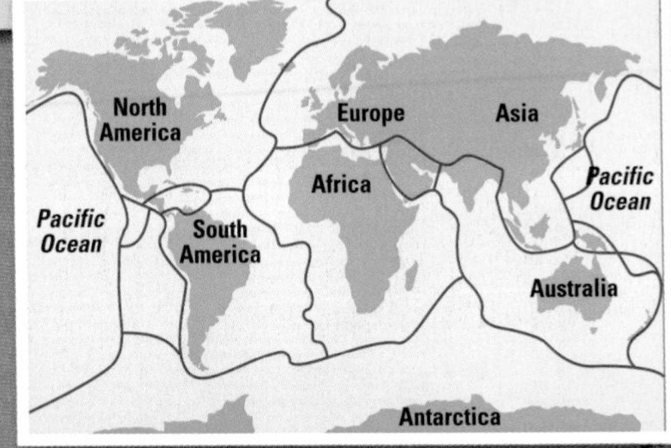

To understand earthquakes, imagine Earth as an egg with a cracked shell. The cracked outer layer (the eggshell) is called the **lithosphere**, and it is divided into huge pieces called **plates** (see map). The plates are constantly moving away from, toward, or past one another. Earthquakes result when plates collide or scrape against each other. The cracks in the lithosphere are called **faults**. Many quakes occur along these fault lines.

What Are TSUNAMIS?

Tsunami (pronounced ***tsoo-NAH-mee***) comes from two Japanese words: "tsu" (harbor) and "nami" (wave). Tsunamis are huge waves. They are sometimes called tidal waves, but they have nothing to do with the tides.

The strongest tsunamis happen when a big part of the sea floor lifts along a fault (see map above), pushing up a huge volume of water. Many times this happens after an undersea earthquake (see table on page 67). The waves move at speeds of up to 500 miles per hour. As they near shore, they slow down, and the great energy forces the water upward into big waves.

MAJOR EARTHQUAKES?

These earthquakes are among the largest and most destructive since 1960.

Year	Location	Magnitude	Deaths (estimated)
1960	near Chile	9.5	5,000
1970	Northern Peru	7.8	66,000
1976	Tangshan, China	8.0	255,000
1988	Soviet Armenia	7.0	55,000
1989	United States (San Francisco area)	7.1	62
1990	Western Iran	7.7	40,000
1995	Kobe, Japan	6.9	5,502
1999	Western Turkey	7.4	17,200
2001	Western India	7.9	30,000
2004	Sumatra, Indonesia	9.0	225,000
2005	Pakistan and India	7.6	80,000
2008	Sichuan, China	7.9	87,652
2010	Haiti	7.0	230,000
2010	Chile	8.8	700
2011	Christchurch, New Zealand	6.3	169
2011	Northeastern Japan	9.0	15,000+

MAJOR TSUNAMIS

These are some of the most destructive tsunamis in recent centuries.

Year	Location	What Happened?	Deaths (estimated)
1707	Hoei, Japan	An 8.6-magnitude earthquake triggered a tsunami with waves up to 30 feet.	30,000
1755	Lisbon, Portugal	Three earthquakes struck Portugal's capital within 10 minutes, creating a tsunami with waves up to 100 feet high.	100,000–200,000
1782	South China Sea near Taiwan	After a major underwater earthquake, a tsunami sent waves inland more than 60 miles.	40,000
1908	Southern Italy	A major earthquake triggered a devastating tsunami.	123,000
2004	Indian Ocean	After a 9.0-magnitude earthquake hit Indonesia, a tsunami with waves up to 100 feet high struck 14 countries.	225,000
2011	Northeastern Japan	A 9.0-magnitude earthquake touched off a huge tsunami.	15,000+

Tsunami, Japan 2011

VOLCANOES

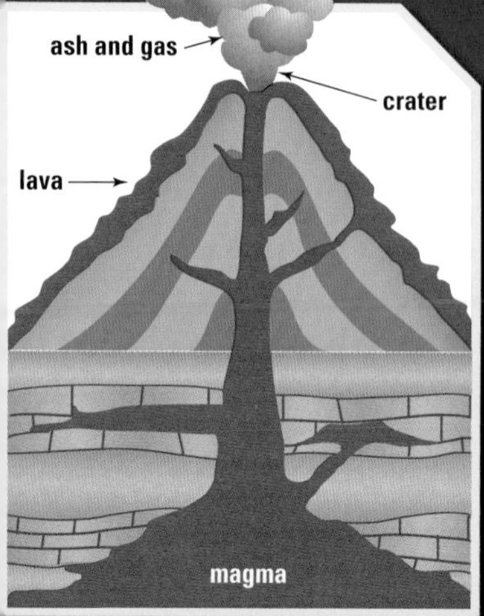

A volcano is a mountain or hill **(cone)** with an opening on top known as a **crater**. Hot melted rock **(magma)**, gases, and other material from inside Earth mix together and rise up through cracks and weak spots. When enough pressure builds up, the magma can escape, erupting through the crater. Magma that comes out of the crater is called **lava**. Lava may be hotter than 2,000°F. The cone of a volcano is often made of layers of lava and ash that have erupted, then cooled.

Some Famous Volcanic Eruptions

Year	Volcano (place)	Deaths (estimated)
79	Mount Vesuvius (Italy)	16,000
1586	Kelut (Indonesia)	10,000
1792	Mount Unzen (Japan)	14,500
1815	Tambora (Indonesia)	10,000
1883	Krakatau, or Krakatoa (Indonesia)	36,000
1902	Mount Pelée (Martinique)	28,000
1980	Mount St. Helens (U.S.)	57
1982	El Chichón (Mexico)	1,880
1985	Nevado del Ruiz (Colombia)	23,000
1986	Lake Nyos (Cameroon)	1,700
1991	Mount Pinatubo (Philippines)	800

Where is the RING of FIRE?

The hundreds of active volcanoes near the edges of the Pacific Ocean make up what is called the **Ring of Fire.** They mark the boundary between the plates under the Pacific Ocean and the plates under the surrounding continents. (Earth's plates are explained on page 66, with the help of a map.) The Ring of Fire runs from Alaska, along the west coast of North and South America, to the southern tip of Chile. The ring also runs down the east coast of Asia, starting in the far north. It continues down past Australia.

How was Hawaii formed?

Hawaii is a 1,500-mile-long chain of islands in the middle of the Pacific Ocean. These islands are the tops of volcanoes, and they were formed by a **hot spot**. This is an area deep inside Earth that spews lava up through the ocean floor. Over time, as more and more lava emerges, cools, and hardens, the volcanic cone rises above the surface. Over thousands of years, the islands drift to the northwest as Earth's plates move (see page 66), and new islands are formed over the hot spot. This process is still going on today.

HURRICANES

HURRICANE CATEGORIES

1 74-95 mph
2 96-110 mph
3 111-130 mph
4 131-155 mph
5 over 155 mph

Hurricanes—called typhoons or cyclones in the Pacific—are Earth's biggest storms. When conditions are right, they form over the ocean from collections of storms and clouds known as tropical disturbances. Strong winds create a wall of clouds and rain that swirl in a circle around a calm center called the **eye.**

The eye develops as **warm, moist air** is forced upward in the storm by **denser, cooler air**. From the outer edge of the storm to the inner eye, the pressure drops and wind speeds rise sharply, creating swirling **convection currents** around the eye. If wind speeds reach 39 mph, the storm is named. If wind speeds top 74 mph, the storm is called a **hurricane**.

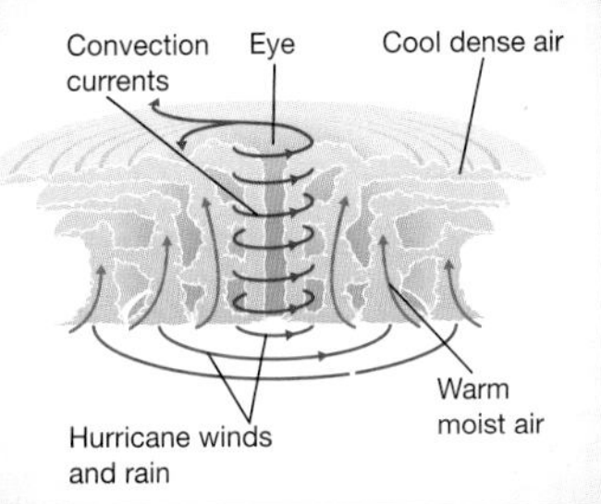

Hurricanes can be up to 300 miles wide. On land, the storm can snap trees and tear buildings apart. Strong winds blowing toward shore can create a rise in the ocean water called a **storm surge**. It can combine with heavy rains to cause flooding and massive damage.

For the Atlantic Ocean, Caribbean Sea, and Gulf of Mexico, hurricane season runs from June 1 to November 30. Most hurricanes happen in August, September, and October, when the oceans are warmest.

NOTABLE U.S. HURRICANES

Date	Location	What Happened?	Deaths
Sept. 8, 1900	Galveston, TX	Category 4 storm flooded the island with 15-foot waves.	8,000+
Sept. 19, 1938	NY, CT, RI, MA	"The Long Island Express," with storm surges rising 10-25 feet, caused $306 million in damages.	600+
Aug. 24-26, 1992	FL, LA	Hurricane Andrew swept across the Gulf of Mexico, leaving 250,000 homeless.	65
Aug. 25-29, 2005	LA, MS, AL, GA, FL	Hurricane Katrina, with 175 mph winds and a 25-foot high storm surge, caused about $125 billion in damage.	1,833

HURRICANE NAMES

The U.S. began using women's names for hurricanes in 1953 and added men's names in 1979. When all letters (except Q, U, X, Y, and Z) are used in one season, any additional storms are named with Greek letters. Six Greek letters were needed to name 2005 storms.

2012 Atlantic Hurricane Names: Alberto, Beryl, Chris, Debby, Ernesto, Florence, Gordon, Helene, Isaac, Joyce, Kirk, Leslie, Michael, Nadine, Oscar, Patty, Rafael, Sandy, Tony, Valerie, William

did you Know?

The strongest hurricane ever recorded in the U.S. hit the Florida Keys on Labor Day in 1935. More than 400 people were killed by this Category 5 storm.

Tornadoes

TORNADO CATEGORIES

WEAK

EF0: 65-85 mph

EF1: 86-110 mph

STRONG

EF2: 111-135 mph

EF3: 136-165 mph

VIOLENT

EF4: 166-200 mph

EF5: over 200 mph

Tornadoes are rapidly spinning columns of air. They usually form when winds change direction, speed up, and spin around in or near a thunderstorm.

Tornadoes can happen any time that the weather is right, but they are more common between March and July. They can happen in any state, but strong tornadoes often touch down in the U.S. Midwest and Southeast.

According to the National Oceanic and Atmospheric Administration (NOAA), about 1,000 tornadoes occur in the U.S. each year.

Tornadoes are measured by how much damage they cause. In February 2007, the U.S. began using the Enhanced Fujita (EF) Scale (top left) to measure tornadoes. The EF-Scale provides an estimate of a tornado's wind speed based on the amount of damage. If a tornado doesn't hit anything, it may be hard to classify it.

Wind speeds are difficult to measure directly, because measuring instruments can be destroyed in more violent winds. The highest wind speed ever recorded—318 mph—was taken in May 1999 in an Oklahoma tornado.

The part of the U.S. where the most tornadoes usually happen each year is known as Tornado Alley. It has no exact boundaries, but it includes large areas of Texas, Oklahoma, Kansas, Nebraska, Iowa, and South Dakota.

U.S. Tornado Records

(since record keeping began in 1950)

YEAR: The 1,817 tornadoes reported in 2004 topped the previous record of 1,424 in 1998.

MONTH: In April 2011, there were a total of 875 tornadoes, easily passing the old record of 542 set in May 2003.

SINGLE EVENT: On April 25-28, 2011, an estimated 305 tornadoes touched down in Alabama and a number of other states, mostly in the Southeast, causing more than 300 deaths.

OTHER MAJOR DISASTERS

Hindenburg disaster

Aircraft Disasters

Date	Location	What Happened?	Deaths
May 6, 1937	Lakehurst, NJ	German zeppelin (blimp) *Hindenburg* caught fire as it prepared to land.	36
March 27, 1977	Tenerife, Canary Islands	Two Boeing 747s collide on the runway of Los Rodeos airport.	582
Sept. 11, 2001	New York, NY; Arlington, VA; Shanksville, PA	Two hijacked planes crashed into the World Trade Center, one into the Pentagon, one went down in a PA field.	Nearly 3,000

Explosions and Fires

Date	Location	What Happened?	Deaths
March 25, 1911	New York, NY	Triangle Shirtwaist Factory caught fire. Workers were trapped inside.	146
Nov. 28, 1942	Boston, MA	Fire swept through the Coconut Grove nightclub; patrons panicked. Deadliest nightclub fire in U.S. history.	146
Dec. 3, 1984	Bhopal, India	A pesticide factory explosion spread toxic gas; worst industrial accident in history.	15,000

Floods

Date	Location	What Happened?	Deaths
Aug. 1931	China	Vast flooding on the Huang He River. Highest known death toll from a flood.	3,700,000
2009	Philippines	Two tropical storms dumped about 60 inches of rain in a week, causing more $250 million in damages.	540
2011	Australia	Severe flooding in southeast Australia around Brisbane caused about $1 billion in property damage.	39

Ship Disasters

Date	Location	What Happened?	Deaths
April 14, 1912	near Newfoundland	Luxury liner *Titanic* collided with iceberg.	1,503
May 7, 1915	Atlantic Ocean, near Ireland	British steamer *Lusitania* torpedoed and sunk by German submarine.	1,198
Jan. 30, 1945	Baltic Sea	Liner *Wilhelm Gustloff* carrying German refugees and soldiers sunk by Soviet sub. Highest death toll for a single ship.	9,000

ENERGY

How much electricity in the U.S. is produced by burning coal? → page 73

Energy can take many forms. Heat, light, and electricity are forms of energy. The Sun's warmth is energy in the form of heat. We extract energy from natural resources and put it to use, providing heat, electricity, and mechanical power. Some resources—like sunlight, water, and wind—will always be around or—like biomass—will always be made by nature. These are renewable resources. Nonrenewable resources, like fossil fuels and uranium, are not naturally replenished.

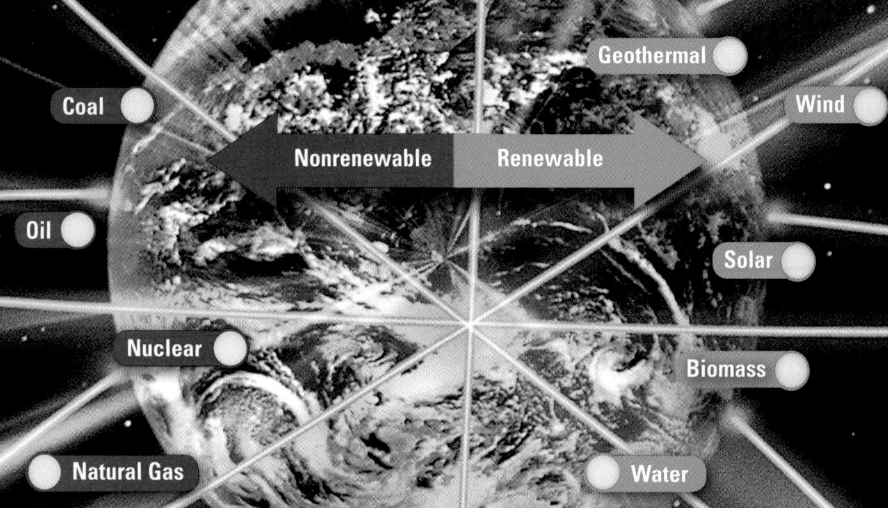

Who Produces and Uses the MOST ENERGY?

The United States produces about 15% of the world's energy—more than any other country except China—but it also uses 20% of the world's supply. The table on the left lists the world's top ten energy producers and the percent of the world's production that each nation was responsible for in 2008. One of these countries—Saudi Arabia—is the world's largest oil producer. The table on the right lists the world's top energy users and the percent of the world's energy that each nation consumed that same year.

TOP ENERGY PRODUCERS		TOP ENERGY USERS	
China	16%	United States	20%
United States	15%	China	17%
Russia	11%	Russia	6%
Saudi Arabia	5%	Japan	5%
Canada	4%	India	4%
India	3%	Germany	3%
Iran	3%	Canada	3%
Indonesia	3%	France	2%
Australia	3%	Brazil	2%
Norway	2%	South Korea	2%

SOURCES OF ENERGY

Where Does Energy Come From?

Nonrenewable resources come in limited supply. The "fossil fuels"—mainly **coal, oil,** and **natural gas**—are the most common sources of energy in the U.S. They are the decayed remains of ancient animals and plants. These fossil fuels took millions of years to form. If we run out, it will take millions of years for new supplies to be made. **Uranium**, the element that is split to power U.S. nuclear reactors, is fairly abundant. However, U-235, the type of uranium used for fuel in nuclear power plants, is relatively rare.

Coal mine

Renewable sources of energy will never run out. The force of moving water, such as a river or waterfall, can create **hydropower**. It is one of the oldest sources of energy. **Ocean energy** uses the motion of the tides or the power of breaking waves to produce energy. The Sun's light can be converted into **solar power**. Steady winds can be used to spin giant propellers, generating **wind power**. **Biomass** is renewable material made from plants or animals. This material, including wood or garbage, can be burned to make energy. Heat from the Earth's mantle, called **geothermal energy**, can be collected at natural hot springs where hot magma boils surface water.

How Do We Power Homes?

The most common uses of energy in the home are to control heating and cooling and provide electricity for lighting and appliances.

Most electricity is generated at power stations by wheel-shaped engines called **turbines**. Water, wind, or steam can be used to push turbines. Water is heated into steam by burning biomass or fossil fuels, by splitting uranium atoms during nuclear fission, or by using the heat of sunlight. More than two-fifths of America's electricity is generated from burning coal.

Some homes have solar "collectors" that capture the Sun's energy for use in heating water or solar panels that convert sunlight directly into electricity. Many people in the U.S. use natural gas, delivered to their home through pipes, for heat and hot water.

Renewable Energy in Action

Washington state is the nation's biggest producer of hydroelectricity and gets about 70 percent of its power from renewable resources. The Grand Coulee Dam, which spans the Columbia River in northern Washington, is the biggest hydroelectric dam in the U.S.

Grand Coulee Dam

WHERE DOES U.S. ENERGY COME FROM?

In 2009, about 83% of the energy used in the U.S. came from fossil fuels, mainly petroleum, natural gas, or coal. The rest came mostly from nuclear power, renewable resources such as hydroelectric power, geothermal, solar, and wind energy, and from alternative fuels such as biomass (including wood, animal waste, and fuels made from plant materials).

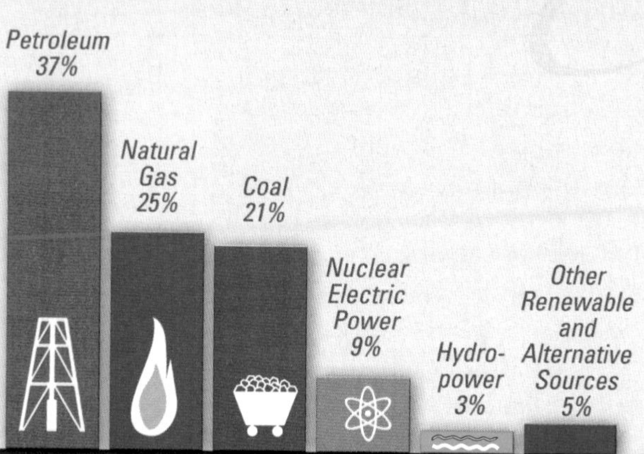

How Does a Nuclear Power Plant Work?

There are different types of nuclear power plants, but they all rely on one basic fact: when the nucleus of an atom of uranium is split, a tremendous amount of energy is produced.

Atoms are made up of three different kinds of particles: protons, neutrons, and electrons. Protons and neutrons are found in the atom's nucleus, or core. Electrons orbit around the nucleus. When the nucleus is split, in a process called **nuclear fission**, two new nuclei are created. In addition, energy is released.

The energy produced by fission is used to boil water, so that it turns into steam. This steam turns the blades of a machine called a turbine, producing electricity.

The uranium used as fuel is in long rods. Neutrons hit these **fuel rods** to split the uranium atoms. By having the right number of neutrons hit the right amount of fuel at the right speed, scientists can create a **chain reaction** in which atoms keep splitting at a controlled rate, producing a steady supply of energy. Cool water and devices called **control rods** keep the fuel rods from getting too hot and keep the chain reaction from getting out of control. The chain reaction takes place inside thick concrete **containment structures**, so that radioactivity doesn't leak out of the plant.

Nuclear power plants do not cause the kinds of air pollution created by plants burning fossil fuels. But there are other potential problems. See page 75 for some pros and cons of nuclear power.

did you Know? *Some countries get a lot more of their electricity from nuclear plants than the U.S. In Europe, for example, Lithuania gets about 78% of its power from nuclear energy, and France gets about 77%.*

Producing Electricity: Pros & Cons

Nuclear Fission

Pros: No greenhouse gases; produces a large amount of energy from a small amount of fuel; cannot explode like a nuclear bomb.

Cons: Creates dangerous nuclear waste that takes thousands of years to become safe; accidents might contaminate large areas with radiation; expensive.

Hydroelectric

Pros: Does not pollute or heat the water or air; no waste products, runs nonstop; very inexpensive.

Cons: Massive dams are expensive and difficult to build; alters the environment around the dam; can affect fish migratory patterns.

Biomass

Pros: Reduces trash in landfills; cuts down on release of methane; plants, such as corn for ethanol, are a renewable resource.

Cons: Burning some trash releases toxins and some greenhouse gases into the air; leaves ash; plants require large farms and specific climate conditions; could raise food prices.

Wind

Pros: Clean; land for wind farms can be used for other purposes like farming; can be built offshore.

Cons: Wind farms take up a lot of space; can kill birds if placed in migratory paths; require winds of at least 12 to 14 mph; can be noisy.

Solar

Pros: No pollution; little maintenance required.

Cons: Solar panels are expensive and take up a lot of space; energy can't be gathered when the Sun isn't shining; manufacturing the solar cells produces waste products.

Solar-powered home

Fossil Fuels

(primarily coal)

Pros: Affordable because equipment is in wide use; needs smaller space to generate power compared to most other sources.

Cons: Limited supply; major contributor to global warming; causes chemical reactions that create acid rain and smog; releases pollutants that cause breathing problems like asthma, can harm land and pollute water.

"Greener" Cars, Cleaner Air

More than 600 million motor vehicles, most of them passenger cars, fill the world's roads. Nearly all of these vehicles burn fossil fuels, mainly gasoline or diesel fuel, putting gases and dust particles into the air. The gases and particles that come out of a vehicle's tail pipe are called **emissions**, and some of them are harmful to people's health. Some emissions contribute to **smog** and other types of air pollution. Some, such as carbon dioxide, are known as **greenhouse gases**, which promote global warming. The 21st century has seen a surge of interest in reducing the harmful emissions from cars and trucks in order to reduce harm to the environment. More and more "green" cars, offering reduced or even zero emissions, have come on the market. Additional models are in the works.

ELECTRIFYING!

One way to deal with the emission problem is to replace gasoline or diesel fuel with some other power source for cars—such as electricity. **Electric cars** don't give off any emissions at all. They first appeared at the end of the 19th century but failed to catch on, largely because the batteries they used had a very limited capacity. Batteries are better today, and electric cars are beginning to make a comeback. The Nissan Leaf, for example, can go about 100 miles on a single charge, so it's useful for people who don't need to drive long distances.

Nissan Leaf

Batteries are not the only possible source of electricity. A lot of effort has been devoted, for example, to studying **hydrogen fuel cells** as a means of powering cars. These devices, when provided with a supply of hydrogen, can make the hydrogen combine with oxygen, a process that yields electricity and a very nonpolluting by-product: water. A few hydrogen fuel cell vehicles have been built, but this technology is not yet ready for use in mass-produced cars.

Hybrid Cars

A popular approach to dealing with automobile emissions in recent years has been not to eliminate them but to reduce them. Carmakers brought out vehicles called **hybrid cars** that feature both a gasoline (or diesel) engine and an electric motor. The two power sources work together to make the vehicle go, and its fossil fuel consumption is much less than in a traditional vehicle.

The first hybrid car to go on sale in the U.S. was the little Honda Insight in December 1999. Seventeen of them were sold that month. Ten years later there were more than 20 models of hybrid cars on the U.S. market. In January 2011, nearly 20,000 hybrids were sold in the United States. The Toyota Prius accounted for more than half of all sales.

CLEANER-BURNING CARS

Carmakers have also brought out nonelectric, fuel-burning cars that are less polluting than those of the past. Some of these vehicles reduce emissions by using alternative fuels, such as biofuels or the relatively clean-burning fossil fuel natural gas. Also, engines in many modern gasoline and diesel cars are simply more efficient and run more cleanly. They offer better fuel economy (and thus a lower rate of emissions per mile). In fact, the 2010 World Green Car title went to the BlueMotion models in Volkswagen's Polo, Passat, and Golf lines.

ON THE JOB: SOLAR ENERGY COMPANY OWNER

Dan Sabia has his own solar energy company that designs and installs rooftop solar energy systems. These systems convert sunlight into electricity. He agreed to talk to *The World Almanac for Kids* about his work.

What do you do in a typical day?

I'm out a lot during the day. I visit buildings where my crews are installing solar panels, to make sure everything is going OK. I also visit and talk with new customers who want a solar energy system. It's important to make sure the building faces south and has no trees shading the roof, so that the solar panels can absorb enough sunlight to produce energy.

What interests and strengths of yours make this job right for you?

Even as a child, I was interested in how things were built and how they worked. At that time, there was no such thing as a career in solar energy. It wasn't until I was much older that I realized I could take my hands-on carpentry, construction, and architectural abilities and put those toward something that's good for our planet.

What kind of education or training did you need to get in order to do your job?

Over the years, I've sharpened both my management and my technical skills. While doing construction and carpentry jobs during high school and college, I took architecture and engineering courses, and I earned a degree in construction. Later, as a major in the National Guard, I handled logistics and operations for a large military camp. I spent many years as a facilities manager for a college and then a large school district, making sure everything operated safely and efficiently. Before starting my own solar energy company, I took courses in renewable energy technology.

What do you like best about your job? What is most challenging?

One of the main challenges is getting the word out that solar energy really is a practical way to produce electricity. Another challenge is that the solar energy business is seasonal. Solar panels can't be installed on rooftops if the temperature is below freezing or the weather is wet. The things I like best about my job are helping the environment and educating people about the advantages of renewable energy. It gives me tremendous satisfaction to know that my efforts are making the planet a cleaner and better place to live.

What are greenhouse gases? → page 80

LIVING GREEN

Protecting the environment is important to humans and every other living thing on Earth. Helping the environment includes keeping air, water, and soil as clean as possible. It also includes preserving Earth's resources for the future, saving the many **biomes** around the world in which different plants and animals live, and reducing the amount of **greenhouse gases** that are being added to the air and are likely changing Earth's climate. Everyone can have an impact, however small, on protecting the environment. Here are some ways people are "living green."

SHOPPING GREEN

- **Rent or reuse:** Every time something new is made, energy and raw materials are used up to make it. If you or your family needs to use something for a short time, find out whether it can be rented, rather than bought new. You also might find used books, toys, party decorations, and even clothing at garage sales or thrift shops.
- **Think about batteries:** When you buy something that requires batteries, use rechargeable batteries rather than batteries that just go into the trash when they're used up.
- **Check out packaging:** The more packaging there is on a food item, toy, or other purchase, the more trash there will be to throw away. When shopping, look for items that don't have a lot of wasteful packaging.
- **Reuse bags:** Bring your own reusable bags to the supermarket to carry your purchases, rather than getting plastic bags at the store.
- **Be aware of ingredients:** Try to buy only products that don't contain harmful chemicals and that are produced in a way that does the least harm to the environment. You can find "green" shampoos, household cleansers, and clothing—all made without harmful chemicals.

TRAVELING GREEN

- **Walk or bike:** Try walking or biking to places that aren't too far away, rather than depending on a car. Most cars burn fuel and put pollution into the air.
- **Use trains and buses:** Encourage your family to think about using a train or a bus the next time you go on vacation, rather than driving.
- **Think about carpooling:** Set up carpools for traveling to places that you and your friends go to all the time, rather than having everyone go in separate cars.

EATING GREEN

- **Think local:** Eat foods that are grown locally, so that they don't have to be shipped long distances. Shipping foods by truck or airplane is a major source of air pollution. Is there a greenmarket or a farmer's market near where you live that sells locally produced food?
- **Remember the season:** Eat fresh fruits and other foods that are in season. When you eat a fruit that's not in season, you're eating something that had to be picked and stored and then shipped a long way to your neighborhood store—all of which uses energy and causes pollution.
- **Check out gardening:** Think about planting a small vegetable garden in your yard. If you don't have a yard, maybe there's a community garden in your neighborhood where people are growing their own food. Could you suggest that your school start a small garden?

THINKING GREEN EVERY DAY

- **Avoid things you use once:** Avoid products that you use just once and then throw away, such as plastic forks, knives, and cups. Try taking your lunch in a container that you can wash and reuse many times, rather than putting it in a paper bag that you'll just throw away.
- **Save water:** Make sure you turn off the faucet tightly to avoid drips that waste water. Don't let the water run when you're not using it—for example, while you brush your teeth. Take showers rather than baths, because they use much less water—and keep your showers short.
- **Use tap water:** Drink tap water rather than bottled water. Making the bottles and shipping the water both use energy. You can fill a glass container with tap water and chill it in the refrigerator so that it will be cold.
- **Be smart about using appliances:** Don't run a half-full washing machine or dishwasher. Wait until the machine is full, and you can clean twice as much using the same amount of water and energy.
- **Conserve electricity:** To save electricity, turn off the lights when you leave a room. Turn off TVs, computers, and other devices when they're not being used.
- **Use the sponge:** Instead of using paper towels to wipe up spills, use a sponge. Paper towels become trash.

did you Know?

Many police departments collect unwanted cell phones and give them to volunteer patrols or to people who might need to contact emergency services but who can't afford to buy a phone. Does your local police department have a program like this?

What Is GLOBAL WARMING?

What Is the Greenhouse Effect?

Global warming is a gradual increase in the average temperature at Earth's surface. Earth reflects back into space about 30% of the Sun's rays that reach it. Some rays are absorbed by Earth's surface and converted into heat energy. The heat radiates from the surface, and some of it escapes into space. But some is prevented from escaping by **greenhouse gases** in the atmosphere. The most common greenhouse gases are water vapor, carbon dioxide, methane, nitrous oxide, ozone, and fluorinated gases. Most greenhouse gases occur naturally, and they help to make life on Earth possible. Without this natural **greenhouse effect**, Earth would be about 60°F colder than it is today.

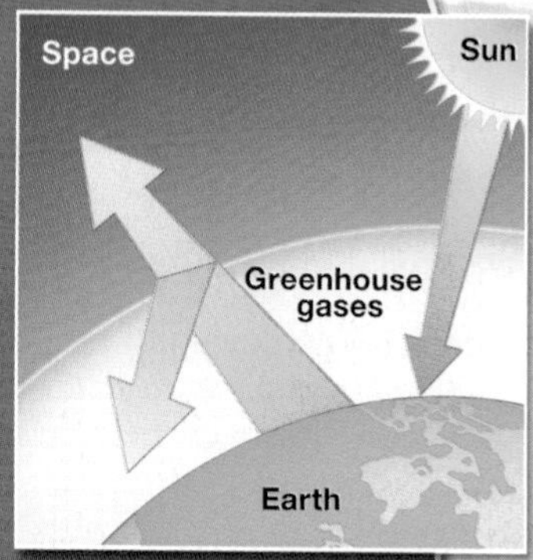

Why Are Greenhouse Gases Increasing?

Since the mid-1700s, humans have been releasing more and more greenhouse gases into the atmosphere. Mostly these additions have come from burning fossil fuels—such as coal, natural gas, and oil—which produce carbon dioxide. Factories, farms, and **landfills** (places where trash is dumped) also give off greenhouse gases. **Deforestation** (cutting down or otherwise destroying forests) adds to the problem, because trees absorb carbon dioxide.

There is more carbon dioxide and methane in the atmosphere today than has been normal for the last 650,000 years, trapping more of the Sun's energy. The decade from 2000 to 2009 was the warmest recorded since good temperature records began in 1880. Scientists find it very likely that humans are the primary cause of this global warming.

Sources of Carbon Dioxide Released by Burning Fossil Fuels*

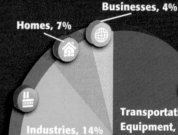

Businesses, 4%
Homes, 7%
Transportation Equipment, 33%
Industries, 14%
Power Plants, 41%

*2009 U.S. figures. Percentages may not add to 100% because of rounding. Source: U.S. Environmental Protection Agency

How Do We Know about Global Warming?

Worldwide records of climate have been kept since around the mid-1800s. They show global increases in air and ocean temperatures, a rise in sea level, and melting glaciers. Today, weather balloons, ocean buoys, and satellites provide even more information.

Scientists drill thousands of feet into ice caps in Antarctica and Greenland to remove ice core samples. The layers of ice and air pockets trapped in them can be read like a timeline of climate change over the past 800,000 years.

What Will Happen?

Rising Sea Levels: Scientists have created computer climate models that identify patterns and make predictions. In the short run, average temperatures may go up or down in a given year. But in the long run, current estimates predict that they will rise. In fact, by the year 2100, Earth's average temperature may increase at least 2°F and oceans will rise 7 inches. The worst-case scenarios suggest that Earth could warm by more than 11°F and sea levels could rise 2 feet or more.

A piece of a glacier falls into the sea.

As Earth warms, sea levels rise:

- Water expands slightly as it warms.
- The ice sheets covering Greenland and the Arctic Sea are melting. Also, chunks of ice (icebergs) are breaking away from ice sheets in Antarctica and Greenland.
- Glaciers and permafrost are melting in non-polar regions, producing more water.
- As ice melts, it exposes darker land or sea, which is less reflective and absorbs more heat.

Melting Polar Ice: The Arctic region may warm up more than many other places because of the albedo effect, or a surface's power to reflect light. Ice reflects the Sun's rays. With less ice on Earth, more of the Sun's heat will be absorbed by the oceans. Warmer water raises sea levels and melts ice faster.

Changing Water Cycle: Warmer air affects the water cycle (see page 82). More water evaporates, and the atmosphere can hold more water vapor. Places with plenty of water will have more rain and floods. But in places where water is scarce, evaporation will dry out the land even more. Vapor will take more time to condense, meaning less rain and more droughts.

Rising sea levels already threaten some coastal settlements and small Pacific islands.

Many scientists believe that warmer oceans will lead to more intense tropical cyclones (also called hurricanes and typhoons).

As environments change, animals must find new homes or they may become extinct. Warmer global climates will allow disease-carrying creatures like mosquitoes to spread to new places.

WATER, WATER EVERYWHERE

Earth is the water planet. More than two-thirds of its surface is covered with water, and every living thing on it needs water to live. Humans can survive for about a month without eating food, but only for about a week without drinking water. People also use water for cooking and cleaning, to produce power, to irrigate farmland, and for recreation.

About 97% of the world's water is salt water in the oceans and inland seas, which can be drunk only after special treatment. Another 2% of the water is frozen in ice caps and glaciers. Half of the 1% left is too far underground to be reached. That leaves only 0.5% for all the people, plants, and animals on Earth.

THE WATER CYCLE

Water is the only thing on Earth that exists naturally in **all three normal physical states**: solid (ice), liquid, and gas (water vapor). The water cycle describes how water changes as it moves through the environment. The cycle has no starting or ending point but is driven by the Sun.

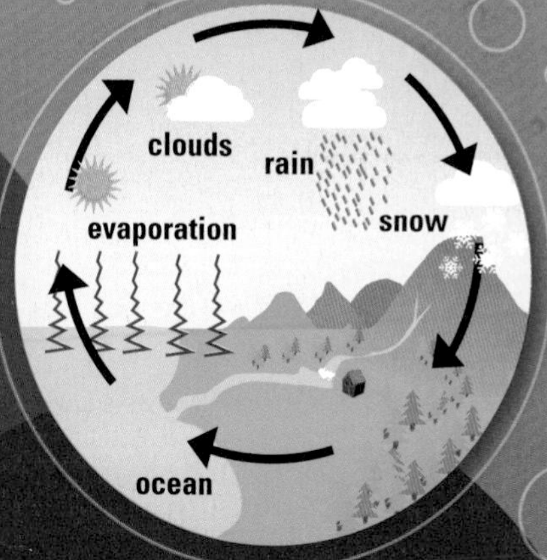

HOW DOES WATER GET INTO THE AIR?

Heat from the Sun causes surface water in oceans, lakes, swamps, and rivers to turn into water vapor. This is called **evaporation**. Plants release water vapor into the air as part of the process called **transpiration**. Animals release a little bit when they breathe and when they perspire.

HOW DOES WATER COME OUT OF THE AIR?

Warm air holds more water vapor than cold air. As the air rises into the atmosphere, it cools and the water vapor **condenses**—changes back into tiny water droplets. These droplets form clouds. As the drops get bigger, gravity pulls them down to Earth as **precipitation** (such as rain, snow, or sleet).

WHERE DOES THE WATER GO?

Depending on where the precipitation lands, it can: **1.** evaporate back into the atmosphere, **2.** run off into streams and rivers, **3.** be absorbed by plants, **4.** soak down into the soil as groundwater, or **5.** fall as snow on a glacier and be trapped as ice for thousands of years.

WATER WOES

Pollution: Polluted water can't be used for drinking, swimming, or watering crops, nor can it provide a good habitat for plants and animals. Major sources of water pollutants are sewage, chemicals from factories, fertilizers and pesticides, and landfills that leak.

Overuse: When more water is taken out of lakes and reservoirs (for drinking, washing, watering lawns, and other uses) than is put back in, the water levels begin to drop. This can be devastating. In some cases, lakes become salty or dry up completely.

WHERE GARBAGE GOES

The disposal of garbage is a serious issue. The problem is that we now produce more garbage than our natural environment can absorb.

WHAT HAPPENS TO THINGS WE THROW AWAY?

Landfills

About half of our trash goes to places called landfills. A **landfill** (or dump) is a low area of land that is filled with garbage. Most modern landfills are lined with a layer of plastic or clay to try to keep dangerous liquids from seeping into the soil and underground water supplies **(groundwater)**. The number of landfills is one-fourth of what it was in 1988, but they're much larger.

The Problem with Landfills

Because of the unhealthy materials many of them contain, landfills do not make good neighbors. But where can we dispose of waste?

Incinerators

One way to get rid of trash is to burn it. Trash can be burned in a furnace-like device called an **incinerator** to make electricity.

The Problem with Incinerators

Leftover ash and smoke from burning trash such as rubber tires may contain harmful chemicals, including greenhouse gases. Pollutants can make it hard for some people to breathe. They can harm plants, animals, and people.

Reduce, Reuse, Recycle

Reducing garbage helps protect the environment. Reuse products. Recycle products so that materials can be used again rather than become garbage.

What Is Made From RECYCLED MATERIALS?

- ***From* RECYCLED PAPER we get newspapers, cereal boxes, wrapping paper, cardboard containers, and insulation.**
- ***From* RECYCLED PLASTIC we get soda bottles, benches, bike racks, cameras, backpacks, carpeting, and clothes.**
- ***From* RECYCLED ALUMINUM we get cans, cars, bicycles, computers, and pots and pans.**
- ***From* RECYCLED GLASS we get glass jars and tiles.**
- ***From* RECYCLED RUBBER we get mousepads, shoe soles, floor tiles, and playground equipment.**

HOME SWEET BIOME

A biome is a large natural area that is home to certain types of plants. The animals, climate, soil, and even the amount of water in the region also help distinguish a biome. There are many kinds of biomes in the world. But the following types cover most of Earth's surface.

Forests

Forests cover about one-third of Earth's land surface. Pines, hemlocks, firs, and spruces grow in the cool **evergreen forests** farthest from the equator. These trees are called evergreens because they keep their leaves year-round. They are also known as **conifers** because they produce cones.

Temperate forests tend to have warm, rainy summers and cool, snowy winters. They often are home to **deciduous trees** (trees that lose their leaves in the fall and grow new ones in the spring), such as maple, oak, beech, and poplar. Mixtures of deciduous trees and evergreens also occur, and some temperate forests are primarily coniferous. Areas where temperate forests can be found include the United States, southern Canada, southern Chile, Europe, Asia, eastern Australia, and New Zealand.

Still closer to the equator are the **tropical rain forests**, home to the greatest variety of plants on Earth. Typically, more than 80 inches of rain fall each year. Tropical trees stay green all year. They grow close together, shading the ground. There are several layers of trees. The top, **emergent layer** has trees that can reach 200 feet in height. The **canopy**, which gets lots of sunlight, comes next, followed by the **understory**. The **forest floor**, covered with roots, gets little sunlight. Many plants cannot grow there.

Tropical rain forests are found mainly in Central America, South America, Africa, Southeast Asia, and Australia and nearby islands. They once covered as much as 12% of Earth's land surface or nearly 7 million square miles. Today, because of destruction by humans, fewer than 2.5 million square miles of rain forest remain. Half the plant and animal species in the world live there. The Amazon rain forest is the world's largest tropical rain forest. It covers more than 2 million square miles—roughly two-thirds the size of the United States.

When rain forests are burned to clear land for agriculture or other activities, carbon dioxide is released into the air. This adds to the **greenhouse effect** (see page 80). As forests are destroyed, the precious soil is easily washed away by the heavy rains.

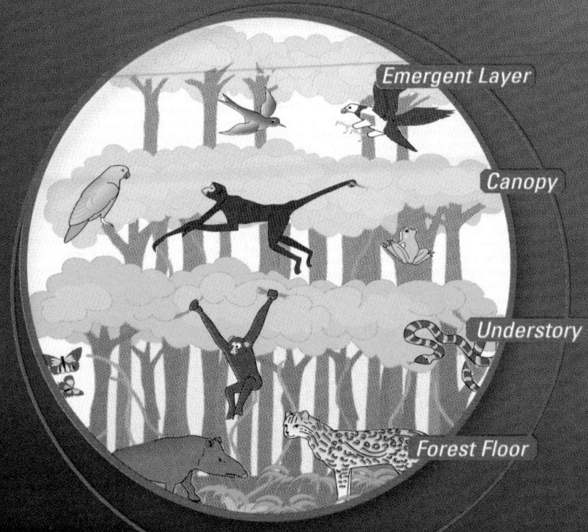

Layers of a tropical rain forest ▲

Tundra

Tundra, the coldest biome, is a treeless plain. In the Arctic tundra—located in the northernmost regions of North America, Europe, and Asia surrounding the Arctic Ocean—the temperature rarely rises above 50°F. Water in the ground freezes the subsoil solid **(permafrost)** so plant and tree roots can't dig down. Most plants are mosses and lichens without roots. In some areas, the top layer of soil thaws for about two months each year. This may allow wildflowers or small shrubs to grow. Alpine tundra is located on top of the world's highest mountains (such as the Himalayas, Alps, Andes, and Rockies). Plants and low shrubs may be found here, and patches of permafrost may occur. Tundra is also found on outer parts of Antarctica and nearby islands.

What Is the Tree Line? On mountains there is an altitude above which trees will not grow. This is the **tree line** or **timberline**.

Deserts

The driest areas of the world are the **deserts**. Hot or cold (Antarctica has desert), they receive less than 10 inches of rain in a year. Many contain an amazing number of plants that store water in thick bodies or roots deep underground. Rain can spur fields of wildflowers to spontaneously bloom. Shrubby sagebrush and spiny cacti are native to dry regions of North and South America. Prickly pear, barrel, and saguaro cacti can be found in the southwestern United States. Date palms grow in desert oases of the Middle East and North Africa.

Desert, Arizona

Savanna, Tanzania

Grasslands

Areas that are too dry to have green forests but not dry enough to be deserts are **grasslands**. The most common plants are grasses. Cooler grasslands are found in the Great Plains of the United States and Canada, in the steppes of Europe and Asia, and in the pampas of Argentina. Drier grasslands called steppes have short grasses and are used for grazing cattle and sheep. In **prairies**, characterized by tall grasses, there is a little more rain. Wheat, rye, oats, and barley grow there. The warmer grasslands, called **savannas**, are found in central and southern Africa, Venezuela, southern Brazil, and Australia. Most savannas have moist summers and cool, dry winters.

Marine

Covering more than two-thirds of Earth's surface, marine regions are the largest biome. The marine biome includes the **oceans, coastal areas, tidal zones,** and **coral reefs**. Reefs are found most often in relatively shallow warm water, including coastal waters of the Caribbean Sea. Like tropical rain forests, reefs are home to thousands of species of plant and animal life. Australia's Great Barrier Reef is the largest in the world.

Reef, Belize

FASHION

Which rapper helped create Rocawear? → page 88

Take a trip through fashion history since the year 1900. What style do you like the best? It's a modern trend for the fashion-forward, especially kids, to borrow from past decades and make their own special styles.

1900s:

THE EDWARDIAN ERA

Women: Formal females favored custom-made dresses, tight corsets, lots of lace, and feathered hats.
Men: High society gents wore tailored wool suits, straw boater hats, and narrow shoes.

1920s:

THE ROARING TWENTIES

Women: Flappers had short, sleek hair and wore drop-waist sequined dresses and fancy costume jewelry.
Men: Distinguished men wore pastel-colored shirts, and silk ties that were secured with tie pins.

1940s:

MAKE DO AND MEND

Women: During World War II, Rosie the Riveter styles (such as blue jeans and drainpipe trousers) were practical and patriotic. Stockings were a luxury.
Men: Materials were scarce during the war. Pillowcases and parachutes were used to make clothing. Instead of wool, suits were made of wood pulp and had fake pockets.

1960s:

FLOWER POWER

Women: A groovy chick would look mod in a bright-colored dress, blue eye shadow, white go-go boots, and long hair.
Men: A hippie guy might wear bell-bottom jeans, a paisley shirt, and a leather vest. Funky peace signs and flower patches were popular.

1970s:

DISCO DAYS

Women: Girls were staying alive in hot pants, polyester pantsuits, bell-bottoms, and platform shoes.

Men: Mr. Disco wore polyester bell-bottoms, brightly colored shirts, and gold chains on the dance floor.

1990s:

ANYTHING GOES

Women: Inspired by the era of grunge music, girls wore big black boots by Dr. Martens, hooded sweatshirts, and layered T-shirts.

Men: Grungy guys kept themselves warm in lumberjack flannels and their money secure with trucker chain wallets. The hip-hoppers, on the other hand, warmed up in puffy athletic jackets and sneakers.

2000s:

FROM HIP-HOP TO *GOSSIP GIRL*

Women: Girls started the decade in low-rise jeans, tight T-shirts with bare midriffs, and bell-bottoms. As the decade continued, girls turned to fashions from teen dramas such as television's *Gossip Girl*, adopting its glamorous yet funky styles.

Men: Hip-hop guys kept a beat in baggy pants, gold chains, and athletic gear. The *Gossip Girl* boys brought back prep-school fashions with their blazers, striped ties, and loafers.

2010s:

GOOD DEALS, CLEAN PLANET

Women: As the U.S. economy took a tumble, girls began re-thinking the luxurious styles of the 2000s. Recessionista became a popular term to describe a girl who could look fashionable on a budget. High-end designers such as Zac Posen and Alice Temperley created affordable clothing for chains like Target.

Men: Men's clothing took on a more relaxed, natural style. In addition to looking for good deals, both girls and guys wanted environmentally friendly clothing. More stores and online retailers began to offer options made with recycled and organic materials.

SOME FAMOUS

Fashion Designers

CALVIN KLEIN

Calvin Klein was born in Brooklyn, New York, in 1942. His grandmother, who was a seamstress, taught him how to sew. He began drawing design sketches as a teenager. After studying at the Fashion Institute of Technology, Klein started his own company. He rose to fame in the 1970s when he created a popular line of jeans with his name on the back pocket. Klein's designs are known for their simplicity and "all-American" look. Although Klein sold his company in 2003, Calvin Klein remains one of the best-known fashion brands in the world.

▲ *Calvin Klein*

STELLA MCCARTNEY

Born in 1971, Stella McCartney is the daughter of singer/songwriter and former Beatle Paul McCartney and his wife Linda. Stella began designing her own clothing as a teenager, and at age 15, she was hired as an intern with designer Christian Lacroix. Her design career took off from there. Linda McCartney was an animal-rights activist, and Stella has followed in her footsteps. She is a committed vegetarian who uses no fur or leather in her designs. Today, Stella McCartney designs both high-end clothing for celebrities and also more affordable fashions sold in stores like H&M and the Gap. She also has a line of organically made skin care products that are never tested on animals.

◀ *Actress Mia Wasikowska wearing a Stella McCartney design*

JAY-Z

Originally named Shawn Corey Carter, Jay-Z was born in Brooklyn, New York, in 1969. He rose to rap stardom in the 1990s. In 1999, Jay-Z expanded his career into fashion design. With partner Damon Dash, he created the clothing company Rocawear. The clothing was inspired by hip-hop culture and sold in department stores. Though Jay-Z sold the rights to the brand in 2007, he kept a stake in the company and continues to oversee the company's products and marketing. Today, Rocawear is extremely successful, with annual sales of about $700 million.

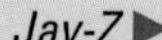

Jay-Z ▶

ON THE JOB: FASHION DESIGNER

Fashion is always changing, and fashion designers are the people who help decide what those changes will be. Meredith Evans, a fashion designer who works for a clothing manufacturer, agreed to talk to *The World Almanac for Kids* about her work.

▲ *Sketches by designer Meredith Evans*

As a fashion designer, what do you do in a typical day?

My days are hectic! I manage a team of people, so I always need to be sure they are clear about what needs to be done that day. I direct the creative part of our clothing line—inspiration for colors, fabrics, silhouettes, prints, and patterns we'll use. And I manage the business side of things, too. I work with our merchandisingand marketing teams to make sure what we are developing fits in with the sales strategy for the season. I also prepare many presentations and have a lot of meetings with clients. These clients are the buyers for the large retail chains that we sell our clothing to.

What interests and strengths of yours make this job right for you?

I am a creative person and love fashion, but I also like business, so this job is a good combination of both.

What kind of education or training did you need to get in order to do your job?

I have a bachelor of fine arts degree from the Parsons School of Design in New York City.

What do you like best about your job? What is most challenging?

I like the fast pace and I like that no two days are ever the same. It's never boring! It is a lot of pressure, however, to always need to be one step ahead of the trends.

GAMES

In what year was the popular game *Tetris* created? → page 90

Kids are spending more time playing video games than ever before. On average, American kids ages 8 to 18 spent 1 hour 13 minutes a day playing video games in 2009. That was 24 minutes more daily gaming time than in 2004. The increase was due mainly to the popularity of "on the go" gaming on cell phones and handheld players.

GAME ON!

Percent of video game time played on each platform:

- CELL PHONES: 23%
- HANDHELD PLAYERS (Nintendo DS, Sony PSP): 29%
- HOME CONSOLES (Wii, PlayStation 3, Xbox 360): 49%

Note: Percentages do not add up to 100% because of rounding.
Source: Kaiser Family Foundation

TOP SELLERS

Since launching the Nintendo Entertainment System (NES) in 1985, Nintendo has created dozens of memorable titles—including the five top-selling games of all time. Each game came bundled with a Nintendo console at some point during its record-setting run.

Game	Console	U.S. Release	Units Sold*
Wii Sports	Wii	2006	76.82 million
Super Mario Bros.	NES	1985	40.24 million
Pokémon Red / Green / Blue	Game Boy	1998	31.37 million
Tetris	Game Boy	1989	30.26 million
Duck Hunt	NES	1985	28.31 million

*Through May 2011; sales figures are worldwide. Source: VGChartz

GAME SPOTLIGHT: TETRIS

One of the simplest games remains among the most popular: *Tetris*. Players have been trying to fit its falling puzzle pieces together for more than 25 years. Created by Russian programmer Alexey Pajitnov in 1984, *Tetris* soon conquered the gaming world. As games moved from home consoles to handhelds to phones, *Tetris*'s popularity grew. Today, it is the best-selling mobile game ever, with more than 100 million paid downloads.

GAMING TIMELINE

1972

The Magnavox Odyssey is the first commercial home video-game console. The system has no sound.

1975

The home version of Atari's *Pong* debuts. It features two lines (or paddles) that players use to hit a dot back and forth.

1977

The Atari VCS (later renamed the 2600) is the first popular system to feature cartridges for different games.

1980

The pie-shaped pellet-eating character Pac-Man chomps its way into arcades.

1985

Known as Famicom in Japan, the Nintendo Entertainment System invades the United States.

1989

Nintendo's first handheld game system, Game Boy, is a huge hit.

1994

The Entertainment Software Rating Board (ESRB) creates rating standards for video games.

1995

Sony releases its popular PlayStation, which uses CD-Roms instead of cartridges.

2001

Home computer giant Microsoft gets into the action with the Xbox.

2004

The Nintendo DS (dual-screen) ushers in a new era of handheld gaming.

2006

Nintendo Wii changes gaming with the introduction of wand-like controllers.

2008

Nintendo *Wii Fit* features a balance board that allows users to exercise as they play.

2010

The motion-sensing Kinect system for the Xbox 360 console allows users to play games without the need of a controller.

2011

The Nintendo 3DS handheld console offers 3-D graphics and effects without the user having to wear 3-D glasses.

WHAT'S NEXT?

Among the most awaited new video games are sequels to some all-time classics.

The Legend of Zelda: Skyward Sword: The latest game in the *Legend of Zelda* series is considered a prequel to 1998's *Ocarina of Time. Skyward Sword* will use the Wii MotionPlus add-on to more accurately capture a player's movements when controlling the actions of the main character, Link.

Madden NFL 12: The newest version of the popular football game promises to be the most realistic to date. Among the dozens of new features offered by *Madden NFL 12* are increased control of players during tackling, the ability to make custom playbooks, and enhanced graphics and animated displays.

GEOGRAPHY

What territory did Daniel Boone explore? ➔ page 95

SIZING UP THE EARTH

The word "geography" comes from the Greek word *geographia*, meaning "writing about the Earth." It was first used by the Greek scholar Eratosthenes, who was head of the great library of Alexandria in Egypt. Around 230 B.C., when many people believed the world was flat, he did a remarkable thing. He calculated the circumference of the Earth. His figure of about 25,000 miles was close to the modern measurement of 24,901 miles!

Actually, the Earth is not perfectly round. It's flatter at the poles and bulges out a little at the middle. This bulge around the equator is due to Earth's rotation. Although Earth seems solid to us, it is really slightly plastic, or flexible. As the Earth spins, material flows toward its middle, piling up and creating a slight bulge. The Earth's diameter is 7,926 miles at the equator, but only 7,900 miles from North Pole to South Pole. The total surface area of the Earth is 196,940,000 square miles.

GEOGRAPHY 1 2 3

Longest Rivers	**1.** Nile (Egypt and Sudan)—4,160 miles **2.** Amazon (Brazil and Peru)—4,000 miles **3.** Chang (China)—3,964 miles (formerly called the Yangtze)
Tallest Mountains	**1.** Mount Everest (Tibet and Nepal)—29,035 feet **2.** K2 (Kashmir)—28,250 feet **3.** Kanchenjunga (India and Nepal)—28,208 feet
Biggest Islands	**1.** Greenland (Atlantic Ocean)—840,000 square miles **2.** New Guinea (Pacific Ocean)—306,000 square miles **3.** Borneo (Pacific Ocean)—280,100 square miles
Biggest Desert Regions	**1.** Sahara Desert (North Africa)—3.5 million square miles **2.** Australian Deserts—1.3 million square miles **3.** Arabian Peninsula—1 million square miles
Biggest Lakes	**1.** Caspian Sea (Europe and Asia)—143,244 square miles **2.** Superior (U.S. and Canada)—31,700 square miles **3.** Victoria (Kenya, Tanzania, Uganda)—26,828 square miles
Highest Waterfalls	**1.** Angel Falls (Venezuela)—3,212 feet **2.** Tugela Falls (South Africa)—2,800 feet **3.** Monge Falls (Norway)—2,540 feet

Reading A Map

DIRECTION Maps usually have a **compass rose** that shows you which way is north. On most maps, like this one, it's straight up. The compass rose on this map is in the upper left corner.

DISTANCE As you can see, the distances on a map are much shorter than the distances in the real world. The **scale** shows you how to estimate the real distance. This map's scale is in the lower left corner.

PICTURES Maps usually have little pictures or symbols to represent real things like roads, towns, airports, or other points of interest. The map **legend** (or **key**) tells what they mean.

FINDING PLACES Rather than use latitude and longitude to locate features, many maps, like this one, use a grid system with numbers on one side and letters on another. An index, listing place names in alphabetical order, gives a letter and a number for each. The letter and number tell you in which square to look for a place on the map's grid. For example, Landisville can be found at A-1 on this map.

Using the map People use maps to help them travel from one place to another. What if you lived in East Petersburgh and wanted to go to the Hands-on-House Children's Museum? First, locate the two places on the map. East Petersburgh is C1, and the Hands-on House Children's Museum is E1. Next, look at the roads that connect them and decide on the best route. (There could be several different ways to go.) One way is to travel east on Route 722, then southeast on Valley Road until you see the Children's Museum.

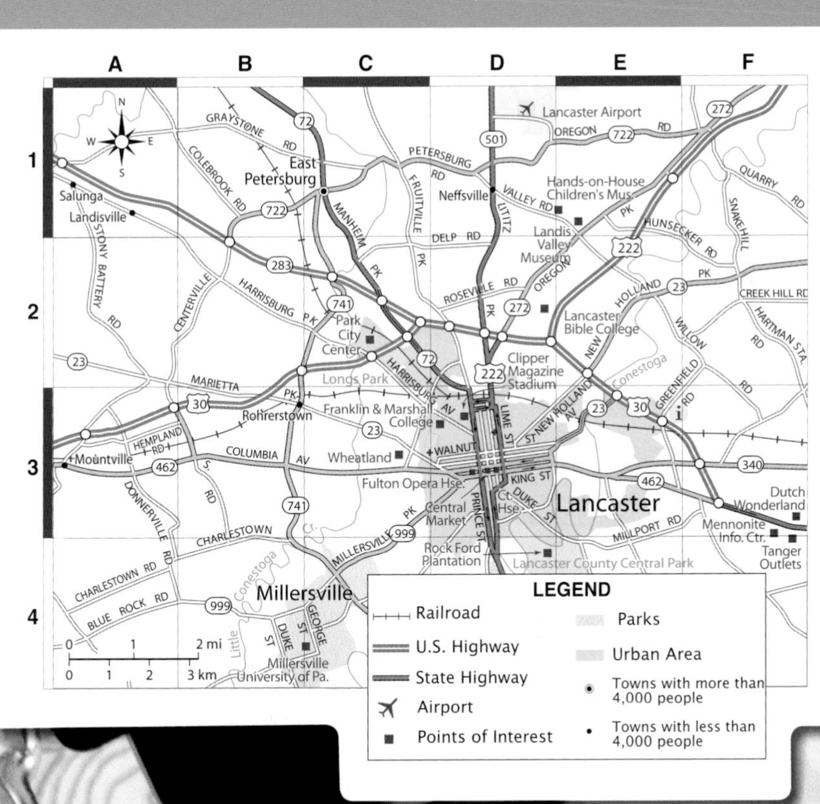

Early Exploration

AROUND 1000 — **Leif Ericson**, from Iceland, explored "Vinland," which may have been the coasts of northeast Canada and New England.

1271–95 — **Marco Polo** (Italian) traveled through Central Asia, India, China, and Indonesia.

1488 — **Bartolomeu Dias** (Portuguese) explored the Cape of Good Hope in southern Africa.

1492–1504 — **Christopher Columbus** (Italian) sailed four times from Spain to America and started colonies there.

1497–98 — **Vasco da Gama** (Portuguese) sailed farther than Dias, around the Cape of Good Hope to East Africa and India.

1513 — **Juan Ponce de León** (Spanish) explored and named Florida.

1513 — **Vasco Núñez de Balboa** (Spanish) explored Panama and reached the Pacific Ocean.

1519–21 — **Ferdinand Magellan** (Portuguese) sailed from Spain around the tip of South America and across the Pacific Ocean to the Philippines, where he died. His expedition continued around the world.

1519–36 — **Hernán Cortés** (Spanish) conquered Mexico, traveling as far west as Baja California.

1527–42 — **Alvar Núñez Cabeza de Vaca** (Spanish) explored the southwestern United States, Brazil, and Paraguay.

1532–35 — **Francisco Pizarro** (Spanish) explored the west coast of South America and conquered Peru.

1534–36 — **Jacques Cartier** (French) sailed up the St. Lawrence River to the site of present-day Montreal.

1539–42 — **Hernando de Soto** (Spanish) explored the southeastern United States and the lower Mississippi Valley.

1603–13 — **Samuel de Champlain** (French) traced the course of the St. Lawrence River and explored the northeastern United States.

1609–10 — **Henry Hudson** (English), sailing from Holland, explored the Hudson River, Hudson Bay, and Hudson Strait.

1682 — **Robert Cavelier, sieur de La Salle** (French), traced the Mississippi River to its mouth in the Gulf of Mexico.

1768–78 — **James Cook** (English) charted the world's major bodies of water and explored Hawaii and Antarctica.

1804–06 — **Meriwether Lewis and William Clark** (American) traveled from St. Louis along the Missouri and Columbia rivers to the Pacific Ocean and back.

1849–59 — **David Livingstone** (Scottish) explored Southern Africa.

Some Famous Explorers

These explorers, and many others, risked their lives on trips to explore faraway and often unknown places. Some sought fame. Some sought fortune. Some just sought challenge. All of them increased people's knowledge of the world.

CHRISTOPHER COLUMBUS (1451–1506), Italian navigator who sailed for Spain. He had hoped to find a fast route to Asia by going west from Europe. Instead he became the first European (other than the Vikings) to reach America, landing in the Bahamas in October 1492.

FERDINAND MAGELLAN (1480–1521), Portuguese navigator and explorer who set sail from Spain in 1519, seeking a western route to the Spice Islands of Indonesia. He became the first European to cross the Pacific Ocean, but was killed by natives in the Philippines. However, because he passed the easternmost point he had reached on an earlier voyage, he is recognized as the first person to circumnavigate the Earth.

DANIEL BOONE (1732–1820), American pioneer and explorer. As a young man, he explored the territory of Kentucky for two years. Using an old Indian trail, he led a group through the Cumberland Gap from Virginia into Kentucky and later went on to blaze hundreds of miles of new trails throughout the territory.

MARY HENRIETTA KINGSLEY (1862–1900), British explorer. At a time when women were discouraged from traveling into remote regions, she made two trips to West Africa, visiting areas never seen by Europeans. She studied and wrote about the customs and natural environment.

MATTHEW HENSON (1866–1955), the first famous African-American explorer. As an assistant to explorer Robert Peary (1856–1920), he traveled on seven expeditions to Greenland and the Arctic region. In April 1909, Peary and Henson became the first to reach, or nearly reach, the North Pole. (Recent research suggests they may have fallen short by about 30 to 60 miles.) ▼

ROALD AMUNDSEN (1872–1928), Norwegian polar explorer. Amundsen was the first person to fly over the North Pole in a dirigible (a large balloon-like aircraft that can be steered), and he was the first person to reach the South Pole, which he reached by dog sled on December 14, 1911.

ROBERT BALLARD ▲ (1942–), American navy commander and underwater archaeologist. Ballard was the first person to locate the remains of the luxury liner *Titanic*, which sank in 1912. He also located other historic ships, such as the World War II battleship *Bismarck*.

MAE C. JEMISON (1956–), the first African-American woman in space. She is a medical doctor and also has training in engineering. Jemison flew on the space shuttle *Endeavour* in September 1992, serving as Mission Specialist.

LOOKING AT OUR WORLD

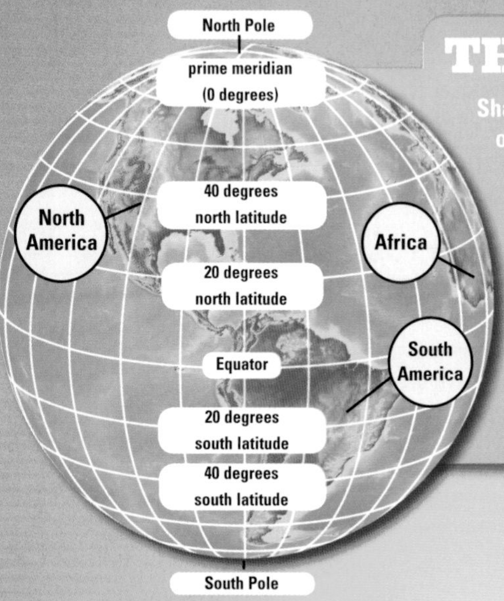

THINKING GLOBAL

Shaped like a ball or sphere, a globe is a model of our planet. Like Earth, it's not perfectly round. It is an oblate spheroid (called a "geoid") that bulges a little in the middle.

In 1569, Gerardus Mercator found a way to project the Earth's curved surface onto a flat map. One problem with a Mercator map (like the one on page 97) is that land closer to the poles appears bigger than it is. Australia looks smaller than Greenland on this type of map, but in reality it's not.

WHICH HEMISPHERES DO YOU LIVE IN?

Draw an imaginary line around the middle of Earth. This is the **equator**. It splits Earth into two halves called **hemispheres**. The part north of the equator, including North America, is the **northern hemisphere**. The part south of the equator is the **southern hemisphere**.

An imaginary line called the **Greenwich meridian** or **prime meridian** divides Earth into east and west. It runs north and south around the globe, passing through the city of Greenwich in England. North and South America are in the **western hemisphere**. Africa, Asia, and most of Europe are in the **eastern hemisphere**.

LATITUDE AND LONGITUDE

Imaginary lines that run east and west around Earth, parallel to the equator, are called **parallels**. They tell you the **latitude** of a place, or how far it is from the equator. The equator is at 0 degrees latitude. As you go farther north or south, the latitude increases. The North Pole is at 90 degrees **north latitude**. The South Pole is at 90 degrees **south latitude**.

Imaginary lines that run north and south around the globe, from one pole to the other, are called **meridians**. They tell you the degree of **longitude,** or how far east or west a place is from the prime meridian (0 degrees).

THE TROPICS OF CANCER AND CAPRICORN

If you find the equator on a globe or map, you'll often see two dotted lines running parallel to it, one above and one below (see pages 150–151). The top one marks the Tropic of Cancer, an imaginary line marking the latitude (about 23°27′ North) where the sun is directly overhead on June 21 or 22, the beginning of summer in the northern hemisphere.

Below the equator is the Tropic of Capricorn (about 23°27′ South). This line marks the sun's path directly overhead at noon on December 21 or 22, the beginning of summer in the southern hemisphere. The area between these dotted lines is the tropics, where it is consistently hot because the sun's rays shine more directly than they do farther north or south.

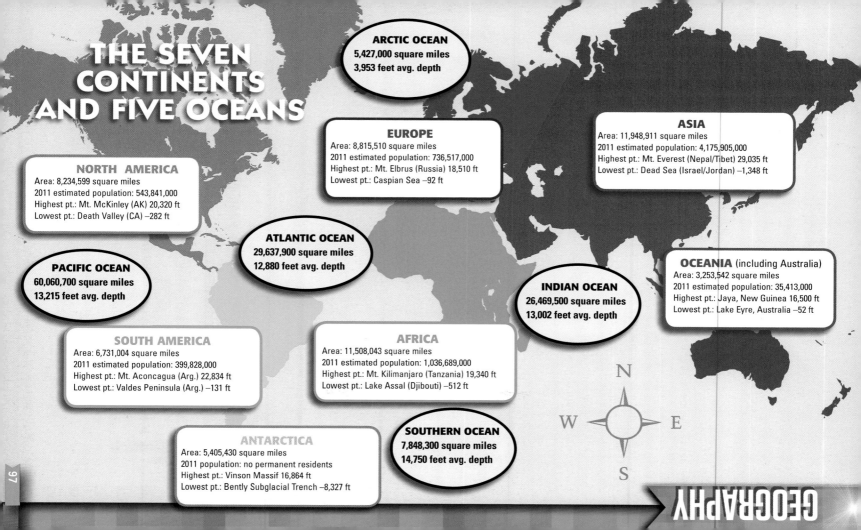

THE SEVEN CONTINENTS AND FIVE OCEANS

ARCTIC OCEAN
5,427,000 square miles
3,953 feet avg. depth

EUROPE
Area: 8,815,510 square miles
2011 estimated population: 736,517,000
Highest pt.: Mt. Elbrus (Russia) 18,510 ft
Lowest pt.: Caspian Sea –92 ft

ASIA
Area: 11,948,911 square miles
2011 estimated population: 4,175,905,000
Highest pt.: Mt. Everest (Nepal/Tibet) 29,035 ft
Lowest pt.: Dead Sea (Israel/Jordan) –1,348 ft

NORTH AMERICA
Area: 8,234,599 square miles
2011 estimated population: 543,841,000
Highest pt.: Mt. McKinley (AK) 20,320 ft
Lowest pt.: Death Valley (CA) –282 ft

ATLANTIC OCEAN
29,637,900 square miles
12,880 feet avg. depth

PACIFIC OCEAN
60,060,700 square miles
13,215 feet avg. depth

OCEANIA (including Australia)
Area: 3,253,542 square miles
2011 estimated population: 35,413,000
Highest pt.: Jaya, New Guinea 16,500 ft
Lowest pt.: Lake Eyre, Australia –52 ft

INDIAN OCEAN
26,469,500 square miles
13,002 feet avg. depth

SOUTH AMERICA
Area: 6,731,004 square miles
2011 estimated population: 399,828,000
Highest pt.: Mt. Aconcagua (Arg.) 22,834 ft
Lowest pt.: Valdes Peninsula (Arg.) –131 ft

AFRICA
Area: 11,508,043 square miles
2011 estimated population: 1,036,689,000
Highest pt.: Mt. Kilimanjaro (Tanzania) 19,340 ft
Lowest pt.: Lake Assal (Djibouti) –512 ft

ANTARCTICA
Area: 5,405,430 square miles
2011 population: no permanent residents
Highest pt.: Vinson Massif 16,864 ft
Lowest pt.: Bently Subglacial Trench –8,327 ft

SOUTHERN OCEAN
7,848,300 square miles
14,750 feet avg. depth

WHAT'S INSIDE THE EARTH?

Starting at the Earth's surface and going down, you find the lithosphere, the mantle, and then the core.

The **lithosphere**, the rocky crust of the Earth, extends for about 60 miles.

The dense, heavy inner part of the Earth is divided into a thick shell, the **mantle**, surrounding an innermost sphere, the **core**. The mantle extends from the base of the crust to a depth of about 1,800 miles and is mostly solid.

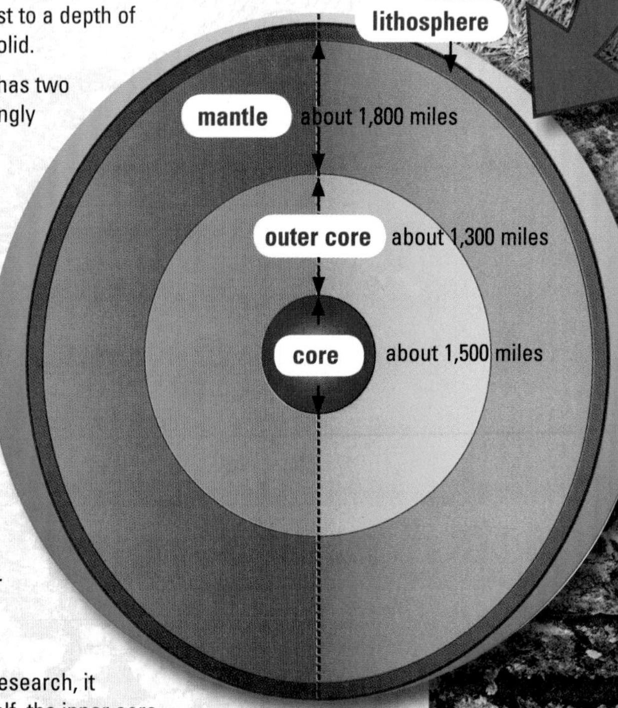

Then there is the Earth's core. It has two parts: an inner sphere of scorchingly hot, solid iron almost as large as the moon and an outer region of molten iron. The inner core is much hotter than the outer core. The intense pressure near the center of Earth squeezes the iron in the inner core into a solid ball nearly as hot as the surface of the Sun. Scientists believe the core formed billions of years ago during the planet's fiery birth. Iron and other heavy elements sank into the planet's hot interior while the planet was still molten. As this metallic soup cooled over millions of years, crystals of iron hardened at the center.

In 1996, after nearly 30 years of research, it was found that, like the Earth itself, the inner core spins on an axis from west to east, but at its own rate, outpacing the Earth by about one degree per year.

HOMEWORK TIP

There are three types of rock:

1 IGNEOUS rocks form from underground magma (melted rock) that cools and becomes solid. Granite is an igneous rock made from quartz, feldspar, and mica.

2 SEDIMENTARY rocks form on low-lying land or the bottom of seas. Layers of small particles harden into rock such as limestone or shale over millions of years.

3 METAMORPHIC rocks are igneous or sedimentary rocks that have been changed by chemistry, heat, or pressure (or all three). Marble is a metamorphic rock formed from limestone.

CONTINENTAL DRIFT

The Earth's landmasses didn't always look the way they do now. The continents are always in motion. It was only in the early 20th century, though, that a geologist named Alfred Lothar Wegener came up with the theory of continental drift. Wegener got the idea by looking at the matching rock formations on the west coast of Africa and the east coast of South America. He named the enormous continent that existed more than 250 million years ago Pangaea. The maps below show how the continents have moved since then. They are still moving, athough most move no faster than your fingernails grow—about 2 inches a year.

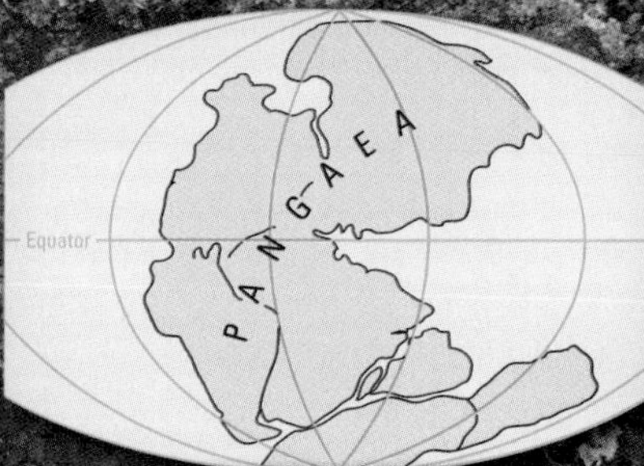

Permian
251 million years ago

Triassic
200 million years ago

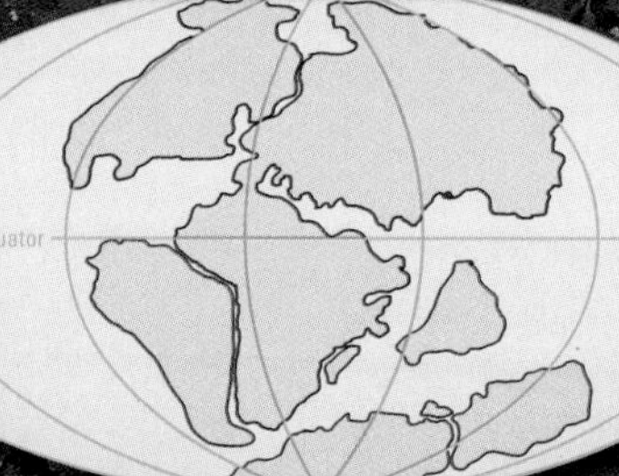

Jurassic
145 million years ago

Cretaceous
65 million years ago

Present Day

HEALTH

Which body system contains the esophagus? → page 104

KIDS' HEALTH ISSUES

ALLERGIES

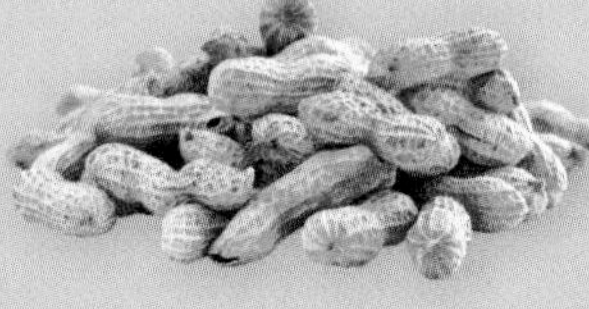

Our immune systems protect us from harmful substances. Certain people's immune systems, however, try to fight off even harmless substances. Common **allergens**—the substances people are allergic to—include pollen and peanuts. If a person inhales, eats, or touches an allergen, he or she might have an allergic reaction. The person might look as if he or she has a cold or have trouble breathing. In severe cases, a person can die from an allergic reaction.

ASTHMA

About 9 million kids in the United States have asthma. Asthma is a condition that makes breathing difficult. It is caused when the airways narrow and can't carry as much air to the lungs. Allergens, polluted air, and exercise are some of the things that can trigger an asthma attack. Asthma can't be cured, but medication can help prevent or treat attacks.

EATING DISORDERS

About 8 million teenagers in the United States have an eating disorder. Some have **anorexia nervosa**, a condition in which the person has an overwhelming desire to be thin. **Anorexics** skip meals and drastically reduce the amount of food they eat. They lose so much weight that they endanger their health. About 5 percent of anorexics die from the disorder.

Other teenagers suffer from **bulimia nervosa**, also known as bulimia. **Bulimics** alternate between bingeing, when they eat huge amounts of food, and purging, when they empty their bodies of everything they've eaten. Unlike anorexics, who are significantly underweight, most bulimics are of normal or above-normal weight.

OBESITY

Generally, someone who is significantly overweight is considered obese. Since 1980, obesity rates have tripled among kids in the United States. Nearly one in three kids today is overweight or obese. When people eat more calories than they burn off through physical activity, their bodies store the extra calories as fat. Being obese can lead to health problems, such as heart disease and diabetes.

First Lady Michelle Obama's Let's ▶ Move campaign encourages kids to eat a healthful diet and stay active.

NEW FOOD PLATE SERVED UP

So long, food pyramid. Hello, nutrition plate. In June 2011, the U.S. Department of Agriculture (USDA) dished up a new symbol—MyPlate—to replace its food pyramid. Some form of pyramid had been used for nearly 20 years to provide guidelines on healthful food choices. So, why the change? The new design, along with a focus on exercise, is part of the campaign against obesity led by First Lady Michelle Obama. Many nutrition experts thought the pyramid was confusing and didn't provide clear enough guidance on how much of different types of foods to eat for good health.

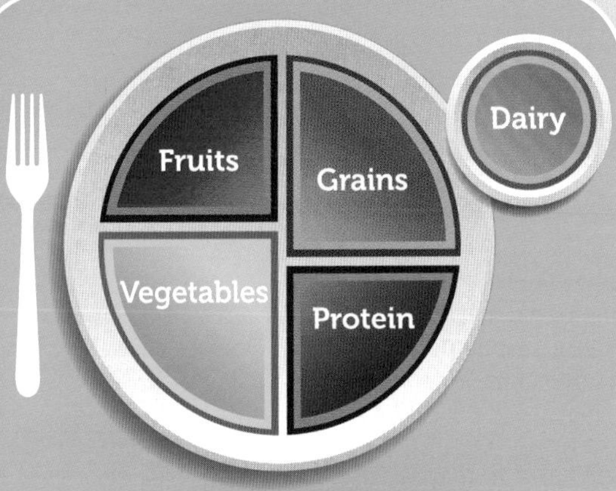

The new plate is divided into four sections—fruits, vegetables, grains, and protein—to show about how much of each food group should be on a person's dish for a healthful meal. A smaller circle next to the plate represents a glass of milk for dairy, since everyone should have some dairy products each day.

FOOD FOR THOUGHT

The USDA shares the following messages along with the new food plate symbol to help people make healthful food choices:

Balancing Calories

- Enjoy your food, but eat less.
- Avoid oversized portions.

Foods to Increase

- Make half your plate fruits and vegetables.
- Drink fat-free or low-fat (1%) milk.
- Make at least half your grains whole grains.

Foods to Reduce

- Compare sodium (salt) in foods such as soup, bread, and frozen meals—and choose the foods with lower numbers.
- Drink water instead of sugary drinks.

For more information, visit ***ChooseMyPlate.gov***

Eating right and keeping active helps keep the body healthy.

YOUR BODY

Know What Goes Into It

HOW TO READ A FOOD LABEL

Every food product approved by the Food and Drug Administration (FDA) has a label that describes its nutrients. For instance, the chips label on this page shows the total calories, fat, cholesterol, sodium, carbohydrate, protein, and vitamin content per serving.

A serving size is always defined (here, it is about 12 chips or 28 grams). This label shows that there are 9 servings per container. Don't be fooled by the calorie count of 140—these are calories per serving and not per container. If you ate the entire bag of chips, you would have eaten 1,260 calories!

Nutrition Facts

Serving Size 1 oz. (28g/About 12 chips)
Servings Per Container About 9

Amount Per Serving	
Calories 140	Calories from Fat 60
	% Daily Value*
Total Fat 7g	**11%**
Saturated Fat 1g	**5%**
Trans Fat 0g	
Cholesterol 0mg	**0%**
Sodium 170mg	**7%**
Total Carbohydrate 18g	**6%**
Dietary Fiber 1g	**4%**
Sugars less than 1g	
Protein 2g	

Vitamin A 0%	•	Vitamin C 0%
Calcium 2%	•	Iron 2%
Vitamin E 4%	•	Thiamin 2%
Riboflavin 2%	•	Vitamin B6 4%
Phosphorus 6%	•	Magnesium 4%

* Percent Daily Values are based on a 2,000 calorie diet. Your daily values may be higher or lower depending on your calorie needs:

	Calories:	2,000	2,500
Total Fat	Less than	65g	80g
Sat Fat	Less than	20g	25g
Cholesterol	Less than	300mg	300mg
Sodium	Less than	2,400mg	2,400mg
Total Carbohydrate		300g	375g
Dietary Fiber		25g	30g

Calories per gram:
Fat 9 • Carbohydrate 4 • Protein 4

WHY YOU NEED TO EAT:

Fats help kids grow and stay healthy. Fats contain nine calories per gram—the highest calorie count of any type of food. So you should limit (but not avoid) fatty foods. Choose unsaturated fats, like the fat in nuts, over saturated fats and trans fats, like the fat in doughnuts.

Carbohydrates are a major source of energy for the body. Simple carbohydrates are found in white sugar, fruit, and milk. Complex carbohydrates, also called starches, are found in bread, pasta, and rice.

Cholesterol is a soft, fat-like substance produced by your body. It's also present in animal products such as meat, cheese, and eggs but not in plant products. Cholesterol helps with cell membrane and hormone production, but there are two main types. Bad cholesterol, or LDL, gets stuck easily in blood vessels, which can lead to a heart attack or stroke. Good cholesterol, or HDL, helps break down bad cholesterol.

Proteins help your body grow and make your immune system stronger. Lean meats and tofu are good options.

Vitamins and Minerals are good for all parts of your body. For example, vitamin A, found in carrots, promotes good vision; calcium, found in milk, helps build bones; and vitamin C, found in fruits, helps heal cuts.

SOME LOW-FAT FOODS

Bananas
Oatmeal
Plain popcorn
Carrots
Sunflower seeds
Lentils

SOME FATTY FOODS

Ice cream
Doughnuts
Cheesecake
Chocolate candy
Potato chips

HAVE FUN GETTING FIT

Why Work Out?

Exercise is a great way to prevent obesity and improve health. Children should get at least 60 minutes of exercise every day. Be sure to make exercise fun. Shoot hoops, bike, swim, or play catch with a friend. The table below shows how many calories you'll burn from different types of activities.

HOW TO WORK OUT

- Begin with a five-minute warm-up! Warm-up exercises heat the body up so muscles are ready for more intense activity. Warm-up exercises include jumping jacks, walking, and stretching.
- After warming up, do an activity that you like, such as running or playing basketball with your friends. This increases your heart rate.
- After working out, cool down for 5 to 10 minutes. Cooling down lets your heart rate slow gradually. Walking is an example of a cool-down activity. Afterward, do some stretching. This helps your muscles remove waste, such as lactic acid, made when you exercise. Be sure to drink water during and after exercise.
- Building up strength through your workouts can be very beneficial. This doesn't mean you should lift the heaviest weights possible! It's better to do more lifts using light weights (1/2 lb or 1 lb) than fewer lifts with very heavy weights. Give your body time to recover between strength workouts.

ACTIVITY	CALORIES PER MINUTE
Racquetball	10
Jogging (6 miles per hour)	8
Martial arts	8
Basketball	7
Soccer	6
Bicycling (10-12 miles per hour)	5
Raking the lawn	4
Skating or rollerblading (easy pace)	4
Swimming (25 yards per minute)	3
Walking (3 miles per hour)	3
Yoga	3
Playing catch	2

did you Know?

It's becoming easier for people with all kinds of disabilities to take part in physical activities. Many groups across the U.S. help out by providing information and chances to compete. Special equipment uses the latest materials (such as light plastics) and improved design to let people with disabilities hold their own in almost any activity.

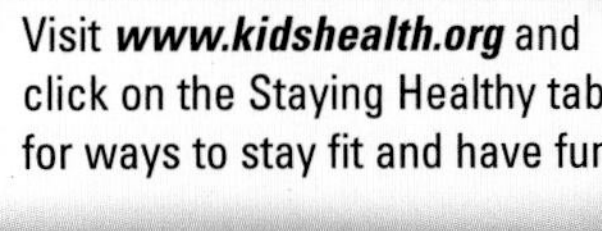

Visit ***www.kidshealth.org*** and click on the Staying Healthy tab for ways to stay fit and have fun.

Body Basics

Your body is made up of many parts. Even though we are all individuals, our bodies share similar structures. These structures make up different systems in the body.

CIRCULATORY SYSTEM In the circulatory system, the **heart** pumps **blood**. Blood travels through tubes, called **arteries**, to all parts of the body. Blood carries oxygen and food that the body needs to stay alive. **Veins** carry blood back to the heart.

DIGESTIVE SYSTEM The digestive system moves food through the **esophagus**, **stomach**, and **intestines**. As food passes through, some of it is broken down into tiny particles called **nutrients**. Nutrients enter the bloodstream and are carried to all parts of the body. The digestive system changes whatever food isn't used into waste that is eliminated from the body.

ENDOCRINE SYSTEM
The endocrine system includes **glands**. There are two kinds of glands. **Exocrine** glands produce liquids such as sweat and saliva. **Endocrine** glands produce chemicals called **hormones**. Hormones control body functions like growth.

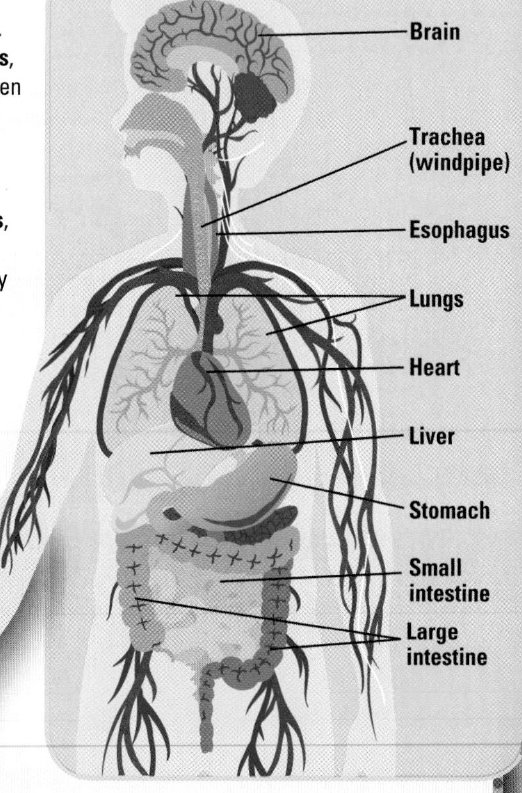

NERVOUS SYSTEM
The nervous system enables us to think, feel, move, hear, and see. It includes the **brain**, the **spinal cord**, and **nerves** throughout the body. Nerves in the spinal cord carry signals between the brain and the rest of the body. The brain has three major parts. The **cerebrum** controls thinking, speech, and vision. The **cerebellum** is responsible for physical coordination. The **brain stem** controls the respiratory, circulatory, and digestive systems.

RESPIRATORY SYSTEM The respiratory system allows us to breathe. Air enters the body through the nose and mouth. It goes through the **windpipe**, or **trachea**, to two tubes called **bronchi**, which carry air to the **lungs**. Oxygen from the air is absorbed by tiny blood vessels in the lungs. The blood then carries oxygen to the heart, from where it is sent to the body's cells.

What the Body's Systems Do

MUSCULAR SYSTEM Muscles are made up of elastic fibers. There are three types of muscle: **skeletal**, **smooth**, and **cardiac**. Skeletal muscles help the body move—they are the large muscles we can see. Smooth muscles are found in our digestive system, blood vessels, and air passages. Cardiac muscle is found only in the heart. Smooth and cardiac muscles are **involuntary** muscles—they work without us having to think about them.

REPRODUCTIVE SYSTEM Through the reproductive system, adult human beings are able to create new human beings. Reproduction begins when a man's **sperm** cell fertilizes a woman's **egg** cell.

URINARY SYSTEM This system, which includes the **kidneys**, cleans waste from the blood and regulates the amount of water in the body.

IMMUNE SYSTEM The immune system protects your body from diseases by fighting against certain outside substances, or **antigens**. This happens in different ways. For example, white blood cells called **B lymphocytes** learn to fight viruses and bacteria by producing **antibodies** to attack them. Sometimes, as with **allergies**, the immune system makes a mistake and creates antibodies to fight a substance that's really harmless.

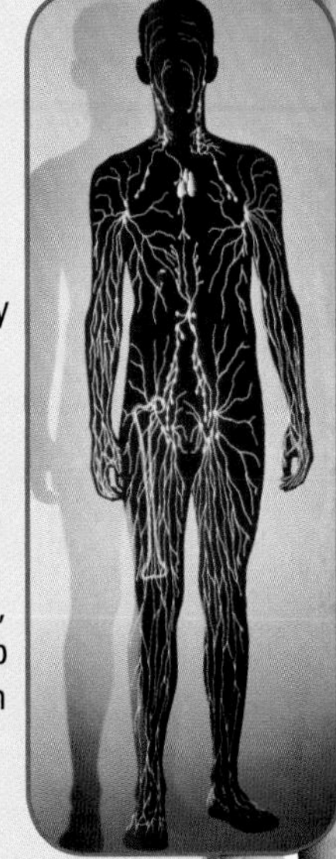

SKELETAL SYSTEM The skeletal system is made up of **bones** that hold the body upright. It also gives your body its shape, protects your organs, and works with your muscles to help you move. Babies are born with 350 bones. By adulthood, some of the bones have grown together for a total of 206.

Brain Power

The typical human brain only weighs about three pounds. But it's like the control center of the body, responsible for making sure everything functions properly. Different parts of the brain do different things.

Right hemisphere of cerebrum

- Controls left side of body
- Location of things relative to other things
- Recognizes faces
- Music
- Emotions

Left hemisphere of cerebrum

- Controls right side of body
- Ability to understand language and speech
- Ability to reason
- Numbers

Cerebrum

Brain stem

Regulates vital activities like breathing and heart rate

Cerebellum

Controls coordination, balance

THE 5 Senses

Your senses gather information about the world around you. The five senses are **hearing, sight, smell, taste,** and **touch.** You need senses to find food, resist heat or cold, and avoid situations that might be harmful. Your ears, eyes, nose, tongue, and skin sense changes in the environment. Nerve receptors send signals about these changes to the brain, where the information is processed.

1 HEARING

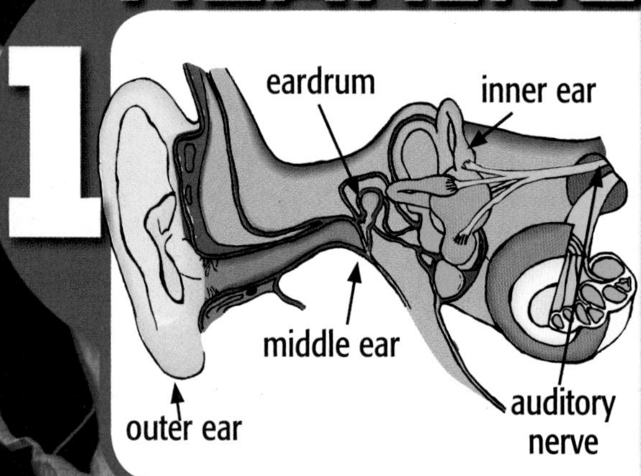

The human ear is divided into three parts—the outer, middle, and inner. The **outer ear** is mainly the flap we can see on the outside. Its shape funnels sound waves into the **middle ear**, where the eardrum is located. The **eardrum** vibrates when sound waves hit it, causing three tiny bones behind it to vibrate as well. These vibrations are picked up in the **inner ear** by tiny filaments of the **auditory nerve**. This nerve changes the vibrations into nerve impulses and carries them to the brain.

did you Know?

The smallest bones in the human body are found in the ear. Located in the middle ear, the hammer, anvil, and stirrup are full size when you are born. The bones are so tiny that all three could fit on a penny together!

2 SIGHT

The **lens** of the eye is the first stop for light waves, which tell you the shapes and colors of things around you. The lens focuses light waves onto the **retina**, located on the back wall of the eye. The retina has light-sensitive nerve cells. These cells translate the light waves into patterns of nerve impulses that travel along the **optic nerve** to your brain, where an image is produced. So in reality, all the eye does is collect light. It is the brain that actually forms the image.

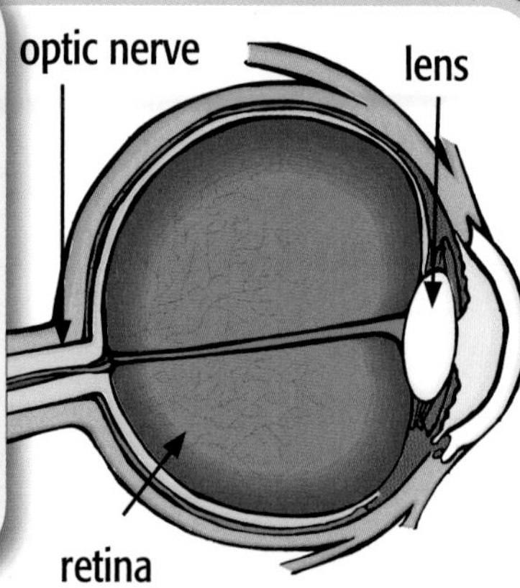

3 SMELL

In our noses are nerve cells called **olfactory receptors**. Tiny mucus-covered hairs from these receptors detect chemicals in the air. These chemicals make what we call odor, or scent. This information then travels along the **olfactory nerves** to the brain. Nerves from the olfactory receptors connect with the **limbic system**, the part of the brain that deals with emotions. That's why we tend to like or dislike a smell right away. The smell can leave a strong impression on our memory, and very often a smell triggers a particular memory.

4 TASTE

Taste buds are the primary receptors for taste. They are located on the surface and sides of the tongue, on the roof of the mouth, and at the back of the throat. These buds can detect five qualities—**sweet** (like sugar), **sour** (like lemons), **salty** (like chips), **bitter** (like coffee), and **umami** or savory flavors (like meat). Taste signals come together with smell signals in the same part of your brain. That's why you need both senses to get a food's full flavor.

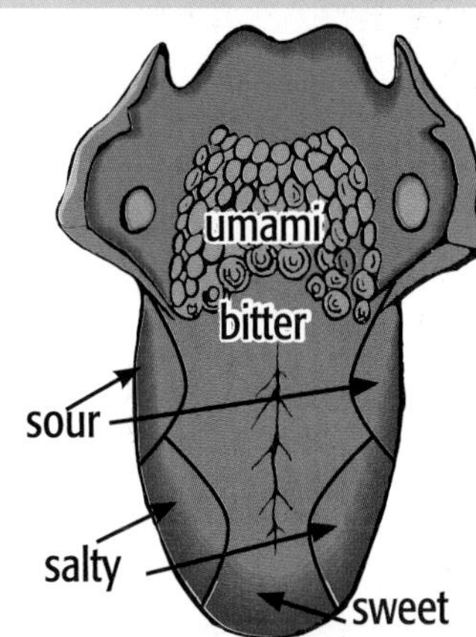

5 TOUCH

Your sense of touch allows you to feel temperature, pain, and pressure. These environmental factors are all sensed by nerve fibers located in the **epidermis**, the outer layer of skin, and the **dermis**, the second layer of skin, throughout the body. As with all the other senses, nerves send information to the brain through the nervous system.

HOMEWORK HELP

How do you prepare a bibliography? → page 110

If you need to study for an exam or write a research paper, there are helpful hints in this chapter.

In other chapters, you can find lots of information on topics you may write about or study in school. **Facts About Nations,** pages 152–177, and **Facts About the States,** pages 292–309, are good places to look. For math tips and formulas, look up the chapter on **Numbers**. For good books to read, and write about, see the **Books** chapter.

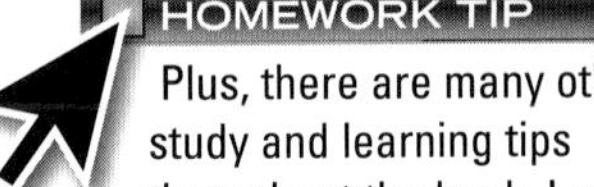

HOMEWORK TIP

Plus, there are many other study and learning tips throughout the book. Look for the **"Homework Tip"** icon!

THOSE TRICKY TESTS

GETTING READY

Being prepared for a test can relieve some of your jitters and can make test taking a lot easier! Here are some tips to help you get ready.

- Take good notes in class and keep up with assignments, so you don't have to learn material at the last minute! Just writing down the notes helps you remember the information.
- Make a study schedule and stick to it! Don't watch TV or listen to distracting music while studying.
- Start reviewing early if you can—don't wait until the night before the test.
- Go over the headings, summaries, and questions in each chapter to review key points. Read your notes and highlight the most important topics.
- Take study breaks so you can concentrate and stay alert.
- Get a good night's sleep and eat a good breakfast before the test.

THE BIG EVENT

Follow these suggestions for smooth sailing during test time:

- Take a deep breath and relax! That will help calm your nerves.
- If you are allowed, skim through the entire exam so you know what to expect and how long it may take.
- As you start each part of the exam, read directions carefully.
- Read each question carefully before answering. For a multiple-choice question, check every possible answer before you decide on one. The best answer could be the last one.
- Don't spend too much time on any one question. Skip hard questions and go back to them at the end.
- Keep track of time so you can pace yourself. Use any time left at the end to go back and review your answers. Make sure you've written the answer you meant to select.

WHICH ONE DO I USE?

When you need to write answers for a school assignment or write a research paper, you'll want to be careful to use words correctly. There are many examples in English of two words (or even three) that sound alike but that mean different things. Words that sound alike but have different meanings are called **homonyms**. Here are a few.

Its/It's

Its is a possessive. That means that it shows ownership. For example:

Each sport has its own rules.

It's, on the other hand, is a contraction of *it is*. For example:

It's time to leave for school.

Affect/Effect

These two words are often confused. *Affect* is a verb that means *to change* or *to influence*. Here's an example:

Our picnic was affected by the rain.

Effect is a noun that means *result* or *impact*. For example:

What *effect* did the rain have on your picnic?

Principal/Principle

Here's another pair of words that often confuse people. *Principal* means *most important*. For example:

What are the *principal* products of France?

The head of a school is also usually called a *principal*.

A *principle*, on the other hand, is a standard or rule that people live by. For example:

An important *principle* stated in the Declaration of Independence is that all men are created equal.

Compliment/Complement

Compliment and *complement* are two very different words. A compliment is a flattering remark:

He paid me a nice *compliment* about my new dress.

To *complement* something means to *complete* it or to *supply a needed portion* of it. Here's an example:

My partner's work on the research paper complemented my own efforts.

They're/There/Their

This time we have three words that sound the same but mean different things. *They're* is a contraction of *they are:*

They're coming to visit at noon.

There refers to a place and means the opposite of *here*.

Put the dishes over *there*.

Finally, the third form, *their*, is a possessive adjective and means *belonging to them*.

Where are *their* coats?

Capital/Capitol

This pair is a bit tricky. *Capital* means the city where a state or country has its government.

The *capital* of the United States is Washington, D.C.

Capitol, on the other hand, is the name of the building where members of the government meet.

The U.S. *Capitol* is the building where Congress meets in Washington, D.C.

Got that? The U.S. *Capitol* is in the *capital* city of Washington, D.C.

HOW TO WRITE A RESEARCH PAPER

Doing Research

To start any research paper or project, the first thing to do is research.

- **Encyclopedias are a good place to start.** They can give you a good overview of the subject.
- **The electronic catalog** of your school or public library will probably be your main source for finding books and articles about your subject. A librarian can help show you how this works.
- You can also use **the Internet** as a research tool (see opposite page).
- As you read each source, **write down the facts and ideas** that you may need. Include the title and author for each source and the page numbers or the web site and address for the web page where you found the particular information.

Writing It Down

The next step is to organize your facts. **Develop a rough outline** of your ideas in the order in which they'll appear. Then, write a draft of your paper. It should contain three main parts:

INTRODUCTION The paper's introduction, or first paragraph, explains your topic and your point of view on it. It should draw readers into the paper and let them know what to expect.

BODY The body of the paper develops your ideas. Use specific facts, examples, and details to make your points clear and convincing. Use separate paragraphs for each new idea and use words and phrases that link one paragraph to the next so your ideas flow smoothly.

CONCLUSION Summarize your main points in the final paragraph, or conclusion.

Showing Your Sources

You may need to do a **bibliography** at the end of your paper. This is a list of all the sources you used to prepare the report. Here are some guidelines for how to cite commonly used types of sources.

FOR A BOOK: Author. *Title.* City Published: Publisher, Year.

Jones, Phil. *Science Foundations: Kingdoms of Life.* New York: Chelsea House, 2011.

FOR A MAGAZINE ARTICLE: Author. "Article Title." *Magazine Title,* Date of Issue, Pages.

Miller, James S. "Moth Masquerade." *Natural History,* November 2010, 14–15.

FOR ONLINE (INTERNET): Author. "Entry Title." *Database Name,* Date of Publication. Database Company. URL (date accessed).

Matlis, Sean. "Glass Gets Tougher Than Steel." *Today's Science,* March 2011. Facts On File, Inc. http://www.2facts.com/tsof_story.aspx?PIN=s1900019 (accessed March 24, 2011).

RESEARCH ON THE INTERNET

Using Library Resources

Your school or public library is a great place to start. It probably has a list (catalog) of its books and of periodicals (newspapers and magazines) available from computers at the library, or even from home over the Internet through your library's web site. You can search using **keywords** (words that describe your subject) in three basic ways: by **author**, by **title**, or by **subject**.

For example, doing a subject search for "Benjamin Franklin" will give you a list of books and articles about him, along with their locations in the library.

Your library may also subscribe to online reference databases that companies create especially for research. These are accessible over the Internet and could contain almanacs, encyclopedias, reference books, other nonfiction books, or collections of articles. You can access these databases from the library, and maybe even from home from your library's web site.

When you write your report, don't copy directly from books, articles, or the Internet—that's **plagiarism**, a form of cheating. Keep track of all your **sources**—the books, articles, and web sites you use—and list them in a **bibliography**. (See page 110 for some examples.)

Why shouldn't I just search the Internet?

The library's list may look just like other information on the Internet. But these sources usually have been checked by experts. This is not true of all the information on the Internet. It could come from almost anybody, and it may not be trustworthy.

When can I use the Internet?

The Internet is still a great way to look things up. You can find addresses or recipes, listen to music, or find things to do. You can look up information on hobbies or musical instruments, or read a magazine or newspaper online.

If you search the Internet on your own, make sure the web site you find is reliable. A U.S. government site or a site produced by a well-known organization or publication is usually your best bet.

Using a Search Engine

The best way to find web sites is to use a search engine. Here are some helpful ones:

Yahoo Kids (kids.yahoo.com)
Kidsclick (www.kidsclick.org)

Start by typing one or two search terms—words that describe your topic. The search engine scans the Internet and gives you a list of sites that contain them. The results appear in a certain order, or **rank**. Search engines use different ways of measuring which web sites are likely to be the most helpful. One way is by counting how many times your search terms appear on each site. The site that's listed first may not have what you want. Explore as many of the sites as possible.

NVENTIONS

en was the parachute invented? → page 112

Invention TIME LINE

YEAR	INVENTION	INVENTOR (COUNTRY)
105	paper	Cai Lun (China)
1440s	printing press/movable type	Johann Gutenberg (Germany)
1590	2-lens microscope	Zacharias Janssen (Netherlands)
1608	telescope	Hans Lippershey (Netherlands)
1714	mercury thermometer	Gabriel D. Fahrenheit (Germany)
1752	lightning rod	Benjamin Franklin (U.S.)
1783	parachute	Sebastien Lenormand (France)
1800	electric battery	Alessandro Volta (Italy)
1804	steam locomotive	Richard Trevithick (England)
1837	telegraph	Samuel F. B. Morse (U.S.), Charles Wheatstone & William F. Cooke (England)
1842	anesthesia (ether)	Crawford W. Long (U.S.)
1870s	telephone*	Antonio Meucci (Italy), Alexander G. Bell (U.S.)
1879	practical light bulb	Thomas A. Edison (U.S.)
1886	automobile (gasoline)	Karl Benz (Germany)
1892	moving picture viewer	Thomas A. Edison & William K. Dickson (U.S.)
1894	cereal flakes	Will Keith Kellogg (U.S.)
1897	diesel engine	Rudolf Diesel (Germany)
1902	air conditioning	Willis Carrier (U.S.)
1923	television**	Vladimir K. Zworykin (U.S.)
1926	liquid-fuel rocket engine	Robert H. Goddard (U.S.) ▶
1928	tape recorder	Fritz Pfleumer (Germany)
1928	penicillin	Alexander Fleming (Scotland)
1930	packaged quick-frozen food	Clarence Birdseye (U.S.)
1933	FM radio	Edwin Armstrong (U.S.)
1938	Frisbee	Fred Morrison (U.S.)
1939	jet airplane	Hans von Ohain (Germany)
1942	electronic computer	John V. Atanasoff & Clifford Berry (U.S.)
1955	TV wireless remote control	Eugene Polley (U.S.)
1955	Velcro®	George de Mestral (Switzerland)
1957	digital image	Russell Kirsch (U.S.)
1957	laser***	Gordon Gould (U.S.)
1971	CAT scanner	Godfrey N. Hounsfield (England)
1973	personal computer	André Thi Truong (France)
1975	digital camera	Steven Sasson (U.S.) ▶
1989	World Wide Web	Tim Berners-Lee (England)
2007	iPhone	Apple (U.S.) ▶
2009	3D digital camera	Fujifilm (Japan)

* Meucci developed a type of telephone (early 1870s); Bell received a patent for a telephone in 1876.

** Others who helped invent the television in the 1920s were Philo T. Farnsworth and John Baird.

*** First working laser built in 1960 by Theodore Maiman.

CURRENT Inventions

AN ELECTRONICS REVOLUTION

If you could go back in time to the 1980s, you'd be amazed at what you saw. Many of the ways people today play games, listen to music, watch TV and movies, communicate, study, and work didn't exist. Or if they did, they existed only in simple forms. The use of electronics has grown at a fantastic pace since then.

Inventors came up with new materials for electronic devices, improvements in old materials, new forms of wireless linkups, new ideas for using the Internet, and new ways of storing, displaying, and using information.

Actually, information was key to many of these developments. Information—whether words, or numbers, or pictures, or whatever—is represented by electronic signals. Scientists and engineers keep developing better and faster ways of processing such signals. More and more information can be handled by smaller and smaller devices.

Smaller but More POWERFUL

Because of this miniaturization trend, little pieces of equipment can now carry enormous computing power. Today's tiny digital cameras do many more things, and do them better, than the film cameras that everyone once used.

The same is true of cell phones. Cell phones were rare in the 1980s. Those that existed looked like bricks compared to today's small phones. Almost all mobile phones today take advantage of efficient digital technology. Many are "smart" phones that carry powerful computer chips and can do things—surf the Web, handle e-mail, show videos, play music, and run games, among dozens of other applications—unthinkable in a phone just 20 or 25 years ago.

▲*Computer chips*

Thanks to advances in chips, people now enjoy such conveniences as robot vacuum cleaners, highly computerized cars, digital video recorders, digital televisions, electronic readers such as Amazon's Kindle, portable media players such as Apple's iPod, and laptop and tablet computers far more powerful than the biggest desktop machines of the 1980s.

did you Know?

Tablet computers like the iPad rely on a lot of new technology, but their roots lie in a 19th-century invention. To use a tablet you touch the screen with your fingers or with a special pen, or stylus. The tablet converts the touch into electric signals. In 1888, Elisha Gray received a U.S. patent for a "teleautograph." This was a device that could take a message (or picture) made with a stylus and send it through wires to a receiving point, where another stylus automatically reproduced the original.

Elisha Gray

LANGUAGE

How do you say "happy birthday" in Arabic? → page 115

More people speak some form (dialect) of Chinese than any other language in the world. Spanish ranks as the second most common native, or first, language. The table below and the map show the languages with at least 100 million native speakers.*

*2009 estimates

LANGUAGE	KEY PLACES WHERE SPOKEN	NATIVE SPEAKERS
Chinese	China, Taiwan	1,213 million
Spanish	Latin America, Spain	329 million
English	U.S., Canada, Britain, Australia	328 million
Arabic	Middle East, North Africa	221 million
Hindi	India	182 million
Bengali	Bangladesh, India	181 million
Portuguese	Portugal, Brazil	178 million
Russian	Russia	144 million
Japanese	Japan	122 million

Which LANGUAGES Are SPOKEN in the UNITED STATES?

Most Americans speak English at home. But since the beginning of American history, immigrants have come to the U.S. from all over the world. Many have brought other languages with them.

The table at the right lists the most frequently spoken languages in the U.S., according to a 2009 Census Bureau report.

	LANGUAGE USED AT HOME	SPEAKERS 5 YEARS AND OLDER
1	Speak only English	228,699,523
2	Spanish, Spanish Creole	35,468,501
3	Chinese	2,600,150
4	Tagalog (Philippines)	1,513,734
5	French	1,305,503
6	Vietnamese	1,251,468
7	German	1,109,216
8	Korean	1,039,021
9	Russian	881,723
10	Arabic	845,396
11	Other Asian languages	783,140
12	African languages	777,553
13	Italian	753,992
14	Portuguese, Portuguese Creole	731,282
15	Other Indic languages	668,596
16	French Creole	659,053
17	Polish	593,598
18	Hindi	560,983
19	Other Indo-European languages	455,483
20	Japanese	445,471

LANGUAGE EXPRESS

Ciao! (Italian)

Hello! (English)

Surprise your friends and family with words from other languages.

English	Arabic*	Chinese	French	Italian
January	yanāyir	yi-yue	janvier	gennaio
February	fibrāyir	er-yue	février	febbraio
March	māris	san-yue	mars	marzo
April	abrīl *or* ibrīl	si-yue	avril	aprile
May	māyū	wu-yue	mai	maggio
June	yūnyū *or* yūnya	liu-yue	juin	giugno
July	yūlyū *or* yūlia	qi-yue	juillet	luglio
August	aġustus	ba-yue	août	agosto
September	sibtambir	jiu-yue	septembre	settembre
October	uktūbar	shi-yue	octobre	ottobre
November	nūfambir	shi-yi-yue	novembre	novembre
December	dīsambir	shi-er-yue	décembre	dicémbre
blue	asrag	lan	bleu	azzurro
red	ahmar	hong	rouge	rosso
green	akhdar	lu	vert	verde
yellow	asfar	huang	jaune	giallo
black	aswad	hei	noir	nero
white	abyad	bai	blanc	bianco
Happy birthday!	Eid meelad sa'eed!	Sheng-ri kuai le!	Joyeux anniversaire!	Buon compleanno!
Hello!	Salam!	Ni hao!	Bonjour!	Ciao!
Good-bye!	Ma salamah!	Zai-jian!	Au revoir!	Arrivederci!
fish	samakah	yu	poisson	pesci
bird	altair	niao	oiseau	uccello
horse	hisan	ma	cheval	cavallo
one	wahed	yi	un	uno
two	ithnaan	er	deux	due
three	thalatha	san	trois	tre
four	arba'a	si	quatre	quattro
five	khamsa	wu	cinq	cinque

***The line over a vowel indicates a long sound.**

did you Know?

The word vuvuzela *appeared in English-language dictionaries for the first time in 2010. Soccer fans blew this long horn at the World Cup in South Africa that year. Some say thousands of vuvuzelas played at once sound like a swarm of wasps. In fact, played at full volume, the instrument may cause permanent hearing loss. It has also been found to spread germs. Organizers of the 2012 Olympic Games are likely to ban the use of the plastic horn.*

¡SAY IT IN ESPAÑOL!

After English, Spanish is the most commonly spoken language in the U.S. More than 35 million people speak Spanish at home. That's more than 11 percent of all people in the U.S.

Pronouncing Spanish Words

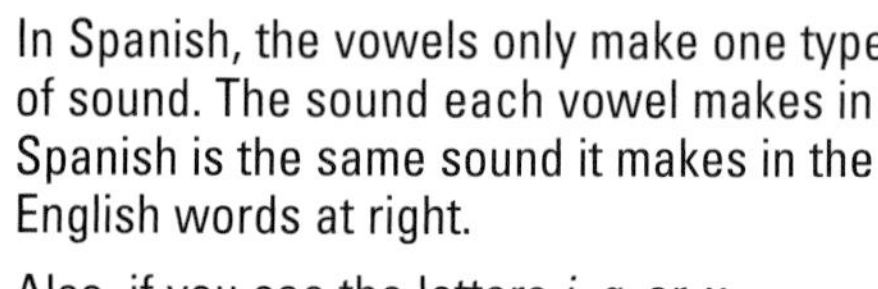

In Spanish, the vowels only make one type of sound. The sound each vowel makes in Spanish is the same sound it makes in the English words at right.

Also, if you see the letters *j*, *g*, or *x* followed by a vowel, pronounce them like the English *h*. So, *frijoles* (beans) sounds like free-HOLE-lehs. *México* sounds like MAY-hee-co. The *h* in Spanish is always silent. So *hermano* (brother) sounds like er-MAN-o.

A	water
E	bet
I	feet
O	slow
U	tube

Try pronouncing the Spanish on this page.

SISTER Languages

There are some words that sound alike in Spanish and English. These are called cognates. See if you can guess each kid's answer to the question:

What do you want to be when you grow up?

Julio	Yo quiero ser *músico.*
Maria	Un dia, yo quisiera ser *autora.*
Juan	Yo quiero ser *banquero.*
Olivia	Un dia, yo quisiera ser *arquitecta.*
Andrés	Yo quiero ser *piloto.*

Answers: Julio—musician; María—author; Juan—banker; Olivia—architect; Andrés—pilot.

Basic Spanish Phrases

Hello	Hola
Good-bye	Adiós
How are you?	¿Cómo estás?
Please	Por favor
Thank you	Gracias
What is your name?	¿Cómo te llamas?

FOOD

Next time you're having dinner, ask your father to pass the *jugo.*

Salad
Ensalada

Shrimp
Camarones

Juice
Jugo

Rice
Arroz

Chicken
Pollo

Paella
Traditional Rice Dish

Use your *boca* to say these parts of the body (*cuerpo*) in Spanish. Use your *cabeza* to remember how to say them!

Head	Cabeza
Ears	Orejas
Eyes	Ojos
Hair	Cabello

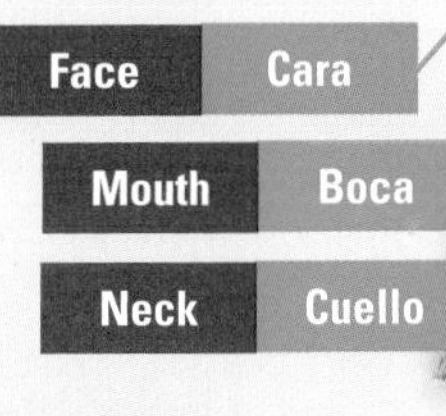

Arm	Brazo
Belly	Barriga
Hand	Mano
Leg	Pierna
Knee	Rodilla
Foot	Pie

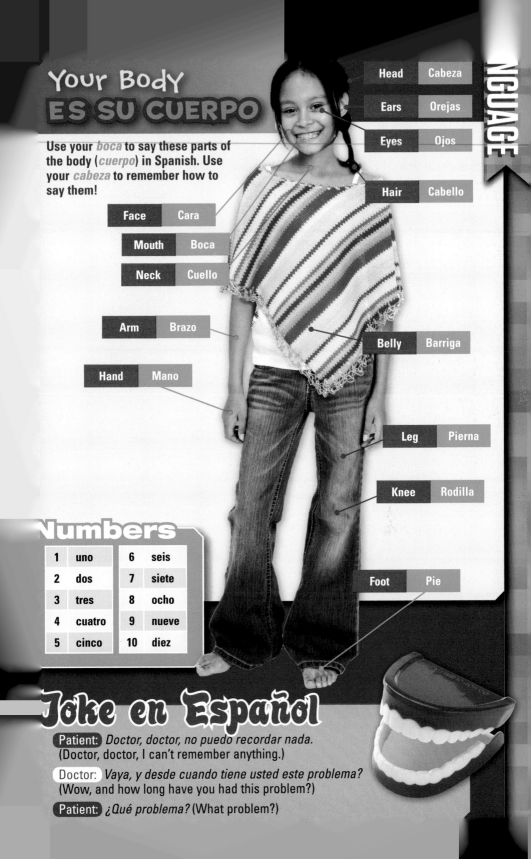

Numbers

1	uno	6	seis
2	dos	7	siete
3	tres	8	ocho
4	cuatro	9	nueve
5	cinco	10	diez

Joke en Español

Patient: *Doctor, doctor, no puedo recordar nada.* (Doctor, doctor, I can't remember anything.)

Doctor: *Vaya, y desde cuando tiene usted este problema?* (Wow, and how long have you had this problem?)

Patient: *¿Qué problema?* (What problem?)

THE ENGLISH LANGUAGE

Facts About English

- According to the *Oxford English Dictionary*, the English language contains between 250,000 and 750,000 words. (Some people count different meanings of the same word as separate words and include unusual technical terms.)
- The most frequently used letters of the alphabet are *e, t, a,* and *o,* in that order.
- The 30 most common words in the English language are: *the, of, and, a, to, in, is, that, it, was, he, for, as, on, with, his, be, at, you, I, are, this, by, from, had, have, they, not, or, one.*

New Words

English is always changing as new words are born and old ones die out. Many new words come from the latest technology, from the media, or from slang.

ambitexterous: able to type text messages with the right and left hand

Belieber: a fan of Canadian singer Justin Bieber

bracketology: the process of determining the winners in a sports tournament

halflogue: an overheard one-sided cell phone conversation

matchy-matchy: overly color coordinated

unfriend: to remove a person from one's contact list on a social networking site

In Other Words: SIMILES

Similes are comparisons of two dissimilar things that use "as" or "like." Here are some to wrap your brain around:

fast as lightning = "moves quickly." Lightning travels speedily through the sky, in the same way that a runner might move rapidly.

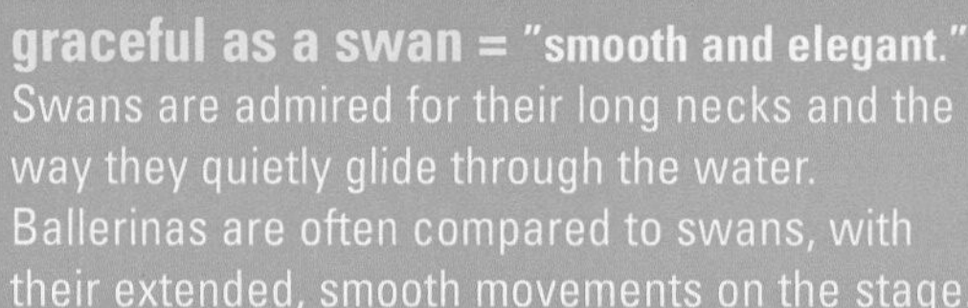

graceful as a swan = "smooth and elegant." Swans are admired for their long necks and the way they quietly glide through the water. Ballerinas are often compared to swans, with their extended, smooth movements on the stage.

flat as a pancake = "completely flat" Pancakes are always flat, in the same way that land without hills might be.

GETTING TO THE ROOT

Many English words and parts of words can be traced back to Latin or Greek. If you know the meaning of parts of a word, you can probably guess what it means. A root (also called a stem) is the part of the word that gives its basic meaning but can't be used by itself. Roots need other word parts to complete them: either a prefix at the beginning, or a suffix at the end, or sometimes both. The following tables give some examples of Latin and Greek roots, prefixes, and suffixes.

LATIN

root	basic meaning	example
-alt-	high	*altitude*
-dict-	to say	*dictate*
-port-	to carry	*transport*
-scrib-/ -script-	to write	*prescription*
-vert-	turn	*invert*

prefix	basic meaning	example
de-	away, off	*defrost*
in-/im-	not	*invisible*
non-	not	*nontoxic*
pre-	before	*prehistoric*
re-	again, back	*rewrite*
trans-	across, through	*transatlantic*

suffix	basic meaning	example
-ation	(makes verbs into nouns)	*invitation*
-fy/-ify	make or cause to become	*horrify*
-ly	like, to the extent of	*highly*
-ment	(makes verbs into nouns)	*government*
-ty/-ity	state of	*purity*

GREEK

root	basic meaning	example
-anthrop-	human	*anthropology*
-bio-	life	*biology*
-dem-	people	*democracy*
-phon-	sound	*telephone*
-psych-	soul	*psychology*

prefix	basic meaning	example
anti-/ant-	against	*antisocial*
auto-	self	*autopilot*
biblio-/ bibl-	book	*bibliography*
micro-	small	*microscope*
tele-	far off	*television*

suffix	basic meaning	example
-graph	write, draw, describe, record	*photograph*
-ism	act, state, theory of	*realism*
-ist	one who believes in, practices	*capitalist*
-logue/ -log	speech, to speak	*dialogue*
-scope	see	*telescope*

MILITARY

What country has the largest armed forces? → page 122

American Revolution

George Washington

Why? The British king sought to control American trade and tax the 13 colonies without their consent. The colonies wanted independence from Great Britain.

Who? British vs. Americans with French support

When? 1775–1783

Result? The colonies gained independence.

War of 1812

Why? Britain interfered with American commerce and forced American sailors to join the British navy.

Who? Britain vs. United States

Battle of Lake Erie

When? 1812–1814

Result? There was no clear winner.
The U.S. unsuccessfully invaded Canada, a British colony. The British burned Washington, D.C., and the White House but were defeated in other battles.

did you Know?

In 1814, First Lady Dolley Madison fled the White House just hours before the British arrived. She had been preparing a large dinner party, and she left the food on the table. So the British feasted—and then set fire to the White House.

Mexican War

Why? The U.S. annexed Texas. It also sought control of California, a Mexican province.

Who? Mexico vs. United States

When? 1846–1848

Result? Mexico gave up its claim to Texas and ceded to the U.S. California and all or part of six other Western states.

Civil War

Why? Eleven Southern states seceded from the U.S. The U.S. fought to keep them.

Civil War soldier

Who? Confederacy vs. Union

When? 1861–1865

Result? The United States remained a unified country. Slavery was abolished.

Spanish-American War

Why? The Americans supported Cuban independence from Spain.

Who? United States vs. Spain

The wreck of the U.S.S. *Maine*

When? 1898

Result? Spain handed the Philippines, Guam, and Puerto Rico over to the U.S. Cuba became independent.

did you Know?

The U.S. battleship **Maine** ***exploded in Havana harbor on January 25, 1898, when a mine was set off underneath the ship. The cry "Remember the*** **Maine!"** ***helped fuel the war fever in the U.S.***

World War I

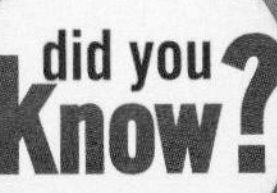

Why? Colonial and military competition between European powers.

Who? Allies (including the U.S., Britain, France, Russia, Italy, and Japan) vs. Central Powers (including Germany, Austria-Hungary, and Turkey)

When? 1914–1918 (U.S. entered in 1917)

Result? The Allies defeated the Central Powers. An estimated 8 million soldiers and close to 10 million civilians were killed.

World War II

U.S. troops land in France on D-Day, June 6, 1944

Why? The Axis sought world domination.

Who? Axis (including Germany, Italy, and Japan) vs. Allies (including the U.S., Britain, France, and the Soviet Union). The U.S. did not enter the war until Japan attacked Pearl Harbor in 1941.

When? 1939–1945 (U.S. dropped atomic bombs on Hiroshima and Nagasaki in August 1945.)

Result? The Allies defeated the Axis. The Holocaust (the Nazi effort to wipe out the Jews and other minorities) was stopped. The U.S. helped rebuild Western Europe and Japan. The Soviet Union set up Communist governments in Eastern Europe.

did you Know? ***More than 16 million Americans served in the military in World War II, by far the highest number for any war in which the United States has fought.***

Korean War

Why? North Korea invaded South Korea. In many ways, the conflict was part of the Cold War between the Communist and non-Communist nations.

Who? North Korea with support from China and the Soviet Union vs. South Korea backed by the United States and its allies

When? 1950–1953

Result? The war ended in a stalemate. Korea remains divided.

did you Know? ***The Korean War Veterans Memorial in Washington, D.C., honors American military personnel who fought in Korea.***

Vietnam War

Why? Communists (Viet Cong) backed by North Vietnam attempted to overthrow South Vietnam's government.

Who? North Vietnam with support from the Soviet Union and China vs. South Vietnam with support from the U.S. and its allies

When? 1959–1975

Result? The U.S. withdrew its troops in 1973. In 1975, South Vietnam surrendered. Vietnam became a unified Communist country.

Persian Gulf War

Why? Iraq invaded and annexed Kuwait. It refused to withdraw despite United Nations demands.

Who? Iraq vs. U.S.-led coalition

When? 1991

Result? The coalition drove out Iraqi forces from Kuwait.

A-10A Thunderbolt II ground attack plane flying during the Persian Gulf War, 1991

Where Are We Now?

Afghanistan War

Why? The U.S. demanded that Afghanistan's Taliban regime turn over Osama bin Laden, the man who planned the 9/11 terrorist attacks in 2001. The Taliban claimed not to know bin Laden's whereabouts.

Who? Taliban vs. Afghani forces, supported by the U.S. and its allies.

When? 2001–

Result? The Taliban was driven from power but later regained control over large parts of the country. In 2009 and 2010, President Barack Obama increased U.S. troop strength to around 100,000, but the U.S. announced plans to begin withdrawing troops in 2011.

did you Know? ***The first U.S. Air Force combat mission in which all fight crew personnel were women took place in Afghanistan on March 30, 2011.***

Iraq War

Why? The U.S. accused Iraq of hiding weapons of mass destruction (WMDs) and supporting terrorists.

Who? Iraq vs. United States, Great Britain, and their allies

When? 2003–

Result? Saddam Hussein's government was toppled. Hussein was captured, put on trial, and hanged. No WMDs were found. The U.S. withdrew the last American combat troops in 2010, although some support troops remained.

TOP 10 NATIONS WITH LARGEST ARMED FORCES*

Rank	Country	Troops
1.	China	2,285,000
2.	United States	1,580,000
3.	India	1,325,000
4.	North Korea	1,106,000
5.	Russia	1,027,000
6.	South Korea	687,000
7.	Pakistan	617,000
8.	Iraq	578,000
9.	Iran	523,000
10.	Turkey	511,000

*Troops on active duty in 2010. Source: The Military Balance/International Institute for Strategic Studies

THE MILITARY: Mother of Inventions

When you think about the military, you probably think of tanks, fighter planes, and submarines. But all kinds of inventions that have become part of everyday life were developed for use by the armed forces—to help the military carry out its missions or to help those who were injured while serving. Here are a few of those inventions:

Anesthesia: Chloroform, an early anesthetic, was first widely used in the United States during the Civil War to keep wounded soldiers from suffering terrible pain as doctors treated their wounds. After the war, private civilian hospitals began using it. Soon the use of anesthesia during surgery and other medical procedures became widespread.

The Internet: An early version of the Internet—a system of connected computer networks—was developed for the U.S. military in the 1960s and 1970s. Called ARPAnet, it was used for military communications and transmission of information, and it was seen as a way to keep essential information from being destroyed in the event of an attack on any one military location.

Penicillin: Although penicillin had been discovered in the 1920s, research on its ability to kill bacteria and on ways to make large amounts of it was spurred by World War II. Doctors were eager to find a drug that could prevent and treat infections in millions of wounded soldiers. By the end of the war, penicillin had saved the lives of countless soldiers, and soon after, it was widely being used by doctors worldwide.

Microwave Oven: In World War II, a tube called a magnetron, which produces microwaves, was used by the Allies in radar to spot German planes. Soon after the war, a scientist working on improving radar systems noticed that a candy bar in his pocket had melted when he went near a magnetron. He experimented with other foods and found that they all got hot when near this type of tube. He created a metal box, fed the microwaves from the tube into it—and created the first microwave oven.

All About Helping Japan

After a powerful earthquake and huge sea wave (tsunami) struck part of Japan on March 11, 2011, the U.S. military was quick to offer its services. Within one day of the quake, an aircraft carrier was off the coast of Japan, serving as a refueling and reloading base for helicopters ferrying relief supplies to survivors. In Japan, U.S. troops flew helicopters and cargo planes to deliver food, water, and medical supplies; helped locate survivors trapped in the rubble; transported survivors to hospitals and refugee centers; and helped clear rubble so that access to the devastated area could be restored.

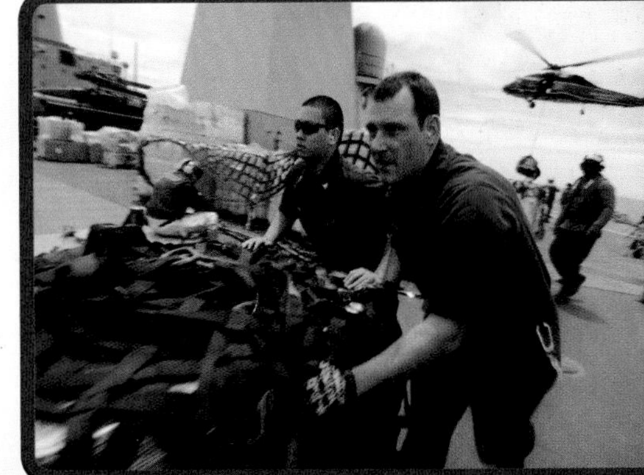

MONEY

Which four presidents appeared on new dollar coins in 2011? → page 125

World's Ten Richest People*

Name	Age	Country	Industry	Worth (in billions)
Carlos Slim Helú†	71	Mexico	Communications	$74.0
Bill Gates	55	United States	Software (Microsoft)	56.0
Warren Buffett	80	United States	Investments	50.0
Bernard Arnault	62	France	Luxury goods (LMVH)	41.0
Lawrence Ellison	66	United States	Data Management (Oracle)	39.5
Lakshmi Mittal	60	India	Steel	31.1
Amancio Ortega	75	Spain	Fashion	31.0
Eike Batista	54	Brazil	Mining, oil	30.0
Mukesh Ambani	53	India	Manufacturing, oil	27.0
Christy Walton†	56	United States	Walmart, inherited	26.5

*As of May 2011 (Source: www.forbes.com) †Includes other family members

World's Youngest Billionaires*

Name	Age	Country	Industry	Worth (in billions)
Dustin Moskovitz	26	United States	Technology (Facebook, Asana)	$2.7
Mark Zuckerberg	26	United States	Technology (Facebook)	13.5
Prince Albert von Thurn und Taxis	27	Germany	Diversified investments	2.0
Scott Duncan	28	United States	Inherited energy company	3.1
Eduardo Saverin	29	United States	Technology (Facebook)	1.6
Yang Huiyan	29	China	Property development	4.1
Fahd Hariri	30	Lebanon	Technology, real estate	1.5
Sean Park	30	United States	Technology (Facebook)	1.6
Ayman Hariri	32	Lebanon	Technology, real estate	1.5
Yoshikazu Tanaka	34	Japan	Technology (Gree)	2.2

*As of March 2011 (Source: www.forbes.com)

WHAT'S NEW IN COINS

The U.S. Mint is making one-dollar coins that show the faces of the presidents. The coins are being released in the order in which the presidents served in office. The Mint plans to issue four presidential $1 coins per year through 2016.

The George Washington dollar coin was the first. It was released on February 15, 2007. Coins with Presidents John Adams, Thomas Jefferson, and James Madison were also released in 2007. In 2008, the coins honored Presidents James Monroe, John Quincy Adams, Andrew Jackson, and Martin Van Buren.

The coins released in 2009 featured William Henry Harrison, John Tyler, James K. Polk, and Zachary Taylor. The 2010 coins portrayed Millard Fillmore, Franklin Pierce, James Buchanan, and Abraham Lincoln. In 2011, another four coins were introduced, honoring Andrew Johnson, Ulysses S. Grant, Rutherford B. Hayes, and James Garfield.

The U.S. Mint is also releasing quarters honoring National Park Service sites and other "National Sites." The first five quarters, released in 2010, featured Yellowstone National Park, Hot Springs National Park, Yosemite National Park, Grand Canyon National Park, and Mount Hood National Forest. In 2011, new quarters honored Gettysburg National Military Park, Glacier National Park, Olympic National Park, Vicksburg National Military Park, and Chickasaw National Recreation Area.

For more information on all these coins, visit the U.S. Mint's website at *www.usmint.gov*

The U.S. $1 Bill: AN OWNER'S MANUAL

Everybody knows that George Washington is on the U.S. one-dollar bill, but did you ever wonder what all that other stuff is?

Plate position
Shows where on the 32-note plate this bill was printed.

The Treasury Department seal: The balancing scales represent justice. The pointed stripe across the middle has 13 stars for the original 13 colonies. The key represents authority.

Serial number
Each bill has its own.

Plate serial number
Shows which printing plate was used for the face of the bill.

Federal Reserve District Number
Shows which district issued the bill.

Treasurer of the U.S. Signature

Series indicator (year note's design was first used)

Secretary of the Treasury signature

(Since 1949, every Treasurer of the U.S. has been a woman.)

Federal Reserve District Seal
The name of the Federal Reserve Bank that issued the bill is printed in the seal. The letter tells you quickly where the bill is from. Here are the letter codes for the 12 Federal Reserve Districts:

A: Boston
B: New York
C: Philadelphia
D: Cleveland
E: Richmond
F: Atlanta
G: Chicago
H: St. Louis
I: Minneapolis
J: Kansas City
K: Dallas
L: San Francisco

Front of the Great Seal of the United States: The bald eagle is the national bird. The shield has 13 stripes for the 13 original colonies. The eagle holds 13 arrows (symbol of war) and an olive branch (symbol of peace). Above the eagle is the motto "E Pluribus Unum," Latin for "out of many, one," and a constellation of 13 stars.

Plate serial number
Shows which plate was used for the back.

Back of the Great Seal of the United States:
The pyramid symbolizes something that lasts for ages. It is unfinished because the U.S. is always growing. The eye, known as the "Eye of Providence," probably comes from an ancient Egyptian symbol. The pyramid has 13 levels; at its base are the Roman numerals for 1776, the year of American independence. "Annuit Coeptis" is Latin for "God has favored our undertaking." "Novus Ordo Seclorum" is Latin for "a new order of the ages." Both phrases are from the works of the Roman poet Virgil.

WORLD CURRENCY

Most countries have their own currency. Sometimes two countries call their currency by the same name, but the money usually has different designs and may have different values. Most currency is decorated with cultural symbols and pictures of important people in the country's history. The designs are colorful and interesting, and they also make it harder to counterfeit the money.

An exchange rate is the price of a country's currency in terms of another. For example, one U.S. dollar cost, or could buy, 6.56 yuan in China in March 2011. These rates are based on a country's economy, the value of products it makes and buys, and inflation, the increase in how much money is needed to buy goods.

When people want to buy goods or services from someone in another country, they need to exchange their money for, or buy, some of the other country's currency.

THE EURO

For most of their histories, countries in Europe, like countries around the world, all had their own currencies. France, for example, used the franc. Germany's currency was called the mark, and Italy's was called the lira. Because Europe is so small and because many European countries wanted to make it easier for companies in one country to do business with companies in other countries, an organization was formed to find ways to eliminate barriers to trade. This organization, now called the European Union (EU), decided, among other things, to create one currency that could be used by many countries.

The euro, whose symbol is €, became the official currency of 12 EU members on January 1, 2002. Today, it is used by 17 EU countries, called the Eurozone: Austria, Belgium, Cyprus, Estonia, Finland, France, Germany, Greece, Ireland, Italy, Luxembourg, Malta, the Netherlands, Portugal, Slovakia, Slovenia, and Spain. The euro is also now used by agreement in six other countries as well.

HOW MUCH IS A DOLLAR WORTH?

In March 2011, here is about how much one dollar could buy of 12 other currencies:

0.61	British pounds
0.97	Canadian dollars
6.56	Chinese yuan
0.74	euros
45.00	Indian rupees
3.53	Israeli new shekels

81.04	Japanese yen
11.99	Mexican pesos
28.27	Russian rubles
4.00	Saudi Arabian riyals
1,121.80	South Korean won
1.57	Turkish lira

MOVIES & TV

Which actors will star in *The Hunger Games* in 2012? → page 129

MOVIE & TV FACTS

Royal Ratings Nearly 23 million Americans turned on their TVs early on April 29, 2011, to watch the London wedding of Kate Middleton and Prince William, grandson of Queen Elizabeth II of England. Millions more watched online from the United States, although coverage of the event began at 4:00 A.M. U.S. Eastern time. Worldwide, it is estimated that perhaps as many as 3 billion people watched the royal wedding.

Historic Host Actress Anne Hathaway broke a record in 2011 when she hosted the Academy Awards with James Franco. At 28 years old, she was the youngest host in the show's history. The record had previously been held by actor Donald O'Connor, who was a few months older when he hosted in 1954.

James Franco and Anne Hathaway ▶

ALL-TIME TOP ANIMATED MOVIES*			ALL-TIME TOP MOVIES*		
1	*Shrek 2* (2004)	$436.7	1	*Avatar* (2009)	$760.5
2	*Toy Story 3* (2010)	415.0	2	*Titanic* (1997)	600.8
3	*Finding Nemo* (2003)	339.7	3	*The Dark Knight* (2008)	533.3
4	*Shrek the Third* (2007)	322.7	4	*Star Wars* (1977)	461.0
5	*The Lion King* (1994)	312.9	5	*Shrek 2* (2004)	436.7
6	*Up* (2009)	293.0	6	*E.T. the Extra-Terrestrial* (1982)	435.0
7	*Shrek* (2001)	267.7	7	*Star Wars: Episode I—The Phantom Menace* (1999)	431.1
8	*The Incredibles* (2004)	261.4	8	*Pirates of the Caribbean: Dead Man's Chest* (2006)	423.3
9	*Monsters, Inc.* (2001)	255.9	9	*Toy Story 3* (2010)	415.0
10	*Despicable Me* (2010)	251.5	10	*Spider-Man* (2002)	403.7

Source: © 2011 by Rentrak Corporation. Rankings are for movies rated G, PG, or PG-13.
*Through May 4, 2011. Gross in millions of dollars based on box office sales in the U.S. and Canada.

TOP TV SHOWS IN 2010–2011

AGES 6–11

NETWORK	CABLE
1. *American Idol*	1. *Kids' Choice Awards*
2. *Wipeout*	2. *iCarly*
3. *Curious George 2: Follow That Monkey!*	3. *The Boy Who Cried Werewolf*
4. *FOX NFL Sunday*	4. *Bolt*
5. *NFL on CBS*	5. *Victorious*

Wipeout ▶

AGES 12–17

NETWORK	CABLE
1. *American Idol*	1. *BCS National Championship*
2. *Glee*	2. *iCarly*
3. *FOX NFL Sunday*	3. *Kids' Choice Awards*
4. *Family Guy*	4. *The Boy Who Cried Werewolf*
5. *NFL on CBS*	5. *The Rose Bowl*

Source: © 2011, The Nielsen Company. Top 5 programs, September 20, 2010, through April 24, 2011.

HITTING THEATERS

IN THE SECOND HALF OF 2011

- Jessica Alba and Jeremy Piven star in *Spy Kids 4: All the Time in the World.* (August)
- Brad Pitt and Jonah Hill star in *Moneyball,* adapted from the bestselling book about the Oakland A's. (September)
- A popular character from the Shrek series gets his own movie in *Puss in Boots.* (November)
- *Breaking Dawn Part 1*, the next Twilight film, begins the final chapter of Edward and Bella's story. (November)
- Steven Spielberg directs *The Adventures of Tintin: The Secret of the Unicorn.* (December)

...AND IN 2012

- Jennifer Lawrence and Josh Hutcherson fight for their lives in *The Hunger Games*, which hits theaters in March.
- Zac Efron and Taylor Swift provide voices for characters in *Dr. Seuss' The Lorax*, due in June.
- Christian Bale ▶ returns as Batman in *The Dark Knight Rises*, coming in July.
- The Twilight series comes to an end in November with *Breaking Dawn Part II.*

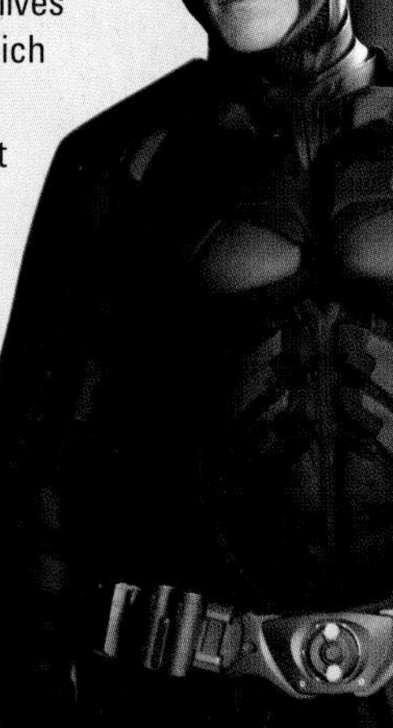

BOOKS TO FILM

Movie: ***Mr. Popper's Penguins*** **(2011)**
Book: ***Mr. Popper's Penguins*** **(1938)**
by Richard and Florence Atwater

The book *Mr. Popper's Penguins* has been beloved by children all over the world since it was published in 1938, but it was not made into a movie until 2011. Jim Carrey played the role of Mr. Popper, a man whose life is changed when he inherits six penguins. (In the book, Mr. Popper has only one penguin at first.) The movie was set in the present day and filmed with live penguins.

Movie: ***I Am Number Four*** **(2011)**
Book: ***I Am Number Four*** **(2010)**
by Pittacus Lore

I Am Number Four was written by James Frey and Jobie Hughes, using the pseudonym Pittacus Lore. The movie rights were purchased before the book was published, and the movie came to theaters just six months after the book was released. It starred Alex Pettyfer as teenage alien John Smith, who comes to Earth to hide from his enemies. Actress Teresa Palmer co-starred in the film. The second book in the series, *The Power of Six*, hits stores in August 2011.

Movies: ***Breaking Dawn*** **(2011 and 2012)**
Book: ***Breaking Dawn*** **(2008)**

Stephenie Meyer is the author of four books, known as the Twilight series, about Bella Swan, a girl who falls in love with a vampire named Edward Cullen. Each of Meyer's Twilight books has been or will be made into a movie. As with the Harry Potter books, the last title in the series has been made into two movies. Robert Pattinson, Kristen Stewart, and Taylor Lautner star in the films.

The Twilight Series

1 *Twilight* (book: 2005; movie: 2008)

2 *New Moon* (book: 2006; movie: 2009)

3 *Eclipse* (book: 2007; movie: 2010)

4 *Breaking Dawn* (book: 2008; movies: 2011 and 2012)

Movies: ***Harry Potter and the Deathly Hallows*** **(2010 and 2011)**
Book: ***Harry Potter and the Deathly Hallows*** **(2007)**

Each of the books in the tremendously popular Harry Potter series by J. K. Rowling has been made into a movie. The seventh book, more than 700 pages long, was split into two films. All of the movies have also been very popular. British actor Daniel Radcliffe has starred in all seven films.

Harry Potter Retrospective

1 *Harry Potter and the Sorcerer's Stone* (book: 1997; movie: 2001)

2 *Harry Potter and the Chamber of Secrets* (book: 1998; movie: 2002)

3 *Harry Potter and the Prisoner of Azkaban* (book: 1999; movie: 2004)

4 *Harry Potter and the Goblet of Fire* (book: 2000; movie: 2005)

5 *Harry Potter and the Order of the Phoenix* (book: 2003; movie: 2007)

6 *Harry Potter and the Half-Blood Prince* (book: 2005; movie: 2009)

7 *Harry Potter and the Deathly Hallows* (book: 2007; movies: 2010 and 2011)

MOVIES & TV WORD SEARCH

Find the name of each movie or TV show listed. The names may appear running up, down, forward, backward, or diagonally.

Names to Find:

American Idol
Avatar
Eclipse
Family Guy
Glee
iCarly
Shrek
Wipeout

T	A	V	S	O	Z	X	X	X	O	R	D	V	K	S
A	U	U	X	G	W	I	Q	K	S	B	U	A	E	I
M	R	O	H	S	K	R	K	H	F	V	Z	N	H	I
E	A	E	E	A	T	E	L	A	T	A	V	F	S	N
R	T	K	P	P	R	O	M	E	S	P	I	L	C	E
I	A	E	H	H	I	I	Q	O	D	W	V	M	D	T
C	V	W	S	M	L	W	U	V	R	G	G	N	N	G
A	A	Z	I	Y	L	Q	T	P	B	V	E	L	L	Z
N	B	E	G	J	B	K	R	T	S	I	E	H	C	Q
I	L	U	M	X	C	T	X	I	L	Q	M	P	M	P
D	Y	I	W	J	D	R	L	C	W	G	L	E	E	Z
O	F	D	E	I	Z	V	E	A	F	D	M	Y	Y	B
L	R	N	X	J	L	M	O	R	L	G	F	L	V	A
H	B	O	N	F	Q	F	L	L	C	B	P	N	O	I
Z	C	N	O	K	W	O	P	Y	S	A	L	A	O	G

MUSIC & DANCE

Who were the winners of *Dancing with the Stars* in Season 12? → page 134

TOP ALBUMS OF 2010

1. *I Dreamed a Dream* ....Susan Boyle
2. *Recovery* ....Eminem ▶
3. *Need You Now* ....Lady Antebellum
4. *The Fame* ....Lady Gaga
5. *My World 2.0* ....Justin Bieber
6. *My Christmas* ....Andrea Bocelli
7. *Fearless* ....Taylor Swift
8. *My World*.......................Justin Bieber
9. *Speak Now* ....Taylor Swift
10. *The E.N.D.* ....The Black Eyed Peas

Source: *Billboard 200*/The Nielsen Company

All About American Idol

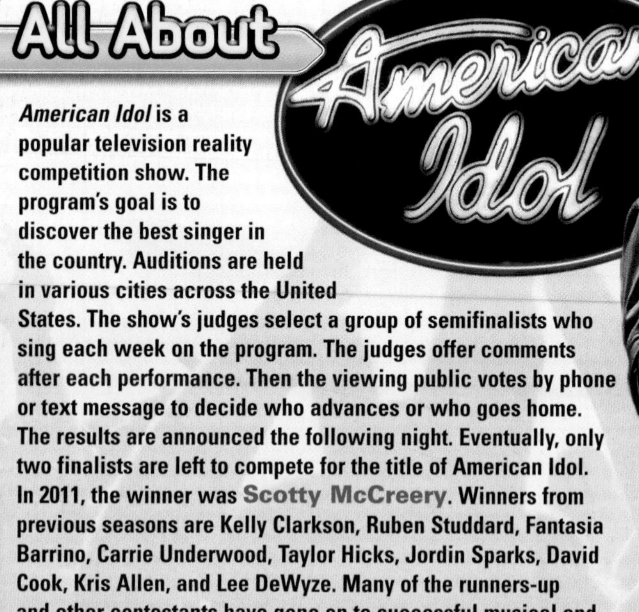

American Idol is a popular television reality competition show. The program's goal is to discover the best singer in the country. Auditions are held in various cities across the United States. The show's judges select a group of semifinalists who sing each week on the program. The judges offer comments after each performance. Then the viewing public votes by phone or text message to decide who advances or who goes home. The results are announced the following night. Eventually, only two finalists are left to compete for the title of American Idol. In 2011, the winner was **Scotty McCreery**. Winners from previous seasons are Kelly Clarkson, Ruben Studdard, Fantasia Barrino, Carrie Underwood, Taylor Hicks, Jordin Sparks, David Cook, Kris Allen, and Lee DeWyze. Many of the runners-up and other contestants have gone on to successful musical and acting careers, including Adam Lambert and Jennifer Hudson.

WHO'S HOT NOW

ADELE

Born: May 5, 1988, in London, England

Albums: *19* (2008), *21* (2011)

Singer-songwriter Adele was born Adele Laurie Blue Adkins in London, England. She wrote her first single, "Hometown Glory," when she was just 16 years old. Like many well-known British performers—including Leona Lewis and Amy Winehouse—Adele attended the BRIT School for Performing Arts and Technology. Her first album, *19*, was released in 2008. Several songs from the album, including "Chasing Pavements" and "Cold Shoulder," were hits. She became known to many more Americans that year when she performed on a popular episode of *Saturday Night Live* featuring then-vice presidential nominee Sarah Palin. In 2009, Adele won Grammy awards for Best New Artist and Best Female Pop Vocal Performance. Her second album, *21*, was released in 2011. Within three months of its release, more than 7 million copies had been sold.

BRUNO MARS

Born: October 8, 1985

Album: *Doo-Wops & Hooligans* (2010)

Born Peter Gene Hernandez, producer and singer-songwriter Bruno Mars grew up in Honolulu, Hawaii. He was part of a musical family—his mother was a singer and his father a percussionist. Mars moved to Los Angeles after graduating from high school and began to write and produce songs for other artists, including Travie McCoy's "Billionaire" and Flo Rida's "Right Round." In 2010, he released his own album, *Doo-Wops & Hooligans*. The album's first single, "Just the Way You Are," earned Mars a Grammy award in 2011 for Best Male Pop Vocal Performance. His "Hooligans in Wondaland" tour took him to sold-out venues across North America and Europe.

DANCING with the STARS

Dancing with the Stars is a television reality-competition show that pairs a celebrity with a professional ballroom dancer. The professional dancer teaches the celebrity how to perform various ballroom dances.

Each pair dances live on the show every week. The dancers receive scores from three professional dance judges. Program viewers may also cast their votes by calling a toll-free number, online at the ABC website, or by text messaging. The judges' scores and the viewer votes are combined to create a score. The pair with the lowest score is eliminated from the competition each week.

The winners of the show's 12th season were football player Hines Ward and professional dancer Kym Johnson. It was the second win for Johnson, who won the 9th season with partner Donny Osmond.

All About Dance Classes

Dance classes are a great way to have fun, stay healthy (dancing can be great exercise), and make new friends. In some areas, there are organizations that offer free classes. If that's not an option, many dance studios will at least allow you to take a free class, to see how you like it, before signing up. Here are just a few types of dance classes that might be available near you:

BALLET is a formal type of dancing, usually performed to classical music. Beginning classes will often teach stretching exercises, the five basic positions of ballet, and simple movements. Ballet dancers begin with flat shoes. Some dancers eventually use pointe shoes, which allow them to dance on the tips of the toes. But dancing "en pointe" takes lots of practice and help from a trained instructor.

TAP dancing requires a special kind of shoes that make a tapping sound on a dance floor. Beginning tap dancing classes will teach basic steps—these steps are eventually combined to create more complicated routines. Tap dancing usually moves at a faster pace than ballet.

JAZZ dance is less formal than either ballet or tap, though it may use similar steps and moves. It does not require any special equipment. Jazz dance routines may start slow, then have bursts of energy. Beginning classes may focus on stretching and learning how to find the beat in different types of music.

MUSICAL INSTRUMENTS

There are many kinds of musical instruments. Instruments in an orchestra are divided into four groups, or sections: string, woodwind, brass, and percussion.

ERCUSSION instruments make ınds when they are struck. They lude **drums**, cymbals, triangles, ıgs, bells, and xylophones. Keyboard truments, like the piano, are sometimes luded in rcussion truments.

STRING instruments make sounds when the strings are either stroked with a bow or plucked with the fingers. The **violin**, viola, cello, bass, and harp are used in an orchestra. The guitar, banjo, and mandolin are other stringed instruments.

OODWINDS are cylindrical and low inside. They make sounds when air is blown into them. The clarinet, **flute**, oboe, bassoon, and piccolo are woodwinds.

BRASSES are hollow inside. They make sounds when air is blown into a mouthpiece. The trumpet, French horn, trombone, and **tuba** are brasses.

?

Thirteen-year-old Greyson Chance took the music world by storm in 2010 after the sixth-grader performed Lady Gaga's hit song "Paparazzi" at his middle school in Edmond, Oklahoma. A video of the performance posted on YouTube quickly attracted more than 28 million viewers. Talk show host Ellen DeGeneres invited him to appear on her show and signed him to a record contract. Chance again performed "Paparazzi" on NBC's New Year's Eve telecast from Times Square in New York City on December 31, 2010.

MYTHOLOGY

What was Greek goddess Aphrodite's Roman name? → page 136

MYTHS OF THE GREEKS

As the ancient Greeks went about their daily lives, they believed that a big family of gods and goddesses was watching over them from Mount Olympus. Farmers planting crops, sailors crossing the sea, and poets writing verses thought that these powerful beings could help or harm them. Stories of the gods and goddesses are called **myths.**

After the Romans conquered Greece, in 146 B.C., they adopted Greek myths but gave Roman names to the main gods and goddesses. Except for Earth, the planets in our solar system are named after Roman or Greek gods.

Greek & Roman Gods

The family of Greek and Roman gods and goddesses was large. Their family tree would have more than 50 figures on it. The deities listed are the Olympian gods, the most important of the gods, who lived on Mount Olympus. Those with * are children of Zeus (Jupiter).

Greek Name	Roman Name	Description
Aphrodite	Venus	Goddess of beauty and of love
*Apollo	Apollo	God of prophecy, music, and medicine
*Ares	Mars	God of war; protector of the city
*Artemis	Diana	Goddess of the Moon and of the hunt
*Athena	Minerva	Goddess of wisdom and of war
Cronus	Saturn	Father of Zeus (Jupiter), Poseidon (Neptune), Hades (Pluto), Hera (Juno), and Demeter (Ceres)
Demeter	Ceres	Goddess of crops and harvest, sister of Zeus (Jupiter)
*Dionysus	Bacchus	God of wine, dancing, and theater
Hades	Pluto	Ruler of the Underworld, brother of Zeus (Jupiter)
Hephaestus	Vulcan	God of fire
Hera	Juno	Queen of the gods, wife of Zeus (Jupiter), goddess of marriage
*Hermes	Mercury	Messenger god, had winged helmet and sandals
Poseidon	Neptune	God of the sea and of earthquakes, brother of Zeus (Jupiter)
Zeus	Jupiter	Sky god (grandson of Uranus), ruler of gods and mortals

MAKING SENSE of the WORLD

Unlike folklore or fables, myths were once thought to be true. Most ancient peoples explained many things in nature by referring to gods and heroes with superhuman qualities. To the Greeks a rough sea meant that **POSEIDON** was angry. Lightning was **THOR'S** hammer in Norse mythology. Egyptians worshipped the sun god **RE**, who sailed across the sky in a ship each day. In Japan, **AMATERASU** was the Shinto sun goddess who gave light to the land. Her brother **SUSANOO** was the storm god who ruled the sea.

There are even stories of gods or heroes who chose brain over brawn to get what they wanted. **COYOTE** was wild and cunning, a true trickster for many Native American tribes throughout the West. He was usually a loner and was never simply good or bad. **ANANSI** was a spider in the stories of the Akan tribes of West Africa. The tiny spider used his wits to capture the hornet, python, and leopard. In return, the sky god **NYAME** let him own every story ever told.

Re

Myths have remained popular long after people knew they weren't true because the stories hold important life lessons and morals for cultures around the world. Myths have also inspired countless stories and works of art.

Greek & Roman Heroes

Besides stories about the gods, Greek and Roman mythology has many stories about other heroes with amazing qualities.

- **ODYSSEUS**, the king of Ithaca, was a hero of the Trojan War in the epic poem the *Iliad*. It was his idea to build a huge wooden horse, hide Greek soldiers inside, and smuggle them into the city of Troy to capture it. The long poem the *Odyssey* is the story of his long and magical trip home after the war.
- **PANDORA** was the first woman created by the Greek gods. Zeus ordered Hephaestus to create a beautiful woman out of earth. All the Olympian gods gave her gifts. Hera's gift was curiosity. When Pandora was finished, she received a box which she was never to open. But because of her curiosity, Pandora could not resist. She opened the box and released all the evil spirits into the world.
- **JASON** and the Argonauts set out on a quest to find the golden fleece so that Jason could reclaim his rightful throne. Among the Argonauts were Herakles and Orpheus. After many adventures and with the help of Medea, Jason slew the Minotaur and claimed the fleece. He later betrayed Medea and eventually died when a beam from his ship, the Argo, fell off and hit him on the head.

Hercules

The most popular hero was Herakles, or **Hercules**. The most famous of his deeds were his 12 labors. They included killing the **Hydra**, a many-headed monster, and capturing the three-headed dog **Cerberus**, who guarded the gates of the Underworld. Hercules was so great a hero that the gods granted him immortality. When his body lay on his funeral pyre, Athena came and carried him off to Mount Olympus in her chariot.

NATIONS

How many nations does Russia border? → page 170

GOVERNMENTS

As of early 2011, the world had 195 independent nations, with various kinds of governments.

Totalitarianism In **totalitarian** countries, the rulers have strong power, and the people have little freedom. Elections are controlled, so that people do not have a real choice. North Korea is an example of a totalitarian country.

Monarchy A **monarchy** is a country headed by a king or queen (or occasionally by a ruler with a different title), who usually has inherited the title from a parent or other relative. There still are some monarchies in the world today. The United Kingdom (Great Britain) is one.

Democracy The word **democracy** comes from the Greek words *demos* ("people") and *kratos* ("rule"). In modern democracies, people govern themselves through the leaders they choose in elections. The United States and many other countries are democracies. Some monarchies, like the United Kingdom, are also democracies because the main decisions are actually made by elected leaders.

The European Union (EU) The EU is an organization of 27 member countries, with more than 500 million people. The EU sets many common policies for its members. People and goods can usually move easily from one EU country to another. Many EU countries share a common currency, the euro.

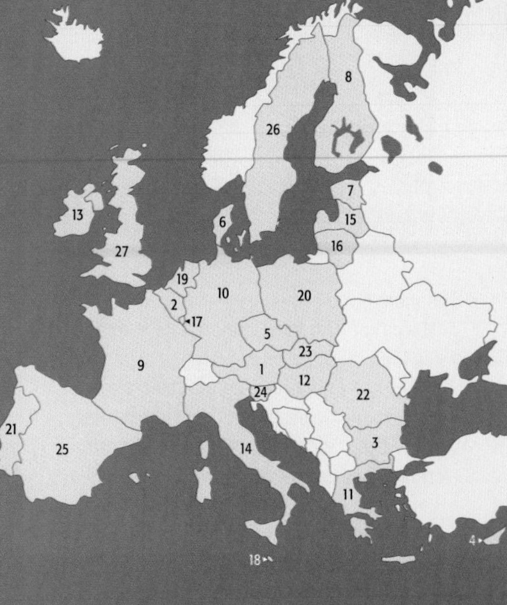

EU Members

1. Austria*	15. Latvia
2. Belgium*	16. Lithuania
3. Bulgaria	17. Luxembourg*
4. Cyprus*	18. Malta *
5. Czech Republic	19. Netherlands*
6. Denmark	20. Poland
7. Estonia*	21. Portugal*
8. Finland*	22. Romania
9. France*	23. Slovakia*
10. Germany*	24. Slovenia*
11. Greece*	25. Spain*
12. Hungary	26. Sweden
13. Ireland*	27. United Kingdom
14. Italy*	

*** People in these countries use the euro.**

A COMMUNITY OF NATIONS

The UN emblem shows the world surrounded by olive branches of peace.

The **United Nations (UN)** was started in 1945 after World War II. The first members were 51 nations, 50 of which met in San Francisco, California. They signed an agreement known as the UN Charter. In early 2011, the UN had 192 members. Kosovo, Taiwan, and Vatican City were not members.

HOW THE UN IS ORGANIZED

- **GENERAL ASSEMBLY** **What It Does:** Discusses world problems, admits new members, appoints the secretary-general, decides the UN budget. **Members:** All UN members; each country has one vote.
- **SECURITY COUNCIL** **What It Does:** Handles questions of peace and security. **Members:** Five permanent members (China, France, the United Kingdom, Russia, and the United States) who must all vote the same way before certain proposals can pass; ten elected by the General Assembly to two-year terms. In 2011 the ten temporary members were Bosnia and Herzegovina, Brazil, Gabon, Lebanon, and Nigeria (terms ending December 31, 2011) and Colombia, Germany, India, Portugal, and South Africa (terms ending December 31, 2012).
- **ECONOMIC AND SOCIAL COUNCIL** **What It Does:** Deals with issues related to economic development, population, education, health, and human rights. **Members:** 54 member countries elected to three-year terms.
- **INTERNATIONAL COURT OF JUSTICE (WORLD COURT)** located in The Hague, Netherlands. **What It Does:** UN court for disputes between countries. **Members:** 15 judges, each from a different country, elected to nine-year terms.
- **SECRETARIAT** **What It Does:** Carries out the UN's day-to-day operations. **Members:** UN staff, headed by the secretary-general.

For more information, go to ***www.un.org***

A New Nation

After 20 years of bloody civil war, the northern and southern parts of the African nation of Sudan reached a peace agreement in 2005, and in January 2011, the people of southern Sudan voted for independence. It was agreed that the region would officially become the world's newest independent nation on July 9, 2011.

People line up to vote in southern Sudan.

Maps showing Nations of the World

Maps showing the continents and nations of the world appear on pages 140–151. Flags of the nations appear on pages 152–177. A map of the United States appears on pages 288–289.

AUSTRALIA

- ⊛ National Capital
- ★ State Capital
- • Other City

PACIFIC ISLANDS

- ⊛ National Capital
- ★ Territorial Capital
- • Other City

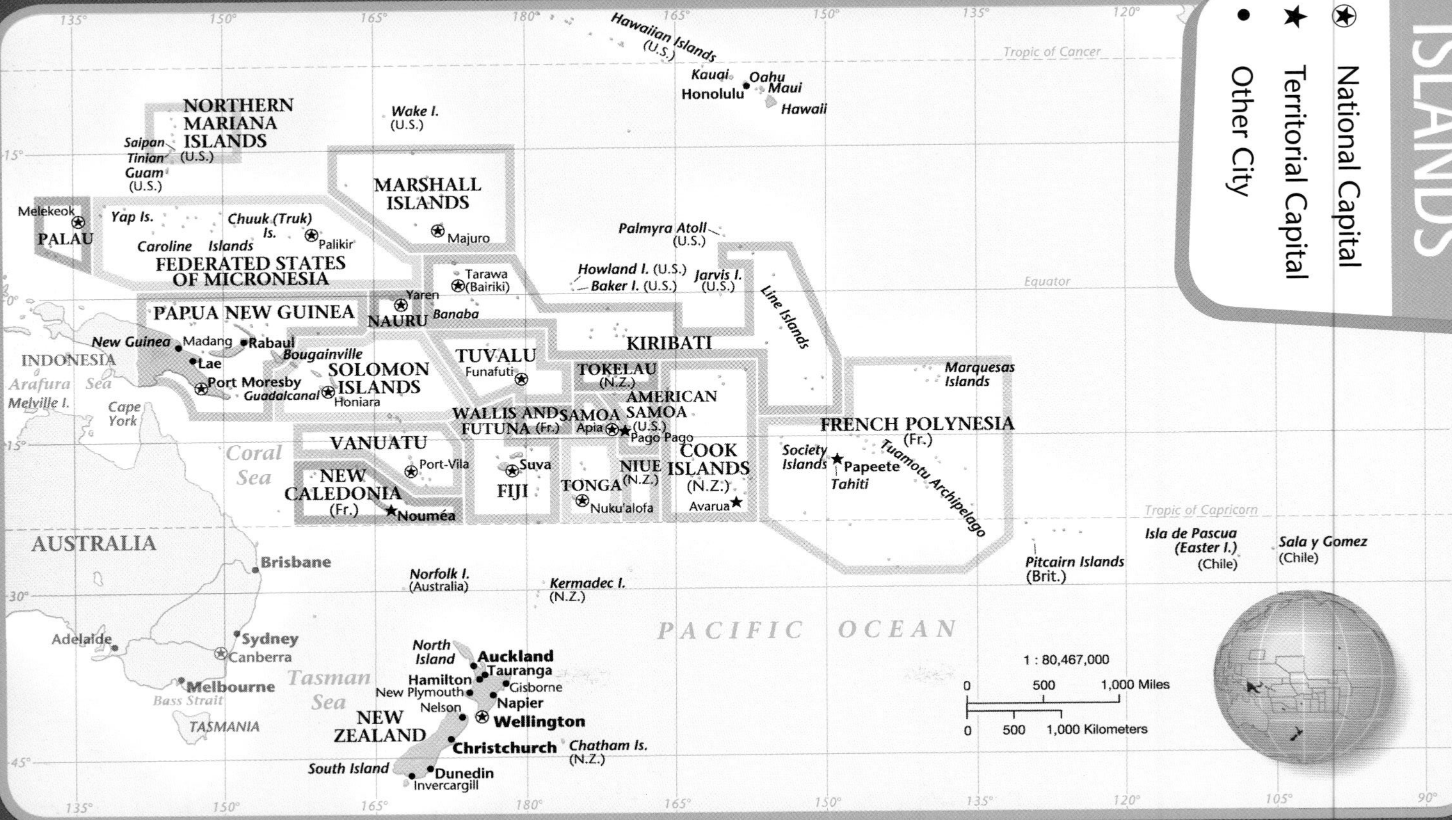

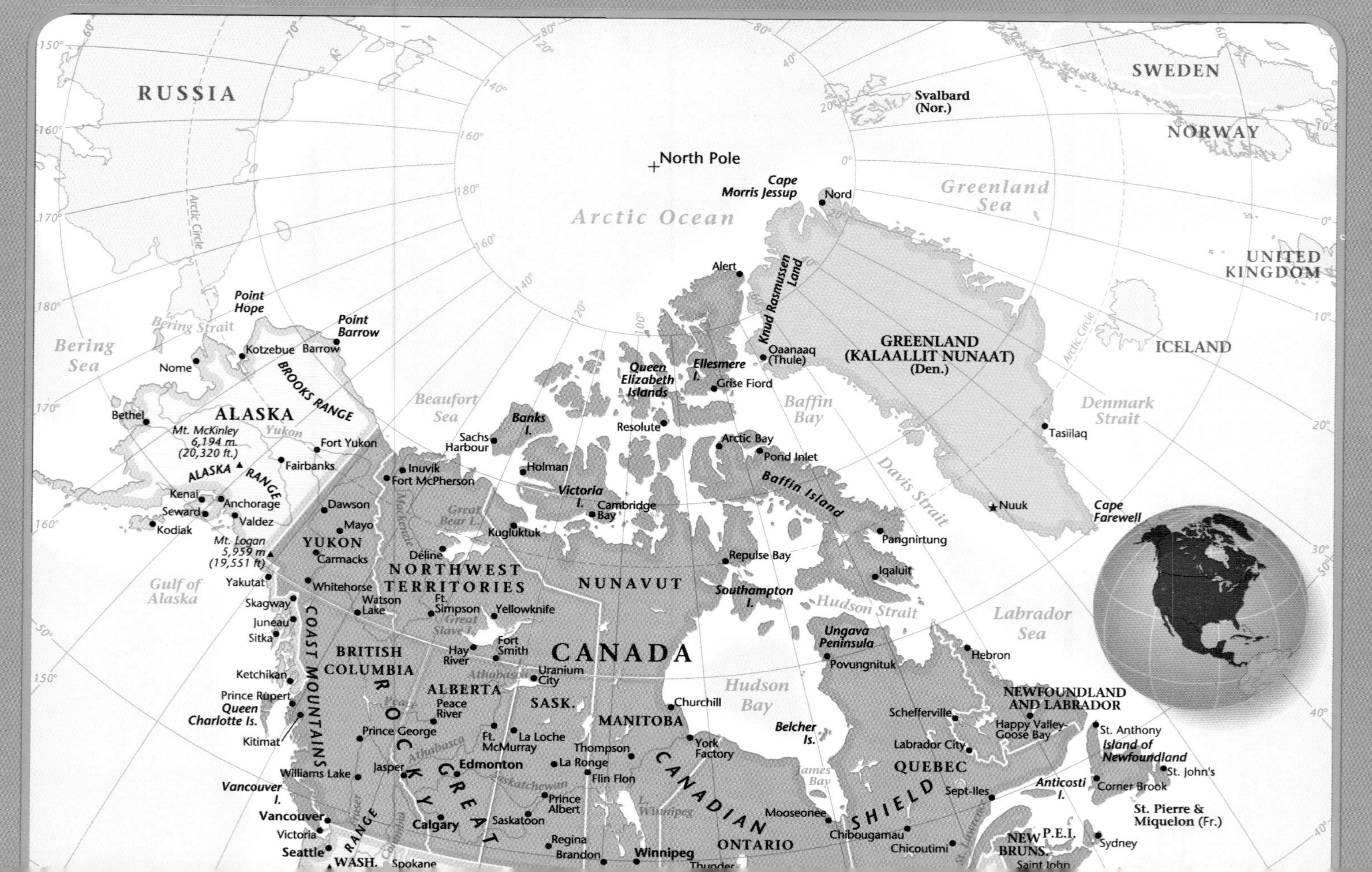

RUSSIA
SWEDEN
NORWAY
Svalbard (Nor.)
North Pole
Cape Morris Jessup
Nord
Greenland Sea
Arctic Ocean
UNITED KINGDOM
ICELAND
Alert
Knud Rasmussen Land
GREENLAND (KALAALLIT NUNAAT) (Den.)
Oaanaaq (Thule)
Queen Elizabeth Islands
Ellesmere I.
Grise Fiord
Baffin Bay
Denmark Strait
Tasiilaq
Point Hope
Point Barrow
Bering Strait
Bering Sea
Kotzebue
Barrow
Nome
BROOKS RANGE
Beaufort Sea
Banks I.
Resolute
Arctic Bay
Pond Inlet
Bethel
ALASKA
Mt. McKinley 6,194 m. (20,320 ft.)
Yukon
Fort Yukon
Sachs Harbour
Fairbanks
Inuvik
Fort McPherson
Holman
Baffin Island
Davis Strait
Nuuk
Cape Farewell
ALASKA RANGE
Kenai
Anchorage
Seward
Valdez
Kodiak
Dawson
Mackenzie
Great Bear L.
Victoria I.
Cambridge Bay
Kugluktuk
Pangnirtung
Mt. Logan 5,959 m (19,551 ft)
Mayo
YUKON
Carmacks
Déline
NORTHWEST TERRITORIES
Repulse Bay
NUNAVUT
Iqaluit
Gulf of Alaska
Yakutat
Whitehorse
Southampton I.
Hudson Strait
Labrador Sea
Skagway
Watson Lake
Ft. Simpson
Yellowknife
Great Slave L.
Juneau
Sitka
COAST MOUNTAINS
Ungava Peninsula
Fort Smith
Hay River
CANADA
Hebron
Povungnituk
BRITISH COLUMBIA
Ketchikan
Athabasca
Uranium City
Hudson Bay
ALBERTA
Prince Rupert
Queen Charlotte Is.
Peace
Peace River
SASK.
Churchill
NEWFOUNDLAND AND LABRADOR
MANITOBA
Schefferville
Belcher Is.
Happy Valley-Goose Bay
St. Anthony
Kitimat
Prince George
Ft. McMurray
La Loche
Thompson
York Factory
Labrador City
Island of Newfoundland
QUEBEC
St. John's
Williams Lake
Jasper
Edmonton
La Ronge
James Bay
Vancouver I.
Flin Flon
Anticosti I.
Corner Brook
Sept-Iles
Saskatchewan
Prince Albert
L. Winnipeg
Vancouver
Mooseonee
St. Pierre & Miquelon (Fr.)
Calgary
Saskatoon
GREAT ROCKY RANGE
CANADIAN SHIELD
Victoria
Chibougamau
P.E.I.
NEW BRUNS.
Sydney
Seattle
Regina
Brandon
Winnipeg
ONTARIO
Chicoutimi
St. Lawrence
WASH.
Spokane
Saint John

NORTH AMERICA
National Capital
Territorial Capital
Other City
1 : 39,835,000
0 500 1,000 Miles
0 500 1,000 Kilometers
PACIFIC OCEAN
ATLANTIC OCEAN
Gulf of Mexico
Caribbean Sea
Bay of Campeche
Gulf of California
Straits of Florida
Tropic of Cancer
UNITED STATES
MEXICO
COAST RANGES
SIERRA NEVADA
Mt. Whitney 4,418 m. (14,494 ft.)
Columbia Plateau
Colorado Plateau
ROCKY MOUNTAINS
GREAT PLAINS
APPALACHIAN MTS.
SIERRA MADRE OCCIDENTAL
SIERRA MADRE ORIENTAL
BAJA CALIFORNIA
YUCATAN PENINSULA
Orizaba Pk. (18,405 ft) 5,610 m
Eureka
Sacramento
San Francisco
Reno
Fresno
Las Vegas
Santa Barbara
Los Angeles
San Diego
Tijuana
Mexicali
CALIF.
NEVADA
OREG.
IDAHO
Boise
Pocatello
UTAH
Salt Lake City
Great Salt L.
ARIZONA
Phoenix
WYO.
Casper
Cheyenne
Billings
COLORADO
Denver
NEW MEXICO
Albuquerque
El Paso
S. DAK.
Rapid City
Bismarck
Fargo
MINN.
Minneapolis
Duluth
NEB.
Omaha
IOWA
KANSAS
Kansas City
Wichita
OKLA.
Oklahoma City
TEXAS
Dallas
Austin
San Antonio
Houston
Shreveport
MO.
St. Louis
ARK.
Little Rock
LA.
Baton Rouge
New Orleans
WIS.
Milwaukee
Lake Michigan
Chicago
ILL.
Indianapolis
IND.
MICH.
Detroit
Lake Huron
Lake Erie
Lake Ontario
Toronto
Cleveland
OHIO
Columbus
Cincinnati
KY.
Louisville
TENN.
Nashville
Memphis
MISS.
Jackson
ALA.
Birmingham
Mobile
GA.
Atlanta
Savannah
FLA.
Jacksonville
Tampa
St. Petersburg
Miami
S.C.
Charlotte
N.C.
Raleigh
VA.
Richmond
W. VA.
Pittsburgh
PENN.
Buffalo
Rochester
N.Y.
New York City
Philadelphia
Baltimore
Washington, D.C.
NEW JERSEY
DELAWARE
MARYLAND
CONN.
R.I.
MASS.
Boston
VT.
N.H.
Portland
Mississippi
Ohio
Arkansas
Platte
Snake
Colorado
Rio Grande
Bermuda (Brit.)
Nogales
Ciudad Juárez
Hermosillo
Chihuahua
Ciudad Obregón
La Paz
Torreón
Durango
Mazatlán
Monterrey
San Luis Potosí
León
Guadalajara
Mexico City
Puebla
Veracruz
Acapulco
Oaxaca
Villahermosa
Tuxtla Gutiérrez
Mérida
Campeche
BELIZE
Belmopan
GUATEMALA
Guatemala City
San Salvador
EL SALVADOR
HONDURAS
Tegucigalpa
NICARAGUA
Managua
San José
COSTA RICA
PANAMA
Panama City
THE BAHAMAS
Nassau
CUBA
Havana
Santiago de Cuba
CAYMAN IS. (Brit.)
JAMAICA
Kingston
HAITI
Port-au-Prince
DOMINICAN REPUBLIC
Santo Domingo
TURKS & CAICOS IS. (Brit.)
PUERTO RICO (U.S.)
San Juan
VIRGIN IS.(U.S.,Brit.)
ST. KITTS & NEVIS
ANTIGUA & BARBUDA
GUADELOUPE (Fr.)
BARBADOS
DOMINICA
MARTINIQUE (Fr.)
ST. LUCIA
ST. VINCENT & THE GRENADINES
GRENADA
TRINIDAD & TOBAGO
Port-of-Spain
Curaçao (Neth.)
Aruba (Neth.)
Bonaire (Neth.)
VENEZUELA
COLOMBIA
BRAZIL

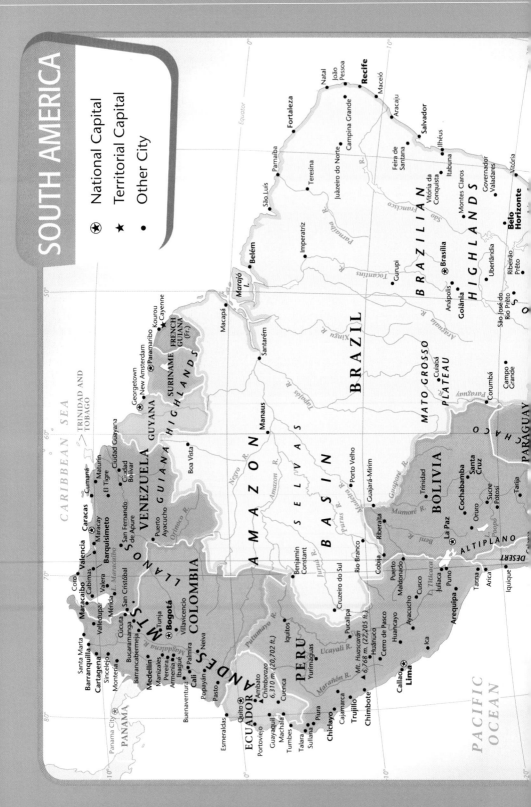

SOUTH AMERICA

- ⊛ National Capital
- ★ Territorial Capital
- • Other City

CARIBBEAN SEA
TRINIDAD AND TOBAGO
PACIFIC OCEAN
Equator
80° 70° 60° 50°
10° 0° 10° 20°

PANAMA
Panama City
COLOMBIA
Santa Marta
Barranquilla
Cartagena
Sincelejo
Montería
Valledupar
Cúcuta
Bucaramanga
Barrancabermeja
Medellín
Manizales
Pereira
Armenia
Ibagué
Tunja
Bogotá
Villavicencio
Buenaventura
Palmira
Cali
Neiva
Popayán
Pasto
Magdalena R.
VENEZUELA
Coro
Maracaibo
Cabimas
Valencia
Caracas
Maracay
Barquisimeto
Valera
Mérida
L. Maracaibo
San Cristóbal
San Fernando de Apure
Cumaná
Maturín
El Tigre
Ciudad Guayana
Ciudad Bolívar
Puerto Ayacucho
Orinoco R.
LLANOS
ANDES MTS.
GUIANA HIGHLANDS
GUYANA
Georgetown
New Amsterdam
SURINAME
Paramaribo
FRENCH GUIANA (Fr.)
Kourou
Cayenne
ECUADOR
Esmeraldas
Quito
Portoviejo
Ambato
Chimborazo 6,310 m. (20,702 ft.)
Guayaquil
Machala
Cuenca
Tumbes
PERU
Talara
Sullana
Piura
Chiclayo
Cajamarca
Trujillo
Chimbote
Iquitos
Yurimaguas
Putumayo R.
Marañón R.
Ucayali R.
Pucallpa
Mt. Huascarán 6,768 m. (22,205 ft.)
Huánuco
Cerro de Pasco
Huancayo
Callao
Lima
Ayacucho
Cusco
Ica
Arequipa
Juliaca
Puno
L. Titicaca
Tacna
Arica
Iquique
ALTIPLANO
DESERT
Calama
BOLIVIA
Cobija
Riberalta
Puerto Maldonado
Beni R.
Mamoré R.
Trinidad
La Paz
Cochabamba
Santa Cruz
Oruro
L. Poopó
Sucre
Potosí
Tarija
CHACO
PARAGUAY
BRAZIL
AMAZON BASIN
SELVAS
Boa Vista
Negro R.
Amazon R.
Manaus
Benjamin Constant
Juruá R.
Purus R.
Madeira R.
Cruzeiro do Sul
Rio Branco
Porto Velho
Guajará-Mirim
Guaporé R.
Macapá
Marajó I.
Belém
Santarém
Tapajós R.
Xingu R.
Tocantins R.
Araguaia R.
Paraguay R.
MATO GROSSO PLATEAU
Cuiabá
Corumbá
Campo Grande
São Luís
Parnaíba
Parnaíba R.
Fortaleza
Imperatriz
Teresina
Natal
Juàzeiro do Norte
João Pessoa
Campina Grande
Recife
Maceió
Aracaju
São Francisco R.
Gurupi
Feira de Santana
Salvador
BRAZILIAN HIGHLANDS
Vitória da Conquista
Ilhéus
Itabuna
Anápolis
Brasília
Goiânia
Montes Claros
Uberlândia
Governador Valadares
São José do Rio Prêto
Ribeirão Prêto
Belo Horizonte
Vitória

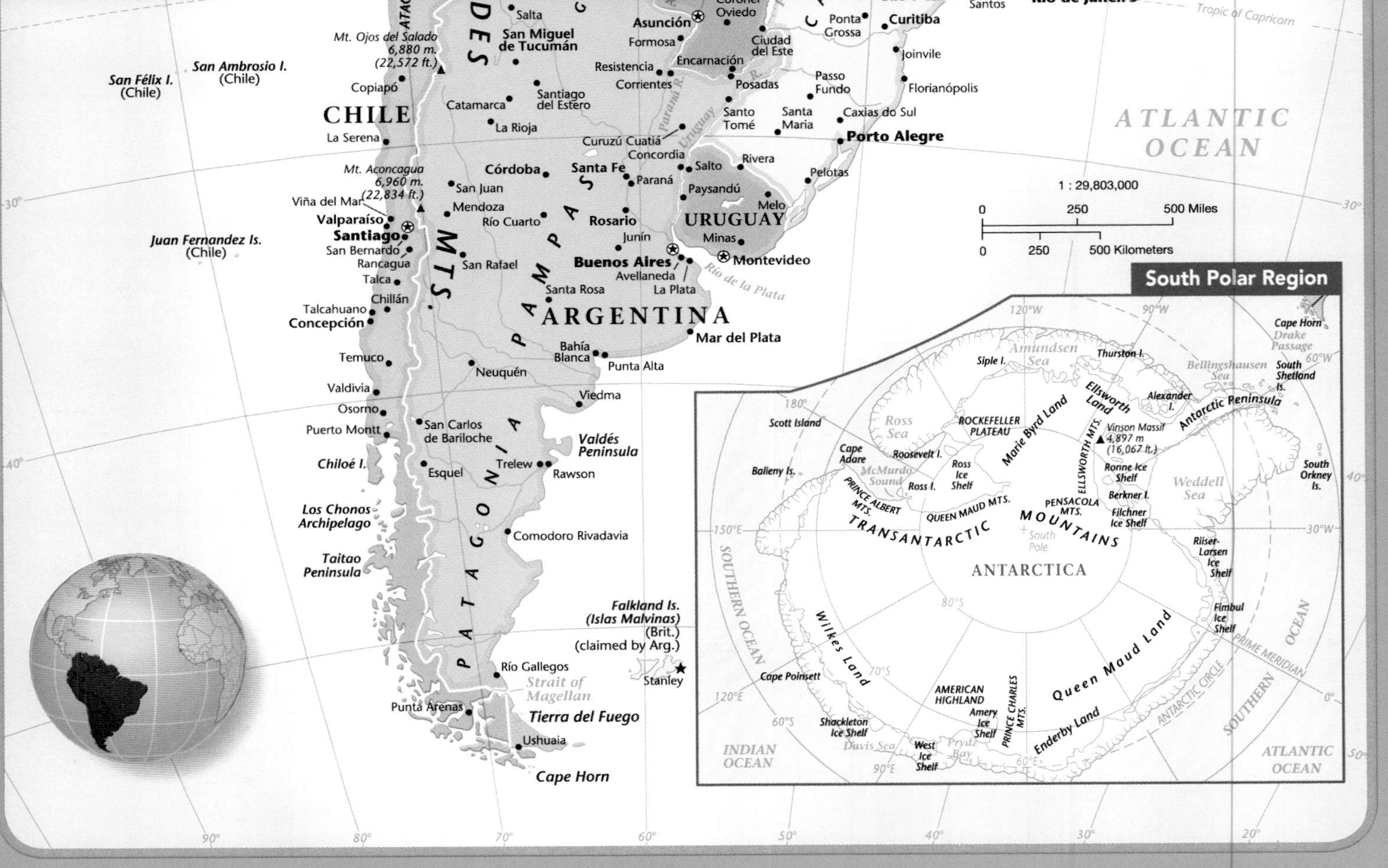

ATLANTIC OCEAN
Tropic of Capricorn
CHILE
ARGENTINA
URUGUAY
ANDES MTS.
PAMPAS
PATAGONIA
Mt. Ojos del Salado 6,880 m. (22,572 ft.)
Mt. Aconcagua 6,960 m. (22,834 ft.)
San Félix I. (Chile)
San Ambrosio I. (Chile)
Juan Fernandez Is. (Chile)
Copiapó
La Serena
Viña del Mar
Valparaíso
Santiago
San Bernardo
Rancagua
Talca
Chillán
Talcahuano
Concepción
Temuco
Valdivia
Osorno
Puerto Montt
Chiloé I.
Los Chonos Archipelago
Taitao Peninsula
Salta
San Miguel de Tucumán
Catamarca
Santiago del Estero
La Rioja
Córdoba
San Juan
Mendoza
Río Cuarto
San Rafael
Santa Fe
Paraná
Rosario
Junín
Buenos Aires
Avellaneda
La Plata
Santa Rosa
Bahía Blanca
Punta Alta
Mar del Plata
Neuquén
Viedma
San Carlos de Bariloche
Esquel
Trelew
Rawson
Valdés Peninsula
Comodoro Rivadavia
Río Gallegos
Strait of Magellan
Punta Arenas
Tierra del Fuego
Ushuaia
Cape Horn
Falkland Is. (Islas Malvinas) (Brit.) (claimed by Arg.)
Stanley
Asunción
Formosa
Resistencia
Corrientes
Encarnación
Posadas
Ciudad del Este
Coronel Oviedo
Curuzú Cuatiá
Concordia
Salto
Paysandú
Rivera
Melo
Minas
Montevideo
Río de la Plata
Paraná R.
Uruguay
Santo Tomé
Santa Maria
Passo Fundo
Ponta Grossa
Curitiba
Joinvile
Florianópolis
Caxias do Sul
Porto Alegre
Pelotas
Santos
1 : 29,803,000
0 250 500 Miles
0 250 500 Kilometers
South Polar Region
ANTARCTICA
South Pole
Cape Horn
Drake Passage
South Shetland Is.
South Orkney Is.
Antarctic Peninsula
Alexander I.
Bellingshausen Sea
Thurston I.
Amundsen Sea
Siple I.
Ellsworth Land
ELLSWORTH MTS.
Vinson Massif 4,897 m (16,067 ft.)
Marie Byrd Land
ROCKEFELLER PLATEAU
Ross Sea
Roosevelt I.
Ross Ice Shelf
Ross I.
McMurdo Sound
Cape Adare
Scott Island
Balleny Is.
PRINCE ALBERT MTS.
QUEEN MAUD MTS.
TRANSANTARCTIC MOUNTAINS
PENSACOLA MTS.
Ronne Ice Shelf
Berkner I.
Filchner Ice Shelf
Weddell Sea
Riiser-Larsen Ice Shelf
Fimbul Ice Shelf
Queen Maud Land
Enderby Land
PRINCE CHARLES MTS.
AMERICAN HIGHLAND
Amery Ice Shelf
Prydz Bay
West Ice Shelf
Davis Sea
Shackleton Ice Shelf
Wilkes Land
Cape Poinsett
SOUTHERN OCEAN
INDIAN OCEAN
ATLANTIC OCEAN
ANTARCTIC CIRCLE
PRIME MERIDIAN

EUROPE
National Capital
Other City
1 : 22,667,000
0 250 500 Miles
0 250 500 Kilometers
Reykjavík
Akureyri
ICELAND
Arctic Circle
Norwegian Sea
Faroe Is. (Den.)
Shetland Is. (Brit.)
Orkney Is.
Hebrides
Tromsø
Kiruna
Bodø
Trondheim
Sundsvall
NORWAY
SWEDEN
Bergen
Oslo
Stavanger
Uppsala
Stockholm
Linköping
Skagerrak
Kattegat
Göteborg
Gotland
Öland
Jutland
Århus
Copenhagen
Helsingborg
Malmö
DENMARK
Odense
Baltic
Aberdeen
Glasgow
Edinburgh
Belfast
UNITED KINGDOM (GREAT BRITAIN)
Newcastle
Irish Sea
Dublin
IRELAND
Cork
Liverpool
Leeds
Manchester
Sheffield
Birmingham
North Sea
Cardiff
Bristol
London
Portsmouth
Land's End
ATLANTIC OCEAN
English Channel
Channel Is. (Brit.)
Brest
Le Havre
Rouen
NETHERLANDS
Amsterdam
Rotterdam
Antwerp
Brussels
Lille
BELGIUM
Liège
LUXEMBOURG
Luxembourg
Paris
Hamburg
Bremen
Hannover
Berlin
Essen
Cologne
Bonn
GERMANY
Leipzig
Dresden
Frankfurt
Gdańsk
Szczecin
Poznań
Łódź
Wrocław
Oder
Vistula
Elbe
Prague
Katowice
CZECH REP.
Brno
Ostrava
Mannheim
Stuttgart
Munich
Strasbourg
Rhine
Danube
Nantes
Loire
Bay of Biscay
FRANCE
Dijon
Bern
Zürich
LIECHTENSTEIN
Linz
Vienna
Bratislava
SLOVAKIA
AUSTRIA
Budapest
HUNGARY
Graz
SWITZERLAND
Geneva
Lyon
ALPS
Mt. Blanc 4807 m (15,771 ft)
Milan
SLOVENIA
Ljubljana
Pécs
Zagreb
DINARIC ALPS
Cape Finisterre
Gijón
Vigo
Bilbao
Bordeaux
Rhône
Toulouse
Turin
Verona
Venice
Po
Bologna
Genoa
CROATIA
SAN MARINO
BOSNIA & HERZEGOVINA
Sarajevo
Porto
Ebro
Valladolid
PYRENEES
Marseille
Nice
MONACO
Ligurian Sea
Florence
APENNINES
Adriatic Sea
Split
MONTENEGRO
Dubrovnik
Podgorica
PORTUGAL
Lisbon
IBERIAN PENINSULA
Pico de Aneto 3404 m (11,168 ft)
Zaragoza
ANDORRA
Toulon
Madrid
Tagus
Badajoz
Barcelona
Corsica (Fr.)
Elba
VATICAN CITY
Rome
ITALY
Bari
SPAIN
Valencia
Balearic Sea
Majorca
Minorca
Palma
Balearic Is. (Sp.)
Cape St. Vincent
Córdoba
Sevilla
Cádiz
Granada
Málaga
Alicante
Sardinia (It.)
Naples
Salerno
Tyrrhenian Sea
Cagliari
Corfu
Ionian Sea
Strait of Gibraltar
GIBRALTAR (Brit.)
Mediterranean Sea
Palermo
Catania
Mt. Etna 3323 m (10,902 ft)
Sicily
Rabat
Casablanca
Algiers
Tunis
Valletta
MALTA
MOROCCO
ATLAS MOUNTAINS
ALGERIA
TUNISIA

North Cape
Hammerfest
Barents Sea
Nar'yan-Mar
Pechora
Murmansk
KOLA PENINSULA
Apatity
Arctic Circle
LAPLAND
Ukhta
URAL MOUNTAINS
White Sea
Arkhangel'sk
RUSSIA
Ob
Irtysh
Serov
Oulu
Belomorsk
Syktyvkar
Bereznikí
Petropavl
Divina
FINLAND
Lake Onega
Kotlas
Yekaterinburg
Perm'
Petrozavodsk
Kirov
Chelyabinsk
Tampere
Lahti
Lake Ladoga
PLAIN
Izhevsk
Kama
Qostanay
Ufa
Helsinki
Vologda
Naberezhnyye Chelny
St. Petersburg
Cherepovets
Gulf of Finland
Magnitogorsk
Tallinn
Kazan
ESTONIA
Velikiy Novgorod
Yaroslavl'
Nizhniy Novgorod
Tartu
Ivanovo
Pskov
EUROPEAN
Ul'yanovsk
Tol'yatti
Orenburg
Orsk
Tver'
Samara
Riga
LATVIA
Saransk
Moscow
Daugavpils
Ryazan'
Penza
Aktobe
LITHUANIA
Vitsyebsk
Smolensk
Tula
Volga
Oral
Kaunas
Vilnius
Tambov
Mahilyow
Lipetsk
Saratov
Ural
KAZAKHSTAN
Minsk
Bryansk
Aral Sea
Hrodna
Voronezh
BELARUS
Homyel'
Kursk
Brest
Atyraū
Warsaw
Volgograd
Kyiv
Kharkiv
UZBEKISTAN
Luhans'k
L'viv
UKRAINE
Dnieper
Donets'k
Don
Astrakhan'
Dniester
Dnipropetrovs'k
Rostov na Donu
Zaporizhzhia
Aktaū
Chernivtsi
Košice
MOLDOVA
Kryvyy Rih
Mariupol'
Caspian Sea
Chişinău
Mykolaiv
Sea of Azov
Stavropol'
Debrecen
MTS.
Iaşi
Groznyy
Makhachkala
Odesa
TURKMENISTAN
ROMANIA
CRIMEA
Krasnodar
Mt. Elbrus 5642 m (18,510 ft)
Timişoara
Simferopol'
CAUCASUS
Türkmenbashy
Sevastopol'
GEORGIA
Ploieşti
Bucharest
Constanţa
Tbilisi
Baku
Black Sea
AZERBAIJAN
ARMENIA
Danube
Varna
BULGARIA
Yerevan
Burgas
Trabzon
Pristina
Sofia
Plovdiv
Skopje
Tabriz
İstanbul
Tehran
Thessaloniki
Ankara
TURKEY
Larisa
IRAN
Aegean Sea
İzmir
Athens
Adana
Tigris
PELOPONNESE
Cyclades
SYRIA
Baghdad
Rhodes
Euphrates
Sea of Crete
Nicosia
IRAQ
LEBANON
CYPRUS
Crete
Iraklion
Beirut
Damascus
Persian Gulf

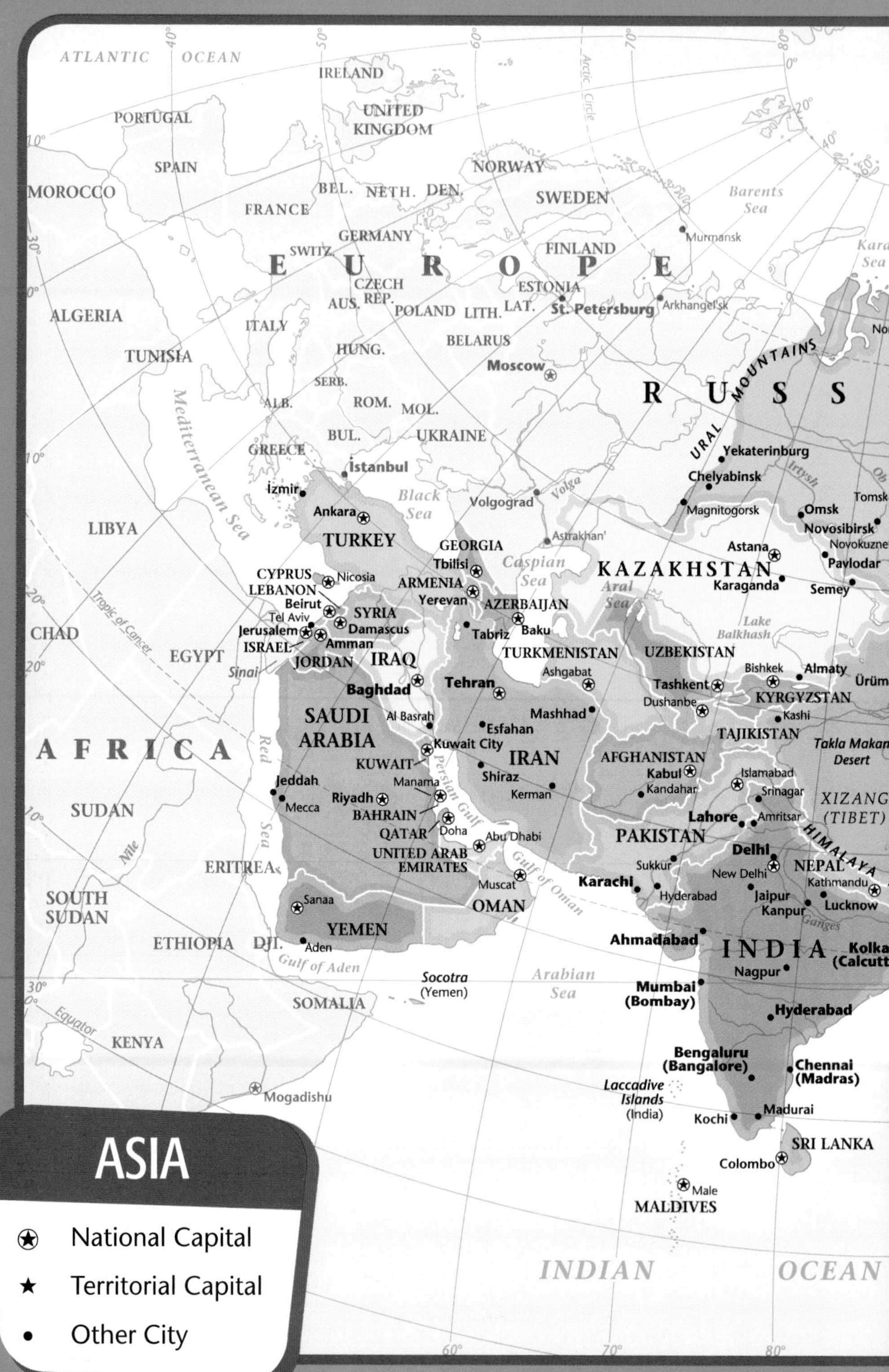
ASIA
National Capital
Territorial Capital
Other City
ATLANTIC OCEAN
IRELAND
UNITED KINGDOM
PORTUGAL
SPAIN
MOROCCO
BEL.
NETH.
DEN.
NORWAY
SWEDEN
FRANCE
GERMANY
SWITZ.
FINLAND
E U R O P E
CZECH REP.
AUS.
POLAND
LITH.
LAT.
ESTONIA
St. Petersburg
Arkhangel'sk
Murmansk
Barents Sea
Kara Sea
ALGERIA
ITALY
HUNG.
BELARUS
Moscow
TUNISIA
SERB.
ALB.
ROM.
MOL.
UKRAINE
BUL.
GREECE
Mediterranean Sea
İstanbul
İzmir
Black Sea
Volgograd
Volga
Astrakhan'
Ankara
TURKEY
GEORGIA
Tbilisi
Caspian Sea
ARMENIA
Yerevan
AZERBAIJAN
Baku
Tabriz
LIBYA
CYPRUS
Nicosia
LEBANON
Beirut
Tel Aviv
Jerusalem
ISRAEL
SYRIA
Damascus
Amman
JORDAN
IRAQ
Baghdad
Tropic of Cancer
CHAD
EGYPT
Sinai
SAUDI ARABIA
Al Basrah
Kuwait City
KUWAIT
Tehran
Esfahan
IRAN
Shiraz
Kerman
Mashhad
TURKMENISTAN
Ashgabat
UZBEKISTAN
Tashkent
Dushanbe
TAJIKISTAN
KYRGYZSTAN
Bishkek
Almaty
Kashi
KAZAKHSTAN
Astana
Karaganda
Semey
Pavlodar
Aral Sea
Lake Balkhash
R U S S
URAL MOUNTAINS
Yekaterinburg
Chelyabinsk
Magnitogorsk
Omsk
Novosibirsk
Tomsk
Novokuznet
Irtysh
A F R I C A
Red Sea
Persian Gulf
Jeddah
Mecca
Riyadh
Manama
BAHRAIN
QATAR
Doha
Abu Dhabi
UNITED ARAB EMIRATES
Muscat
Gulf of Oman
OMAN
SUDAN
Nile
ERITREA
SOUTH SUDAN
ETHIOPIA
DJI.
Sanaa
YEMEN
Aden
Gulf of Aden
Socotra (Yemen)
SOMALIA
Equator
KENYA
Mogadishu
AFGHANISTAN
Kabul
Kandahar
Islamabad
Srinagar
PAKISTAN
Lahore
Amritsar
Takla Makan Desert
XIZANG (TIBET)
HIMALAYA
Delhi
New Delhi
NEPAL
Kathmandu
Lucknow
Sukkur
Karachi
Hyderabad
Jaipur
Kanpur
Ganges
Ahmadabad
INDIA
Nagpur
Arabian Sea
Mumbai (Bombay)
Hyderabad
Bengaluru (Bangalore)
Chennai (Madras)
Laccadive Islands (India)
Kochi
Madurai
SRI LANKA
Colombo
Male
MALDIVES
INDIAN OCEAN
Arctic Circle

North Pole
ARCTIC OCEAN
Chukchi Sea
East Siberian Sea
Bering Sea
ALASKA
Laptev Sea
Anadyr
KAMCHATKA PENINSULA
Magadan
Petropavlovsk-Kamchatskiy
Sea of Okhotsk
Yakutsk
SIBERIA
Sakhalin
Kuril Islands (Russia)
Komsomolsk na Amure
Khabarovsk
Blagoveshchensk
Krasnoyarsk
Bratsk
Lake Baikal
Chita
Irkutsk
Ulan-Ude
Sapporo
Harbin
JAPAN
Vladivostok
Sea of Japan (East Sea)
Sendai
Ulaanbaatar
Changchun
Tokyo
Shenyang
Yokohama
MONGOLIA
N. KOREA
Kyoto
Pyongyang
Kobe
Osaka
GOBI DESERT
Beijing
Dalian
Seoul
Hohhot
Tianjin
S. KOREA
Hiroshima
PACIFIC OCEAN
XINJIANG
Jinan
Qingdao
Nagasaki
Taiyuan
Yellow Sea
Zhengzhou
Lanzhou
Shanghai
Xi'an
Nanjing
East China Sea
CHINA
Wuhan
Okinawa (Japan)
Ryukyu Islands
Everest
Chengdu
Wenzhou
Changsha
Fuzhou
Chongqing
Lhasa
Xiamen
Taipei
BHUTAN
TAIWAN
Guangzhou
Philippine Sea
Hong Kong
Kunming
Nanning
Macao
Dhaka
Hanoi
Gulf of Tonkin
LUZON
Mandalay
LAOS
1 : 51,914,000
Nay Pyi Taw
0
500
1,000 Miles
MYANMAR (BURMA)
Vientiane
Manila
Da Nang
PHILIPPINES
South China Sea
0
500
1,000 Kilometers
Yangon (Rangoon)
THAILAND
VIETNAM
Cebu
MINDANAO
CAMBODIA
Bangkok
Davao
Phnom Penh
Ho Chi Minh City
Sulu Sea
Andaman Sea
Gulf of Thailand
Kota Kinabalu
Celebes Sea
NEW GUINEA
Bandar Seri Begawan
Manado
Nicobar Islands (India)
BRUNEI
MALAYSIA
Medan
Kuching
BORNEO
Kuala Lumpur
SINGAPORE
Singapore
INDONESIA
Banda Sea
Arafura Sea
SUMATRA
Padang
Banjarmasin
Makassar
Dili
Timor Sea
Palembang
Java Sea
TIMOR-LESTE
Jakarta
Surabaya
Bandung
JAVA
Kupang
AUSTRALIA

ATLANTIC OCEAN
AZORES (Port.)
MADEIRA (Port.)
CANARY IS. (Sp.)
Las Palmas
PORTUGAL
Lisbon
SPAIN
Madrid
FRANCE
Paris
SWITZ.
GERMANY
CZECH REP.
AUSTRIA
SLOVE.
CRO.
ITALY
Rome
BOS. & HER.
MONT.
SERB.
KOS.
MAC.
ALBANIA
GREECE
Athens
SLOVAKIA
HUNGARY
ROMANIA
Bucharest
MOLDOVA
UKRAINE
BULGARIA
İstanbul
Black Sea
RUSSIA
KAZAKHSTAN
Caspian Sea
Aral Sea
UZBEKISTAN
TURKMENISTAN
GEORGIA
ARMENIA
AZERBAIJAN
TURKEY
Ankara
CYPRUS
SYRIA
Damascus
LEBANON
ISRAEL
Jerusalem
JORDAN
IRAQ
Baghdad
IRAN
Tehran
KUWAIT
Persian Gulf
BAHRAIN
QATAR
SAUDI ARABIA
Riyadh
Tropic of Cancer
OMAN
YEMEN
Sanaa
Gulf of Aden
DJIBOUTI
Djibouti
SOMALIA
Berbera
Hargeysa
Red Sea
Suez Canal
MALTA
Mediterranean Sea
Gulf of Sidra
MOROCCO
Tangier
Rabat
Casablanca
Safi
Marrakech
Fez
Oujda
Oran
Algiers
Constantine
Annaba
Bizerte
Tunis
Sfax
TUNISIA
ATLAS MOUNTAINS
Béchar
Ghardaia
ALGERIA
I-n-Salah
AHAGGAR MTS.
Tamanrasset
WESTERN SAHARA (occ. by Morocco)
Laayoune
Nouadhibou
MAURITANIA
Nouakchott
SAHARA
LIBYA
Tripoli
Misratah
Benghazi
al-Bayda
Tobruk
al-Jawf
LIBYAN DESERT
EGYPT
Alexandria
Port Said
Cairo
Siwa
Luxor
Aswan
L. Nasser
NUBIAN DESERT
Port Sudan
Atbara
Nile
SUDAN
Omdurman
Khartoum
Kassala
Wad Medani
Blue Nile
El Obeid
El Fasher
ERITREA
Asmara
Assab
Gonder
L. Tana
ETHIOPIAN HIGHLANDS
Addis Ababa
Jima
Harer
GREAT RIFT VALLEY
ETHIOPIA
Kelafo
L. Turkana
SOUTH SUDAN
Malakal
Juba
Wau
White Nile
TIBESTI
CHAD
Faya-Largeau
Abéché
N'Djamena
L. Chad
Sarh
CENTRAL AFRICAN REPUBLIC
Bangui
Bouar
Ubangi
AIR
NIGER
Agadez
Zinder
Niamey
SAHEL
MALI
Timbuktu
Niger
Ségou
Bamako
Kayes
SENEGAL
Dakar
Kaolack
Senegal
THE GAMBIA
Banjul
GUINEA-BISSAU
Bissau
GUINEA
Labé
Conakry
Kankan
SIERRA LEONE
Freetown
LIBERIA
Monrovia
CÔTE D'IVOIRE
Yamoussoukro
Bouake
Abidjan
BURKINA FASO
Ouagadougou
Bobo-Dioulasso
GHANA
Kumasi
Accra
Sekondi-Takoradi
TOGO
Lomé
BENIN
Porto-Novo
NIGERIA
Sokoto
Kano
Zaria
Abuja
Maiduguri
Ogbomosho
Ibadan
Lagos
Enugu
Onitsha
Port Harcourt
Benue
Garoua
Maroua
CAMEROON
Douala
Yaoundé
Malabo
40°
30°
20°
10°

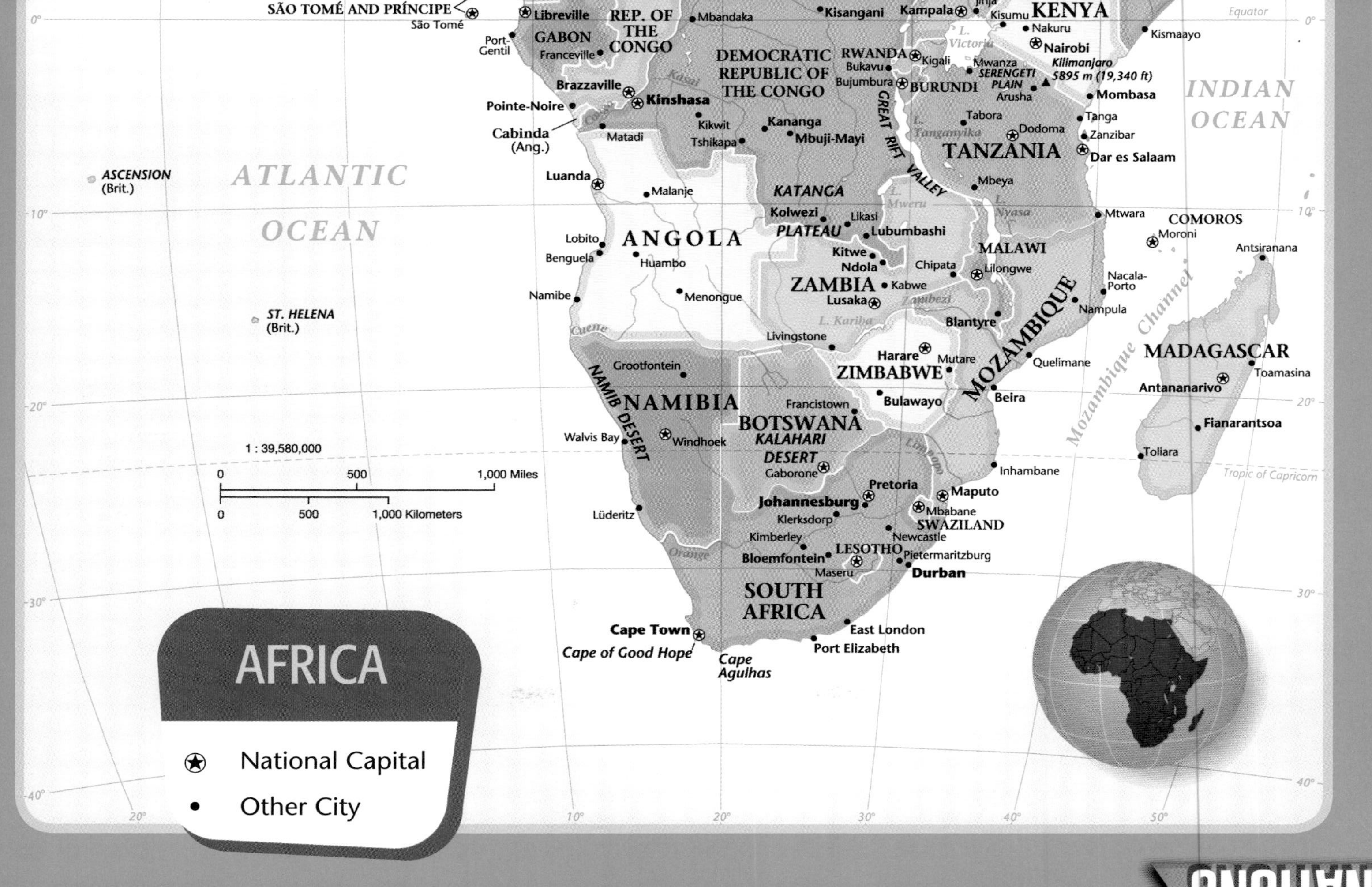
AFRICA
National Capital
Other City
1 : 39,580,000
0
500
1,000 Miles
0
500
1,000 Kilometers
ATLANTIC OCEAN
INDIAN OCEAN
Equator
Tropic of Capricorn
SÃO TOMÉ AND PRÍNCIPE
São Tomé
ASCENSION (Brit.)
ST. HELENA (Brit.)
Libreville
GABON
Port-Gentil
Franceville
REP. OF THE CONGO
Brazzaville
Pointe-Noire
Cabinda (Ang.)
Kinshasa
Matadi
Mbandaka
DEMOCRATIC REPUBLIC OF THE CONGO
Kisangani
Kikwit
Tshikapa
Kananga
Mbuji-Mayi
KATANGA
Kolwezi
Likasi
PLATEAU
Lubumbashi
Kampala
Jinja
Kisumu
KENYA
Nakuru
Nairobi
Kismaayo
Kilimanjaro 5895 m (19,340 ft)
Mombasa
RWANDA
Kigali
Bukavu
Bujumbura
BURUNDI
Mwanza
SERENGETI PLAIN
Arusha
GREAT RIFT VALLEY
Tabora
Dodoma
TANZANIA
Tanga
Zanzibar
Dar es Salaam
Mbeya
Mtwara
COMOROS
Moroni
Antsiranana
Luanda
Malanje
ANGOLA
Lobito
Benguela
Huambo
Namibe
Menongue
MALAWI
Lilongwe
Chipata
Kitwe
Ndola
ZAMBIA
Kabwe
Lusaka
Blantyre
MOZAMBIQUE
Nacala-Porto
Nampula
Quelimane
Beira
Mozambique Channel
MADAGASCAR
Toamasina
Antananarivo
Fianarantsoa
Toliara
Livingstone
Harare
Mutare
ZIMBABWE
Bulawayo
Grootfontein
NAMIBIA
NAMIB DESERT
Walvis Bay
Windhoek
Lüderitz
Francistown
BOTSWANA
KALAHARI DESERT
Gaborone
Pretoria
Johannesburg
Klerksdorp
Maputo
Mbabane
SWAZILAND
Newcastle
Inhambane
Kimberley
LESOTHO
Bloemfontein
Maseru
Pietermaritzburg
Durban
SOUTH AFRICA
Cape Town
Cape of Good Hope
Cape Agulhas
East London
Port Elizabeth

FACTS ABOUT NATIONS

Here are basic facts about the world's independent nations. The color of the heading for each country tells you what continent it belongs in. The population is an estimate for 2011. The area includes both land and inland water. The language entry gives official languages and other common languages.

Afghanistan

Capital: Kabul
Population: 29,835,392
Area: 250,001 sq mi (647,500 sq km)
Language: Afghan Persian (Dari), Pashtu
Did You Know? The people of Afghanistan speak about fifty different languages or dialects.

VILLAGE IN AFGHANISTAN

Albania

Capital: Tirana
Population: 2,994,667
Area: 11,100 sq mi (28,748 sq km)
Language: Albanian, Greek
Did You Know? Some twenty years after the fall of its Communist government, Albania is attracting tourists with its beautiful beaches and historic cities.

Algeria

Capital: Algiers (El Djazair)
Population: 34,994,937
Area: 919,595 sq mi (2,381,740 sq km)
Language: Arabic, French, Berber dialects
Did You Know? Algeria is the biggest country in Africa, if you count land area only. (Nigeria is bigger if you count inland water.)

Andorra

Capital: Andorra la Vella
Population: 84,825
Area: 181 sq mi (468 sq km)
Language: Catalan, French, Castilian
Did You Know? Tiny Andorra is ruled by two "co-princes" from neighboring countries: the president of France and the bishop of Urgel in Spain.

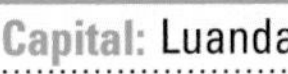

Angola

Capital: Luanda
Population: 13,338,541
Area: 481,354 sq mi (1,246,700 sq km)
Language: Portuguese, African languages
Did You Know? Angola has about 9 billion barrels of oil reserves, more than any other country in Sub-Saharan Africa except Nigeria.

Antigua & Barbuda

Capital: St. John's
Population: 87,884
Area: 171 sq mi (443 sq km)
Language: English
Did You Know? On August 1, 1834, Antigua became the first of the British Caribbean colonies to free its slaves.

COLOR KEY

- Africa
- Asia
- Australia
- Europe
- North America
- Pacific Islands
- South America

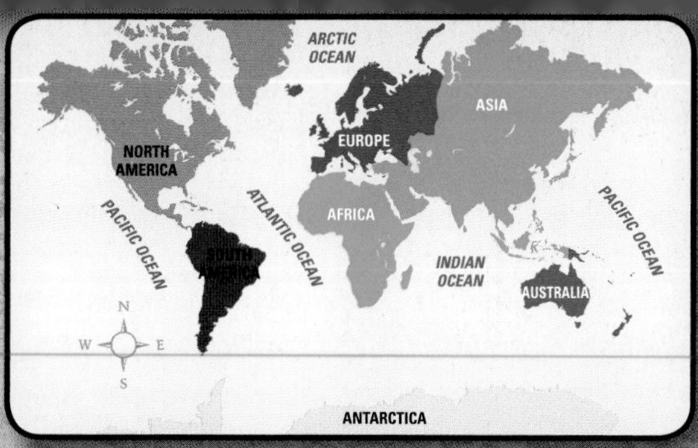

Argentina

Capital: Buenos Aires

Population: 41,769,726

Area: 1,068,302 sq mi (2,766,890 sq km)

Language: Spanish, English, Italian, German, French

Did You Know? Ushuaia, at the tip of Argentina, attracts many tourists. It is the world's southernmost city and lies about 700 miles from Antarctica.

Armenia

Capital: Yerevan

Population: 2,967,975

Area: 11,484 sq mi (29,743 sq km)

Language: Armenian, Russian

Did You Know? Armenia considers itself the first country to have formally adopted Christianity as a state religion, in the year 301.

Australia

Capital: Canberra

Population: 21,766,711

Area: 2,967,909 sq mi (7,686,850 sq km)

Language: English, Aboriginal languages

Did You Know? Heavy flooding that began in late 2010 spread over an area larger than France and Germany combined. More than 200,000 Australians were affected.

BEACH IN AUSTRALIA

Austria

Capital: Vienna

Population: 8,217,280

Area: 32,382 sq mi (83,870 sq km)

Language: German, Slovene, Croatian, Hungarian

Did You Know? Austria's most popular foods include wiener schnitzel, a tasty veal dish, and apple strudel, one of many delicious desserts.

Azerbaijan

Capital: Baku

Population: 8,372,373

Area: 33,436 sq mi (86,600 sq km)

Language: Azeri, Russian, Armenian

Did You Know? Azerbaijan became an independent nation in 1991, when the Soviet Union broke up.

The Bahamas

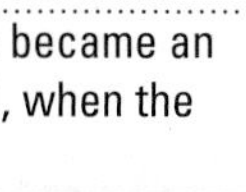

Capital: Nassau

Population: 313,312

Area: 5,382 sq mi (13,940 sq km)

Language: English, Creole

Did You Know? Columbus first set foot in America when he landed on an island in the Bahamas, probably Watling Island, on October 12, 1492.

Bahrain

Capital: Manama

Population: 1,214,705

Area: 257 sq mi (665 sq km)

Language: Arabic, English, Farsi, Urdu

Did You Know? Most of the people in this small island kingdom in the Persian Gulf are Shiite Muslims. However, Sunni Muslims have most of the power in the government.

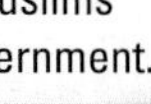

Bangladesh

Capital: Dhaka

Population: 158,570,535

Area: 55,599 sq mi (144,000 sq km)

Language: Bangla, English

Did You Know? The saltwater crocodile, found mainly in India and Bangladesh, can measure more than 20 feet long.

Barbados

Capital: Bridgetown

Population: 286,705

Area: 166 sq mi (431 sq km)

Language: English

Did You Know? The so-called green monkeys of Barbados arrived about 350 years from West Africa. Their fur looks greenish in certain light.

Belarus

Capital: Minsk

Population: 9,577,552

Area: 80,155 sq mi (207,600 sq km)

Language: Belarusian, Russian

Did You Know? Contamination from the 1986 Chernobyl nuclear power plant explosion, in neighboring Ukraine, continues to affect Belarus. High numbers of children have been diagnosed with cancer. Many people are unemployed because farmland was contaminated.

Belgium

Capital: Brussels

Population: 10,431,477

Area: 11,787 sq mi (30,528 sq km)

Language: Dutch, French, German

Did You Know? Belgium produces about 170,000 tons of chocolate every year, supporting about 300 chocolate makers and more than 2,000 shops.

Belize

Capital: Belmopan

Population: 321,115

Area: 8,867 sq mi (22,966 sq km)

Language: English, Spanish, Mayan, Garifuna, Creole

Did You Know? Belize Barrier Reef is the second largest coral reef system (a diverse underwater habitat) in the world.

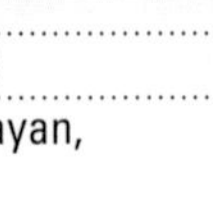

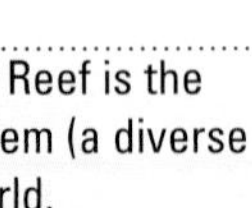

Benin

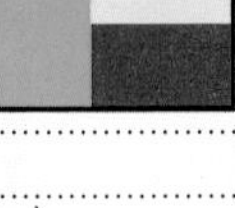

Capital: Porto-Novo (constit.); Cotonou (admin.)

Population: 9,325,032

Area: 43,483 sq mi (112,620 sq km)

Language: French, Fon, Yoruba

Did You Know? Most of present-day Benin was part of the Kingdom of Abomey for almost 300 years, until the area came under French control around 1900.

Bhutan

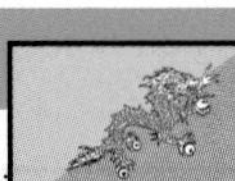

Capital: Thimphu

Population: 708,427

Area: 18,147 sq mi (47,000 sq km)

Language: Dzongkha, Tibetan dialects

Did You Know? People in Bhutan must wear traditional clothes when in public. Women wear an ankle-length dress or skirt, called a *kira* or *half kira*.

Bolivia

Capital: La Paz (admin.); Sucre (legislative/judiciary)

Population: 10,118,683

Area: 424,164 sq mi (1,098,580 sq km)

Language: Spanish, Quechua, Aymara

Did You Know? Bolivia is named after Simón Bolívar, a military leader who freed much of South America from Spanish rule.

BRUSSELS, BELGIUM

Bosnia and Herzegovina

Capital: Sarajevo
Population: 4,622,163
Area: 19,772 sq mi (51,209 sq km)
Language: Bosnian, Croatian, Serbian
Did You Know? On June 28, 1914, Archduke Franz Ferdinand of Austria and his wife were shot and fatally wounded as they rode in an open car in Sarajevo. The event helped set off World War I.

Botswana

Capital: Gaborone
Population: 2,065,398
Area: 231,804 sq mi (600,370 sq km)
Language: Setswana, English
Did You Know? After diamond deposits were discovered in 1967, Botswana became one of Africa's most prosperous countries.

Brazil

Capital: Brasília
Population: 203,429,773
Area: 3,286,488 sq mi (8,511,965 sq km)
Language: Portuguese, Spanish, English, French
Did You Know? About 180 million people in the world speak Portuguese. Most of them live in Brazil.

RIO DE JANEIRO, BRAZIL

Brunei

Capital: Bandar Seri Begawan
Population: 401,890
Area: 2,228 sq mi (5,770 sq km)
Language: Malay, English, Chinese
Did You Know? The same royal family has ruled Brunei since the 1400s.

Bulgaria

Capital: Sofia
Population: 7,093,635
Area: 42,823 sq mi (110,910 sq km)
Language: Bulgarian, Turkish
Did You Know? Plovdiv, Bulgaria's second largest city, is one of Europe's oldest cities. There is evidence that people were living at the site as early as 6,000 years ago.

Burkina Faso

Capital: Ouagadougou
Population: 16,751,455
Area: 105,869 sq mi (274,200 sq km)
Language: French, indigenous languages
Did You Know? "Burkina Faso" means "land of honest people."

Burundi

Capital: Bujumbura
Population: 10,216,190
Area: 10,745 sq mi (27,830 sq km)
Language: Kirundi, French, Swahili
Did You Know? The Twa, a Pygmy group (adult males average about 5 feet tall), are thought to be Burundi's original inhabitants.

Cambodia

Capital: Phnom Penh
Population: 14,701,717
Area: 69,900 sq mi (181,040 sq km)
Language: Khmer, French, English
Did You Know? More than half of all Cambodians are under the age of 21.

COLOR KEY

- Africa
- Asia
- Australia
- Europe
- North America
- Pacific Islands
- South America

Cameroon

Capital: Yaoundé
Population: 19,711,291
Area: 183,568 sq mi (475,440 sq km)
Language: English, French, African languages
Did You Know? Some 1,700 people were killed in 1986 when a cloud of poisonous gas rose from a volcanic lake.

Canada

Capital: Ottawa
Population: 34,030,589
Area: 3,855,103 sq mi (9,984,670 sq km)
Language: English, French
Did You Know? In 1994, Canada's Parliament declared ice hockey the country's national winter sport and lacrosse the national summer sport.

PARLIAMENT HILL, OTTAWA, CANADA

Cape Verde

Capital: Praia
Population: 516,100
Area: 1,557 sq mi (4,033 sq km)
Language: Portuguese, Crioulo
Did You Know? More Cape Verdeans live abroad than live on the nation's islands.

Central African Republic

Capital: Bangui
Population: 4,950,027
Area: 240,535 sq mi (622,984 sq km)
Language: French, Sangho
Did You Know? In 1976, Jean-Bedel Bokassa proclaimed himself emperor, but he was overthrown a few years later.

Chad

Capital: N'Djamena
Population: 10,758,945
Area: 495,755 sq mi (1,284,000 sq km)
Language: French, Arabic, Sara
Did You Know? There are some 200 native ethnic groups living in Chad.

Chile

Capital: Santiago
Population: 16,888,760
Area: 292,260 sq mi (756,950 sq km)
Language: Spanish
Did You Know? The Atacama Desert in northern Chile is one of the earth's driest places. In some areas, rain has never been recorded.

China

Capital: Beijing
Population: 1,336,718,015
Area: 3,705,407 sq mi (9,596,960 sq km)
Language: Mandarin, and many dialects
Did You Know? China has more than 150 cities with a population of more than 1 million.

Colombia

Capital: Bogotá
Population: 44,725,543
Area: 439,736 sq mi (1,138,910 sq km)
Language: Spanish
Did You Know? The town of Lloro, on the slopes of the Andes Mountains, may be the world's rainiest place. It gets an average of more than 500 inches of rain each year.

COLOR KEY

- Africa
- Asia
- Australia
- Europe
- North America
- Pacific Islands
- South America

Comoros

Capital: Moroni
Population: 794,683
Area: 838 sq mi (2,170 sq km)
Language: Arabic, French, Shikomoro
Did You Know? The endangered Livingstone's flying fox, a fruit bat native to the islands of Comoros, has a wing span of more than 4 feet.

Congo, Democratic Republic of the

Capital: Kinshasa
Population: 71,712,867
Area: 905,568 sq mi (2,345,410 sq km)
Language: French, Lingala, Kingwana, Kikongo, Tshiluba
Did You Know? This country in the heart of Africa was ruled by Belgium for about 80 years, until it won independence in 1960.

Congo, Republic of the

Capital: Brazzaville
Population: 4,243,929
Area: 132,047 sq mi (342,000 sq km)
Language: French, Lingala, Monokutuba, Kikongo
Did You Know? The Bantu people of the Congo have lived in the region since before A.D. 1000.

Costa Rica

Capital: San José
Population: 4,576,562
Area: 19,730 sq mi (51,100 sq km)
Language: Spanish, English
Did You Know? Almost one-fourth of the land in Costa Rica has been set aside as protected areas for the nation's many kinds of plants and animals.

Côte d'Ivoire (Ivory Coast)

Capital: Yamoussoukro
Population: 21,504,162
Area: 124,503 sq mi (322,460 sq km)
Language: French, Dioula
Did You Know? The largest Christian church in the world is in Côte d'Ivoire's capital city of Yamoussoukro.

Croatia

Capital: Zagreb
Population: 4,483,804
Area: 21,831 sq mi (56,542 sq km)
Language: Croatian, Serbian
Did You Know? Croatia has more than 1,000 islands off its coast in the Adriatic Sea. Only about 50 are inhabited.

Cuba

Capital: Havana
Population: 11,087,330
Area: 42,803 sq mi (110,860 sq km)
Language: Spanish
Did You Know? One of the world's few remaining Communist countries, Cuba lies just 90 miles away from the tip of Florida.

Cyprus

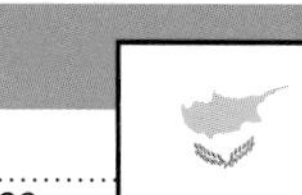

Capital: Nicosia
Population: 1,120,489
Area: 3,571 sq mi (9,250 sq km)
Language: Greek, Turkish, English
Did You Know? Halloumi, a salty cheese made from a mixture of goat and sheep milk, is a traditional food in Cyprus.

SEA CAVES NEAR CAPE GRECO, CYPRUS

Czech Republic

Capital: Prague

Population: 10,190,213

Area: 30,450 sq mi (78,866 sq km)

Language: Czech, Slovak

Did You Know? The so-called "Velvet Revolution" brought about the end of communism in Czechoslovakia in 1989. The term "Velvet Divorce" was used to describe the 1993 division of the Czech Republic and Slovakia.

Denmark

Capital: Copenhagen

Population: 5,529,888

Area: 16,639 sq mi (43,094 sq km)

Language: Danish, Faroese

Did You Know? The statue of the Little Mermaid in Copenhagen's harbor was created in honor of the Danish fairy tale author Hans Christian Andersen.

Djibouti

Capital: Djibouti

Population: 757,074

Area: 8,880 sq mi (23,000 sq km)

Language: French, Arabic, Somali, Afar

Did You Know? Most of the country is barren. It receives little rainfall, and few plants survive in Djibouti's rocky deserts.

Dominica

Capital: Roseau

Population: 72,969

Area: 291 sq mi (754 sq km)

Language: English, French patois

Did You Know? The Sisserou parrot, seen on Dominica's flag, is the national bird. Dominica's tropical rain forests are its only home in the world.

Dominican Republic

Capital: Santo Domingo

Population: 9,956,648

Area: 18,815 sq mi (48,730 sq km)

Language: Spanish

Did You Know? Sancocho, a stew with vegetables and chunks of different meats, is a favorite dish in the Dominican Republic.

Ecuador

Capital: Quito

Population: 15,007,343

Area: 109,483 sq mi (283,560 sq km)

Language: Spanish, Quechua

Did You Know? The tortoises in Ecuador's Galapagos Islands can weigh more than 500 pounds and live for 150 years or more. Scientists have been working to save them from becoming extinct.

Egypt

Capital: Cairo

Population: 82,079,636

Area: 386,662 sq mi (1,001,450 sq km)

Language: Arabic, English, French

Did You Know? The Great Pyramid of Giza, built around 2250 B.C., is made up of more than 2 million stone blocks.

PYRAMID AT GIZA, EGYPT

El Salvador

Capital: San Salvador

Population: 6,071,774

Area: 8,124 sq mi (21,040 sq km)

Language: Spanish, Nahua

Did You Know? El Salvador is the most densely-populated country on the mainland of the Americas, with more than 900 people per square mile.

COLOR KEY

- Africa
- Asia
- Australia
- Europe
- North America
- Pacific Islands
- South America

Equatorial Guinea

Capital: Malabo
Population: 668,225
Area: 10,831 sq mi (28,051 sq km)
Language: Spanish, French, Fang, Bubi
Did You Know? Equatorial Guinea is the only African country in which Spanish is an official language.

Eritrea

Capital: Asmara
Population: 5,939,484
Area: 46,842 sq mi (121,320 sq km)
Language: Afar, Arabic, Tigre, Kunama, Tigrinya
Did You Know? Eritrea was once a colony of Italy, then occupied by British forces, and finally annexed by Ethiopia before it achieved independence in 1993.

Estonia

Capital: Tallinn
Population: 1,282,963
Area: 17,462 sq mi (45,226 sq km)
Language: Estonian, Russian
Did You Know? In January 2011, Estonia became the 17th nation of the European Union to use the euro as its currency.

Ethiopia

Capital: Addis Ababa
Population: 90,873,739
Area: 435,186 sq mi (1,127,127 sq km)
Language: Amharic, Tigrinya, Oromigna, Guaragigna, Somali, Arabic
Did You Know? Ethiopia was taken over by Italy in 1936 but was freed by British forces five years later during World War II.

Fiji

Capital: Suva
Population: 883,125
Area: 7,054 sq mi (18,270 sq km)
Language: English, Fijian, Hindustani
Did You Know? Wearing a hat is a sign of disrespect in Fijian culture.

Finland

Capital: Helsinki
Population: 5,259,250
Area: 130,559 sq mi (338,145 sq km)
Language: Finnish, Swedish
Did You Know? In Finland, fines for speeding are based on income. One of Finland's richest citizens was fined $216,900 for driving too fast.

France

Capital: Paris
Population: 65,102,719
Area: 248,429 sq mi (643,427 sq km)
Language: French
Did You Know? The Tour de France bicycle race is a three-week-long event that covers more than 2,000 miles.

PALACE OF VERSAILLES, FRANCE

Gabon

Capital: Libreville
Population: 1,576,665
Area: 103,347 sq mi (267,667 sq km)
Language: French, Fang, Myene, Nzebi
Did You Know? Oil and other natural resources have helped make Gabon one of Africa's more prosperous countries.

Capital: Banjul

Population: 1,797,860

Area: 4,363 sq mi (11,300 sq km)

Language: English, Mandinka, Wolof

Did You Know? The Gambia is the smallest country by area on the continent of Africa.

Georgia

Capital: T'bilisi

Population: 4,585,874

Area: 26,911 sq mi (69,700 sq km)

Language: Georgian, Russian, Armenian, Azeri, Abkhaz

Did You Know? The Georgian alphabet is one of only a few alphabets still in use today. It is believed to have been created in the 5th century.

Germany

Capital: Berlin

Population: 81,471,834

Area: 137,847 sq mi (357,021 sq km)

Language: German

Did You Know? Sauerbraten, a favorite German dish, used to be made with horse meat. Today, it is usually made with beef, and it is often served with potato dumplings and red cabbage.

BRANDENBURG GATE, BERLIN, GERMANY

Ghana

Capital: Accra

Population: 24,791,073

Area: 92,456 sq mi (239,460 sq km)

Language: English, Akan, Moshi-Dagomba, Ewe, Ga

Did You Know? In 1957, the British colony known as the Gold Coast was merged with another territory to form Ghana.

Greece

Capital: Athens

Population: 10,760,136

Area: 50,942 sq mi (131,940 sq km)

Language: Greek, English, French

Did You Know? More than 2,000 islands are part of the country of Greece. Many are quite small, and fewer than 200 are inhabited.

Grenada

Capital: Saint George's

Population: 108,419

Area: 133 sq mi (344 sq km)

Language: English, French patois

Did You Know? Grenada is sometimes referred to as the "Spice of the Caribbean" because its top export is nutmeg.

Guatemala

Capital: Guatemala City

Population: 13,824,463

Area: 42,043 sq mi (108,890 sq km)

Language: Spanish, Amerindian languages

Did You Know? Before the arrival of the Spanish, the Mayan Indian empire flourished for more than 1,000 years in what is today Guatemala.

Guinea

Capital: Conakry

Population: 10,601,009

Area: 94,926 sq mi (245,857 sq km)

Language: French, Susu, Pulaar, Malinke

Did You Know? In its first five decades as an independent country (1958–2008), Guinea had only two different rulers.

COLOR KEY

- Africa
- Asia
- Australia
- Europe
- North America
- Pacific Islands
- South America

Guinea-Bissau

Capital: Bissau
Population: 1,596,677
Area: 13,946 sq mi (36,120 sq km)
Language: Portuguese, Crioulo, African languages
Did You Know? At carnival time, the people of Guinea-Bissau wear masks to make them look like sharks, hippos, and bulls.

Guyana

Capital: Georgetown
Population: 744,768
Area: 83,000 sq mi (214,970 sq km)
Language: English, Amerindian dialects, Creole, Hindi
Did You Know? Christopher Columbus explored the coast of Guyana in 1498, and almost 100 years later, Sir Walter Raleigh searched for gold there.

Haiti

Capital: Port-au-Prince
Population: 9,719,932
Area: 10,714 sq mi (27,750 sq km)
Language: French, Creole
Did You Know? An earthquake in January 2010 killed more than 200,000 Haitians and left many more homeless. Haiti was already the poorest country in the Americas.

Honduras

Capital: Tegucigalpa
Population: 8,143,564
Area: 43,278 sq mi (112,090 sq km)
Language: Spanish, Amerindian dialects
Did You Know? Christopher Columbus was the first European to reach Honduras, where he landed in 1502.

Hungary

Capital: Budapest
Population: 9,976,062
Area: 35,919 sq mi (93,030 sq km)
Language: Hungarian (Magyar)
Did You Know? In the course of Hungary's history, large parts of the country have been part of the Roman Empire, the Mongol Empire, and Turkey's Ottoman Empire.

Iceland

Capital: Reykjavik
Population: 311,058
Area: 39,769 sq mi (103,000 sq km)
Language: Icelandic, English
Did You Know? Glaciers, lakes, and a lava desert cover about three-fourths of Iceland's surface area.

India

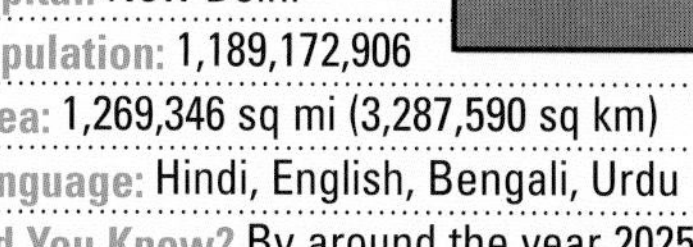

Capital: New Delhi
Population: 1,189,172,906
Area: 1,269,346 sq mi (3,287,590 sq km)
Language: Hindi, English, Bengali, Urdu
Did You Know? By around the year 2025, India is expected to have the largest population of any country in the world.

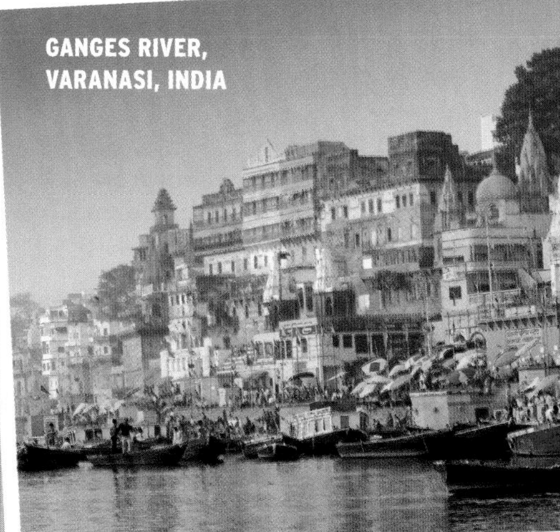

GANGES RIVER, VARANASI, INDIA

Indonesia

Capital: Jakarta
Population: 245,613,043
Area: 741,100 sq mi (1,919,440 sq km)
Language: Bahasa Indonesian, English, Dutch, Javanese
Did You Know? There are over 200 million Muslims in Indonesia, more than in any other country.

Iran

Capital: Tehran
Population: 77,891,220
Area: 636,296 sq mi (1,648,000 sq km)
Language: Farsi (Persian), Turkic, Kurdish
Did You Know? The Persians settled in Iran around 1500 B.C. and made it the center of a vast empire in the 6th century B.C. But the empire fell to Alexander the Great.

Iraq

Capital: Baghdad
Population: 30,399,572
Area: 168,754 sq mi (437,072 sq km)
Language: Arabic, Kurdish
Did You Know? The Sumerians settled in the region more than 5,000 years ago. They built walled cities and an advanced civilization that lasted for 3000 years.

Ireland

Capital: Dublin
Population: 4,670,976
Area: 27,135 sq mi (70,280 sq km)
Language: English, Irish
Did You Know? In the mid-1800s, Ireland's potato crop failed and caused a huge famine. About 1 million people died, and another 2 million fled to other countries.

KILKENNY CASTLE, IRELAND

Israel

Capital: Jerusalem
Population: 7,473,052
Area: 8,019 sq mi (20,770 sq km)
Language: Hebrew, Arabic, English
Did You Know? Almost 3.5 million tourists visited Israel in 2010, a record-high number.

Italy

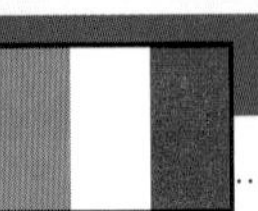

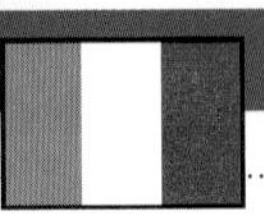
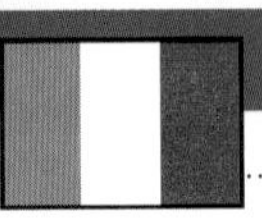
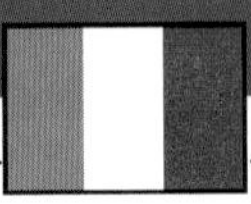

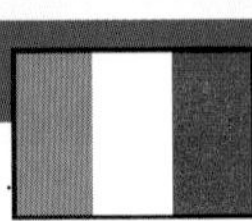
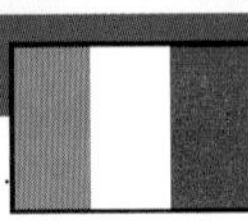
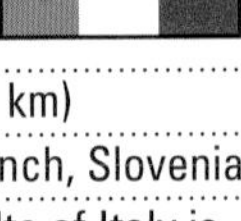

Capital: Rome
Population: 61,016,804
Area: 116,306 sq mi (301,230 sq km)
Language: Italian, German, French, Slovenian
Did You Know? Alessandro Volta of Italy is credited with inventing an early version of the battery. The electrical unit *volt* is named for him.

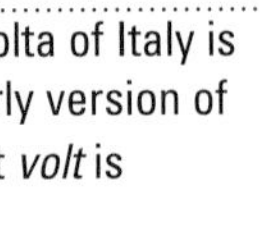

Jamaica

Capital: Kingston
Population: 2,868,380
Area: 4,244 sq mi (10,991 sq km)
Language: English, Jamaican Creole
Did You Know? Reggae, a mixture of native, rock, and soul music, was developed in Jamaica.

Japan

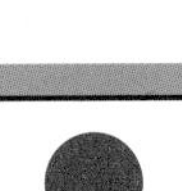

Capital: Tokyo
Population: 126,475,664
Area: 145,883 sq mi (377,835 sq km)
Language: Japanese
Did You Know? Many newer buildings in Japan are designed to withstand earthquakes. The March 2011 earthquake in Japan, however, created a huge tsunami, or sea wave. It was the tsunami that caused most of the damage and loss of life Japan suffered.

Jordan

Capital: Amman
Population: 6,508,271
Area: 35,637 sq mi (92,300 sq km)
Language: Arabic, English
Did You Know? Philadelphia was the name in ancient times for the city that is now Amman.

COLOR KEY

- Africa
- Asia
- Australia
- Europe
- North America
- Pacific Islands
- South America

Kazakhstan

Capital: Astana

Population: 15,522,373

Area: 1,049,155 sq mi (2,717,300 sq km)

Language: Kazakh, Russian

Did You Know? Like Russia, and unlike the other former Soviet republics, Kazakhstan has large oil reserves.

Kenya

Capital: Nairobi

Population: 41,070,934

Area: 224,962 sq mi (582,650 sq km)

Language: Kiswahili, English

Did You Know? A worldwide ban on ivory trading in 1989 helped save Kenya's elephants from possibly becoming extinct. But illegal hunting of elephants continues to be a problem.

SAVANNA IN KENYA

Kiribati

Capital: Tarawa

Population: 100,743

Area: 313 sq mi (811 sq km)

Language: English, I-Kiribati

Did You Know? Kiribati's islands are spread across an area of the Pacific Ocean about the same size as the continental U.S.

Korea, North

Capital: Pyongyang

Population: 24,457,492

Area: 46,541 sq mi (120,540 sq km)

Language: Korean

Did You Know? North and South Korea have officially been at war for more than 50 years. A ceasefire ended the Korean War in 1953, but there has never been a peace treaty.

Korea, South

Capital: Seoul

Population: 48,754,657

Area: 38,023 sq mi (98,480 sq km)

Language: Korean

Did You Know? Ban Ki-moon, a former foreign minister of South Korea, became secretary-general of the UN in 2007.

Kosovo

Capital: Pristina

Population: 1,825,632

Area: 4,203 sq mi (10,887 sq km)

Language: Albanian, Serbian, Bosnian, Turkish, Roma

Did You Know? Kosovo declared its independence from Serbia in 2008 and has its own government, but some countries do not accept it as an independent nation.

Kuwait

Capital: Kuwait City

Population: 2,595,628

Area: 6,880 sq mi (17,820 sq km)

Language: Arabic, English

Did You Know? In 2005, women were granted full political rights for the first time, including the right to vote and run in parliamentary elections.

Kyrgyzstan

Capital: Bishkek

Population: 5,587,443

Area: 76,641 sq mi (198,500 sq km)

Language: Kyrgyz, Russian

Did You Know? The region that is now Kyrgyzstan was conquered by the Mongol emperor Genghis Khan in the early 1200s.

VIENTIANE, LAOS

Laos

Capital: Vientiane
Population: 6,477,211
Area: 91,429 sq mi (236,800 sq km)
Language: Lao, French, English
Did You Know? The first kingdom in what is now Laos was called *Lan Xang*, or "Kingdom of the Million Elephants."

Latvia

Capital: Riga
Population: 2,204,708
Area: 24,938 sq mi (64,589 sq km)
Language: Latvian, Russian, Lithuanian
Did You Know? The president's official home is a castle built in the early 1300s.

Lebanon

Capital: Beirut
Population: 4,143,101
Area: 4,015 sq mi (10,400 sq km)
Language: Arabic, French, English, Armenian
Did You Know? The cedar of Lebanon is one of four cedar species in the world. The tree is mentioned in myths and even appears on the country's flag.

Lesotho

Capital: Maseru
Population: 1,924,886
Area: 11,720 sq mi (30,355 sq km)
Language: English, Sesotho, Zulu, Xhosa
Did You Know? The Kingdom of Lesotho is completely surrounded by South Africa.

Liberia

Capital: Monrovia
Population: 3,786,764
Area: 43,000 sq mi (111,370 sq km)
Language: English, ethnic languages
Did You Know? Liberia was founded in 1822 by freed African slaves from the U.S. It became an independent republic in 1847.

Libya

Capital: Tripoli
Population: 6,597,960
Area: 679,362 sq mi (1,759,540 sq km)
Language: Arabic, Italian, English
Did You Know? Most of Libya is desert. Only about 1 percent of the land is naturally suitable for farming.

Liechtenstein

Capital: Vaduz
Population: 35,236
Area: 62 sq mi (160 sq km)
Language: German, Alemannic dialect
Did You Know? Nearly half of all the workers in tiny Liechtenstein commute there each day from their homes in Austria, Switzerland, or Germany.

Lithuania

Capital: Vilnius
Population: 3,535,547
Area: 25,213 sq mi (65,300 sq km)
Language: Lithuanian, Russian, Polish
Did You Know? Lithuania and France rely on nuclear power for their energy needs more than any other countries in the world.

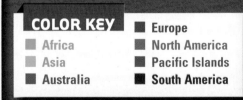

COLOR KEY
- Africa
- Asia
- Australia
- Europe
- North America
- Pacific Islands
- South America

Luxembourg

Capital: Luxembourg
Population: 503,302
Area: 998 sq mi (2,586 sq km)
Language: French, German, Luxembourgish
Did You Know? Tiny Luxembourg has been ruled by Burgundy, Spain, Austria, and France, and it was overrun by Germany in two world wars.

Macedonia

Capital: Skopje
Population: 2,077,328
Area: 9,781 sq mi (25,333 sq km)
Language: Macedonian, Albanian, Turkish
Did You Know? Skopje was rebuilt after an earthquake in 1963 destroyed more than half of the city.

Madagascar

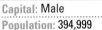

Capital: Antananarivo
Population: 21,926,221
Area: 226,657 sq mi (587,040 sq km)
Language: Malagasy, French
Did You Know? Lemurs are monkey-like animals with big eyes and, usually, long bushy tails. They can be found only in Madagascar and nearby islands.

BAOBAB TREES, MADAGASCAR

Malawi

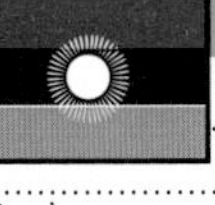
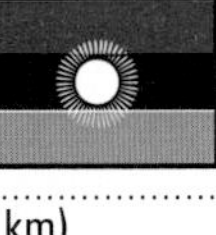

Capital: Lilongwe
Population: 15,879,252
Area: 45,745 sq mi (118,480 sq km)
Language: English, Chichewa
Did You Know? Malawi means "flaming waters" and is named for the sun setting on Lake Malawi, Africa's third-largest lake.

Malaysia

Capital: Kuala Lumpur
Population: 28,728,607
Area: 127,317 sq mi (329,750 sq km)
Language: Malay, English, Chinese, Tamil
Did You Know? During the late 20th century, Malaysia grew into a major industrial power.

Maldives

Capital: Male
Population: 394,999
Area: 116 sq mi (300 sq km)
Language: Maldivian Divehi, English
Did You Know? The capital island of this 1,190-island nation is so overcrowded that Hulhumale, an artificial island, was created nearby.

Mali

Capital: Bamako
Population: 14,159,904
Area: 478,767 sq mi (1,240,000 sq km)
Language: French, Bambara
Did You Know? Until the 15th century, this area was part of the great Mali Empire in Africa.

Malta

Capital: Valletta
Population: 408,333
Area: 122 sq mi (316 sq km)
Language: Maltese, English
Did You Know? This island nation is located midway between Europe and Africa, but it considers itself part of Europe and joined the European Union in 2004.

Marshall Islands

Capital: Majuro

Population: 67,182

Area: 70 sq mi (181 sq km)

Language: English, Marshallese

Did You Know? The United States occupied this island nation for several decades after World War II and the country still uses the U.S. dollar as its currency.

Mauritania

Capital: Nouakchott

Population: 3,281,634

Area: 397,955 sq mi (1,030,700 sq km)

Language: Arabic, Wolof, Pulaar

Did You Know? Ben Amera, one of the biggest monoliths (large single rocks) in the world, lies in the desert sands of Mauritania.

Mauritius

Capital: Port Louis

Population: 1,303,717

Area: 788 sq mi (2,040 sq km)

Language: Creole, Bhojpuri, French, English

Did You Know? About 70% of the people are descended from immigrants who came from India to work on Mauritius's sugar plantations.

Mexico

Capital: Mexico City

Population: 113,724,226

Area: 761,606 sq mi (1,972,550 sq km)

Language: Spanish, Mayan languages

Did You Know? Near Mexico City lie the ruins of an ancient city. It was abandoned in the eighth century A.D., and even its name was lost. The Aztecs later called it Teotihuacán, or "City of the Gods."

Micronesia

Capital: Palikir

Population: 106,836

Area: 271 sq mi (702 sq km)

Language: English, Trukese, Pohnpeian, Yapese

Did You Know? Micronesia is made up of 607 separate islands in the Pacific Ocean, spread over a path about 2,000 miles long.

Moldova

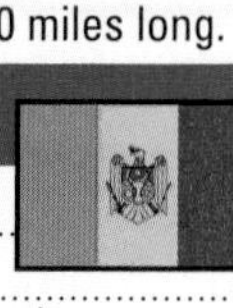

Capital: Chisinau

Population: 4,314,377

Area: 13,067 sq mi (33,843 sq km)

Language: Moldovan, Russian

Did You Know? On March 1, Moldovans celebrate the beginning of spring by wearing a pin with braided threads of red (symbolizing blood) and white (symbolizing life).

COASTLINE OF MONACO

Monaco

Capital: Monaco

Population: 30,539

Area: 0.76 sq mi (1.96 sq km)

Language: French, English, Italian, Monegasque

Did You Know? Children born in Monaco today can be expected to live to be almost 90 years old, a longer life expectancy than in any other country.

Mongolia

Capital: Ulaanbaatar

Population: 3,133,318

Area: 603,909 sq mi (1,564,116 sq km)

Language: Khalkha Mongolian

Did You Know? There is plenty of space in Mongolia, the most thinly populated country in the world.

COLOR KEY

- Africa
- Asia
- Australia
- Europe
- North America
- Pacific Islands
- South America

Montenegro

Capital: Cetinje; Podgorica (admin.)

Population: 661,807

Area: 5,415 sq mi (14,026 sq km)

Language: Serbian, Bosnian, Albanian, Croatian

Did You Know? Montenegro adopted its first constitution in 2007, a little more than a year after it declared its independence from Serbia. Both countries had been a part of Yugoslavia.

Morocco

Capital: Rabat

Population: 31,968,361

Area: 172,414 sq mi (446,550 sq km)

Language: Arabic, Berber dialects, French

Did You Know? One of the world's most grueling foot races is the Marathon des Sables ("Marathon of Sands"), a 7-day, 143-mile trek across the Sahara Desert in Morocco.

Mozambique

Capital: Maputo

Population: 22,948,858

Area: 309,496 sq mi (801,590 sq km)

Language: Portuguese, Bantu languages

Did You Know? Mozambique has been hurt by colonial rule, civil war, and famine. But after a peace deal in 1992 ended 16 years of civil conflict, the country has enjoyed a period of rapid economic growth.

Myanmar (Burma)

Capital: Nay Pyi Taw

Population: 53,999,804

Area: 261,970 sq mi (678,500 sq km)

Language: Burmese

Did You Know? The Mogok Stone Tract in northern Myanmar is known for producing some of the world's most brilliant rubies.

Namibia

Capital: Windhoek

Population: 2,147,585

Area: 318,696 sq mi (825,418 sq km)

Language: Afrikaans, English, German

Did You Know? The largest naturally occurring piece of iron on Earth is a meteorite that fell in Namibia.

Nauru

Capital: Yaren district

Population: 9,322

Area: 8 sq mi (21 sq km)

Language: Nauruan, English

Did You Know? Named "Pleasant Island" by its first European visitors, Nauru is the world's smallest island nation in area.

Nepal

Capital: Kathmandu

Population: 29,391,883

Area: 56,827 sq mi (147,181 sq km)

Language: Nepali, Maithali, Bhojpuri, English

Did You Know? More than 3,000 people have made it to the top of Mount Everest, on the Nepal-China border. Over 200 others have died in the attempt.

MOUNT EVEREST, NEPAL

Netherlands

Capital: Amsterdam; The Hague (admin.)

Population: 16,847,007

Area: 16,033 sq mi (41,526 sq km)

Language: Dutch, Frisian

Did You Know? For breakfast Dutch people like to eat bread with different kinds of toppings, as well as cheeses and cold meats.

New Zealand

Capital: Wellington

Population: 4,290,347

Area: 103,738 sq mi (268,680 sq km)

Language: English, Maori

Did You Know? The first European to see the New Zealand coast was the 17th-century Dutch navigator Abel Tasman. The Maori natives did not let him land.

Nicaragua

Capital: Managua

Population: 5,666,301

Area: 49,998 sq mi (129,494 sq km)

Language: Spanish, Miskito, indigenous languages

Did You Know? The islands of the Miskito Cays, once an area for pirate hideouts, are now a protected area for coral reefs and wildlife.

Niger

Capital: Niamey

Population: 16,468,886

Area: 489,192 sq mi (1,267,000 sq km)

Language: French, Hausa, Djerma

Did You Know? Niger is the 22nd-largest country in the world. It is about twice the size of Texas.

Nigeria

Capital: Abuja

Population: 155,215,573

Area: 356,669 sq mi (923,768 sq km)

Language: English, Hausa, Yoruba, Ibo

Did You Know? Nigeria has more people than any other African country. It also exports the most oil of any nation on the continent.

COLOR KEY

- Africa
- Asia
- Australia
- Europe
- North America
- Pacific Islands
- South America

Norway

Capital: Oslo

Population: 4,691,849

Area: 125,021 sq mi (323,802 sq km)

Language: Norwegian, Sami

Did You Know? The UN ranks Norway as the nation with the highest "quality of life."

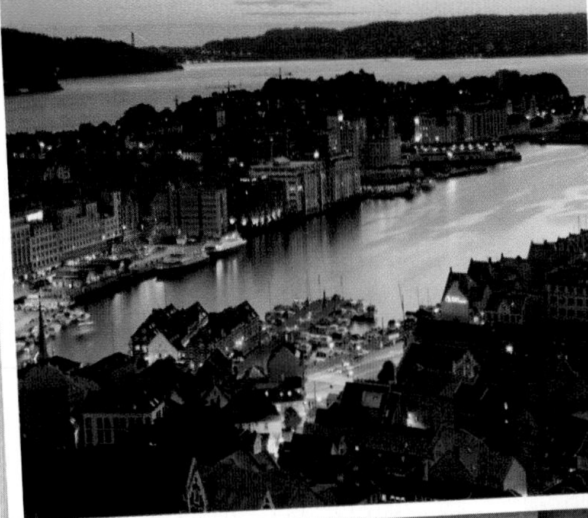

BERGEN, NORWAY

Oman

Capital: Muscat

Population: 3,027,959

Area: 82,031 sq mi (212,460 sq km)

Language: Arabic, English, Indian dialects

Did You Know? As part of their traditional clothing, Omani men carry an ornate dagger called a khanjar tucked in the front of a special belt.

Pakistan

Capital: Islamabad

Population: 187,342,721

Area: 310,403 sq mi (803,940 sq km)

Language: Urdu, English, Punjabi, Sindhi

Did You Know? Pakistan and Syria both have close to 2 million refugees living within their borders, more than any other countries in the world.

Palau

Capital: Melekeok

Population: 20,956

Area: 177 sq mi (458 sq km)

Language: English, Palauan, Sonsoral, Tobi, Angaur

Did You Know? Palau's marine life is among the world's most diverse—more than 1,400 species of fish and 500 species of coral can be found here.

Panama

Capital: Panama City

Population: 3,460,642

Area: 30,193 sq mi (78,200 sq km)

Language: Spanish, English

Did You Know? Panama is the shortest link between the Atlantic and Pacific Oceans in the Americas, making its 50-mile-long (80-km) canal of great strategic importance.

Papua New Guinea

Capital: Port Moresby

Population: 6,187,591

Area: 178,704 sq mi (462,840 sq km)

Language: English, Motu, Melanesian pidgin

Did You Know? There are only six species of poisonous birds in the world, and they all live in Papua New Guinea.

Paraguay

Capital: Asunción

Population: 6,459,058

Area: 157,047 sq mi (406,750 sq km)

Language: Spanish, Guarani

Did You Know? Paraguay is one of two landlocked countries in South America. It and Bolivia are the only countries on the continent without a coastline.

Peru

Capital: Lima

Population: 29,248,943

Area: 496,226 sq mi (1,285,220 sq km)

Language: Spanish, Quechua, Aymara

Did You Know? More than 16,700 feet above sea level, the mining town of La Rinconada, in the Andes Mountains of Peru, is said to be the highest town in the world.

Philippines

Capital: Manila

Population: 101,833,938

Area: 115,831 sq mi (300,000 sq km)

Language: Filipino, English

Did You Know? The Battle of Leyte Gulf, fought in 1944 off the Philippines, was the biggest naval battle in history. It involved 282 Allied and Japanese ships and about 2,000 planes.

Poland

Capital: Warsaw

Population: 38,441,588

Area: 120,726 sq mi (312,679 sq km)

Language: Polish, Ukrainian, German

Did You Know? Famous people born in Poland include composer Frederic Chopin, Nobel Prize-winning scientist Marie Curie, and Pope John Paul II.

WAWEL CASTLE, POLAND

Portugal

Capital: Lisbon

Population: 10,760,305

Area: 35,672 sq mi (92,391 sq km)

Language: Portuguese

Did You Know? The national style of music, called *fado*, originated in Lisbon. It has a sad and longing sound.

Qatar

Capital: Doha

Population: 848,016

Area: 4,416 sq mi (11,437 sq km)

Language: Arabic, English

Did You Know? Qatar and Liechtenstein are the two richest countries in the world, as measured by economic output per person.

Romania

Capital: Bucharest

Population: 21,904,551

Area: 91,699 sq mi (237,500 sq km)

Language: Romanian, Hungarian, German

Did You Know? Prince Vlad Tepes ("the Impaler"), who once ruled part of Romania, was the inspiration for the fictional Dracula.

Russia

Capital: Moscow

Population: 138,739,892

Area: 6,592,772 sq mi (17,075,200 sq km)

Language: Russian, many minority languages

Did You Know? The world's biggest country, Russia spans two continents (Europe and Asia) and borders 14 other nations.

ST. BASIL'S CATHEDRAL, MOSCOW, RUSSIA

GORILLA IN VOLCANOES NATIONAL PARK, RWANDA

Rwanda

Capital: Kigali

Population: 11,370,425

Area: 10,169 sq mi (26,338 sq km)

Language: French, English, Kinyarwanda, Kiswahili

Did You Know? Volcanoes National Park is home to one of only two remaining mountain gorilla populations in the world.

Saint Kitts and Nevis

Capital: Basseterre

Population: 50,314

Area: 101 sq mi (261 sq km)

Language: English

Did You Know? This two-island state is the smallest independent nation in the Caribbean, in both size and population.

Saint Lucia

Capital: Castries

Population: 161,557

Area: 238 sq mi (616 sq km)

Language: English, French patois

Did You Know? The Caribbean island is a popular spot to visit because of its beautiful beaches, unusual plants, and the Qualibou volcano with its boiling sulphur springs.

COLOR KEY

- Africa
- Asia
- Australia
- Europe
- North America
- Pacific Islands
- South America

Saint Vincent and the Grenadines

Capital: Kingstown

Population: 103,869

Area: 150 sq mi (389 sq km)

Language: English, French patois

Did You Know? Christopher Columbus landed on the island of St. Vincent in January 1498.

Samoa (formerly Western Samoa)

Capital: Apia

Population: 193,161

Area: 1,137 sq mi (2,944 sq km)

Language: English, Samoan

Did You Know? This Pacific island nation has temperatures in the 70s and 80s (Fahrenheit) all year round.

San Marino

Capital: San Marino

Population: 31,817

Area: 24 sq mi (61 sq km)

Language: Italian

Did You Know? San Marino, a tiny nation surrounded entirely by Italy, claims to be the oldest country in Europe, dating back to the fourth century.

São Tomé and Príncipe

Capital: São Tomé

Population: 179,506

Area: 386 sq mi (1,001 sq km)

Language: Portuguese, Creole

Did You Know? Cocoa is the country's chief export, but output has declined in recent years, putting strains on the already weak economy.

Saudi Arabia

Capital: Riyadh

Population: 26,131,703

Area: 830,000 sq mi (2,149,960 sq km)

Language: Arabic

Did You Know? Saudi Arabia is the birthplace of Islam, and just about all Saudis today are Muslims. Only Muslim religious services are permitted in public.

MECCA, SAUDI ARABIA

Senegal

Capital: Dakar

Population: 12,643,799

Area: 75,749 sq mi (196,190 sq km)

Language: French, Wolof, Pulaar

Did You Know? Dakar is the westernmost point on the continent of Africa.

Serbia

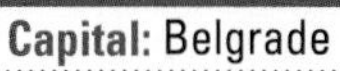

Capital: Belgrade

Population: 7,310,555

Area: 29,913 sq mi (77,474 sq km)

Language: Serbian, Albanian, Romanian

Did You Know? The Roma (Gypsies), one of Serbia's largest minority groups, have helped to maintain the country's folk music tradition.

Capital: Victoria

Population: 89,188

Area: 176 sq mi (455 sq km)

Language: Creole, English, French

Did You Know? The colors of Seychelles' flag represent the sky and sea (blue), the sun (yellow), the people and their work (red), social justice and harmony (white), and the environment (green).

Sierra Leone

Capital: Freetown

Population: 5,363,669

Area: 27,699 sq mi (71,740 sq km)

Language: English, Mende, Temne, Krio

Did You Know? The lakes and rivers of Sierra Leone are home to crocodiles and hippos.

Singapore

Capital: Singapore

Population: 4,740,737

Area: 269 sq mi (697 sq km)

Language: Chinese, Malay, Tamil, English

Did You Know? In Singapore you can be given a big fine for spitting in public, carrying chewing gum, or bringing a toy weapon or toy money into the country.

SKYLINE OF SINGAPORE

Slovakia

Capital: Bratislava

Population: 5,477,038

Area: 18,859 sq mi (48,845 sq km)

Language: Slovak, Hungarian

Did You Know? Slovakia and the Czech Republic were joined together after World War I (as the country of Czechoslovakia), but they broke up into separate nations in 1993.

Slovenia

Capital: Ljubljana

Population: 2,000,092

Area: 7,827 sq mi (20,273 sq km)

Language: Slovenian, Serbo-Croatian

Did You Know? Slovenia was part of Yugoslavia from 1918 to 1991, when it declared independence. It later became a member of the European Union and the UN.

Solomon Islands

Capital: Honiara

Population: 571,890

Area: 10,985 sq mi (28,450 sq km)

Language: English, Melanesian pidgin

Did You Know? Because so many different languages are spoken in the Solomon Islands, many people communicate using a simplified English called Melanesian pidgin.

Somalia

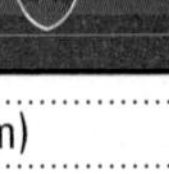

Capital: Mogadishu

Population: 9,925,640

Area: 246,201 sq mi (637,657 sq km)

Language: Somali, Arabic, Italian, English

Did You Know? As of early 2011, pirates from Somalia were holding more than 50 ships and 800 people for ransom.

South Africa

Capital: Pretoria (admin.); Cape Town (legis.); Bloemfontein (judicial)
Population: 49,004,031
Area: 471,011 sq mi (1,219,912 sq km)
Language: Afrikaans, English, Ndebele, Sotho, Zulu, Xhosa
Did You Know? South Africa is a leading source of valuable minerals, such as gold, diamonds, and platinum.

GAME RESERVE, SOUTH AFRICA

Spain

Capital: Madrid
Population: 46,754,784
Area: 194,897 sq mi (504,782 sq km)
Language: Castilian Spanish, Catalan, Galician
Did You Know? In 2010, Spain defeated the Netherlands in the finals to win its first-ever World Cup soccer championship.

Sri Lanka

Capital: Colombo
Population: 21,283,913
Area: 25,332 sq mi (65,610 sq km)
Language: Sinhala, Tamil, English
Did You Know? Ceylon tea takes its name from this country, which used to be called Ceylon while under European rule.

Sudan*

Capital: Khartoum
Population*: 45,047,502
Area*: 967,499 sq mi (2,505,810 sq km)
Language: Arabic, Nubian, Ta Bedawie
Did You Know? Khartoum is located where the White Nile and the Blue Nile rivers meet to form the main Nile River.

*Includes South Sudan, scheduled to become an independent country on July 9, 2011.

Suriname

Capital: Paramaribo
Population: 491,989
Area: 63,039 sq mi (163,270 sq km)
Language: Dutch, English, Sranang Tongo
Did You Know? Suriname is one of the most heavily forested countries in the world. Forests cover about 95 percent of the land.

Swaziland

Capital: Mbabane
Population: 1,370,424
Area: 6,704 sq mi (17,363 sq km)
Language: English, siSwati
Did You Know? Most people in Swaziland live in the countryside. Only about one out of every five people lives in a city.

Sweden

Capital: Stockholm
Population: 9,088,728
Area: 173,732 sq mi (449,964 sq km)
Language: Swedish, Sami, Finnish
Did You Know? Recent data show that Sweden has a smaller gap between rich and poor families than any other country in the world.

COLOR KEY

- Africa
- Asia
- Australia
- Europe
- North America
- Pacific Islands
- South America

MOUNT KILIMANJARO, TANZANIA

Switzerland

Capital: Bern (admin.); Lausanne (judicial)

Population: 7,639,961

Area: 15,942 sq mi (41,290 sq km)

Language: German, French, Italian, Romansch

Did You Know? The Gotthard Base tunnel is expected to be the world's longest railway tunnel when it is finished in a few years. It will extend for 35 miles through the Swiss Alps.

Syria

Capital: Damascus

Population: 22,517,750

Area: 71,498 sq mi (185,180 sq km)

Language: Arabic, Kurdish, Armenian

Did You Know? Tablets found in the ancient city of Ugarit contain one of the world's oldest alphabets, dating back to around 1400 B.C.

Taiwan

Capital: Taipei

Population: 23,071,779

Area: 13,892 sq mi (35,980 sq km)

Language: Mandarin Chinese, Taiwanese

Did You Know? Although Taiwan set up its own government in 1949, China considers Taiwan to be one of its provinces and still under its control.

Tajikistan

Capital: Dushanbe

Population: 7,627,200

Area: 55,251 sq mi (143,100 sq km)

Language: Tajik, Russian

Did You Know? Tajikistan's main source of energy is hydroelectricity. Its Nurek Dam is the highest dam in the world.

Tanzania

Capital: Dar es Salaam; Dodoma (legislative)

Population: 42,746,620

Area: 364,900 sq mi (945,087 sq km)

Language: Kiswahili (Swahili), English, Arabic

Did You Know? Mount Kilimanjaro, the tallest mountain in Africa, stands all by itself. There are no other mountains around it.

Thailand

Capital: Bangkok

Population: 66,720,153

Area: 198,457 sq mi (514,000 sq km)

Language: Thai, English

Did You Know? The king of Thailand is said to be the richest royal person in the world, worth about $30 billion.

BANGKOK, THAILAND

Timor-Leste (East Timor)

Capital: Dili

Population: 1,177,834

Area: 5,743 sq mi (14,874 sq km)

Language: Tetum, Portuguese, Indonesian, English

Did You Know? This country occupies the eastern half of Timor island; the island's western half (except for an area on the coast) belongs to Indonesia.

Togo

Capital: Lomé

Population: 6,771,993

Area: 21,925 sq mi (56,785 sq km)

Language: French, Ewe, Mina, Kabye, Dagomba

Did You Know? Togo is one of the world's leading producers of phosphates.

Tonga

Capital: Nuku'alofa

Population: 105,916

Area: 289 sq mi (748 sq km)

Language: Tongan, English

Did You Know? Tonga is ruled by the only surviving monarchy in Polynesia, though it does have a parliament in which most of the members are elected.

Trinidad and Tobago

Capital: Port-of-Spain

Population: 1,227,505

Area: 1,980 sq mi (5,128 sq km)

Language: English, Hindi, French, Spanish

Did You Know? Many people from India came to Trinidad in the 1800s to work on sugar cane plantations. Today, about 40 percent of Trinidad's population is of Indian descent.

Tunisia

Capital: Tunis

Population: 10,629,186

Area: 63,170 sq mi (163,610 sq km)

Language: Arabic, French

Did You Know? The ancient city of Carthage was located in what is now Tunisia.

Turkey

Capital: Ankara

Population: 78,785,548

Area: 301,384 sq mi (780,580 sq km)

Language: Turkish, Kurdish, Arabic

Did You Know? The Bosporus Bridge, in Istanbul, spans two continents, linking Asia with Europe. About 3% of Turkey is in Europe, and the rest in Asia.

ISTANBUL, TURKEY

Turkmenistan

Capital: Ashgabat

Population: 4,997,503

Area: 188,456 sq mi (488,100 sq km)

Language: Turkmen, Russian, Uzbek

Did You Know? Turkmenistan has the world's fourth-largest reserves of natural gas, after Russia, Iran, and Qatar.

Tuvalu

Capital: Funafuti

Population: 10,544

Area: 10 sq mi (26 sq km)

Language: Tuvaluan, English

Did You Know? Some scientists predict that because of global warming and rising sea levels these nine small islands could disappear within the next fifty years.

COLOR KEY

- Africa
- Asia
- Australia
- Europe
- North America
- Pacific Islands
- South America

LONDON EYE FERRIS WHEEL, UNITED KINGDOM

Uganda

Capital: Kampala

Population: 34,612,250

Area: 91,136 sq mi (236,040 sq km)

Language: English, Ganda, Swahili

Did You Know? The crested crane is a national symbol and appears on Uganda's flag.

Ukraine

Capital: Kiev (Kyiv)

Population: 45,134,707

Area: 233,090 sq mi (603,700 sq km)

Language: Ukrainian, Russian

Did You Know? Ukraine has the biggest area of any country in Europe, except Russia. Both Ukraine and Russia were once part of the Soviet Union.

United Arab Emirates

Capital: Abu Dhabi

Population: 5,148,664

Area: 32,278 sq mi (83,600 sq km)

Language: Arabic, Persian, English, Hindi, Urdu

Did You Know? In 2010, the Burj Khalifa (Khalifa Tower) skyscraper opened in Dubai, becoming the world's tallest building.

United Kingdom (Great Britain)

Capital: London

Population: 62,698,362

Area: 94,526 sq mi (244,820 sq km)

Language: English, Welsh, Scottish Gaelic

Did You Know? Queen Elizabeth I, Sir Isaac Newton, Charles Darwin, and Charles Dickens are among many famous people buried in London's Westminster Abbey.

United States

Capital: Washington, D.C.

Population: 308,745,538*

Area: 3,795,951 sq mi (9,831,513 sq km)

Language: English, Spanish

Did You Know? The United States uses more energy than any other country—about one-fifth of the world's total energy consumption.

*2010 U.S. Census

Uruguay

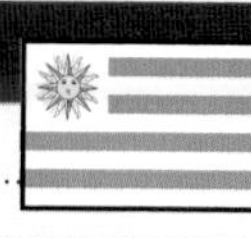

Capital: Montevideo

Population: 3,308,535

Area: 68,039 sq mi (176,220 sq km)

Language: Spanish, Portunol

Did You Know? The leaves of the *yerba maté* shrub are used to brew a popular drink in Uruguay. The tea is often drunk from a gourd using a metal straw.

Uzbekistan

Capital: Tashkent
Population: 28,128,600
Area: 172,742 sq mi (447,400 sq km)
Language: Uzbek, Russian, Tajik
Did You Know? Uzbekistan and Liechtenstein are the only two countries that are "doubly landlocked." They are surrounded entirely by other countries that also have no seacoast.

Vanuatu

Capital: Port-Vila
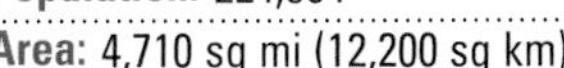
Population: 224,564
Area: 4,710 sq mi (12,200 sq km)
Language: French, English, Bislama, local languages
Did You Know? More than 100 local languages and dialects are spoken on the 80-plus islands that make up this Pacific nation.

Vatican City

Population: 832
Area: 0.17 sq mi (0.44 sq km)
Language: Italian, Latin, French
Did You Know? For many centuries before Italy was unified in the late 1800s, popes ruled over a large part of central Italy. The "Papal States" once had a population of about 3 million people.

Venezuela

Capital: Caracas
Population: 27,635,743
Area: 352,144 sq mi (912,050 sq km)
Language: Spanish, indigenous dialects
Did You Know? Venezuela produces about 2.5 million barrels of oil a day, making it the largest oil producer in South America.

ANGEL FALLS, VENEZUELA

Vietnam

Capital: Hanoi
Population: 90,549,390
Area: 127,244 sq mi (329,560 sq km)
Language: Vietnamese, English, French, Chinese
Did You Know? In 2010, Hanoi celebrated the 1,000th anniversary of its founding as a city.

Yemen

Capital: Sana'a
Population: 24,133,492
Area: 203,850 sq mi (527,970 sq km)
Language: Arabic
Did You Know? One of Yemen's chief crops is coffee. "Mocha" coffee beans take their name from the Yemeni port city of Mocha.

Zambia

Capital: Lusaka
Population: 13,881,336
Area: 290,586 sq mi (752,614 sq km)
Language: English, indigenous languages
Did You Know? Victoria Falls, one of the world's largest waterfalls, provides Zambia with a source of hydroelectric power.

Zimbabwe

Capital: Harare
Population: 12,084,304
Area: 150,804 sq mi (390,580 sq km)
Language: English, Shona, Sindebele
Did You Know? The nation takes its name from the famous stone ruins of Great Zimbabwe, a city built by wealthy Shona-speaking cattlemen between the 13th and 14th centuries.

COLOR KEY

- Africa
- Asia
- Australia
- Europe
- North America
- Pacific Islands
- South America

NUMBERS

What is a perfect number? → page 179

To Infinity...and Beyond

The set of numbers includes all different types—positive and negative numbers, fractions and decimals, and even irrational numbers that cannot be expressed as a fraction. In math, numbers are thought of as infinite because you can always imagine a larger number. For example, what's the biggest number you know? Add 1 to that number and you have a bigger number! Both positive and negative numbers go on to infinity.

The symbol for infinity looks like an eight lying on its side.

Prime Time

All numbers—except 0 and 1—are either prime numbers or composite numbers. A prime number is a number that can be divided only by itself and the number 1. So, prime numbers include 2, 3, 5, 7, 11, 13, 17, and so on. All other positive numbers (other than 1) are called composite numbers, because they have at least two factors (numbers they can be divided by evenly) other than 1. For example, 6 is a composite number. Its factors are 1, 2, 3, and 6.

Integers

Integers are whole numbers, both positive and negative. Zero is an integer. Fractions, decimals, and percentages are not.

The Prefix Tells the Number

After each number shown below, there are one or more prefixes, which are used to form words that include that number. Knowing what the prefix stands for can help you understand the meaning of the word. For example, a **bi**cycle has two wheels. The pieces in the video game *Tetris* have four squares.

1	uni-, mono-	unicorn, monorail
2	bi-	binoculars
3	tri-	triangle
4	quadr-, tetr-	quadrangle, tetrahedron
5	pent-, quint-	pentagon, quintuplet
6	hex-, sext-	hexagon, sextuplet
7	hept-, sept-	heptathlon, septuplet

8	oct-	octopus
9	non-	nonagon
10	dec-	decade
100	cent-	century
1,000	kilo-	kilometer
million	mega-	megabyte
billion	giga-	gigabyte

ROMAN NUMERALS

People have been counting since the earliest of times. The counting system used by the ancient Romans is still in use today. Roman numerals are built from different letters. The chart below shows some common Roman numerals.

1	I	16	XVI
2	II	17	XVII
3	III	18	XVIII
4	IV	19	XIX
5	V	20	XX
6	VI	30	XXX
7	VII	40	XL
8	VIII	50	L
9	IX	60	LX
10	X	70	LXX
11	XI	80	LXXX
12	XII	90	XC
13	XIII	100	C
14	XIV	500	D
15	XV	1,000	M

If one Roman numeral is followed by one with a greater value, the first is subtracted from the second. For example, IX means 10 – 1 = 9. Think of it as "one less than ten." On the other hand, if a Roman numeral is followed by one or more others that are equal or of lesser value, add them together. Thus, LXI means 50 + 10 + 1 = 61.

A Roman numeral can be repeated only three times to express a number. For example, XXX equals 30. You would have to write XL (50 minus 10) to show the number 40.

One place you might see Roman numerals used is in the Super Bowl. In 2011, the Green Bay Packers won Super Bowl XLV. What number Super Bowl was that? How would you write 2011 in Roman numerals?

Super Bowl I was played in 1967. What was the Roman numeral used for the Super Bowl played in 1977?

ANSWERS ON PAGES 334–336.

Zero

Do you know the Roman numeral for 0? Probably not, because there isn't one! The Babylonians in Asia, Hindus in India, and Mayans in the Americas were among the first peoples to use the idea of zero as a "placeholder." In our number system "10" means 1 "ten" and 0 "ones." The 0 in 10 is a placeholder in the ones column.

Zero has some interesting properties. Any number multiplied by 0 equals 0. Any number added to 0 equals the original number.

Super Bowl XLV

***A perfect number** is a whole number that is equal to the sum of all of its factors (numbers it can be divided by evenly) less than itself. For example, the smallest perfect number is six (1 + 2 + 3 = 6), and the second-smallest is 28 (1 + 2 + 4 + 7 + 14 = 28). Greek mathematicians knew about the first four perfect numbers (6, 28, 496, and 8,128) more than 2,000 years ago.*

Fractions, Decimals, and Percents

FRACTIONS

A fraction is part of a whole. It helps to think of a fraction as a slice of a circle, with the circle being the whole (represented by the number 1). Check out the common fractions at right.

1/2

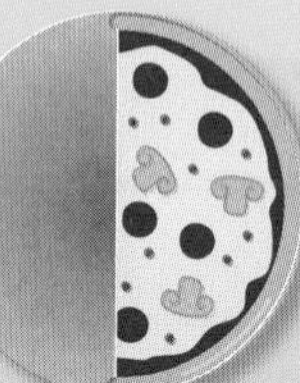

1/2 is missing

2/3

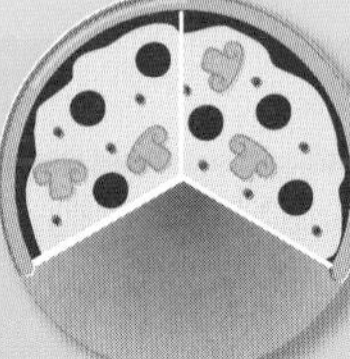

1/3 is missing

7/8

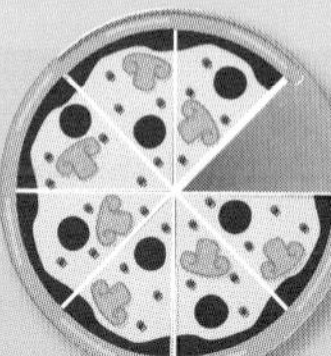

1/8 is missing

HOMEWORK TIP

To reduce a fraction to its lowest terms, divide both the numerator (top number) and the denominator (bottom number) by the largest number by which both can be divided evenly. For example, to reduce 8/16 to its lowest terms, divide the numerator and denominator by 8. You end up with 1/2.

PERCENTS

Percents also represent part of a whole. The word *percent* means "per hundred." So, a percent is like a fraction with a denominator of 100. You see percents every day. If you scored 80 percent on a test at school, you received 80 points out of a possible 100. Changing percents to fractions is not hard. Here are two examples:

80% = 80/100; reduced to its lowest terms, 80/100 becomes 4/5
23% = 23/100, which cannot be reduced

DECIMALS

Decimals are also part of a whole. They are represented with numerals placed to the right of a decimal point. Each position—or place—in a decimal has its own name.

7.75

ones place **tenths place** **hundredths place**

HOMEWORK TIP

To convert a decimal to a fraction or a percent, you have to pay attention to the placement after the decimal point. For example, 0.2 means 2 tenths, or 2/10, which can be reduced to 1/5. And think of 0.25 as 25 hundredths, or 25/100, which can be reduced to 1/4. To convert a decimal to a percent, just move the decimal point to the right of the hundredths place:
0.25 = 25% and 0.025 = 2.5%

Can you change these decimals to fractions that are reduced to lowest terms?
0.4 0.75 0.9

ANSWERS ON PAGES 334–336.

Go Figure

Grab your thinking cap—and a calculator! It's time to put your numbers knowledge to the test. Solve the math problem or puzzle in each clue. Then fill in the correct answer in the puzzle. (Write out the word or words. Don't use numerals.) We've filled in one of them for you. Ready? 1-2-3 go!

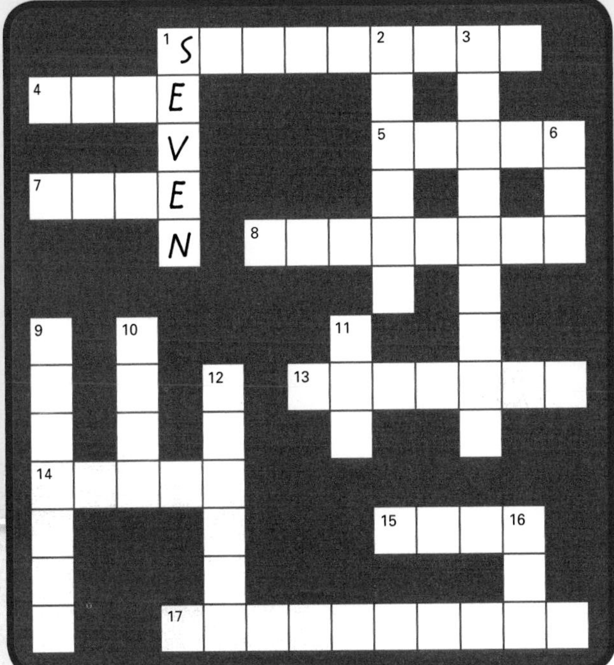

ACROSS

1. 7, 11, 13, __, 19, 23

4. XLVIII minus XXXIX

5. Jacob made 40 percent of the 20 shots he took at his basketball game. How many baskets did he sink?

7. How many more sides does an octagon have than a triangle?

8. XIII multiplied by IV

13. Grandpa Max has been alive for three decades less than a century. How many years old is he?

14. Emma has 12 pieces of gum. If she gives 1/2 of her gum to friends and chews 1/4 of it herself, how many pieces does she have left?

15. 101 x 0

17. Your favorite TV show starts in one hour and 2,400 seconds. In how many minutes will it begin?

DOWN

1. 420 minutes = __ hours

2. 6.85 + 8.77 + 4.38

3. 3, 9, __, 6,561

6. What is the lowest prime number?

9. Michael has a 25-percent discount coupon that he plans to use to buy a video game that sells for $20. How many dollars will the game cost him with the discount?

10. Olivia has $1.82 in her change purse. She has five quarters, three nickels, and two pennies. The rest of her change is dimes. How many dimes does she have?

11. If a rabbit hops 100 feet in one minute, how many feet does it travel in six seconds?

12. 1, 3, 4, 7, __, 18

16. 3/14 + 5/14 + 3/7

ANSWERS ON PAGES 334–336.

POPULATION

What state grew the fastest between 2000 and 2010? → page 184

WHERE DO PEOPLE LIVE?

In 1959, there were 3 billion people in the world. By 1999, there were 6 billion. The United Nations estimated that the world population would reach 7 billion during 2011 and pass 9 billion by 2050.

Russia is the largest nation in area, with over 6.5 million square miles of land. China is a distant second, with 3.6 million square miles. China and India are the biggest nations in population, with more than a billion people each.

POPULATIONS

LARGEST (2011)

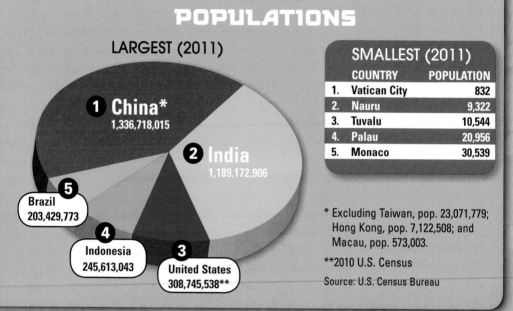

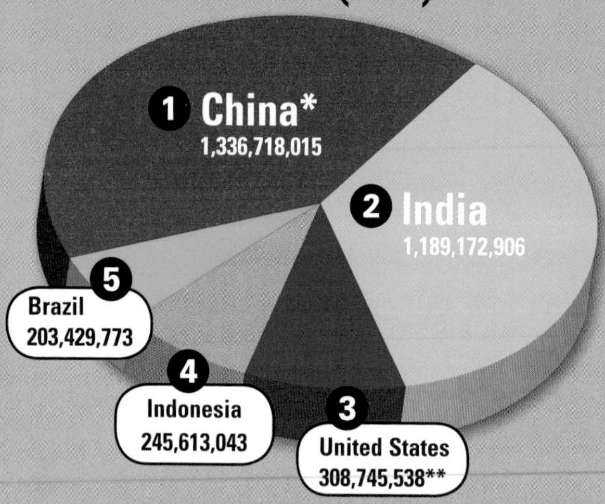

SMALLEST (2011)

	COUNTRY	POPULATION
1.	Vatican City	832
2.	Nauru	9,322
3.	Tuvalu	10,544
4.	Palau	20,956
5.	Monaco	30,539

* Excluding Taiwan, pop. 23,071,779; Hong Kong, pop. 7,122,508; and Macau, pop. 573,003.

**2010 U.S. Census

Source: U.S. Census Bureau

MOST SPARSELY POPULATED

	COUNTRY	PERSONS PER SQ MI
1.	Mongolia	5.2
2.	Namibia	6.8
3.	Australia	7.3
4.	Iceland	8.0
5.	Suriname	8.2

To get the population density, divide the population by the area. Density is calculated here according to land area and is based on 2011 population.

MOST DENSELY POPULATED

	COUNTRY	PERSONS PER SQ MI*
1.	Monaco	39,661
2.	Singapore	17,890
3.	Vatican City	4,894
4.	Bahrain	4,247
5.	Maldives	3,435

* For comparison, New Jersey is the most densely populated U.S. state, with about 1,196 people per square mile in 2010.

ALL ABOUT POPULATION GROWTH

There are more people in the world now than ever before. Historically, population growth rates were low, but they started to increase in the 17th and 18th centuries. The world grew very fast in the 20th century. While growth is expected to slow down, the United Nations estimates the world population will still increase by 2 billion people between now and 2050.

Almost all this growth will be in poorer countries. In developed countries, more people are older, and families also have fewer children. In some of these countries, the population is falling. Japan's population is projected to decline about 20% by 2050. People aged 65 or older will then make up almost 40% of the population.

About four in every ten people on Earth today live in China or India. India is expected to overtake China to become the world's most populous country by around 2025. Its current population is projected to climb by about 30% by 2050, to over 1.6 billion. About two-thirds of the people will be between 15 and 64 years old.

What does all that mean? For Japan, there will be fewer workers and fewer people to take care of the older population. Having more workers may help India develop its economy. But high population growth puts a strain on land and resources, especially in developing countries, where many people are poor.

YOUNGEST AND AGING POPULATIONS

Here are the countries that have the highest and lowest percentages of people who are under 15 years of age. (In the United States, 20.2% of the population is under 15 years old.)

YOUNGEST:	% under 15 years old
Uganda	49.9%
Niger	49.6%
Mali	47.3%
Zambia	46.7%

OLDEST:	% under 15 years old
Monaco	12.3%
Japan	13.1%
Germany	13.3%
Slovenia	13.4%

Source: *CIA World Factbook;* estimates for 2011.

THE WORLD'S BIGGEST MEGA CITIES

Many people live in and around cities, in a large area sometimes called a "mega-city" or an "urban agglomeration." The area may include more than one city when the cities are close together. These are the biggest mega-cities according to United Nations estimates for 2010. (See page 185 for the 10 biggest U.S. cities.)

Mumbai, India

CITY, COUNTRY	POPULATION
1. Tokyo, Japan	36,669,000
2. Delhi, India	22,157,000
3. Sao Paulo, Brazil	20,262,000
4. Mumbai, India	20,041,000
5. Mexico City, Mexico	19,460,000
6. New York/Newark, U.S.	19,425,000

Source: *World Urbanization Prospects*

CENSUS 2010

COUNTING THE AMERICAN PEOPLE

As required by the Constitution, the federal government carries out a census every ten years, to try to count all the people living in the United States. The latest census was in 2010. The Census Bureau mailed out forms in March to every house or other place where people lived. Places such as hospitals and prisons were included. People were asked to complete the form and mail it back by Census Day, April 1, 2010. Census workers tried to visit every place that did not send back a form. They also tried to find homeless people.

The census population for each state determines how many of the 435 seats it will get in the U.S. House of Representatives. After every census, some states gain seats and some lose seats (see page 260 for the gainers and losers). Census population figures are also used to determine how seats in state legislatures are distributed within each state. In addition, the census information about people and where they live is used to help the government decide where to spend money for different services.

After every census there are complaints that some people—often members of minority groups—were left uncounted. But no census can be perfect, and census results are not usually changed.

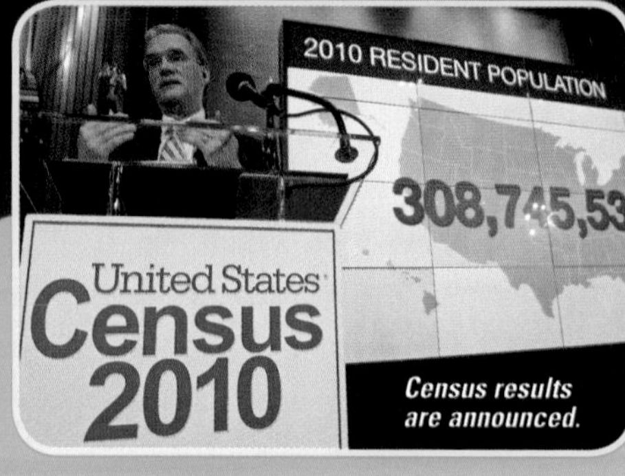

Census results are announced.

2010 Census Facts

- The 2010 U.S. Census counted 308,745,538 people living in the United States.
- From 2000 to 2010 the nation's population grew by 9.7%, the slowest percentage growth since the 1930s.
- Most of the growth was in the South and West. Nevada's population rose the fastest, by 35%.
- California and Texas are the biggest states in population. Wyoming is the smallest.
- New immigrants, and children born to them, accounted for about three-fourth of the nation's population growth from 2000 to 2010.
- Hispanic Americans, who may be of any race, accounted for more than half of the nation's growth. Hispanic Americans are now the largest minority group (making up 16% of the population).
- African Americans make up about 13% of the population.
- Asian Americans account for only about 5% of the population, but they are the fastest growing racial group (up 43.3% from 2000 to 2010).
- American Indians, native Hawaiians, and Alaska natives together account for about 1%.

THE GROWING U.S. POPULATION

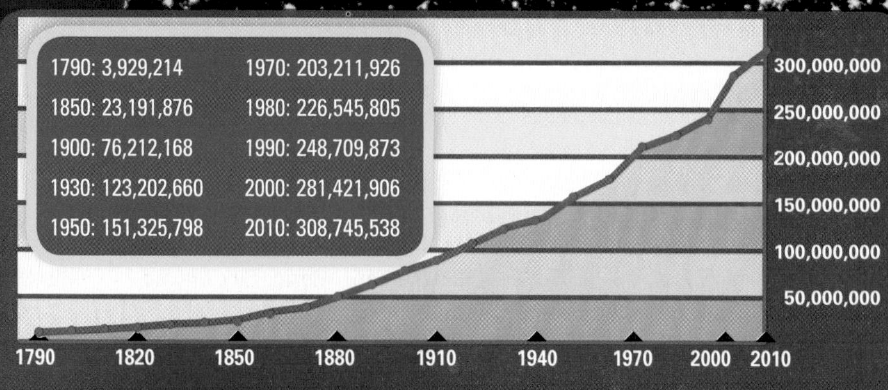

POPULATION OF THE UNITED STATES, 2010

as of April 1, 2010, based on U.S. Census figures

RANK & STATE NAME	POPULATION	RANK & STATE NAME	POPULATION
1. California (CA)	37,253,956	27. Oregon (OR)	3,831,074
2. Texas (TX)	25,145,561	28. Oklahoma (OK)	3,751,351
3. New York (NY)	19,378,102	29. Connecticut (CT)	3,574,097
4. Florida (FL)	18,801,310	30. Iowa (IA)	3,046,355
5. Illinois (IL)	12,830,632	31. Mississippi (MS)	2,967,297
6. Pennsylvania (PA)	12,702,379	32. Arkansas (AR)	2,915,918
7. Ohio (OH)	11,536,504	33. Kansas (KS)	2,853,118
8. Michigan (MI)	9,883,640	34. Utah (UT)	2,763,885
9. Georgia (GA)	9,687,653	35. Nevada (NV)	2,700,551
10. North Carolina (NC)	9,535,483	36. New Mexico (NM)	2,059,179
11. New Jersey (NJ)	8,791,894	37. West Virginia (WV)	1,852,994
12. Virginia (VA)	8,001,024	38. Nebraska (NE)	1,826,341
13. Washington (WA)	6,724,540	39. Idaho (ID)	1,567,582
14. Massachusetts (MA)	6,547,629	40. Hawaii (HI)	1,360,301
15. Indiana (IN)	6,483,802	41. Maine (ME)	1,328,361
16. Arizona (AZ)	6,392,017	42. New Hampshire (NH)	1,316,470
17. Tennessee (TN)	6,346,105	43. Rhode Island (RI)	1,052,567
18. Missouri (MO)	5,988,927	44. Montana (MT)	989,415
19. Maryland (MD)	5,773,552	45. Delaware (DE)	900,877
20. Wisconsin (WI)	5,686,986	46. South Dakota (SD)	814,180
21. Minnesota (MN)	5,303,925	47. Alaska (AK)	710,231
22. Colorado (CO)	5,029,196	48. North Dakota (ND)	672,591
23. Alabama (AL)	4,779,736	49. Vermont (VT)	625,741
24. South Carolina (SC)	4,625,364	50. District of Columbia (DC)	601,723
25. Louisiana (LA)	4,533,372	51. Wyoming (WY)	563,626
26. Kentucky (KY)	4,339,367	TOTAL U.S. POPULATION	308,745,538

LARGEST CITIES IN THE UNITED STATES

Cities grow and shrink in population. Below is a list of the largest U.S. cities in 2010. Their 1950 populations are shown for comparison. Populations are for people living within the city limits only.

RANK & CITY	2010	1950
1. New York, NY	8,175,133	7,891,957
2. Los Angeles, CA	3,792,621	1,970,358
3. Chicago, IL	2,695,598	3,620,962
4. Houston, TX	2,099,451	596,163
5. Philadelphia, PA	1,526,006	2,071,605
6. Phoenix, AZ	1,445,632	106,818
7. San Antonio, TX	1,327,407	408,442
8. San Diego, CA	1,307,402	434,462
9. Dallas, TX	1,197,816	334,387
10. San Jose, CA	945,942	95,280

Source: U.S. Census Bureau, 1950 and 2010 Census results

THE MANY FACES OF AMERICA: IMMIGRATION

The number of Americans who were born in another country (foreign-born) has risen in recent decades. It reached 38 million in 2007, or almost 13% of the population. That was the highest percentage since 1930. There has been some falloff in immigration since 2007, mostly because of the U.S. economic recession, but immigration levels remain high. In contrast to the early 1900s, when most immigrants came from Europe, most now come from other parts of the world. In 2009, 53% of foreign-born Americans could trace their origins to Latin America, and 28% to Asia. Only 13% were born in Europe.

Immigrants come for various reasons, such as to escape poverty or oppression and to make better lives for themselves and their children. The figures below, from the Department of Homeland Security, cover legal immigrants only. Each year hundreds of thousands of people come across the border illegally or overstay a temporary visa. (Visas are official government documents that grant permission for a person to visit, work, or attend school in another country.) The U.S. government estimated there were about 11 million unauthorized immigrants in the country in 2010, including almost 7 million from Mexico.

What Countries Do Immigrants Come From?

A total of 619,913 immigrants were naturalized—that is, were sworn in—as U.S. citizens in the 12-month period ending September 30, 2010. The table below shows the countries where the largest numbers of these immigrants came from.

COUNTRY	Number	Percent of total
Mexico	67,062	10.8
India	61,142	9.9
Philippines	35,465	5.7
China*	33,969	5.5
Vietnam	19,313	3.1
Colombia	18,417	3.0
Dominican Republic	15,451	2.5
Cuba	14,050	2.3
Haiti	12,291	2.0
Jamaica	12,070	1.9
Pakistan	11,601	1.9
South Korea	11,170	1.8
El Salvador	10,343	1.7
Iran	9,337	1.5
Nigeria	9,126	1.5

*Excluding Taiwan, Hong Kong, and Macau

Where Do Immigrants Settle?

In the 12 months ending September 30, 2010, 1,042,625 people from foreign countries became "legal permanent residents" of the U.S. One out of five of these immigrants, including large numbers from Vietnam, Mexico, and the Philippines, settled in California. Around half of those born in the Dominican Republic settled in New York. Florida was the destination for most of the immigrants from Haiti and the vast majority of those from Cuba.

State	Number
California	208,446
New York	147,999
Florida	107,376
Texas	87,750
New Jersey	56,920
Illinois	37,909
Massachusetts	31,069

The states shown here were home to two out of three immigrants who became legal permanent residents of the U.S. in 2010.

New U.S. citizens are sworn in.▼

All About Hispanic Americans

Hispanics, or Latinos, are people of any race who trace their heritage back to Mexico, Puerto Rico, Cuba, the Dominican Republic, or any other Spanish-speaking culture in the Americas or elsewhere in the world. In 2010, there were more than 50 million Hispanics in the U.S., making up about 16% of the population. Six out of ten were born in the U.S.

Hispanics are the largest minority group in the U.S., and their numbers are growing rapidly. By 2050, they are expected to make up close to 30% of the population.

According to the 2010 U.S. Census, there were about 14 million Hispanics living in California, more than in any other state. Texas ranked second, with a Hispanic population of 9.5 million. Florida followed, with about 4.2 million Hispanics, and New York ranked fourth, with 3.4 million.

New Mexico had the highest percentage of Hispanics in its population. In 2010, about 46% of New Mexico's residents were Hispanic. California and Texas had the second- and third-highest percentage of Hispanic people, with about 38% each.

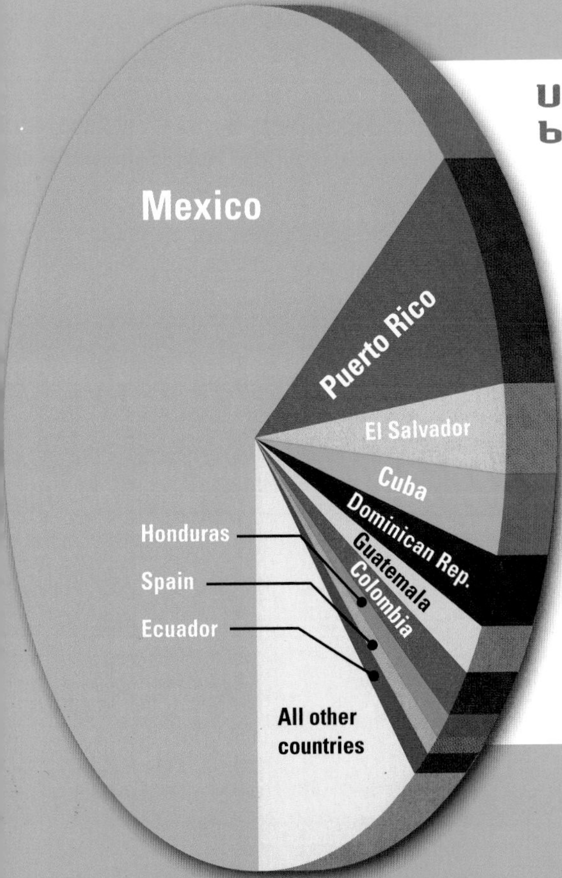

U.S. Hispanic Population by Place of Origin, 2009

Place	Number	Percent of All Hispanics
Mexico	31,673,700	65.5
Puerto Rico	4,411,604	9.1
El Salvador	1,736,221	3.6
Cuba	1,677,158	3.5
Dominican Rep.	1,640,180	2.8
Guatemala	1,077,412	2.2
Colombia	916,616	1.9
Honduras	624,533	1.3
Spain	613,585	1.3
Ecuador	611,457	1.3
All other countries	3,365,678	7.5

Source: Pew Hispanic Center; American Community Survey, U.S. Census Bureau

PRIZES & CONTESTS

Who won the Kids' Choice Award for TV Actress? → page 189

NOBEL PRIZES

The Nobel Prizes are named after Alfred B. Nobel (1833–1896), a Swedish scientist who invented dynamite and who left money for most of the prizes. They are given every year for promoting peace, as well as for achievements in physics, chemistry, physiology or medicine, literature, and economics.

◄ In 2010, writer and political activist **Liu Xiaobo** was awarded the Nobel Peace Prize "for his long and non-violent struggle for fundamental human rights in China."

Past winners of the Nobel Peace Prize include:

2009 Barack Obama, U.S. president, for his efforts in international diplomacy

2007 Al Gore Jr. (former U.S. vice president) and the International Panel on Climate Change, for their efforts in educating the world about global warming

2004 Wangari Maathai, Kenyan environmentalist and social reformer ▼

2002 Jimmy Carter, former U.S. president and peace negotiator

1997 Jody Williams and the International Campaign to Ban Landmines

1993 Nelson Mandela, leader of South African blacks; **F. W. de Klerk,** president of South Africa

1991 Aung San Suu Kyi, activist for democracy in Myanmar (Burma)

1989 Dalai Lama, Tibetan Buddhist leader, forced into exile in 1959

1986 Elie Wiesel, Holocaust survivor and author

1979 Mother Teresa, leader of the order of the Missionaries of Charity, who cared for the sick and dying in India

1964 Martin Luther King Jr., civil rights leader

1954 Albert Schweitzer, missionary, surgeon

1919 Woodrow Wilson, U.S. president who played a key role in founding the League of Nations

1906 Theodore Roosevelt, U.S. president who helped negotiate a peace treaty between Japan and Russia

ENTERTAINMENT AWARDS

2011 KIDS' CHOICE AWARDS

The 2011 Kids' Choice Awards were held Saturday, April 2, 2011, and hosted by Jack Black (above). More than 200 million votes were cast by kids to choose the winners. For more information, go to: ***www.nick.com***

Kids' Choice Award winners in 2011 included:

- Music Group . . . . The Black Eyed Peas
- Movie . . . . *The Karate Kid*
- Book . . . . *Diary of a Wimpy Kid* series
- Video Game . . . . *Just Dance 2*
- Favorite Buttkicker . . Jackie Chan
- Reality TV Show. . . . . *American Idol*
- TV Show . . . . *iCarly*
- Cartoon . . . . *SpongeBob SquarePants*
- TV Actor . . . . Dylan Sprouse
- TV Actress . . . . Selena Gomez
- TV Sidekick . . . . Jennette McCurdy
- Movie Actor . . . . Johnny Depp
- Movie Actress . . . . Miley Cyrus
- Animated Movie. . . . . *Despicable Me*
- Voice from an Animated Movie . . . . Eddie Murphy *(Shrek Forever After)*
- Male Singer . . . . Justin Bieber
- Female Singer. . . . . Katy Perry
- Song . . . . "Baby," Justin Bieber
- Male Athlete. . . . . Shaquille O'Neal
- Female Athlete. . . . . Lindsey Vonn
- Big Help Award . . . . Justin Timberlake

did you Know? ***The Big Help Award is given to someone who has taken action to make the world better. In 2011, Justin Timberlake received the award in part for his efforts to raise money for children's health care.***

BEE INVOLVED

If you have a knack for spelling or an interest in world geography, then these two national contests may be for you.

NATIONAL SPELLING BEE

The National Spelling Bee was started in Louisville, Kentucky, by the *Courier-Journal* in 1925. Today, newspapers across the U.S. run spelling bees for kids 15 and under. Winners may qualify for the Scripps National Spelling Bee held in Washington, D.C., in late May or early June. If interested, ask your school principal about enrolling your school. (For a behind-the-scenes look at the National Spelling Bee, try the 2002 film *Spellbound*.)

Sukanya Roy, 14, from South Abington Township, Pennsylvania, won the 84th annual Scripps National Spelling Bee contest on June 2, 2011. She won the bee by correctly spelling the word "cymotrichous," an adjective that means having wavy hair. "I went through the dictionary once or twice," she said, "and I guess some of the words really stuck."

For more information, visit: *www.spellingbee.com*

Here are some of the words used in the 2011 spelling bee. Some of them are just a little bit difficult!

abhinaya	**exsufflation**
capoeira	**galoubet**
cheongsam	**polatouche**
opodeldoc	**bondieuserie**
anaphylaxis	**sorites**
brachygraphy	**rougeot**

NATIONAL GEOGRAPHIC BEE

The 2011 winner is...

Tine Valencic, a 13-year old from Colleyville, Texas. Valencic won the 23rd National Geographic Bee by answering this question: "Thousands of mountain climbers and trekkers rely on Sherpas to aid their ascent of Mount Everest. The southern part of Mount Everest is in which Nepalese national park?" (The answer: Sagarmatha National Park.) Valencic won a $25,000 scholarship for college, a trip to the Galapagos Islands, and a lifetime membership in the National Geographic Society. He has been interested in geography since kindergarten, when he was given an atlas as a gift.

The National Geographic Bee draws 5 million contestants from more than 12,000 schools in all parts of the United States. To enter, you must be in grades 4–8. School-level bees are followed by state-level bees and then the nationals (which are moderated by *Jeopardy!* host Alex Trebek).

For more information, visit: ***www.nationalgeographic.com/geobee***

ODD Contests

It just seems to be part of human nature to find out who is the best at something, no matter what it is! There are state, national, and international competitions in a wide variety of events. Most of them are commonplace ones such as foot races or trivia contests. But then there are others that are more unusual. Here are a few contests that are not very ordinary.

Duct Tape Prom Outfits

Couples entering the Duck® Brand Duct Tape Stuck on Prom Contest must attend a high school prom wearing complete outfits and accessories made from duct tape. The winning couple is chosen based on originality, workmanship, quantity of Duck Tape used, use of colors, and creative use of accessories. The first place couple each receives a $5,000 scholarship and a $5,000 cash prize is awarded to the school that hosted the prom.

For more information, visit: ***www.stuckatprom.com***

Rotten Sneaker Contest

The National Odor-Eaters Rotten Sneaker Contest is held annually in Montpelier, Vermont. In 2011, the panel of judges included NASA "Master Sniffer" George Aldrich, a chemical specialist for space missions. Each year, the winner's sneakers are added to the Odor-Eaters "Hall of Fumes." Other prizes for the 2011 winner included $2,500, the Golden Sneaker Award trophy, a supply of Odor-Eaters® products, and a trip to see the play *Mary Poppins* on Broadway in New York City.

For more information, visit: ***www.odor-eaters.com***

Make It With Wool

The National Make It Yourself with Wool (NMIYWW) competition awards scholarships to creative students who make outfits out of wool. Winners receive $2,000 and $1,000 scholarships. In 2011, finalists from 31 states modeled their creations at the national competition in Denver, Colorado.

For more information, visit: ***www.sheepusa.org***

RELIGION

How many Hindus are there in the world? → page 193

How did the universe begin? Why are we here on Earth? What happens to us after we die? For most people, religion provides answers to questions like these. Believing in a God or gods, or in a higher power, is one way people make sense of the world around them. Religion can also help guide people's lives.

Different religions have different beliefs. For example, Christians, Jews, and Muslims are monotheists, meaning they believe in only one God. Hindus are polytheists, meaning they believe in many gods. On this page and the next are some facts about the world's major religions.

Christianity

WHO STARTED CHRISTIANITY? Christianity is based on the teachings of Jesus Christ. He was born in Bethlehem between 8 B.C. and 4 B.C. and died about A.D. 29.

WHAT WRITINGS ARE THERE? The **Bible**, consisting of the Old Testament and New Testament, is the main spiritual text in Christianity.

WHAT DO CHRISTIANS BELIEVE? There is only one God. God sent his Son, Jesus Christ, to Earth. Jesus died to save humankind but later rose from the dead.

HOW MANY ARE THERE? Christianity is the world's biggest religion. In 2009, there were about 2.3 billion Christians worldwide.

WHAT KINDS ARE THERE? More than one billion Christians are **Roman Catholics**, who follow the Pope's leadership. **Orthodox Christians** accept similar teachings but follow different leadership. **Protestants** disagree with many Catholic teachings. They believe in the Bible's authority.

Buddhism

WHO STARTED BUDDHISM? Siddhartha Gautama (the Buddha), around 525 B.C.

WHAT WRITINGS ARE THERE? The Tripitaka, or "Three Baskets," contains three collections of teachings, rules, and commentaries. There are also other texts, many of which are called sutras.

WHAT DO BUDDHISTS BELIEVE? Buddha taught that life is filled with suffering. Through meditation and deeds, one can end the cycle of endless birth and rebirth and achieve a state of perfect peace known as nirvana.

HOW MANY ARE THERE? In 2009, there were about 484 million Buddhists in the world, 94% of them in Asia.

WHAT KINDS ARE THERE? There are two main kinds: Theravada ("Way of the Elders") Buddhism, the older kind, is more common in countries such as Sri Lanka, Myanmar, and Thailand. Mahayana ("Great Vehicle") Buddhism is more common in China, Korea, Japan, and Tibet.

Hinduism

WHO STARTED HINDUISM? The beliefs of Aryans, who migrated to India around 1500 B.C., intermixed with the beliefs of the people who already lived there.

WHAT WRITINGS ARE THERE? The **Vedas** ("Knowledge") collect the most important writings in Hinduism, including the ancient hymns in the **Samhita** and the teachings in the **Upanishads.** Also important are the stories the **Bhagavad-Gita** and the **Ramayana**.

WHAT DO HINDUS BELIEVE? There is one divine principle, known as **brahman**; the various gods are only aspects of it. Life is an aspect of, yet separate from the divine. To escape a meaningless cycle of birth and rebirth (**samsara**), one must improve one's **karma** (the purity or impurity of one's past deeds).

HOW MANY ARE THERE? In 2009, there were about 935 million Hindus, mainly in India and in places that people from India have immigrated to.

WHAT KINDS ARE THERE? Most Hindus are primarily devoted to a single deity, the most common being the gods **Vishnu** and **Shiva** and the goddess **Shakti**.

Islam

WHO STARTED ISLAM? Muhammad, the Prophet, about A.D. 622.

WHAT WRITINGS ARE THERE? The **Koran** (*al-Qur'an* in Arabic), is regarded as the word of God. The **Sunna**, or example of the Prophet, is recorded in the **Hadith**.

WHAT DO MUSLIMS BELIEVE? People who practice Islam are known as Muslims. There is only one God. God revealed the Koran to Muhammad so he could teach humankind truth and justice. Those who "submit" (literal meaning of "Islam") to God will attain salvation.

HOW MANY ARE THERE? In 2009, there more than 1.5 billion Muslims, mostly in parts of Africa and Asia.

WHAT KINDS ARE THERE? There are two major groups: the Sunnis, who make up about 84% of the world's Muslims, and the Shiites, who broke away in a dispute over leadership after Muhammad died in 632.

Judaism

WHO STARTED JUDAISM? Abraham is thought to be the founder of Judaism, one of the first monotheistic religions. He probably lived between 2000 B.C. and 1500 B.C.

WHAT WRITINGS ARE THERE? The most important is the **Torah** ("Law"), comprising the five books of Moses. The **Nevi'im** ("Prophets") and **Ketuvim** ("Writings") are also part of the Hebrew Bible.

WHAT DO JEWS BELIEVE? There is one God who created and rules the universe. One should be faithful to God and observe God's laws.

HOW MANY ARE THERE? In 2009, there were about 14.5 million Jews around the world. Many live in Israel or the United States.

WHAT KINDS ARE THERE? In the U.S. there are three main forms: **Orthodox**, **Conservative**, and **Reform**. Orthodox Jews are the most traditional, following strict laws about dress and diet. Reform Jews are the least traditional. Conservative Jews are somewhere in-between.

Major Holy Days

FOR CHRISTIANS, JEWS, MUSLIMS, BUDDHISTS, AND HINDUS

CHRISTIAN HOLY DAYS

	2012	2013	2014
Ash Wednesday	February 22	February 13	March 5
Good Friday	April 6	March 29	April 18
Easter Sunday	April 8	March 31	April 20
Easter for Orthodox Churches	April 15	May 5	April 20
Christmas*	December 25	December 25	December 25

*Russian and some other Orthodox churches celebrate Christmas in January.

JEWISH HOLY DAYS

The Jewish holy days begin at sundown the night before the first full day of the observance. The dates of first full days are listed below.

	2012–2013 (5773)	2013–2014 (5774)	2014–2015 (5775)
Rosh Hashanah (New Year)	September 17, 2012	September 5, 2013	September 25, 2014
Yom Kippur (Day of Atonement)	September 26, 2012	September 14, 2013	October 4, 2014
Hanukkah (Festival of Lights)	December 9, 2012	November 28, 2013	December 17, 2014
Passover	March 26, 2013	April 15, 2014	April 4, 2015

ISLAMIC (MUSLIM) HOLY DAYS

The Islamic holy days begin at sundown the night before the first full day of the observance. The dates of first full days are listed below.

	2011–2012 (1433)	2012–2013 (1434)	2013–2014 (1435)
Muharram 1 (New Year)	November 26, 2011	November 15, 2012	November 4, 2013
Mawlid (Birthday of Muhammad)	February 4, 2012	January 24, 2013	January 13, 2014
Ramadan (Month of Fasting)	July 20, 2012	July 9, 2013	June 28, 2014
Eid al-Fitr (End of Ramadan)	August 19, 2012	August 8, 2013	July 28, 2014
Eid al-Adha	October 26, 2012	October 15, 2013	October 4, 2014

BUDDHIST HOLY DAYS

Not all Buddhists use the same calendar to determine holidays and festivals. A few well-known Buddhist observances and the months in which they may fall are listed below.

NIRVANA DAY, **February:** Marks the death of Siddhartha Gautama (the Buddha).

VESAK OR VISAKAH PUJA (BUDDHA DAY), **April/May:** Celebrates the birth, enlightenment, and death of the Buddha.

ASALHA PUJA (DHARMA DAY), **July:** Commemorates the Buddha's first teaching

MAGHA PUJA OR SANGHA DAY, **February:** Commemorates the day when 1,250 of Buddha's followers (**sangha**) visited him without his calling them.

VASSA (RAINS RETREAT), **July-October:** A three-month period during Asia's rainy season when monks travel little and spend more time on meditation and study. Sometimes called Buddhist Lent

HINDU HOLY DAYS

Different Hindu groups use different calendars. A few of the many Hindu festivals and the months in which they may fall are listed below.

MAHA SHIVARATRI, **February/March:** Festival dedicated to Shiva, creator and destroyer.

HOLI, **February/March:** Festival of spring

RAMANAVAMI, **March/April:** Celebrates the birth of Rama, the seventh incarnation of Vishnu.

DIWALI, **October/November:** Festival of Lights

All About Mormonism

The Mormon faith, also known as the Church of Jesus Christ of Latter-day Saints, was founded in the 1830s. Its founder was Joseph Smith Jr. Smith said he was inspired to start the Mormon faith by a vision in which he saw God the Father and Jesus Christ, as well as by other revelations. After Smith died, Brigham Young became the leader of the group. In the 1840s, Young led thousands of Mormons from the Midwest to the church's new base in Utah, where many Mormons still live. Mormons believe that their faith returns Christianity to Christ's own teachings. In addition to the Christian Bible, Mormons accept the *Book of Mormon*, written by Smith, as a religious text. Mormons have often faced discrimination, partly because Mormonism in the past accepted some controversial practices, including polygamy (the marriage of one man to more than one woman at a time).

▲ *Salt Lake Temple in Utah*

What causes auroras? → page 204

THE WORLD OF Science

The Latin root of the word "science" is *scire,* meaning "to know." There are many kinds of knowledge, but when people use the word *science* they usually mean a kind of knowledge that can be discovered and backed up by observation or experiments.

The branches of scientific study can be loosely grouped into four main branches: Physical Science, Life Science (Biology), Earth Science, and Social Science. Each branch has more specific areas of study. For example, zoology includes entomology (study of insects), which in turn includes lepidopterology (the study of butterflies and moths).

In answering questions about our lives, our world, and our universe, scientists must often draw from more than one discipline. Biochemists, for example, deal with the chemistry that happens inside living things. Paleontologists study fossil remains of ancient plants and animals. Astrophysicists study matter and energy in outer space. And mathematics, considered by many to be both an art and a science, is used by all scientists.

Social Science

ANTHROPOLOGY: human cultures and physical characteristics

ECONOMICS: production and distribution of goods and services

POLITICAL SCIENCE: governments

PSYCHOLOGY: mental processes and behavior

SOCIOLOGY: human society and community life

Physical Science

ASTRONOMY: stars, planets, outer space

CHEMISTRY: properties and behavior of substances

PHYSICS: matter and energy

Life Science (Biology)

ANATOMY: structure of the human body

BOTANY: plants

ECOLOGY: living things in relation to their environment

GENETICS: heredity

PATHOLOGY: diseases and their effects on the human body

PHYSIOLOGY: the body's biological processes

ZOOLOGY: animals

Earth Science

GEOGRAPHY: Earth's surface and its relationship to humans

GEOLOGY: Earth's structure

HYDROLOGY: water

METEOROLOGY: Earth's atmosphere and weather

MINERALOGY: minerals

OCEANOGRAPHY: the sea, including currents and tides

PETROLOGY: rocks

SEISMOLOGY: earthquakes

VOLCANOLOGY: volcanoes

HOW DO SCIENTISTS MAKE DISCOVERIES? *THE SCIENTIFIC METHOD*

The scientific method was developed over many centuries. You can think of it as having five steps:

1. Ask a question.
2. Gather information through observation.
3. Based on that information, make an educated guess (hypothesis) about the answer to your question.
4. Design an experiment to test that hypothesis.
5. Evaluate the results.

If the experiment shows that your hypothesis is wrong, make up a new hypothesis. If the experiment supports your hypothesis, then your hypothesis may be correct! However, it is usually necessary to test a hypothesis with many different experiments before it can be accepted as a scientific law—something that is generally accepted as true.

You can apply the **scientific method** to problems in everyday life. For example, suppose you plant some seeds and they fail to sprout. You would probably **ask** yourself, "Why didn't they sprout?"—and that would be step one of the scientific method. The next step would be to make **observations**; for example, you might take note of how deep the seeds were planted, how often they were watered, and what kind of soil was used. Then, you would make an **educated guess** about what went wrong—for example, you might hypothesize that the seeds didn't sprout because you didn't water them enough. After that, you would **test** your hypothesis—perhaps by trying to grow the seeds again, under the exact same conditions as before, except that this time you would water them more frequently.

Finally, you would wait and **evaluate** the results of your experiment. If the seeds sprouted, then you could conclude that your hypothesis may be correct. If they didn't sprout, you'd continue to use the method to find a scientific answer to your original question.

did you Know?

Most scientists think that people from Siberia in Asia were the first to settle in the Western Hemisphere. But when did they arrive? Stone tools and weapons uncovered at several sites date from around 13,000 years ago. A few objects that may be older have also been found, but researchers argue about their significance and age. A discovery reported in March 2011 provided evidence for a much earlier human presence in North America. It involved a large group of tools and weapons found by Buttermilk Creek near Austin, Texas. Some of the items were dated to as far back as 15,500 years ago.

Buttermilk Creek dig

WHAT EVERYTHING IS MADE OF

Everything we see and use is made of basic ingredients called elements. There are more than 100 elements. They are found in nature or made by scientists.

Elements in Earth's Crust
(percent by weight)

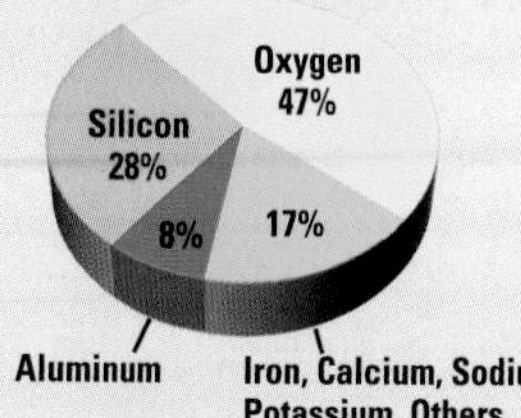

Elements in the Atmosphere
(percent by volume)

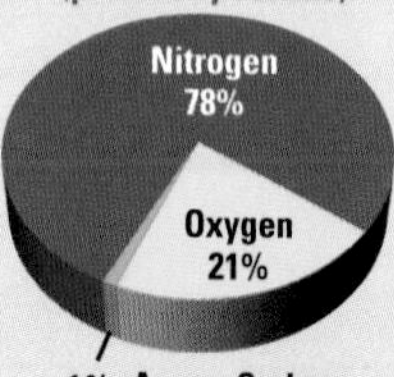

How Elements Are Named

Elements are named after places, scientists, figures in mythology, or properties of the element. But no element gets a name until the International Union of Pure and Applied Chemistry (IUPAC) accepts it. In 2009, the IUPAC officially accepted the 112th element, later given the name copernicium (honoring the 16th-century astronomer Copernicus) and the symbol Cn. Copernicium was first produced by German scientists in 1996. In June 2011, two more new elements were accepted: No. 114 and No. 116. Their official names remained to be decided.

NAME	SYMBOL	WHAT IT IS	WHEN FOUND	NAMED FOR
Argon	Ar	gas	1894	the Greek word *argos,* which means inactive or lazy; it is one of the least reactive of all elements
Californium	Cf	radioactive metal	1950	state of California, and the University of California
Hydrogen	H	non-metal	1766	the Greek words *hydro* and *genes,* which mean water and forming
Iodine	I	nonmetallic solid	1811	the Greek word *iodes,* meaning violet
Iridium	Ir	transitional metal	1804	the Latin word *iridis,* meaning rainbow
Nickel	Ni	transitional metal	1774	the German word *kupfernickel,* meaning devil's copper
Tungsten	W	transitional metal	1783	the Swedish words *tung sten,* meaning heavy stone.
Vanadium	V	metal	1801	Vanadis, the Scandinavian goddess of beauty; its salts have beautiful colors

ALL ABOUT... Compounds

Carbon, hydrogen, nitrogen, and oxygen are the most common chemical elements in the human body. Many other elements may be found in small amounts. These include calcium, iron, phosphorus, potassium, and sodium.

When elements join together, they form compounds. Water is a compound made up of hydrogen and oxygen. Salt is a compound made up of sodium and chlorine.

Common Name	Contains the Compound	Contains the Elements
Chalk	calcium carbonate	calcium, carbon, oxygen
Fool's Gold	iron disulfide	iron, sulfur
Marble	calcium carbonate	calcium, carbon, oxygen
Rust	iron oxide	iron, oxygen
Sugar	sucrose	carbon, hydrogen, oxygen
Toothpaste	sodium fluoride	sodium, fluorine
Vinegar	acetic acid	carbon, hydrogen, oxygen

CHEMICAL SYMBOLS ARE SCIENTIFIC SHORTHAND

When scientists write the names of elements, they often use a symbol instead of spelling out the full name. The symbol for each element is one or two letters. Scientists write O for oxygen and He for helium. The symbols usually come from the English name for the element (C for carbon). The symbols for some of the elements come from the element's Latin name. For example, the symbol for gold is Au, which is short for *aurum*, the Latin word for gold.

TURNING BASE METALS INTO GOLD?

Hundreds of years ago, during the Middle Ages, some people believed that they could change base metals like lead into gold. These people, called alchemists, thought that something called a philosopher's stone and intense faith could combine to cause the change. This belief persisted for centuries; even the great scientist Isaac Newton believed in alchemy!

Medieval physician and alchemist Philippus Aureolus Paracelsus

Physical Science

SOUND and LIGHT

What Is Sound?

Sound is a form of energy that is made up of waves traveling through matter. When you "hear" a sound, it is actually your ear detecting the vibrations of molecules as the sound wave passes through. To understand sound, you first have to understand waves. Take a bowl full of water and drop a penny into the middle of it. You'll see little circular waves move away from the area where the penny hit, spread out toward the bowl's edges, and bounce back. Sound moves in the same way. The waves must travel through a gas, liquid, or a solid. In the vacuum of space, there is no sound because there are no molecules to vibrate. When you talk, your vocal cords vibrate to produce sound waves.

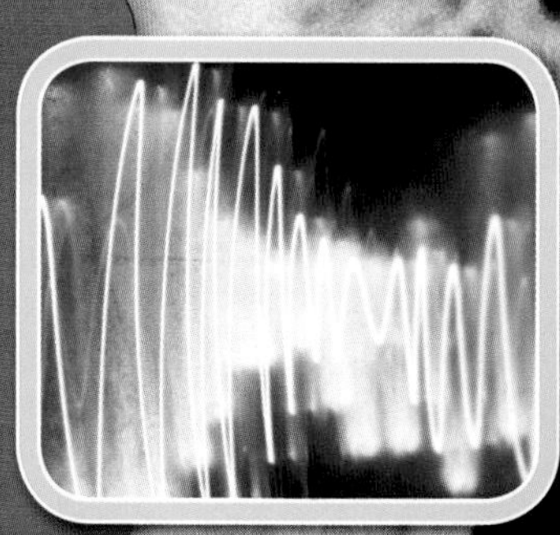

What Is Light?

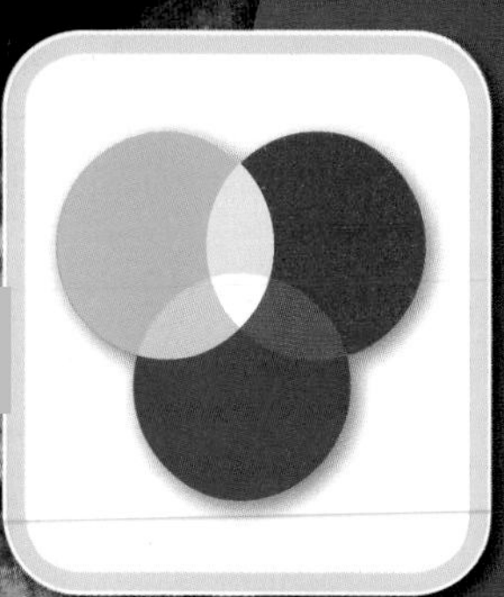

Light is a little tricky. It is a form of energy known as electromagnetic radiation that is emitted from a source. It travels as waves in straight lines and spreads out over a larger area the farther it goes. Scientists also think it goes along as particles known as photons. Light is produced in many ways. They generally involve changes in the energy levels of electrons inside atoms.

Regular white light is made up of all the colors of the spectrum from red to violet. Each color has its own frequency and wavelength. When you see a color on something, such as a red apple, that means that the apple absorbed all other colors of the spectrum and reflected the red light. Things that are white reflect almost all the light that hits them. Things that are black, on the other hand, absorb all the light that hits them.

Light vs. Sound

Sound travels fast but light travels a whole lot faster. You've probably noticed that when you see lightning, you don't hear thunder until several seconds later. That's because the light reaches you before the sound. The speed of sound in air varies depending mainly on temperature (sound also travels faster through liquids and many solids). A jet traveling at about 761 miles per hour is considered to be flying at the "speed of sound." But this is nothing compared to light. In a vacuum, such as in space, it goes 186,000 miles per ***second***! Scientists don't think anything in the universe can travel faster.

How Simple Machines Work

Simple machines are devices that make our lives easier. Cars could not run, skyscrapers couldn't be built, and elevators couldn't carry people up—if it weren't for simple machines.

Inclined Plane When trying to get a refrigerator onto the back of a truck, a worker will use a ramp, or inclined plane. Instead of lifting something heavy a short distance, we can more easily push it over a longer distance, but to the same height.
Examples: escalators, staircases, slides

Lever Any kind of arm, bar, or plank that can pivot on something (known as a fulcrum), is a lever. Depending on where the fulcrum is located on the lever, it can be used for different things.
Examples: shovel, bottle opener, "claw" part of a hammer used for prying out nails, seesaw

Wedge These machines are two inclined planes fastened onto each other to make a point. Wedges are used to pull things apart and even cut.
Examples: axes, knives

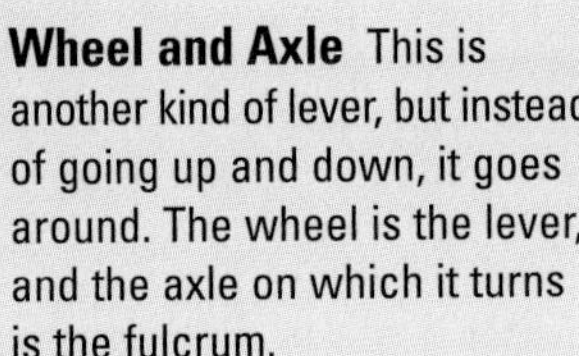

Wheel and Axle This is another kind of lever, but instead of going up and down, it goes around. The wheel is the lever, and the axle on which it turns is the fulcrum.
Examples: cars, bicycles, wagons

Pulley A pulley is similar to a wheel and axle, except that there's no axle. It can be used to change both the direction and level of force needed to move an object. The best example is a crane. An object is tied to a cable, which goes up and around the pulley, and down to the crane engine which is pulling it.
Examples: a block and tackle, a flag pole, tow trucks

Screw A screw is an inclined plane wrapped around a cylinder. In the case of a wood screw, as it is turned it travels deeper into the piece of wood. Another use of a screw is to hold things in place such as the lid on a jar.
Examples: drills, corkscrews

Biological Science

What Are Living Things Made of?

Plant cell

Cells are sometimes called the "building blocks" of living things. Complex life forms have many cells. There are trillions of them in the human body.

There are two main kinds of cells: **eukaryotic** and **prokaryotic**. All the cells in your body—along with the cells of other animals, plants, and fungi—are eukaryotic. These contain several different structures called **organelles**. Like tools in a toolbox, each kind of organelle has its own function. The **nucleus**, for example, contains most of the cell's DNA, while the **mitochondria** provide energy for the cell. The **ribosomes** are involved in making proteins.

Plant and animal cells differ in a few ways. Animal cells rely on mitochondria for energy, but plant cells also have an organelle called a **chloroplast**. This contains chlorophyll, a green chemical plants use to get oxygen and energy from sunlight and water, a process called **photosynthesis**. Unlike animal cells, plant cells have a rigid cell wall made largely of **cellulose**.

Prokaryotes (living things, or organisms, with prokaryotic instead of eukaryotic cells) are all around you—and even inside of you. For example, bacteria are prokaryotes. Most prokaryotes are single-celled. They don't have the variety of organelles that eukaryotic cells do.

WHAT IS DNA?

Every cell has **DNA**, a molecule that holds all the information about the organism containing the cell. The structure of DNA was discovered in 1953 by the British scientist Francis Crick and the American scientist James Watson.

Lengths of connected bits of a DNA molecule, called **genes**, are tiny pieces of code. They determine what each organism is like. Almost all the DNA and genes come packaged in thread-like structures called **chromosomes**. Humans have 46. There are 22 almost identical pairs, plus the X and Y chromosomes, which determine whether a human is male (one X chromosome and one Y chromosome) or female (two X chromosomes).

Genes are passed on from parents to children, and no two organisms (except clones or identical twins) have the same DNA.

Many things—the color of our eyes or hair, whether we're tall or short, our chances of getting certain diseases—depend on our genes.

What Is the Human Genome?

A genome is all the DNA in an organism, including its genes. The human genome contains 20,000 to 25,000 genes. That's fewer than the 50,000-plus genes of a rice plant! Human genes can produce more than one kind of protein. Proteins perform most life functions and make up a large part of cellular structures.

Tiny Creatures

SCIENCE

Microbes Anton van Leeuwenhoek (pronounced Lay-wen-ook) made the first practical microscope in 1674. When he looked through it, he saw tiny bacteria, plant cells, and fungi, among other things. When he wrote about his findings, Leeuwenhoek called the creatures "wee beasties." We call them **microorganisms** ("micro" means *little*), or microbes. Before the microscope, people had no idea that there were millions of tiny living things crawling all over them.

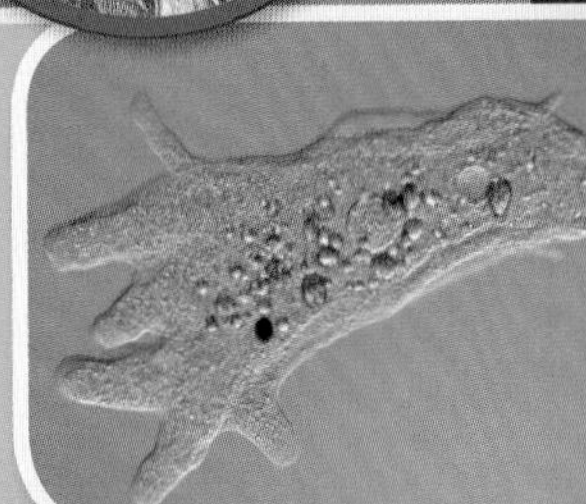

Amoebas Amoebas (uh-ME-buhz) are eukaryotic jelly-like blobs of protoplasm that ooze through their microscopic world. They eat by engulfing their food and slowly digesting it. To move around, the cell extends a part of its goo to create something called a **pseudopod** (SOO-doh-pod), which means "false foot." The amoeba uses this to pull the rest of its "body" along. Amoebas normally live in water or on moist surfaces. In humans, most kinds of amoebas are harmless, but some cause diseases.

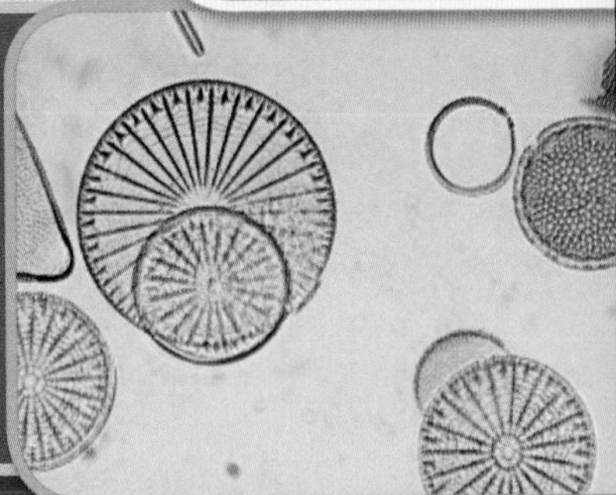

Diatoms Diatoms are one-celled algae that make glass shells to protect themselves. When they die, their shells collect at the bottom of the ocean in great numbers and form something called **diatomaceous earth**. It's gritty like sandpaper. Diatomaceous earth was once used in toothpaste to help scrape plaque off teeth. Nowadays, among other things, it is used as a pesticide—when sprayed in the air, it gets caught in the lungs of insects and slowly suffocates them.

WHAT ABOUT VIRUSES?

Mimivirus

Viruses are often thought of as not really alive. But it depends on how you define life. Tiny in size and lacking cells, viruses consist of genetic material—either DNA or the similar RNA—and a protein coat. They don't grow. They don't appear to react to the environment. They don't do anything—unless they are located inside a living thing, in which case they can reproduce, by borrowing the living thing's genetic machinery. In recent years super-sized viruses, dubbed the mimivirus and mamavirus, have been discovered in amoebas. They are as big as small bacteria. Scientists have also found a very tiny virus that appears to use the mamavirus's genetic machinery to reproduce.

SCIENCE Q&A

WHY DOES ICE FLOAT? When most liquids are cooled until they freeze, or turn into a solid, they shrink. They become "denser"—which means that more matter is crammed into their solid form than into their liquid form. That is why people often think of solid objects as being heavier than liquids. But there are exceptions. Water is one. It actually expands when it freezes into ice. As a result, ice cubes and icebergs are lighter than water, and so they float instead of sinking.

WHAT MAKES AURORAS? People in northern parts of the world often see a shimmering or pulsating light in the night sky. Known as the aurora borealis, or the northern lights, it may look like a billowing curtain. It may also take the form of a broad glow, a rainbow-like arc, bright thin rays, or moving streamers. The same kind of light can be seen in the southern hemisphere, where it is called the aurora australis, or the southern lights. Auroras are caused by particles such as electrons given off by the Sun. Earth's magnetic field pulls some of these particles toward the north and south poles, and they interact with oxygen and nitrogen atoms in the atmosphere to produce light.

HOW LONG CAN YOU SURVIVE IN FREEZING WATER? It depends. If you fall into really cold water, the shock of the sudden cold can make you start hyperventilating—breathing very fast and deep. If you are underwater when this happens, you will drown right away. If you survive the cold shock, the next worry is that your body temperature may get too low. This condition, called hypothermia, can be fatal. In 41°F water, you might last 10 to 20 minutes before starting to feel weak. A heavier person may last longer than a thin one, since body fat serves as insulation. Also, the less of your body that is in the water, the longer you'll tend to survive, since water carries heat away faster than air.

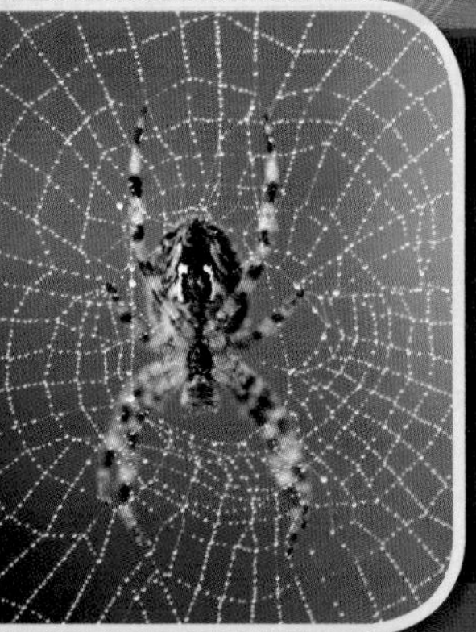

WHAT MAKES SPIDER SILK SO STRONG? Dragline silk—the silk a spider uses to hang from a ceiling—is only about one-tenth as thick as a human hair, but it is several times stronger than steel. Other strong materials, such as ceramics, tend to be stiff or breakable. Spider silk can stretch and bend without breaking. Its secret is its structure. It contains proteins that help make the silk stretchable. It also has proteins that form stacks of thin flat crystals connected by the normally weak type of chemical link called a hydrogen bond. As long as the crystals are small enough, the bonds work together, taking on great strength and letting the silk stretch and bend rather than break.

SOME FAMOUS SCIENTISTS

NICOLAUS COPERNICUS (1473–1543), Polish scientist who is known as the founder of modern astronomy. He came up with the theory that Earth and other planets revolve around the Sun. But most thinkers continued to believe that Earth was the center of the universe.

JOHANNES KEPLER (1571–1630), German astronomer who developed three laws of planetary motion. He was the first to propose a force (later named gravity) that governs planets' orbits around the Sun.

JOSEPH HENRY (1797–1878), American physicist who made key discoveries about electromagnetism. The henry, a commonly used unit of measure for the property of an electric circuit known as inductance, was named in his honor. In 1846 he became the first secretary, or head, of the Smithsonian Institution in Washington, D.C.

CHARLES DARWIN (1809–1882), British scientist who is best known for his theory of **evolution by natural selection**. According to this theory, living creatures, by gradually changing so as to have the best chances of survival, slowly developed over millions of years into the forms they have today.

GEORGE WASHINGTON CARVER (1864–1943), African-American scientist and inventor best known for his work with plants and soils. He came up with hundreds of products from peanuts, pecans, sweet potatoes, and soybeans and developed a hardy new hybrid cotton.

MARIE CURIE (1867–1934), Polish-born French physicist who discovered the radioactive elements polonium and radium with her husband, Pierre, and later carried out important research on radium. Marie and Pierre Curie shared the Nobel Prize for Physics in 1903, and Marie by herself won the Nobel Prize for Chemistry in 1911.

ALBERT EINSTEIN (1879–1955), German-American physicist who developed revolutionary theories about the relationships between time, space, matter, and energy. Probably the most famous and influential scientist of the 20th century, he won a Nobel Prize in 1921.

ROSALIND FRANKLIN (1920–1958), British physical chemist whose use of X rays to reveal molecular structure played a key role in the 1953 discovery of the structure of DNA. Her early death, from cancer, kept her from being considered for a share of the Nobel Prize that was awarded in 1962 for the discovery.

NEIL DEGRASSE TYSON (1959–), American astrophysicist who heads the Hayden Planetarium at New York's American Museum of Natural History but is best known for his popular books and TV programs on science. He has received the NASA Distinguished Public Service Medal, and an asteroid has been named after him.

What is the coldest planet? → page 207

THE SOLAR SYSTEM

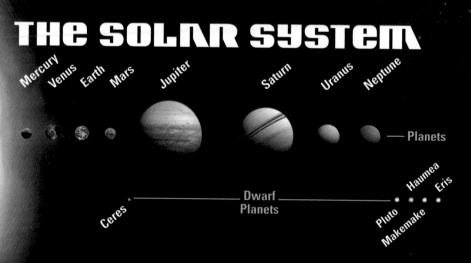

Mercury Venus Earth Mars Jupiter Saturn Uranus Neptune — Planets

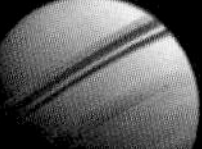

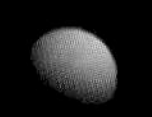

Ceres — Dwarf Planets — Pluto Haumea Makemake Eris

The SUN Is a STAR

Did you know that the Sun is a star, like the other stars you see at night? It is a typical, medium-size star. But because the Sun is much closer to our planet than any other star, we can study it in great detail. The diameter of the Sun is 865,000 miles—more than 100 times Earth's diameter. The gravity of the Sun at its surface is nearly 28 times the gravity of Earth.

How hot is the Sun? The surface temperature of the Sun is close to 10,000° F, and it is believed that the Sun's inner core may reach temperatures around 28 million degrees! The Sun provides enough light and heat energy to support life on our planet.

HOMEWORK TIP

Here's a useful way to remember the names of planets in order of their distance from the Sun. Think of this sentence: My Very Excellent Mother Just Sent Us Nachos.

M = Mercury, **V** = Venus, **E** = Earth, **M** = Mars, **J** = Jupiter, **S** = Saturn, **U** = Uranus, **N** = Neptune

The Planets Are in Motion

The planets in the solar system move around the Sun in oval-shaped paths called **orbits**. One complete trip around the Sun is called a **revolution**. Earth takes one year, or 365¼ days, to make one revolution. Planets farther away from the Sun take longer. Most planets have one or more moons. A moon orbits a planet in much the same way that the planets orbit the Sun. Each planet also spins, or rotates, on its axis. An axis is an imaginary line running through the center of a planet. The time it takes Earth to rotate on its axis equals one day.

Saturn

Planet Champions

Largest planet:
Jupiter (88,846 miles diameter)

Smallest planet:
Mercury (3,032 miles diameter)

Shortest orbit:
Mercury (88 days)

Longest orbit:
Neptune (164.8 years)

Tallest mountain:
Mars (Olympus Mons, 16.8 miles high)

Hottest planet:
Venus (867° F)

Coldest planet:
Neptune (–330° F)

Shortest day:
Jupiter (9 hours, 55 minutes, 33 seconds)

Longest day:
Mercury (175.94 days)

No moons:
Mercury, Venus

Most moons:
Jupiter (63 known satellites)

WHAT IS AN ECLIPSE?

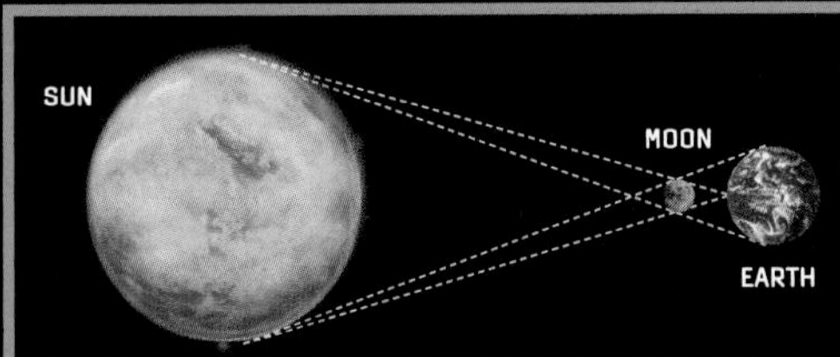

During a solar eclipse, the Moon casts a shadow on part of Earth. A total solar eclipse is when the Sun is completely blocked out. When this happens, the halo of gas around the Sun, called the **corona**, can be seen.

The next total solar eclipse is predicted to take place on November 13, 2012. It will be seen in northern Australia and the South Pacific Ocean. An annular eclipse—in which only the central portion of the Sun is blocked out—will be visible in China, Japan, and the western U.S. on May 12, 2012.

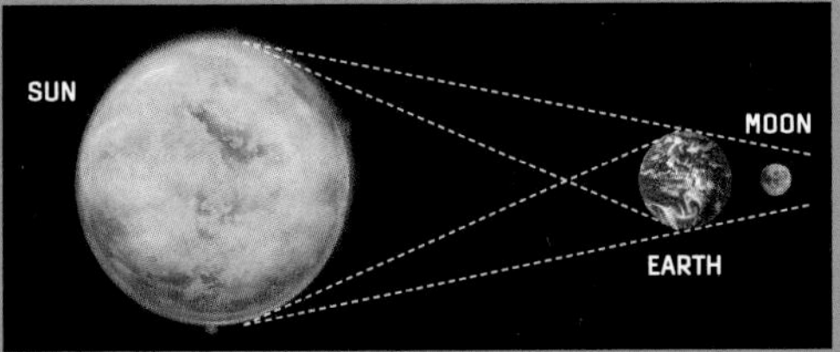

Sometimes Earth casts a shadow on the Moon. During a total lunar eclipse, the Moon remains visible, but it looks dark.

In 2011, total lunar eclipses were expected on June 15 and December 10. Only the second one could be seen in North America. Total lunar eclipses will not occur again until 2014, when two are predicted.

THE PLANETS

1 MERCURY

Average distance from the Sun: 36 million miles

Diameter: 3,032 miles

Average temp.: 333° F

Surface: silicate rock

Time to revolve around the Sun: 88 days

Day (synodic—midday to midday): 175.94 days

Number of moons: 0

Mercury has the most extreme differences in temperature in the solar system. It is close to the Sun, and so temperatures can get very high. But the side facing away from the Sun can be very cold.

2 VENUS

Average distance from the Sun: 67 million miles

Diameter: 7,521 miles

Average temp.: 867° F

Surface: silicate rock

Time to revolve around the Sun: 224.7 days

Day (synodic): 116.75 days

Number of moons: 0

From Earth, Venus usually appears brighter than any other planet or star. At certain times, Venus can even be seen in daylight.

3 EARTH

Average distance from the Sun: 93 million miles

Diameter: 7,926 miles

Average temp.: 59° F

Surface: water, basalt, and granite rock

Time to revolve around the Sun: 365 ¼ days

Day (synodic): 24 h

Number of moons: 1

When a gigantic earthquake shook Japan on March 11, 2011, Earth's mass shifted. This caused Earth to rotate a little faster, shortening the day by about 1.8 millionths of a second.

4 MARS

Average distance from the Sun: 142 million miles

Diameter: 4,222 miles

Average temp.: –81° F

Surface: iron-rich basaltic rock

Time to revolve around the Sun: 687 days

Day (synodic): 24 h 39 min 35 s

Number of moons: 2

NASA's **Mars Reconnaissance Orbiter** *went into orbit around the Red Planet in 2006. Since then, it has sent more data to Earth than all other interplanetary spacecraft put together.*

5 JUPITER

Average distance from the Sun: 484 million miles

Diameter: 88,846 miles

Average temp.: –162° F

Surface: liquid hydrogen

Time to revolve around the Sun: 11.9 years

Day (synodic): 9 h 55 min 33 s

Number of moons: 63

A comet or asteroid slammed into Jupiter in mid-2009, producing a black area 5,000 miles long.

6 SATURN

Average distance from the Sun: 887 million miles

Diameter: 74,898 miles

Average temp.: –218° F

Surface: liquid hydrogen

Time to revolve around the Sun: 29.5 years

Day (synodic): 10 h 34 min 13 s

Number of moons: 62

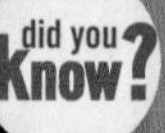

Saturn's large moon Titan boasts rain, lakes, and seas. The liquid in them is not water but, probably, methane, which generally occurs as a gas on the much warmer Earth.

7 URANUS

Average distance from the Sun: 1.8 billion miles
Diameter: 31,763 miles
Average temp.: –323° F
Surface: liquid hydrogen and helium
Time to revolve around the Sun: 84 years
Day (synodic): 17 h 14 min 23 s
Number of moons: 27

William Herschel, who discovered Uranus in 1781, worked as a music teacher and organist until a stipend from King George III allowed him to study astronomy full-time in 1782. He went on to make several other important discoveries.

8 NEPTUNE

Average distance from the Sun: 2.8 billion miles
Diameter: 30,775 miles
Average temp.: –330° F
Surface: liquid hydrogen and helium
Time to revolve around the Sun: 164.8 years
Day (synodic): 16 h 6 min 36 s
Number of moons: 13

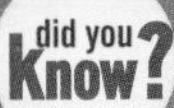

Neptune, Jupiter, Saturn, and Uranus are often called gas-giant planets because they consist largely of gas (and liquid). But they all also are thought to have rocky cores.

DWARF PLANETS AND PLUTOIDS

In 2006 the International Astronomical Union (IAU) officially changed the definition of "planet." It decided that a planet must "clear the neighborhood" around its orbit. In other words, a planet has to have strong enough gravity that nearby bodies either merge with it or orbit around it. As a result, Pluto, an object that travels around the Sun in an orbit lying mostly past Neptune's, lost planet status. Pluto is rather small—smaller even than Earth's Moon—and it does not clear its neighborhood, which happens to be part of a collection of objects called the Kuiper Belt. The IAU put Pluto in a new category called **dwarf planet**.

Like a planet, a dwarf planet orbits the Sun. It doesn't have enough gravity to clear its neighborhood, but the gravity must be strong enough to give the dwarf a rounded shape. The first objects to be officially classified as dwarf planets were Pluto, Ceres, and Eris in 2006 and Haumea and Makemake in 2008. Ceres orbits the Sun in the asteroid belt between Mars and Jupiter. Dwarf planets with orbits beyond Neptune's are called **plutoids** by the IAU. Pluto, Eris, Haumea, and Makemake are all plutoids.

CERES

Average distance from the Sun: 257 million miles
Diameter: 592 miles
Number of moons: 0

PLUTO

Average distance from the Sun: 3.67 billion miles
Diameter: 1,430 miles
Number of moons: 3

did you Know? ***Pluto was discovered by American astronomer Clyde Tombaugh in 1930.***

HAUMEA

Average distance from the Sun: 4 billion miles
Diameter: roughly 900 miles
Number of moons: 2

MAKEMAKE

Average distance from the Sun: 4.2 billion miles
Diameter: 930 miles
Number of moons: 0

ERIS

Average distance from the Sun: 6.3 billion miles
Diameter: 1,600 miles
Number of moons: 1

PLANET EARTH SEASONS

The Earth spins on its axis of rotation. That's how we get day and night. But the Earth's axis isn't straight up and down. It is tilted about 23½ degrees. Because of this tilt, different parts of the globe get different amounts of sunlight during the year as the Earth orbits the Sun. This is why we have seasons.

23.5°

WINTER Winter begins at the winter solstice (around December 21) in the Northern Hemisphere (north of the equator, where we live). Our hemisphere is tilted away from the Sun, so the Sun's rays reach us less directly. While days get longer during winter, they are still shorter than in spring and summer, so it's cold. Everything is reversed in the Southern Hemisphere, where it's summer!

SPRING At the vernal equinox (around March 21), daylight is 12 hours long throughout the world because Earth is not tilted toward or away from the Sun. Days continue to get longer and the sunlight gets more direct in the Northern Hemisphere during spring.

Vernal Equinox

Summer Solstice

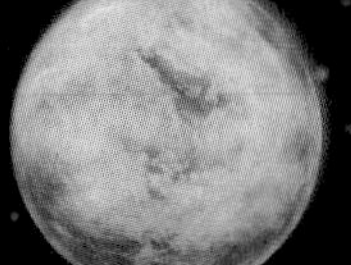

Winter Solstice

Autumnal Equinox

SUMMER The summer solstice (around June 21) marks the longest day of year in the Northern Hemisphere and the beginning of summer. The build-up of heat caused by more-direct sunlight during the long late spring and early summer days in the Northern Hemisphere makes summer our warmest season.

FALL After the autumnal equinox (around September 21) the Northern Hemisphere tilts away from the Sun; sunlight is less direct and lasts less than 12 hours. The hemisphere cools off as winter approaches.

THE MOON

The Moon is about 238,900 miles from Earth. It is 2,160 miles in diameter and has almost no atmosphere. The dusty surface is covered with craters. The Moon takes the same time for to rotate on its axis as it does to orbit Earth (27 days, 7 hours, 43 minutes). This is why one side of the Moon is always facing Earth. The Moon has no light of its own but reflects light from the Sun. The lighted part of the Moon that we see changes in a regular cycle, waxing (growing) and waning (shrinking). It takes the Moon about 29½ days to go through all the "phases" in this cycle. This is called a lunar month.

PHASES OF THE MOON

New Moon

Waxing Crescent

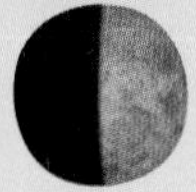
First Quarter

Waxing Gibbous

Full Moon

Waning Gibbous

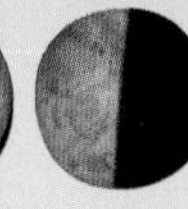
Last Quarter

Waning Crescent

New Moon

MOON Q&A

Why are there dark spots on the face of the Moon?

The dark spots you see on the face of the Moon are called *maria*. They were once thought to be seas. ("Maria" means "seas" in Latin.) Maria actually are low plains made out of basalt, a fine, dark volcanic rock. The paler areas on the Moon's surface are mountains and highlands.

Does the Moon really cause the ocean tides?

Yes. Because the Moon is so big, its gravity causes the water in our seas and oceans to rise and fall as the Moon revolves around Earth. The Sun's gravitational pull also has an effect on ocean tides, but it is much weaker than the Moon's. That's because the Moon is so much closer to Earth than the Sun.

Are there any plans to go back to the Moon?

Countries such as the U.S., China, Russia, and India plan to use unmanned spacecraft to explore the Moon in coming years. In October 2010, China put *Chang'e-2* (named for a mythical moon goddess) into orbit around the Moon. *Chang'e-3*, expected to launch in 2013, will try to place a rover on the lunar surface. The U.S. planned to launch two spacecraft in late 2011 on a mission, called *GRAIL*, to learn about the Moon's inner structure by studying its gravity. The U.S. and some other countries have also talked about sending humans to the Moon in the future.

SOME UNMANNED MISSIONS in the Solar System

LAUNCH DATE	
1959	**Luna 2** First spacecraft to hit the surface of the Moon
1962	**Mariner 2** First successful flyby of Venus
1964	**Mariner 4** First probe to reach Mars, 1965
1972	**Pioneer 10** First probe to reach Jupiter, 1973
1973	**Mariner 10** First probe to reach Mercury, 1974
1975	**Viking 1 and 2** Landed on Mars in 1976
1977	**Voyager 1** Reached Jupiter in 1979 and Saturn in 1980
1977	**Voyager 2** Reached Jupiter in 1979, Saturn in 1981, Uranus in 1986, Neptune in 1989
1989	**Magellan** Orbited Venus and mapped its surface
1989	**Galileo** Reached Jupiter in 1995
1997	**Cassini** Reached Saturn in June 2004
2003	**Mars rovers Spirit and Opportunity** Landed on Mars in early 2004
2004	**Messenger** Flew past Mercury in 2008 and 2009 and entered into orbit around the planet in 2011. Sent back first up-close data since 1975
2005	**Deep Impact** Reached comet Tempel 1 July 4, 2005
2006	**New Horizons** Due to reach Pluto in 2015
2007	**Phoenix** Landed in 2008 to search for signs that Mars once held life
2007	**Dawn** Due to reach asteroid Vesta in 2011 and Ceres in 2015
2009	**LCROSS** Slammed into the Moon, kicking up debris for study. Scientists detected signs of water
2010	**Hayabusa** Brought to Earth first samples ever obtained from the surface of an asteroid

Phoenix Mars Lander

Artist's concept of the New Horizons spacecraft as it approaches Pluto and its three moons

MILESTONES in Human Spaceflight

The U.S. formed NASA in 1958. It was in response to the Soviet Union's launching of the first artificial satellite *Sputnik I* on October 4, 1957. Since then, more than 500 astronauts have made trips into space to conduct research, visit orbiting space stations, and explore the Moon. Below are some of the biggest moments in human spaceflight.

1961	On April 12, Soviet cosmonaut Yuri Gagarin, in *Vostok 1*, became the first person to orbit Earth. On May 5, U.S. astronaut Alan B. Shepard Jr. during the *Mercury 3* mission became the first American in space.
1962	On February 20, U.S. astronaut John H. Glenn Jr. during the *Mercury 6* mission became the first American to orbit Earth.
1963	From June 16 to 19, the Soviet spacecraft *Vostok 6* carried the first woman into space, Valentina V. Tereshkova.
1965	On March 18, Soviet cosmonaut Aleksei A. Leonov became the first person to "walk" in space.
1966	On March 16, U.S. *Gemini 8* became the first craft to dock with (become attached to) another vehicle (an unmanned Agena rocket).
1969	On July 20, U.S. *Apollo 11's* lunar module *Eagle* landed on the Moon's surface in the area known as the Sea of Tranquility. Neil Armstrong was the first person ever to walk on the Moon.
1970	In April, *Apollo 13* astronauts returned safely to Earth after an explosion damaged their spacecraft and prevented them from landing on the Moon.
1973	On May 14, the U.S. put its first space station, *Skylab*, into orbit. The last *Skylab* crew left in February 1974.
1975	American and Soviet spacecraft docked in July, and for several days their crews worked and spent time together in space.
1981	*Columbia* was launched on April 12 and became the first space shuttle to reach space.
1986	On January 28, space shuttle *Challenger* exploded 73 seconds after takeoff. All seven astronauts, including teacher Christa McAuliffe, died. In February, the Soviet space station *Mir* was launched into orbit, where it remained for 15 years.
1998	In December, space shuttle *Endeavour* carried into orbit *Unity*, a U.S.-built part of the International Space Station (ISS). *Unity* was linked up to the Russian-built *Zarya* control module, which had been carried into orbit the preceding month. The first ISS crew arrived in November 2000.
2001	In April, U.S. businessman Dennis Tito rode a Russian Soyuz rocket to the ISS, becoming the first paying space tourist.
2003	On February 1, space shuttle *Columbia* disintegrated during its reentry into the Earth's atmosphere, killing the seven-member crew. China launched its first manned spacecraft on October 15.
2004	On June 21, Mike Melvill piloted *SpaceShipOne*, the first privately funded spacecraft, into space.
2009	A May mission by space shuttle *Atlantis* repaired and enhanced the aging Hubble Space Telescope, which was launched in 1990.
2011	Last flights scheduled for space shuttle program, to carry into orbit nearly all the final major components for completion of the ISS.

SPACE NEWS 2012

Milestone Year

April 12, 2011, was a big anniversary for manned spaceflight. It marked exactly 50 years since Soviet cosmonaut Yuri Gagarin became the first human in space. It also marked exactly 30 years since a U.S. space shuttle flew around Earth for the first time. The space shuttle program was expected to end in 2011, with all three remaining operational shuttles—*Discovery*, *Endeavour*, and *Atlantis*—making their final flight.

After the Shuttles

With the retirement of the shuttles, the job of ferrying crew, supplies, and equipment to and from the International Space Station (ISS) will be handled, at least for the immediate future, by Russian spacecraft, with a little help from Japanese and European Space Agency craft.

The U.S. hopes private companies will eventually also supply transportation into "near-Earth" space—such as the orbit of the ISS. In June 2010 a test flight of the Falcon 9 rocket, developed by Space Exploration Technologies (SpaceX), placed an object in Earth orbit. Six months later, a Falcon 9 carried into orbit SpaceX's Dragon cargo carrier.

Private companies also moved ahead with plans to offer short, nonorbital flights into space for tourists. Virgin Galactic's air-launched *Enterprise* made its first solo test flight in October 2010. The company hopes to begin regular tourist flights by 2012.

Space Plane

Despite the end of the space shuttle era, the idea of a reusable "space plane" capable of flying into orbit and back lives on—but in a smaller and unmanned form. The U.S. Air Force has a secret experimental robot space plane called the X-37B. In December 2010 the craft, about a quarter the size of the shuttle, finished its maiden voyage after more than 220 days in space. An X-37B began another flight three months later.

The Moon and Beyond

In addition to *GRAIL*, NASA's upcoming Moon missions include *LADEE* ("Lunar Atmosphere and Dust Environment Explorer"), set to take off in 2013. Mars is the goal of two upcoming NASA missions. The *Mars Science Laboratory*, expected to launch in 2011, involves landing a rover named *Curiosity* on the Red Planet. *MAVEN* ("Mars Atmosphere and Volatile EvolutioN") is slated for launch in 2013. A 2011 launch is expected for NASA's *Juno*, which will take five years to travel to Jupiter and then will go into orbit around the giant planet to study its atmosphere, gravity, and magnetic field.

WHAT'S OUT THERE?

Spiral galaxy M100

What else is in space besides planets?

A **GALAXY** is a group of billions of stars held close together by gravity. The universe may have more than 100 billion galaxies! The one we live in is called the Milky Way. Our Sun and planets are only a small part of it. Scientists think there are as many as 200 billion stars in the Milky Way!

NEBULA is the name astronomers give to any fuzzy patch in the sky, even galaxies and star clusters. Planetary nebulas come from the late stages of some stars, while star clusters and galaxies are groups of stars. Emission nebulas, reflection nebulas, and dark dust clouds are regions of gas and dust that may be hundreds of light-years wide and are often birthplaces of stars. Emission nebulas often give off a reddish glow, caused when their hydrogen gas is heated by hot, newly formed stars nearby. Dust particles in some areas reflect hot blue starlight and appear as reflection nebulas. Dark dust clouds, though still mainly gas, contain enough dust to absorb starlight and appear as dark nebulas.

BLACK HOLE is the name given to a region in space with gravity so strong that nothing can get out—not even light. Many black holes are probably formed when giant stars at least 20 times as massive as our Sun burn up their fuel and collapse, creating very dense cores. Scientists think bigger, "supermassive" black holes may form from the collapse of many stars, or from the merging of smaller black holes, in the centers of galaxies. Black holes can't be seen, because they do not give off light. Astronomers watch for signs, such as effects on the orbits of nearby stars, X-ray bursts from matter being sucked into the black hole, or long jets of particles.

SATELLITES are objects that move in an orbit around a planet. Moons are natural satellites. Artificial satellites, launched into orbit by humans, are used as space stations and observatories. They are also used to take pictures of Earth's surface and to transmit communications signals.

ASTEROIDS are solid chunks of rock or metal that range in size from small boulders to hundreds of miles across. Some asteroids orbit other asteroids. Hundreds of thousands of asteroids orbit the Sun in the main asteroid belt between Mars and Jupiter.

Comet Siding Spring (infrared view)

COMETS are chunks of ice, dust, and rock that form long tails as they move nearer to the Sun. One of the most well-known is Halley's Comet. It can be seen about every 76 years and will appear again in the year 2061.

METEOROIDS are small pieces of stone or metal. Most meteoroids are fragments from comets or asteroids that broke off from crashes in space with other objects. A few are actually chunks that blew off the Moon or Mars after an asteroid hit. When a meteoroid enters Earth's atmosphere, it usually burns up completely. This streak of light is called a **meteor**, or **shooting star**. If a piece of a meteoroid manages to land on Earth, it is called a **meteorite**.

SPORTS

In what city did today's Atlanta Braves first play baseball? → page 225

You don't have to serve like Serena or shoot like LeBron to love playing sports. Indoors or out, there are plenty of great ways to have fun and stay fit.

FAVORITE SPORTS

Here are the most popular sports and activities among kids in the United States in 2009.

BOYS (AGES 6–17)		
1.	Bicycling (Road)	8.1 million
2.	Basketball	7.6 million
3.	Bowling	7.3 million
4.	Freshwater Fishing	6.6 million
5.	Running/Jogging	5.8 million
6.	Baseball	5.6 million
7.	Outdoor Soccer	5.2 million
8.	Darts	5.1 million
9.	Walking	4.1 million
10.	Skateboarding	3.9 million

GIRLS (AGES 6–17)		
1.	Bowling	5.9 million
2.	Walking	5.8 million
3.	Bicycling (Road)	5.5 million
4.	Running/Jogging	4.3 million
5.	Freshwater Fishing	3.2 million
6.	Outdoor Soccer	3.1 million
7.	Darts	2.7 million
8.	Ice Skating	2.5 million
9.	Basketball	2.3 million
10.	Inline Skating	2.2 million

Source: Sporting Goods Manufacturers Association's Sports & Participation Report, 2010

Little League

Little League Baseball and Softball is one of the largest youth sports programs in the world. It began in 1939 in Williamsport, Pennsylvania, with 30 boys playing on three teams. Today, more than 2.5 million boys and girls ages 4 to 18 play on nearly 168,000 Little League baseball and softball teams in more than 80 countries.

Find out more at *www.littleleague.org*

GLOBAL GAMES

Football, baseball, and auto racing are among the most popular professional sports in the United States. But around the world, soccer (called football in other countries) rules. What other sports do kids in other countries love to watch and play? Here are a few of them.

Cricket Cricket started in England in the 16th century. Today it is most popular in Great Britain and in former British colonies, such as India, Pakistan, and Australia. In some ways, cricket is like baseball. A pitcher, called a bowler, throws a ball (on a bounce) toward a target, called a wicket. A batsman guards the wicket by hitting the ball in any direction. The batting team scores runs and makes outs, and the matches are divided into innings. Major international matches are four innings, but they can take up to five days to complete. ▶

Rugby Rugby is similar to football but with a bigger ball and much less protective equipment. Teams score a try (much like a touchdown) by crossing the goal line with the ball. They also score by kicking the ball through goalposts. Players cannot pass the ball forward—only backward or sideways. They advance the ball mainly by running with it while trying to avoid being tackled by defenders. There are two popular types of the sport—rugby union has 15 players per team, and rugby league has 13. Rugby sevens, a variation of rugby union featuring seven-player teams, will debut as an Olympic sport in 2016.

Table Tennis Many kids in the United States have fun playing table tennis with friends and family. But table tennis, also known as Ping-Pong, is a serious competitive sports in many countries. Since 1988, table tennis has been an Olympic sport, with nearly all the gold medals being won by Chinese or Korean competitors.

Who Am I?

I was born in Oklahoma City in 1989. My father coached my high school basketball team, which I helped lead to four straight state championships. In college, I played for the Oklahoma Sooners and was chosen National Player of the Year as a sophomore. I then turned pro and was selected by the Los Angeles Clippers as the first pick in the 2009 National Basketball Association (NBA) draft. A knee injury sidelined me for the 2009–2010 season, but the following year I really made my mark with my ferocious dunks and physical play. I won the Slam Dunk contest at the 2011 NBA All-Star Game and was the unanimous choice for the 2010–2011 season's Rookie of the Year.

Answer: Blake Griffin

THE OLYMPIC GAMES

The first Olympics were held in Greece in 776 B.C. They featured one event—a footrace. For more than 1,000 years, the Olympic Games were held every four years. In 393 A.D., the Roman emperor Theodosius put an end to the Olympics. The first modern Games were held in Athens, Greece, in 1896. Since then, the Summer Olympics have taken place every four years at a different location. (The Games were canceled due to world wars in 1916, 1940, and 1944.)

2012 SUMMER OLYMPICS

Olympic Stadium

In 2012, London will host the Olympics for a record third time. (The United Kingdom's capital also was the site of the Summer Games in 1908 and 1948.) About 10,500 athletes from 205 countries or territories are expected to participate in the 2012 Games, which will take place from July 27 to August 12. Events will be held throughout and near London. Other parts of the United Kingdom will get in on the action as well. The new Olympic Park complex, built in London's East End section, will be the main site of the Games. It includes the 80,000-seat Olympic Stadium, where the track & field competitions and the opening and closing ceremonies will take place.

2012 Summer Olympic Sports		
Aquatics (diving, swimming, water polo)	Equestrian	Sailing
	Fencing	Shooting
Archery	Field Hockey	Table Tennis
Athletics (track & field)	Football (soccer)	Taekwondo
Badminton	Gymnastics	Tennis
Basketball	Handball	Triathlon
Boxing	Judo	Volleyball (beach, indoor)
Canoe	Modern Pentathlon	Weightlifting
Cycling	Rowing	Wrestling

NEW IN 2012

For the first time in Olympic history, women will compete in the ring for a chance to win a medal in boxing. Another new 2012 event will be mixed-doubles tennis, which features teams made up of one man and one woman. Two sports included in the 2008 Olympics have been eliminated from the 2012 Games: baseball and softball.

YOUTH OLYMPIC GAMES

The first-ever Youth Olympic Games took place August 14–26, 2010, in Singapore. More than 3,500 athletes ages 14 to 18 from around the world competed in 201 events in 26 different summer sports. China won the most total medals (51) and the most gold medals (30). The International Olympic Committee (IOC) plans to hold the Youth Olympic Games every two years, alternating between summer and winter events. The first Winter Youth Olympic Games are scheduled be held January 13–22, 2012, in Innsbruck, Austria.

LOOKING AHEAD

2014 Winter Olympics | Sochi, Russia | February 7 to February 23, 2014

Sochi, a city on the coast of the Black Sea in southern Russia, will host the 22nd Winter Olympics. The 2014 Games will be the first Olympics held in Russia since it became an independent country. The IOC voted not to add any new sports for these Games.

2016 Summer Olympics | Rio de Janeiro, Brazil | August 5 to August 21, 2016

Rio de Janeiro, Brazil, will host the 2016 Summer Games. The Rio Olympics will be the first ever held in South America. The Games will include two new sports: golf and rugby sevens.

THE WINTER OLYMPICS

The first Winter Olympics were held in Chamonix, France, in 1924. The competition was originally called "the Winter Sports Week." The event wasn't officially recognized as the first Winter Olympics until after the Games were completed. Sixteen countries were represented by 258 athletes. Only 11 were women. Originally, the winter and summer games were both held every four years during the same year. But starting in 1994, the schedule changed. Now the winter and summer games alternate every two years.

2010 WINTER GAMES

Vancouver, Canada, hosted the 21st Winter Games, which took place February 12–28, 2010. More than 2,500 athletes from a record 82 countries competed for 86 gold medals in 15 different sports. The United States sent the most athletes, 212. Seven countries sent athletes to the Winter Games for the first time in 2010: the Cayman Islands, Colombia, Ghana, Montenegro, Pakistan, Peru, and Serbia.

2010 Medal Count

A total of 26 countries won at least one medal in Vancouver. The 37 medals won by the United States were the most by any country in Winter Olympic history. Canada's 14 gold medals were also a Winter Olympic record. Here are the top 10 medal-winning nations.

COUNTRY	Gold	Silver	Bronze	TOTAL
UNITED STATES	9	15	13	**37**
GERMANY	10	13	7	**30**
CANADA	14	7	5	**26**
NORWAY	9	8	6	**23**
AUSTRIA	4	6	6	**16**
RUSSIA	3	5	7	**15**
SOUTH KOREA	6	6	2	**14**
CHINA	5	2	4	**11**
SWEDEN	5	2	4	**11**
FRANCE	2	3	6	**11**

did you Know?

The United States may have won the most total medals at the Vancouver Games, but a woman from Norway took home more medals than any other single competitor. Cross-country skier Marit Bjørgen won the gold in three events—the individual sprint, individual pursuit, and 4 x 5 kilometer relay. She also nabbed a silver in the 30 kilometer classical and a bronze in the 10 kilometer freestyle event, bringing her medal count to five. That's a lot of hardware!

OLYMPIC ALL-STARS

U.S. athletes provided some of the most exciting moments at the 2010 Winter Olympics.

Snowboarder **Shaun White**, who took home the gold medal in the men's half-pipe at the 2006 Winter Olympics in Turin, Italy, wowed the crowds again in Vancouver. The 23-year-old redhead was assured of a second straight gold after notching a high score on his first half-pipe run. White could have taken it easy on his second run, but instead he made history. He ended the run with his new signature move, the Double McTwist 1260, which includes two flips and three-and-a-half spins.

Shaun White

Before the 2010 Olympics, skier **Bode Miller** was largely a forgotten man. After winning two silver medals at the 2002 Olympics, Miller failed to win a single medal in 2006. In Vancouver, though, Miller came back in a big way. He won three medals, including a gold in the super combined event.

Lindsey Vonn was considered the United States' top skier coming into the 2010 Olympics, but a serious shin injury threatened to sideswipe her medal quest. Vonn skied through the pain, though, and won the gold in the downhill competition, becoming the first U.S. woman to do so. She later added a silver in the super G.

Lindsey Vonn

Apolo Ohno entered the Vancouver Games as the most successful short track speed skater in Olympic history. The 27-year-old added three medals to his total: a silver in the 1,500 meters and bronze medals in the 1,000 meters and 5,000-meter relay. He now has more Winter Olympic medals than any other U.S. athlete.

Top U.S. Olympic Winter Games Medal Winners

Athlete	Sport	Years*	G	S	B	Total
Apolo Ohno	short track speed skating	2002, 2006, 2010	2	2	4	8
Bonnie Blair	speed skating	1988, 1992, 1994	5	0	1	6
Eric Heiden	speed skating	1980	5	0	0	5
Bode Miller	alpine skiing	2002, 2010	1	3	1	5
Cathy Turner	short track speed skating	1992, 1994	2	1	1	4

*Only years in which the athlete won medals are listed.

PARALYMPICS

The Paralympic Games are the official Olympic Games for athletes with physical, mental, or sensory disabilities. The Games got their start in 1948, when Sir Ludwig Guttman organized a competition in England for World War II veterans with spinal-cord injuries. When athletes from the Netherlands joined in 1952, the movement went international.

Olympic-style competition began in Rome in 1960, and the first Winter Paralympics were held in Sweden in 1976. Since 1988, the Paralympics have been held just after the Winter and Summer Olympic competitions. Following the 2010 Winter Olympics in Vancouver, about 500 athletes from 44 countries took part in the Paralympic Games at the Vancouver Olympic venues. Athletes from around the world will compete in the 2012 Summer Paralympic Games in London.

OFFICIAL PARALYMPIC SPORTS

Six Competitive Levels: wheelchair, intellectual disabilities, amputees, visual disabilities, cerebral palsy, and other mobility disabilities

Winter: alpine skiing, biathlon, cross-country skiing, ice sledge hockey, wheelchair curling

Summer: archery, boccia, cycling, equestrian, goalball, judo, powerlifting, rowing, sailing, shooting, soccer, swimming, table tennis, track & field, volleyball, wheelchair basketball, wheelchair fencing, wheelchair rugby, wheelchair tennis

Sledge hockey

Find out more at *www.paralympic.org*

SPECIAL OLYMPICS

The Special Olympics is the world's largest program of sports training and athletic competition for children and adults with intellectual disabilities. Founded in 1968, Special Olympics has offices in all 50 states, Washington, D.C., and throughout the world. The organization offers training and competition to more than 3 million athletes in about 175 countries.

Special Olympics holds World Games every two years. These alternate between summer and winter sports. The last Special Olympics World Summer Games took place June 25 to July 4, 2011, in Athens, Greece. The next World Winter Games are scheduled to be held in 2013 in Pyeongchang, South Korea.

To volunteer or find out more, visit: *www.specialolympics.org*

Special Olympics basketball

Auto Racing

NASCAR

Bill France founded the National Association for Stock Car Auto Racing (NASCAR) in 1947. Stock cars look a lot like the cars that are "in stock" at a car dealership. In 1949, Red Byron won the first NASCAR championship as the top driver of the season. Since 2008, the championship has been known as the Sprint Cup. Races in the Sprint Cup series include the Daytona 500 and the Brickyard 400.

NASCAR CHAMPIONS

Year	Champion	Year	Champion	Year	Champion
1984	Terry Labonte	1993	Dale Earnhardt	2002	Tony Stewart
1985	Darrell Waltrip	1994	Dale Earnhardt	2003	Matt Kenseth
1986	Dale Earnhardt	1995	Jeff Gordon	2004	Kurt Busch
1987	Dale Earnhardt	1996	Terry Labonte	2005	Tony Stewart
1988	Bill Elliott	1997	Jeff Gordon	2006	Jimmie Johnson
1989	Rusty Wallace	1998	Jeff Gordon	2007	Jimmie Johnson
1990	Dale Earnhardt	1999	Dale Jarrett	2008	Jimmie Johnson
1991	Dale Earnhardt	2000	Bobby Labonte	2009	Jimmie Johnson
1992	Alan Kulwicki	2001	Jeff Gordon	2010	Jimmie Johnson

Jimmie Johnson

INDIANAPOLIS 500

The Indianapolis 500 is the biggest event in open-wheel racing. Open-wheel cars have narrow bodies and big uncovered tires. The first Indy 500 was held at the Indianapolis Motor Speedway in 1911. Indy winners traditionally celebrate by drinking milk.

INDY WINNERS

Year	Winner	Speed
1911	Ray Harroun	74.602 mph
1920	Gaston Chevrolet	88.618 mph
1930	Billy Arnold	100.448 mph
1940	Wilbur Shaw	114.277 mph
1950	Johnnie Parsons	124.002 mph
1960	Jim Rathmann	138.767 mph
1970	Al Unser	155.749 mph
1980	Johnny Rutherford	142.862 mph
1990	Arie Luyendyk	185.981 mph*
2000	Juan Montoya	167.607 mph
2001	Helio Castroneves	131.294 mph
2002	Helio Castroneves	166.499 mph
2003	Gil de Ferran	156.291 mph
2004	Buddy Rice	138.518 mph
2005	Dan Wheldon	157.603 mph
2006	Sam Hornish Jr.	157.085 mph
2007	Dario Franchitti	151.774 mph
2008	Scott Dixon	143.567 mph
2009	Helio Castroneves	150.318 mph
2010	Dario Franchitti	161.623 mph
2011	Dan Wheldon	170.265 mph

Dan Wheldon

*Race record for average lap speed.

BASEBALL

The first known game of baseball with rules similar to those of the modern game was played at Elysian Fields in Hoboken, New Jersey, on June 19, 1846. The current National League (NL) was formed in 1876. The American League (AL) was established in 1901. Since the early 1900s, the champions of the NL and AL have met in the World Series.

GIANTS WIN BIG!

The San Francisco Giants kicked off their 2011 season with a loss to their NL West division rivals the Los Angeles Dodgers. At the end of 2010, however, the Giants stood taller than any other Major League Baseball team, as they defeated the powerful Texas Rangers four games to one in the World Series. It was the first world championship for the Giants since 1954, when they still played in New York. (They started playing in San Francisco in 1958.) The Giants hadn't been expected to go very far in the playoffs, but excellent pitching performances from young starters such as Tim Lincecum and Matt Cain combined with clutch hitting helped propel them to victory. Shortstop Edgar Renteria, who hit .412 (7 for 17) with two home runs and six runs batted in, was named World Series MVP.

2010 AWARD WINNERS

MVP	CY YOUNG (top pitcher)	ROOKIE OF THE YEAR
AL: Josh Hamilton, Texas Rangers	AL: Felix Hernandez, Seattle Mariners	AL: Neftali Feliz, Texas Rangers
NL: Joey Votto, Cincinnati Reds	NL: Roy Halladay, Philadelphia Phillies	NL: Buster Posey, San Francisco Giants

Fabulous Fenway

The year 2012 marks the 100th birthday of Fenway Park, the home of the Boston Red Sox and the oldest ballpark in Major League Baseball. On April 20, 1912, Fenway hosted its first official game. During the stadium's first seven years, the Red Sox won four World Series. However, after the 1918 season, the Fenway faithful had to wait 86 years before their beloved team claimed another championship. In recent years, the Red Sox have done their grand old ballpark proud, notching World Series victories in 2004 and 2007. Fenway boasts many unique features, perhaps the most famous being its towering left-field fence. Painted green and standing 36 feet, 2 inches tall, it has long been known as the Green Monster.

SOME MAJOR LEAGUE RECORDS*

BATTERS

Most Home Runs

Career: 762, Barry Bonds (1986–2007)
Season: 73, Barry Bonds (2001)
Game: 4, by 12 different players

Most Hits

Career: 4,256, Pete Rose (1963–86)
Season: 262, **Ichiro Suzuki** (2004)
Game: 7, Rennie Stennett (1975)

Most Stolen Bases

Career: 1,406, Rickey Henderson (1979–2003)

Season: 130, Rickey Henderson (1982)
Game: 6, by four different players

PITCHERS

Most Strikeouts

Career: 5,714, Nolan Ryan (1966–93)
Season: 383, Nolan Ryan (1973)
Game: 20, Roger Clemens (1986, 1996); **Kerry Wood** (1998)

Most Wins

Career: 511, Cy Young (1890–1911)
Season: 41, Jack Chesbro (1904)

Most Saves

Career: 601, **Trevor Hoffman** (1993–2010)
Season: 62, **Francisco Rodriguez** (2008)

*Through the 2010 season. Players in bold played in 2010. Game stats are for nine-inning games only.

Formerly Known As ...

Did you know that most of Major League Baseball's 30 teams used to play under a different name or in a different city—or both? The **Atlanta Braves**, for example, used to be the Boston Braves (and for a time, the Boston Bees) and then were the Milwaukee Braves before starting play in Atlanta in 1966. The **Oakland Athletics** were the Philadelphia Athletics and then the Kansas City Athletics before moving to the West Coast in 1968. Washington, D.C., was the original home of today's **Minnesota Twins** and, after that, of the present-day **Texas Rangers**. The current **Washington Nationals** used to be the Montreal Expos.

The Montreal Expos became the Washington Nationals after the 2004 season.

BASEBALL HALL OF FAME

In 2011, baseball celebrated the 75th anniversary of its first Hall of Fame class. The 1936 inductees were five legendary players: Babe Ruth, Ty Cobb, Honus Wagner, Christy Mathewson, and Walter Johnson. In 1939, the current home of the National Baseball Hall of Fame and Museum officially opened in Cooperstown, New York. Three new members were inducted in 2011: twelve-time All-Star second baseman Roberto Alomar, durable pitcher Bert Blyleven, and baseball executive Pat Gillick. That brought the total number of members to 295.

Find out more about baseball's legends at *www.baseballhall.org*

BASKETBALL

Dr. James Naismith invented basketball in Springfield, Massachusetts, in 1891. He used peach baskets as hoops. At first, each team had nine players instead of five. Big-time pro basketball started in the late 1940s, when the National Basketball Association (NBA) was formed. The Women's National Basketball Association (WNBA) began play in 1997.

New Champions

The 2011 NBA Finals saw the Dallas Mavericks square off against the Miami Heat—a rematch of the 2006 championships. Although the Heat triumphed in 2006, the Mavs emerged victorious this time, taking the series four games to two to capture their first league title. Heading into the 2010–2011 season, the Heat looked to be the team to beat after signing three star free agents: LeBron James, Chris Bosh, and their own Dwyane Wade. However, the strong play of such Dallas veterans as Dirk Nowitzki, Jason Kidd, and Jason Terry powered the Mavs past Miami. Nowitzki was chosen Finals MVP.

The Chicago Bulls finished with the best regular-season record but fell to Miami in the playoffs. Chicago's Derek Rose was named regular-season MVP. The Oklahoma City Thunder's Kevin Durant led the league in scoring for the second straight year. Shaquille O'Neal, the NBA's fifth all-time leading scorer, announced his retirement after his team, the Boston Celtics, was eliminated from the playoffs.

Dirk Nowitzki (41)

HALL OF FAME

The Naismith Memorial Hall of Fame in Springfield, Massachusetts, honors great players, coaches, and others who have had a big impact on the game. The 2011 class included Chris Mullen, who also was inducted as part of the 1992 Olympic "Dream Team" in 2010, and five-time NBA champion Dennis Rodman. The other new members chosen were ABA/NBA star Artis Gilmore, international great Arvydas Sabonis, Boston Celtics forward Tom "Satch" Sanders, four-time Olympic gold medalist Teresa Edwards, NBA coaching legend Tex Winter, NCAA coaches Herb Magee and Tara Vanderveer, and Harlem Globetrotters "clown prince" Reece "Goose" Tatum.

Find out more about the legends of basketball at *www.hoophall.com*

2010-2011 NBA LEADERS

Points per Game:	27.7	Kevin Durant	Oklahoma City Thunder
Rebounds per Game:	15.2	Kevin Love	Minnesota Timberwolves
Assists per Game:	11.4	Steve Nash	Phoenix Suns
Blocks per Game:	2.6	Andrew Bogut	Milwaukee Bucks
Field Goal Percentage:	61.5	Nene	Denver Nuggets
Steals per Game:	2.4	Chris Paul	New Orleans Hornets
Free Throw Percentage:	93.4	Stephen Curry	Golden State Warriors
3-Point Field Goal Percentage:	45.7	Matt Bonner	San Antonio Spurs

Some All-Time NBA Records*

POINTS

Career: 38,387, Kareem Abdul-Jabbar (1969–1989)

Season: 4,029, Wilt Chamberlain (1961–1962)

Game: 100, Wilt Chamberlain (1962)

ASSISTS

Career: 15,806, John Stockton (1984–2003)

Season: 1,164, John Stockton (1990–1991)

Game: 30, Scott Skiles (1990)

REBOUNDS

Career: 23,924, Wilt Chamberlain (1959–1973)

Season: 2,149, Wilt Chamberlain (1960–1961)

Game: 55, Wilt Chamberlain (1960)

3-POINTERS

Career: 2,612, **Ray Allen** (1996–2011)

Season: 269, **Ray Allen** (2005–2006)

Game: 12, **Kobe Bryant** (2003); Donyell Marshall (2005)

*Through the 2010-2011 season. Players in bold played in 2010–2011.

The WNBA

Australian forward/center Lauren Jackson led the Seattle Storm to the 2010 WNBA championship. Seattle defeated the Atlanta Dream three games to none to win its second-ever league crown. Jackson was named MVP of both the regular season and the Finals.

The Storm notched a league-best 28–6 record during the regular season, then marched undefeated through the playoffs. Also in 2010, the Phoenix Mercury's Diana Taurasi won her fourth WNBA scoring title in five years. The Minnesota Lynx selected two-time college player of the year Maya Moore as the first pick in the 2011 WNBA Draft. Moore led the University of Connecticut to back-to-back national championships in 2009 and 2010.

Lauren Jackson (15)

COLLEGE BASKETBALL

The men's National Collegiate Athletic Association (NCAA) Tournament began in 1939. Today, it is a spectacular 65-team extravaganza that is part of March Madness. Games on the Final Four weekend, when the semifinals and finals are played, are watched by millions of viewers. The Women's NCAA Tournament began in 1982 and has soared in popularity.

THE 2011 NCAA TOURNAMENTS

Heroic Huskies

The No. 3-seeded Connecticut Huskies put on a smothering defensive display in the 2011 NCAA men's basketball title game, as they defeated the No. 8 Butler Bulldogs, 53–41. While Connecticut celebrated its third-ever NCAA championship, underdog Butler suffered its second straight title game loss. Huskies point guard Kemba Walker led all scorers with 19 points on the way to being named the tournament's Most Outstanding Player. In the Final Four contests that determined who played for the title, UConn squeaked by the 2nd-seeded Kentucky Wildcats, 66–65, while Butler downed an upstart 11th seed, the Virginia Commonwealth Rams, 70–62.

Kemba Walker (15) ▶

Don't Mess With Texas A&M!

In a match-up of two No. 2 seeds, the Texas A&M Aggies beat the Notre Dame Fighting Irish, 76–70, to claim the 2011 NCAA women's basketball title. It was the Aggies' first-ever NCAA championship. The game featured a dominating performance by Texas A&M center Danielle Adams, the tournament's Most Outstanding Player, who scored 22 of her 30 points in the second half. To reach the finals, each team had to overcome a pair of top-seeded powerhouses. The Aggies bested the Stanford Cardinal, 63–62, in a see-saw battle, while the Fighting Irish upset the defending NCAA champion Connecticut Huskies, 72–63.

Conn-secutive Wins

The University of Connecticut Huskies women's college basketball team pulled off an amazing feat that spanned more than two years. From November 2008 to December 2010, UConn won 90 games in a row, breaking the NCAA record of 88 consecutive wins that was set by the UCLA men's basketball team during 1971–1974. The Huskies' streak began at the start of the 2008–2009 season with an 82–71 victory over Georgia Tech and ended on December 30, 2010, with a 71–59 loss to Stanford. Along the way, Connecticut completed two undefeated seasons, during which the Huskies won the 2009 and 2010 NCAA titles. In their impressive run, the Huskies beat their opponents by an average of more than 33 points!

UConn forward Maya Moore ▶

COLLEGE FOOTBALL

Football began as a college sport in the 1800s. In 1998, the National Collegiate Athletic Association (NCAA) introduced the Bowl Championship Series (BCS), which pits many of the top-ranked college football teams against each other in an effort to determine a national champion.

On January 10, 2011, the Auburn Tigers beat the Oregon Ducks, 22–19, in the BCS National Championship Game in Glendale, Arizona. Both teams entered the game undefeated. The first half ended with Auburn leading 16–11. A third quarter field goal by Tigers kicker Wes Byrum made the score 19–11, but the Ducks tied things up with less than three minutes to play. Auburn then drove down to Oregon's 1-yard line, and Byrum kicked a field goal as time expired, giving the Tigers the victory. Auburn running back Michael Dyer was named Offensive Player of the Game after rushing for 143 yards and helping to set up the winning kick.

Wes Byrum

Bowled Over!

Here are the results of other major bowl games played in January 2011.

Rose Bowl	Pasadena, CA	Texas Christian (TCU) 21, Wisconsin 19
Sugar Bowl	New Orleans, LA	Ohio State 31, Arkansas 26
Fiesta Bowl	Glendale, AZ	Oklahoma 48, Connecticut 20
Orange Bowl	Miami, FL	Stanford 40, Virginia Tech 12

HEISMAN TROPHY

In December 2010, Auburn Tigers quarterback Cam Newton was named the 76th winner of the Heisman Trophy as the top college player in the nation. Newton passed for 2,589 yards and threw 28 touchdowns, while also running for 1,409 yards and scoring 20 rushing touchdowns, in leading Auburn to the BCS National Championship Game.

ALL-TIME DIVISION I NCAA LEADERS*

RUSHING

YARDS

Career: 6,397, Ron Dayne, Wisconsin (1996–1999)
Season: 2,628, Barry Sanders, Okla. St. (1988)
Game: 406, LaDainian Tomlinson, TCU (1999)

TOUCHDOWNS

Career: 73, Travis Prentice, Miami of Ohio (1996–1999)
Season: 37, Barry Sanders, Okla. St. (1988)

PASSING

YARDS

Career: 17,072, Timmy Chang, Hawaii (2000–2004)
Season: 5,833, B.J. Symons, Texas Tech (2003)
Game: 716, David Klingler, Houston (1990)

TOUCHDOWNS

Career: 134, Graham Harrell, Texas Tech (2005–2008)
Season: 58, Colt Brennan, Hawaii (2006)

*Through the 2010 season

NATIONAL FOOTBALL LEAGUE

The professional league that became the modern National Football League (NFL) started in 1920. The rival American Football League began in 1960. The two leagues played the first Super Bowl in 1967. In 1970, the leagues merged to become the NFL as we know it today.

PACKERS POWER

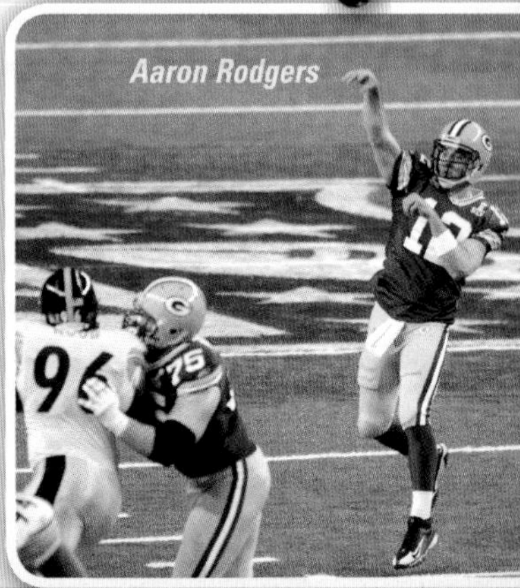
Aaron Rodgers

On February 6, 2011, the Green Bay Packers defeated the Pittsburgh Steelers, 31–25, in Super Bowl XLV. The victory gave the Packers their fourth Super Bowl win. Green Bay jumped out to a 14–0 first quarter lead and led 21–10 at halftime, but the Steelers made things interesting in the fourth quarter when they closed to within 28–25. However, Green Bay tacked on a field goal with just over two minutes to play and held on for the victory. Packers quarterback Aaron Rodgers, who completed 24 of 39 passes for 306 yards and threw three touchdowns, was named Super Bowl MVP.

2011 PRO BOWL

In 2011, for the second straight year, the Pro Bowl was played the week before the Super Bowl. Prior to 2010, the NFL all-star game was played the week after the championship game. In a high-scoring contest, the National Football Conference beat the American Football Conference, 55–41. Washington Redskins cornerback DeAngelo Hall, who returned a fumble for a touchdown and also had an interception, was named MVP.

Tom Brady

2010 NFL LEADERS

Rushing Yards: 1,616, Arian Foster, Houston Texans

Receptions: 115, Roddy White, Atlanta Falcons

Receiving Yards: 1,448, Brandon Lloyd, Denver Broncos

Touchdowns: 18, Arian Foster, Houston Texans

Passing Yards: 4,710, Philip Rivers, San Diego Chargers

Touchdown Passes: 36, Tom Brady, New England Patriots

Points: 143, David Akers, Philadelphia Eagles

Interceptions: 8, Ed Reed, Baltimore Ravens

Sacks: 15.5, DeMarcus Ware, Dallas Cowboys

NFL All-Time Record Holders*

RUSHING YARDS
- Career: 18,355, Emmitt Smith (1990–2004)
- Season: 2,105, Eric Dickerson (1984)
- Game: 296, **Adrian Peterson** (2007)

RECEIVING YARDS
- Career: 22,895, Jerry Rice (1985–2004)
- Season: 1,848, Jerry Rice (1995)
- Game: 336, Willie Anderson (1989)

PASSING YARDS
- Career: 71,838, **Brett Favre** (1991–2010)
- Season: 5,084, Dan Marino (1984)
- Game: 554, Norm Van Brocklin (1951)

POINTS SCORED
- Career: 2,544, Morten Andersen (1982–2004, 2006–2007)
- Season: 186, **LaDainian Tomlinson** (2006)
- Game: 40, Ernie Nevers (1929)

*Through the 2010 season.

Players in **bold** played in 2010.

NFL DRAFT

The 76th annual NFL Draft was held April 28–30, 2011, in New York City. The Carolina Panthers had the first pick, and chose Auburn University Tigers quarterback Cam Newton. NFL teams have been holding a draft to select top college players since 1936. That year, with the first pick in NFL Draft history, the Philadelphia Eagles selected Jay Berwanger of the University of Chicago.

Over the years, many future NFL superstars were taken first overall in the draft. That list includes Peyton Manning (1998) and Hall of Fame quarterbacks Terry Bradshaw (1970), John Elway (1983), and Troy Aikman (1989). A player's draft position is not always an indication of his future success, however. Many high draft picks have had short NFL careers. And many players who were selected in late rounds became stars. For example, star quarterback Tom Brady was the New England Patriots' 199th overall pick in 2000.

Cam Newton

PRO FOOTBALL HALL OF FAME

The Pro Football Hall of Fame in Canton, Ohio, was founded in 1963 to honor outstanding players, coaches, and contributors to the NFL. Running back Marshall Faulk and cornerback/kickoff returner/punt returner Deion Sanders topped the list of seven members who were scheduled to be inducted on August 6, 2011. Faulk rushed for more than 1,000 yards in seven of his first eight NFL seasons. The multi-talented Sanders returned nine interceptions, six punts, and three kickoffs for touchdowns during his career. They were joined by defensive end Richard Dent, linebackers Chris Hanburger and Les Richter, NFL Films creator Ed Sabol, and tight end Shannon Sharpe.

Learn more about football's biggest names at *www.profootballhof.com*

GOLF

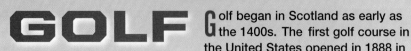

Golf began in Scotland as early as the 1400s. The first golf course in the United States opened in 1888 in Yonkers, New York. The sport has grown to include both men's and women's professional tours. And millions of other golfers play just for fun.

The men's tour in the U.S. is run by the Professional Golfers' Association (PGA). The four major championships (with the year first played) are:

- British Open (1860)
- United States Open (1895)
- PGA Championship (1916)
- Masters Tournament (1934)

The women's tour in the U.S. is guided by the Ladies Professional Golf Association (LPGA). The four major championships are:

- United States Women's Open (1946)
- McDonald's LPGA Championship (1955)
- Kraft Nabisco Championship (1972)
- Women's British Open (1976)

The All-Time "Major" Players

These pro golfers have won the most major championships through June 2011.

MEN	WOMEN
1. Jack Nicklaus, 18	1. Patty Berg, 15
2. Tiger Woods, 14	2. Mickey Wright, 13
3. Walter Hagen, 11	3. Louise Suggs, 11
4. Ben Hogan, 9	4. Babe Didrikson Zaharias, 10
Gary Player, 9	Annika Sorenstam, 10

▲Yani Tseng of Taiwan became the youngest golfer to capture three major LPGA championships when she won the 2010 Women's British Open at age 21.

did you Know?

GYMNASTICS

Although the sport dates back to ancient Egypt, modern-day gymnastics began in Europe in the early 1800s. It has been part of the Olympics since 1896. The first World Gymnastic Championships were held in the city of Antwerp, Belgium, in 1903.

Artistic gymnastics is the most popular form of gymnastics. Men compete in the high bar, parallel bars, rings, vault, pommel horse, floor exercise, individual all-around, and team events. The women's events are the uneven parallel bars, vault, balance beam, floor exercise, individual all-around, and team competition. Only women compete in rhythmic gymnastics, which includes the rope, hoop, ball, clubs, ribbon, and all-around events.

At the World Artistic Gymnastics Championships in October 2010, Japan's Kōhei Uchimura won the men's individual all-around competition. Russia's Aliya Mustafina took home the gold medal in the women's all-around. Finishing third in the men's and women's all-around, respectively, were the United States' Jonathan Horton and Rebecca Bross.

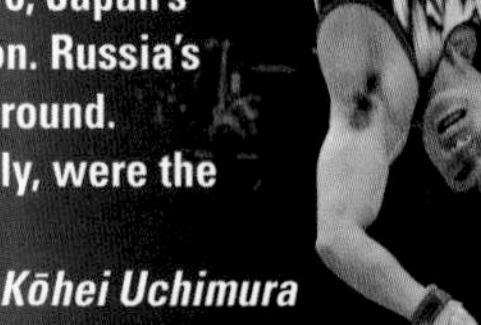

Kōhei Uchimura

ICE HOCKEY

Ice hockey began in Canada in the mid-1800s. The National Hockey League (NHL) was formed in 1917. Today the NHL has 30 teams. During the 2010–2011 season, there were 24 U.S. teams and six Canadian ones. However, the Atlanta Thrashers moved to Winnipeg, Canada, before the 2011–2012 season.

BRUINS WIN!

The Boston Bruins defeated the Vancouver Canucks in seven games to win their first Stanley Cup since 1972. Bruins goaltender Tim Thomas shut out the Canucks in the decisive Game 7 and allowed only eight goals during the entire series. Thomas, who set a record for the most saves in a Stanley Cup finals with 238, was awarded the Conn Smythe Trophy as the playoffs MVP.

SEASON	WINNER	RUNNER-UP
2000–2001	Colorado Avalanche	New Jersey Devils
2001–2002	Detroit Red Wings	Carolina Hurricanes
2002–2003	New Jersey Devils	Anaheim Mighty Ducks
2003–2004	Tampa Bay Lightning	Calgary Flames
2004–2005	Season canceled	
2005–2006	Carolina Hurricanes	Edmonton Oilers
2006–2007	Anaheim Ducks	Ottawa Senators
2007–2008	Detroit Red Wings	Pittsburgh Penguins
2008–2009	Pittsburgh Penguins	Detroit Red Wings
2009–2010	Chicago Blackhawks	Philadelphia Flyers
2010–2011	Boston Bruins	Vancouver Canucks

SOME ALL-TIME NHL RECORDS*

GOALS SCORED

Career: 894, Wayne Gretzky (1979–1999)

Season: 92, Wayne Gretzky (1981–1982)

Game: 7, Joe Malone (1920)

GOALIE WINS

Career: 625, **Martin Brodeur** (1992–2011)

Season: 48, **Martin Brodeur** (2006–2007)

POINTS

Career: 2,857, Wayne Gretzky (1979–1999)

Season: 215, Wayne Gretzky (1985–1986)

Game: 10, Darryl Sittler (1976)

GOALIE SHUTOUTS

Career: 116, **Martin Brodeur** (1992–2011)

Season: 22, George Hainsworth (1928–1929)

* Through the 2010–2011 season. Player in bold played in 2010–2011.

2010–2011 NHL League Leaders

Points: 104, Daniel Sedin, Vancouver Canucks

Goals: 50, Corey Perry, Anaheim Ducks

Assists: 75, Henrik Sedin, Vancouver Canucks

Save Percentage: .938, Tim Thomas, Boston Bruins

Wins: 38, Roberto Luongo, Vancouver Canucks; Carey Price, Montreal Canadiens

Twin brothers Daniel and Henrik Sedin

HALL OF FAME

Located in Toronto, Ontario, Canada, the Hockey Hall of Fame honors contributors to the sport both on and off the ice. The facility also features exhibits celebrating the history of ice hockey and the NHL. **Learn more at *www.hhof.com***

SOCCER

World Cup

The Reign of Spain

Held every four years, the Men's FIFA World Cup is a month-long tournament that is one of the most popular sporting events in the world. The 2010 World Cup kicked off June 11, 2010, in South Africa. Thirty-two teams from across the globe competed in 10 stadiums around South Africa, leading up to a July 11 final match in Johannesburg. Spain, making its first World Cup final appearance, faced off against the Netherlands, which had lost championship matches in 1974 and 1978. At the end of regulation play, the score was tied 0–0. Then, with only four minutes left in overtime, Spain's Cesc Fàbregas passed the ball to teammate Andrés Iniesta, who scored to give his team a 1–0 victory. Earlier in the tournament, the United States advanced to the round of 16, after notching a win and two ties during the group stage. However, the U.S. team was eliminated after a 2–1 loss to Ghana.

Andrés Iniesta

Looking Ahead: The next three men's World Cups will be held in Brazil (2014), Russia (2018), and Qatar (2022).

MEN

Year	Winner	Year	Winner	Year	Winner
1930	Uruguay	1958	Brazil	1986	Argentina
1934	Italy	1962	Brazil	1990	West Germany
1938	Italy	1966	England	1994	Brazil
1942	not held	1970	Brazil	1998	France
1946	not held	1974	West Germany	2002	Brazil
1950	Uruguay	1978	Argentina	2006	Italy
1954	West Germany	1982	Italy	2010	Spain

The Women Kick into Action

The FIFA Women's World Cup is also held every four years, one year after the men's tournament. The latest one began on June 26, 2011, in Germany. Sixteen teams participated in matches held at stadiums in nine different German cities, with the final scheduled to take place July 17 in Frankfurt. The U.S. team—led by Abby Wambach, who has scored more than 100 goals in international play—was trying to win its third tournament and first since 1999.

WOMEN

Year	Winner
1991	United States
1995	Norway
1999	United States
2003	Germany
2007	Germany

Looking Ahead: The next women's World Cup will be hosted by Canada in 2015.

Abby Wambach (17)

Major League Soccer

In 2010, Major League Soccer (MLS) expanded to 16 teams with the addition of the Philadelphia Union. The 2010 season ended with the Colorado Rapids beating FC Dallas, 2–1, in overtime for the MLS Cup. Colorado defender George John deflected a shot by Colorado striker Macoumba Kandji into his own goal to give the Rapids the championship. Colorado striker Conor Casey was named Most Valuable Player of the MLS Cup. FC Dallas star David Ferreira received the regular-season MVP honor. For 2011, MLS further expanded to 18 teams, as the Portland Timbers and the Vancouver Whitecaps FC joined the league.

David Ferreira

Women's Professional Soccer

Women's Professional Soccer (WPS) shrunk from seven teams to six for the 2011 season. The Western New York Flash joined the league, but two original WPS franchises, FC Gold Pride and the Chicago Red Stars, folded. In 2010, FC Gold Pride defeated the Philadelphia Independence, 4-0, in the WPS Championship Game. Gold Pride forward Marta was the league's leading goal scorer and was named the MVP for 2010.

Marta (10)

U.S. Youth Soccer

The United States Youth Soccer Association began in 1974 with 100,000 players. Today, more than 3 million young soccer enthusiasts from ages 5 to 19 are registered to participate. U.S. Youth Soccer seeks to inspire a lifelong passion for the game while promoting physical, emotional, and intellectual growth in its participants.

Find out more at *www.usyouthsoccer.org*

TENNIS

Modern tennis began in 1873. The first championships were held in Wimbledon, near London, four years later. In 1881, the first official U.S. men's championships were held at Newport, Rhode Island. Six years later, the first U.S. women's championships took place in Philadelphia. Today, the four most important tournaments, or Grand Slam events, are the Australian Open, the French Open, the All-England (Wimbledon) Championships, and the U.S. Open.

ALL-TIME GRAND SLAM SINGLES WINS

MEN	Australian	French	Wimbledon	U.S.	Total
Roger Federer (b. 1981)**	4	1	6	5	16
Pete Sampras (b. 1971)	2	0	7	5	14
Roy Emerson (b. 1936)	6	2	2	2	12
Bjorn Borg (b. 1956)	0	6	5	0	11
Rod Laver (b. 1938)	3	2	4	2	11
Rafael Nadal (b. 1986)**	1	6	2	1	10
Bill Tilden (1893–1953)	*	0	3	7	10

WOMEN	Australian	French	Wimbledon	U.S.	Total
Margaret Smith Court (b. 1942)	11	5	3	5	24
Steffi Graf (b. 1969)	4	6	7	5	22
Helen Wills Moody (1905–1998)	*	4	8	7	19
Chris Evert (b. 1954)	2	7	3	6	18
Martina Navratilova (b. 1956)	3	2	9	4	18

**Never played in tournament. **Player active in 2011. Wins through June 2011.*

SLAMMIN' GOOD TENNIS

In 2010 and 2011, Spain's Rafael Nadal loosened the tight grip that his rival Roger Federer of Switzerland long had on the men's tennis world. After Federer won the 2010 Australian Open to extend his men's record Grand Slam victory total to 16, Nadal captured four of the next five major tournaments. In June 2011, Nadal beat Federer to win his record-tying sixth French Open championship. Nadal took over the world number 1 ranking from Federer in 2010 and held onto it well into 2011.

As for the women, Serena Williams won two major titles in 2010 (the Australian Open and Wimbledon) to give her 13 career Grand Slam championships. However, health issues sidelined her during late 2010 and much of 2011. The 2010 U.S. Open and 2011 Australian Open were won by Belgium's Kim Clijsters. Li Na took the 2011 French Open to become the first Chinese player ever to win a Grand Slam singles title.

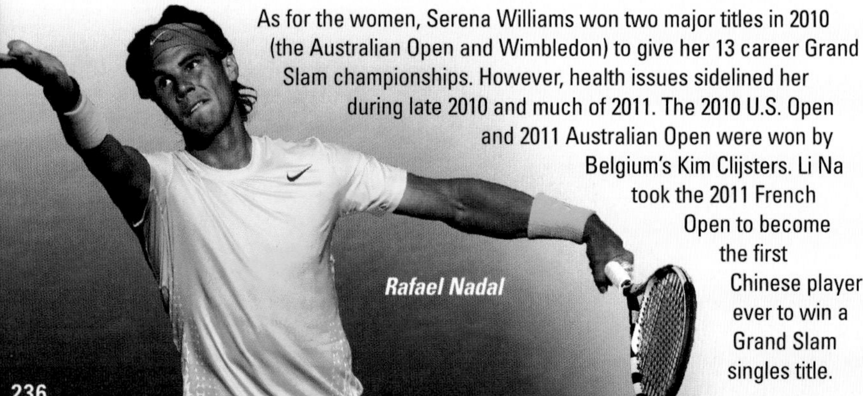

Rafael Nadal

Davis Cup

The Davis Cup is an international team tennis competition for men. It began in 1900 as a contest between just the United States and Great Britain called the International Lawn Tennis Challenge. Now more than 120 countries participate. Teams face off in a best-of-five series of singles and doubles matches to determine who advances. The United States has won the most Davis Cup championships (32), followed by Australia (28), France and Great Britain (9), and Sweden (7). Here are the results of the Davis Cup finals since 2000:

2000	Spain 3, Australia 1
2001	France 3, Australia 2
2002	Russia 3, France 2
2003	Australia 3, Spain 1
2004	Spain 3, United States 2
2005	Croatia 3, Slovakia 2
2006	Russia 3, Argentina 2
2007	United States 4, Russia 1
2008	Spain 3, Argentina 1
2009	Spain 5, Czech Republic 0
2010	Serbia 3, France 2

All in the Family

You know how parents are always telling kids to play nicely together? Well, here are a couple of pairs of siblings who play great together.

Serena Williams and her older sister Venus are known for their success in women's singles tennis, but they also make a pretty unstoppable doubles team. From 1999 through mid-2011, the Williams sisters won 12 Grand Slam doubles titles, including four straight major championships stretching from the 2009 Wimbledon tournament through the 2010 French Open.

Twin brothers Bob and Mike Bryan, meanwhile, have been the most successful men's doubles team in recent years. Since 2003, the twins have collected 10 Grand Slam doubles championships. And back in their college days at Stanford University, the Bryans also won the 1998 NCAA doubles title.

Venus and Serena Williams

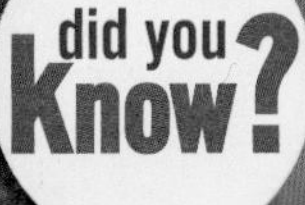

In March 2011, Ivo Karlović of Croatia hit the fastest tennis serve ever recorded. During a match in the Croatian capital of Zagreb, the 6-foot, 10-inch athlete smashed a serve 156 miles per hour (mph). That broke the record of 155 mph set in 2004 by the United States' Andy Roddick. In 2008, Venus Williams set the record for the fastest serve ever by a female player—130 mph.

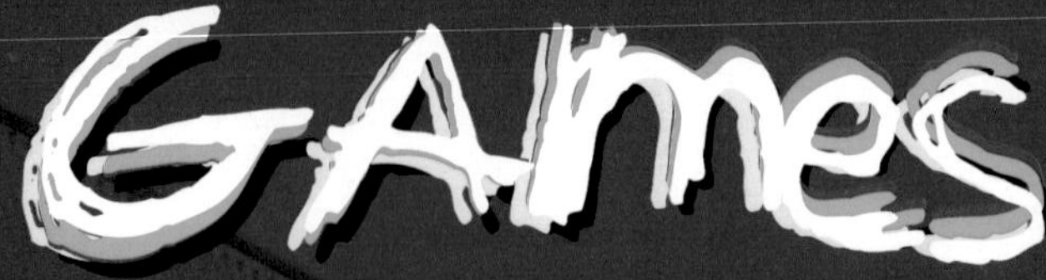

X Games

ESPN held the first X Games (originally called the Extreme Games) in Rhode Island and Vermont in 1995. The first Winter X Games followed two years later, in Big Bear Lake, California. Considered the Olympics of action sports, the X Games showcase fearless athletes who are always looking for new ways to go higher and faster and invent more exciting tricks.

Lindsey Jacobellis (in yellow)

Winter X Games The Winter X Games feature events in snowboarding, skiing, and snowmobiling. The 15th Winter X Games took place in Aspen, Colorado, January 27–30, 2011. Several of the top performances belonged to repeat champions. Shaun White set a record by winning his fourth consecutive men's snowboard superpipe gold medal. Lindsey Jacobellis claimed a fourth straight gold in the women's snowboarder X (snowboard cross)—her seventh time winning the event overall. Sarah Burke of Canada won her fourth career women's skiing superpipe. Kelly Clark became the first woman ever to land a 1080 (three complete revolutions in the air), on her way to winning her second-ever gold in the women's snowboard superpipe.

Summer X Games The Summer X Games feature events in Moto X (motocross), BMX, skateboarding, and rally car racing. The 17th Summer X Games were set to be held in downtown Los Angeles in late July 2011. The 2011 games saw the addition of the Enduro X (endurocross) competition. Both men and women competed, separately, in this indoor motorcycle event, which features a race course filled with logs, mud, rocks, sand, and other obstacles.

Learn more about extreme sports at *http://espn.go.com/action*

Dave Mirra

All-Time X Games Gold Medalists

Here are the X Games competitors who have won the most events at the annual action sports championships.

WINTER X GAMES		
Competitor	**Sport(s)**	**Medals***
Shaun White	snowboarding	11
Tanner Hall	skiing	7
Lindsey Jacobellis	snowboarding	7
Shaun Palmer	skiing, snowboarding	6
Tucker Hibbert	snowmobiling	6
Nate Holland	snowboarding	6
Tara Dakides	snowboarding	5
Blair Morgan	snowmobiling	5

*Through 2011. Athletes in bold competed in 2011 X Games.

SUMMER X GAMES		
Competitor	**Sport(s)**	**Medals***
Dave Mirra	BMX, rally car	14
Travis Pastrana	motocross, rally car	11
Tony Hawk	skateboarding	10
Andy Macdonald	skateboarding	8
Jamie Bestwick	BMX	8
Fabiola de Silva	inline skating	7
Bob Burnquist	skateboarding	7
Pierre-Luc Gagnon	skateboarding	7

*Through 2010. Athletes in bold competed in 2010 X Games.

SPORTS PUZZLES

SPORTS STAR *Spiral*

Use the clues to figure out which athletes' last names spiral around the red rule. Each name after number 1 begins with the last letter of the previous name. The names wind around in a clockwise direction. Hint: Each athlete in the puzzle is featured in the Sports section.

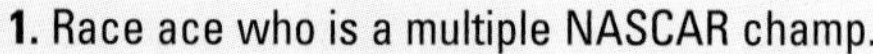

1. Race ace who is a multiple NASCAR champ.

2. Star Tiger who became a Panther on Draft Day.

3. Spaniard who knows about good service and Grand Slam success.

4. Ballplayer who stood tall on the mound at the World Series.

5. BMX cyclist who owns an extreme amount of gold.

6. Aggie b-baller who helped take the fight out of the Irish.

7. Canuck who can really shoot a puck.

8. Golf legend with "major" skills.

9. Speedy and versatile Pro Football Hall of Famer.

1						2
			6			
5			9			
					7	
			8			3
			4			

CHAMPIONSHIP WORD SEARCH

Find the names of the following championship teams discussed in the Sports section. The names are all hidden in the puzzle. They may appear running up, down, forward, backward, or diagonally.

Names to Find:

Aggies
Giants
Gold Pride
Huskies
Packers
Rapids
Storm
Tigers

S	E	I	G	U	S	K	I	E	S
S	I	J	O	Q	D	Z	V	B	T
E	H	U	S	K	I	E	S	O	E
I	O	Y	E	R	P	L	E	C	G
G	I	A	N	F	A	M	S	K	G
G	O	L	D	P	R	I	D	E	I
A	W	P	K	O	R	P	A	R	E
I	A	C	T	I	G	E	R	S	S
R	A	S	T	N	A	I	G	U	X
P	S	R	E	K	C	A	P	S	H

ANSWERS ON PAGES 334–336.

TECHNOLOGY & COMPUTERS

What is cyberbullying? → page 241

COMPUTER HIGHLIGHTS TIME LINE

100 B.C.	The Antikythera Mechanism, which used gears to predict the positions of astronomical bodies, was built by the ancient Greeks. It was the first known mechanical computer.
1623	Wilhelm Schickard built the first machine that could automatically add, subtract, multiply, and divide. He called it a "calculating clock."
1946	The first electronic, programmable, general-purpose computer was invented. It was called ENIAC, for "Electronic Numerical Integrator and Computer."
1967	The Advanced Research Projects Agency (ARPA) allotted money toward creating a computer network. It became ARPAnet, which evolved into the Internet.
1968	The first hypertext system was built by Douglas Engelbart of Stanford Research Institute. Called NLS (oN Line System), the system's design allowed users to move text and data with a mouse (which Engelbart invented in 1963).
1971	The "floppy disk" was introduced by IBM as a means of affordable portable storage.
1975	The Altair 8800 entered the market. It was the first widely sold personal microcomputer.
1975	Bill Gates and Paul Allen founded Microsoft. Later came the first version of Windows.
1990	The World Wide Web was first launched with one server by British physicist Tim Berners-Lee. He also created Uniform Resource Locators (URLs), the Hypertext Transfer Protocol (HTTP), and Hypertext Markup Language (HTML).
1996	Google, the Internet's most popular search engine, began as a graduate student project at Stanford University called BackRub.
2004	Facebook, the popular social networking site, was launched by Harvard University student Mark Zuckerberg. Membership was at first limited to college students but was opened to anyone in 2006.
2005	YouTube, a popular video sharing service, was founded.
2006	Twitter, a Web service letting people send or post short messages, was founded. The messages, called tweets, cannot be longer than 140 characters and are searchable.
2010	Apple introduced the iPad, a tablet computer. An updated model, the iPad 2, was released early in 2011.

did you Know?

Just five years after Facebook was opened to the general public, the social networking site had more than 500 million members around the world in 2011. The United States had the most Facebook users, about 30 percent of the total. Indonesia had the second-highest number of users, with the United Kingdom coming in third.

COMPUTER TALK

BIT The smallest unit of data

BYTE An amount of data equal to 8 bits

COOKIE Information, such as a password for a website, that is stored on your computer. When you go back to that site later, your browser sends the information (the "cookie") to the website.

ENCRYPTION The process of changing information into a code to keep others from reading it

HTTP Hypertext Transfer Protocol is the method of file exchange used on the World Wide Web.

MEGABYTE (MB) An amount of information equal to 1,048,516 bytes, or (in some situations) 1 million bytes

RAM OR RANDOM ACCESS MEMORY Memory your computer uses to open programs and store your work until you save it to a hard drive or disk. Information in RAM disappears when the computer is turned off.

ROM OR READ ONLY MEMORY Memory that contains permanent instructions for the computer and cannot be changed.

SPYWARE Software that observes computer activity without the user's knowledge. May record key strokes or fill the screen with ads

TABLET A portable computer with a touch-sensitive screen

URL OR UNIFORM RESOURCE LOCATOR The technical name for a website address

VIRUS A program that damages other programs and data. It gets into a computer through the Internet or shared disks.

WI-FI OR WIRELESS FIDELITY Technology that allows one computer to link to other computers and the Internet without wires

Social networking websites such as Facebook and MySpace can be a lot of fun. But they can also be a source of problems. To be on the safe side, you should always keep an eye out for risks.

Protect against cyberbullying. Cyberbullying refers to emails or posts sent over the Internet that are intended to embarrass or hurt another person. These posts often spread lies or tell secrets the victim shared in confidence. If you are a victim of a cyberbully, save the posts or emails and show them to an adult you trust. Often the person behind the bullying can be found. To help keep cyberbullying from spreading, refuse to pass along bullying emails about someone else, express disapproval of cyberbullying messages, and report them to an adult.

Be careful about what personal information you make public. Carefully guard your password, birthday, address, phone number, and other personal information. This can make it harder for others to steal your identity online.

Take advantage of the website's security features. Pick a unique, hard-to-guess password. Keep your profile viewable only by friends. If the website allows your username to be different from your real name, make sure yours is different—and does not include personal information, such as your age or town.

Beware of viruses. Antivirus software may not recognize new viruses. For this reason it is important to think twice before downloading an app or any other file from a source that you don't know or don't have reason to trust.

RESEARCH ON THE INTERNET

Limit the Keyword Search

Before you start researching a topic with a search engine, decide exactly what you need. Knowing what you're looking for makes it easier to find sites that have the information you need. It can also help you evaluate the source.

As you search the Internet, keep the following tips in mind:

- Make your search terms as specific as possible. Suppose you have an assignment that asks you to describe three famous inventions of Thomas Edison. Search for: famous inventions Thomas Edison.
- Put words in quotes when you are searching for a specific phrase. To find out which president said, "I cannot live without books," type the exact phrase in quotation marks (as shown) in the search box. Some search engines have an "Advanced Search" tool so that you can search for particular combinations of terms.
- Try using a synonym if you are having trouble with your search. Suppose you are searching for the different ways in which moisture, or water, reaches the ground. Try searching for "forms of precipitation."
- Try different search engines if one isn't producing results. The three most popular general search engines—Google (www.google.com), Yahoo (www.yahoo.com), and Bing (www.bing.com)—usually come up with slightly different sets of results.

Identify the Website

Huge amounts of information are on the Internet. While this makes the Internet great for research, not all sources are reliable. A wide variety of information is available, from facts and data to stories and opinions.

The ending of the main part of a web page's address may offer clues to the type of page. Government sites in the U.S. generally end in **.gov** or **.us**. These sites are reliable sources for data and objective reports. Nonprofit organizations often end in **.org**. Educational institutions end in **.edu**. Business sites usually end in **.com** or **.net**. Many international organizations end in **.int**.

ON THE JOB: SYSTEMS ENGINEER

Systems engineers are responsible for supporting, installing, and maintaining different computer systems, including e-mail systems. Chris Robley is a senior systems engineer in the IT (information technology) department of a worldwide fashion company. He agreed to talk to *The World Almanac for Kids* about his work.

What do you do in a typical day?

My typical day includes checking all of the company's computer systems and making sure that they're functioning properly. Company employees who are working from home or are traveling on business have to be able to access their work e-mail and reach work-related Internet sites. I help people who work for my company all around the world and who are having computer-related problems. My department is also responsible for updating the company's computer systems so that they run faster and so that our users can do more work from home or other remote locations.

What interests and strengths of yours make this job right for you?

The main interest and strength that suits me for this job is my desire to fix things that are broken. This started when I was young. As a kid, I would break my toy train in an attempt to figure out how it worked. Then I would have to fix it. Later, I started playing with bigger toys, like computers, and my curiosity for figuring out how thing worked and fixing them grew.

What kind of education or training did you need to get in order to do your job?

I have a bachelor's degree in mechanical engineering. I have also taken various specialized Microsoft classes.

What do you like best about your job? What is most challenging?

The best thing about my job is being able to help my company's employees with their computer problem anywhere in the world. Our company, like most, has become dependent on e-mails and other computer systems. This makes IT jobs important, but it can also be challenging because users need their problems fixed right away, and sometimes that just isn't possible.

TRANSPORTATION

When was the bicycle invented? → page 245

Getting from There to Here:
A SHORT HISTORY OF TRANSPORTATION

5000 B.C.

5000 B.C. People harness animal-muscle power. Oxen and donkeys carry heavy loads.

3500 B.C. Egyptians create the first sailboat. Before this, people made rafts or canoes and paddled them with poles or their hands.

3500 B.C. In Mesopotamia (modern-day Iraq), vehicles with wheels are invented. But the first wheels are made of heavy wood, and the roads are terrible.

A.D. 800 Fast, shallow-draft longships make Vikings a powerful force in Europe from 800 to 1100.

983 First locks to raise water level are built on China's Grand Canal. By 1400, a 1,500-mile water highway system was developed.

Around 1000 Using magnetic compasses, Chinese are able to sail long distances in flat-bottomed ships called junks.

1450s Portuguese build fast ships with three masts. These plus the compass usher in an age of exploration.

1660s Horse-drawn stagecoaches begin running in France. They stop at "stages" to switch horses and passengers—the first mass transit system.

1681 France's 150-mile Canal du Midi connects the Atlantic Ocean with the Mediterranean Sea.

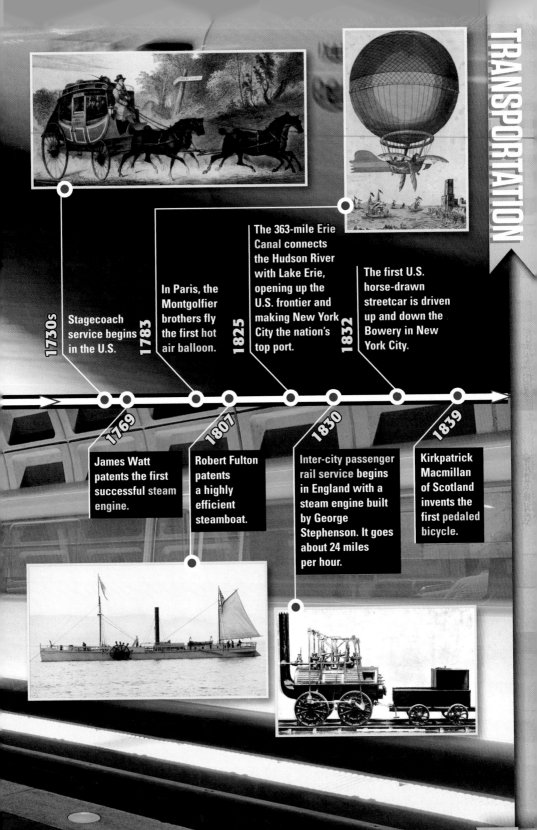

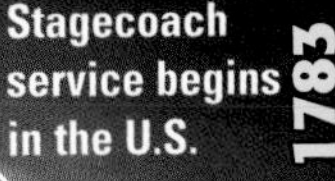

1730s Stagecoach service begins in the U.S.

1769 James Watt patents the first successful steam engine.

1783 In Paris, the Montgolfier brothers fly the first hot air balloon.

1807 Robert Fulton patents a highly efficient steamboat.

1825 The 363-mile Erie Canal connects the Hudson River with Lake Erie, opening up the U.S. frontier and making New York City the nation's top port.

1830 Inter-city passenger rail service begins in England with a steam engine built by George Stephenson. It goes about 24 miles per hour.

1832 The first U.S. horse-drawn streetcar is driven up and down the Bowery in New York City.

1839 Kirkpatrick Macmillan of Scotland invents the first pedaled bicycle.

1860s Paddle-wheel steamboats dominate U.S. river travel.

1862 Etienne Lenoir of Belgium builds the first car with an internal-combustion engine.

1863 Using steam locomotives, the London subway (known as the "tube") opens.

1869 Transcontinental railroad is completed at Promontory Point, Utah. The Suez Canal in Egypt opens, saving ships a long trip around Africa.

1873 San Francisco's cable car system begins service.

1887 First practical electric street railway system opens in the U.S. in Richmond, Virginia. Suburbs soon grow around cities as trolley systems let people live farther away from the workplace.

1897 The first U.S. subway service begins in Boston. New York City follows in 1904.

1903 At Kitty Hawk, North Carolina, the Wright brothers fly the first powered heavier-than-air machine.

1908 Henry Ford builds the first Model T, a practical car for the general public.

TRANSPORTATION

1914
The 50-mile Panama Canal opens, saving ships a nearly 6,000-mile trip around South America.

1939
The first practical helicopter and first jet plane are invented. The jet flies up to 434 mph. Jet passenger service began in 1952.

1964
Shinkansen "bullet train" service (124 mph) begins in Japan.

1969
U.S. astronauts aboard *Apollo 11* land on the Moon.

1981
The first space shuttle is launched on April 12, 1981.

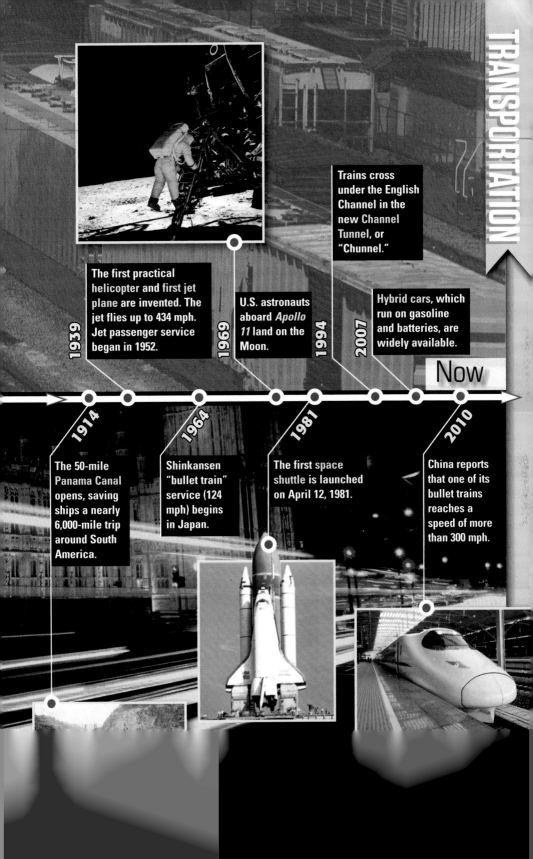

1994
Trains cross under the English Channel in the new Channel Tunnel, or "Chunnel."

2007
Hybrid cars, which run on gasoline and batteries, are widely available.

2010
China reports that one of its bullet trains reaches a speed of more than 300 mph.

Now

TRAVEL

What is the biggest theme park in the United States? ⇒ page 249

In the late 13th century, famed Italian adventurer Marco Polo took a winding 5,600-mile journey overland from Venice, Italy, to Beijing, China. When he returned to Venice, Polo published a chronicle of his travels. The stories were so fantastic that many people didn't believe his tales.

You may not be taking a journey of thousands of miles on your next trip, but the excitement of traveling is the same. People always have the desire to stretch their legs, explore new places, and have adventures that others may—or may not—believe.

The 10 Most Visited

Countries*	U.S. Tourist Sites*
1. France	1. Times Square, NY
2. United States	2. Las Vegas Strip, Las Vegas
3. Spain	3. National Mall and Memorials, Washington, D.C.
4. China	4. Faneuil Hall, Boston
5. Italy	5. Magic Kingdom, Lake Buena Vista, FL
6. United Kingdom	6. Golden Gate National Recreation Area, San Francisco, CA
7. Turkey	7. Disneyland, Anaheim, CA
8. Germany	8. Fisherman's Wharf, San Francisco, CA
9. Malaysia	9. Hollywood Walk of Fame, Los Angeles, CA
10. Mexico	10. Great Smoky Mountains National Park, NC and TN
*2009	*2010

World's Five Most-Visited Amusement Parks*

1. Magic Kingdom, Walt Disney World (Lake Buena Vista, Florida), 17.2 million
2. Disneyland (Anaheim, California), 16.9 million
3. Tokyo Disneyland (Japan), 13.6 million
4. Disneyland Paris (Marne-La-Vallee, France), 12.7 million
5. Tokyo Disney Sea (Japan), 12.0 million

*2009

AMUSEMENT PARKS

The first amusement parks appeared in Europe more than 400 years ago. Attractions included flower gardens, bowling, music, and a few simple rides.

Today's amusement parks are much more impressive. With super-fast roller coasters, parades, shows, and other attractions, amusement parks now have something to amuse just about anyone. Here's a look at some of the most popular amusement parks in the U.S.

FABULOUS FACTS

Biggest Park: Walt Disney World, Lake Buena Vista, Florida, 28,000 acres

Most Rides: 74, Cedar Point, Sandusky, Ohio

Most Roller Coasters: 17, Cedar Point, Sandusky, Ohio

Fastest Roller Coaster: 128 mph, Kingda Ka, Six Flags Great Adventure, Jackson, New Jersey ▶

Tallest Roller Coaster: 456 feet, Kingda Ka, Six Flags Great Adventure, Jackson, New Jersey

▶ **Cedar Point (Sandusky, Ohio)** One of the oldest amusement parks in the U.S., Cedar Point (on Lake Erie) opened in 1870. Its first roller coaster, the Switchback Railway, opened in 1892. It had a then-dizzying 25-foot-high hill, on which riders traveled at about 10 mph. Today at Cedar Point, the Top Thrill Dragster roller coaster reaches a height of 420 feet, and the cars zip along at a top speed of 120 mph! There are also plenty of other attractions, including Soak City, which features water rides and a wave pool.

▶ **Water World (Denver, Colorado)** One of the largest water parks in the United States, Water World opened in 1982. There are 38 rides on its 64 acres. Among a wide variety of attractions are more family tube rides than at any other water park in the U.S. and Wally World for young children. Voyage to the Center of the Earth is an enclosed tube ride that spans more than a quarter of a mile. The park also includes some of the highest water slides in the world (Flatline, Redline, and Pipeline), where riders can reach speeds of up to 40 miles per hour.

▶ **Universal Studios Florida/Islands of Adventure (Orlando, Florida)** Universal Studios opened in 1990, and visitors have been "riding the movies" there ever since. Rides, shows, and other attractions feature favorite movie and TV characters, including Shrek, Spiderman, the Incredible Hulk, and Dr. Doom. In 2010, Universal opened a major new attraction, The Wizarding World of Harry Potter, which has three rides, as well as shops and a restaurant.

SOME MUST-SEE MUSEUMS

As you travel to new places, you can learn a lot—and have a lot of fun—by visiting local museums. Some museums have exhibits about space, the history of life on Earth, and other areas of science. Some display great art. Some focus on American history. And there are museums about almost any subject you can imagine. Here is a small sampling of some of the leading museums in the United States.

▲ *Kennedy Space Center*

√ The **Kennedy Space Center**, near Daytona Beach, Florida, gives visitors the chance to meet real astronauts, experience "liftoff" at the beginning of a space flight, and imagine what the future of space travel will be like. There's an IMAX theater and a real Saturn V rocket like the one that launched the astronauts who landed on the Moon. Soon, the center will display the newly retired space shuttle *Atlantis*.

For more information, see: ***www.kennedyspacecenter.com***

√ The **Metropolitan Museum of Art**, in New York City, is among the largest museums of fine art in the world. Its collection covers art from all parts of the world and includes works by the most important artists in history. The Met also has collections of furniture from past centuries, medieval arms and armor, and a beautiful, peaceful Chinese garden.

For more information, see: ***www.metmuseum.org***

√ The **Field Museum**, in Chicago, Illinois, is an amazing museum that focuses on the history of plant and animal life on Earth. Among its most famous exhibits is Lucy, a cast of the fossil of a woman who lived some 3.2 million years ago in Africa and who is one of the earliest human ancestors yet discovered. The Field also displays a dinosaur nicknamed "Sue," the largest and the most complete *Tyrannosaurus rex* skeleton ever found.

For more information, see: ***www.fieldmuseum.org***

◀ *The huge* T. rex *nicknamed "Sue"*

THE 7 WONDERS OF THE WORLD

These 7 Wonders of the World were chosen in 2007 through an online poll in which over 100 million people from 200 countries cast votes. The 7 Wonders, all equal in rank, are:

The Great Wall of China
(begun 221 B.C.; completed A.D. 1368–1644), China

The Pyramid at Chichén Itzá
(before A.D. 1200), Yucatan Peninsula, Mexico

Petra
(1st century B.C.), Jordan

The Roman Colosseum
(A.D. 70–82), Rome, Italy

Machu Picchu
(A.D. 1460–1470), Peru

Christ the Redeemer
(A.D. 1931), Rio de Janiero, Brazil

The Taj Mahal
(A.D. 1630), Agra, India

*Since it opened in 1925, the **Children's Museum of Indianapolis** has grown to become the largest children's museum in the world. More than 1 million people visit each year to see its thousands of exhibits. There is a display on life in modern Egypt, information on how we can learn from the world around us, an area devoted to dinosaurs, and a planetarium.*

Museum visitors take a pretend ride through the streets of Cairo, Egypt.

NATIONAL PARKS

The world's first national park was Yellowstone, established in 1872. Today in the U.S., there are 58 national parks, including parks in the Virgin Islands, Guam, Puerto Rico, and American Samoa. The National Park Service manages 394 units in all, including national monuments, memorials, battlefields, military parks, historic parks, historic sites, lakeshores, seashores, recreation areas, scenic rivers and trails, wilderness areas, and the White House—more than 84 million acres in all! For more information, you can write to the National Park Service, Department of the Interior, 1849 C Street NW, Washington, D.C. 20240, or go to: ***www.nps.gov/parks.html***

YOSEMITE NATIONAL PARK

This park, established in 1890, covers 761,266 acres in east-central California. It has the world's largest concentration of granite domes—mountain-like rocks that were created by glaciers millions of years ago. You can see many of them rising thousands of feet above the valley floor. Two of the most famous are Half Dome, which looks smooth and rounded, and El Capitan, which is the biggest single granite rock on Earth. Skilled climbers come from all over the world to scale this 3,000-foot-high wall of rock. Yosemite Falls, which drops 2,425 feet, is the highest waterfall in North America. It is actually two waterfalls, called the upper and lower falls, connected by a series of smaller waterfalls. Yosemite also features lakes, meadows, and giant sequoia trees, and is home to bighorn sheep and bears.

GRAND CANYON NATIONAL PARK

This national park, established in 1919, has one of the world's most spectacular landscapes, covering more than a million acres in northwestern Arizona. The canyon is 6,000 feet deep at its deepest point and 15 miles wide at its widest. Most of the 40 identified rock layers that form the canyon's 277-mile-long wall are exposed, offering a detailed look at the Earth's geologic history. The walls display a cross section of the Earth's crust from as far back as two billion years ago. The Colorado River—which carved out the giant canyon—still runs through the park, which is a valuable wildlife preserve with many rare, endangered animals. The pine and fir forests, painted deserts, plateaus, caves, and sandstone canyons offer a wide range of habitats.

ACADIA NATIONAL PARK

Acadia National Park is located in eastern Maine. It offers spectacular views of the rocky Maine coast, the tallest mountain on the U.S. Atlantic seaboard (Cadillac Mountain), and 120 miles of hiking trails. Its 47,000 acres include lakes, ponds, and Mount Desert Island, which was first settled 5,000 years ago by American Indians. In the 1800s, the area's natural beauty attracted many artists from the "Hudson River school," and the region also became popular as a summer resort. Concerned that the land would be ruined by developers, George B. Dorr, a conservationist, started buying up thousands of acres. He donated this land to the U.S. government, and in 1919 the park was created.

EVERGLADES NATIONAL PARK

Located in southern Florida, the Everglades is the largest subtropical wilderness in the U.S. Almost 1.4 million acres of this wilderness are now protected in Everglades National Park. More than 360 species of birds, 40 species of mammals, and 50 kinds of reptiles live in the park's varied ecosystems, which include swamps, saw grass prairies, and mangrove forests. The park's different habitats allow a huge variety of life forms to thrive. As you move from place to place, you may see all kinds of animals, from tiny frogs to free-roaming alligators and crocodiles, graceful herons, several varieties of geckos, and lots of snakes, including boa constrictors. You can visit a mahogany forest and pine forests, and you can walk along raised boardwalks to get beautiful views of miles of swaying saw grass marshes full of wildlife. The park has a visitor's center near the entrance, and there is another visitor's center, called Flamingo, at the southern tip. From the marina at Flamingo, visitors can take boat tours.

YELLOWSTONE NATIONAL PARK

Located mostly in northwestern Wyoming and partly in eastern Idaho and southwestern Montana, Yellowstone is known for its 10,000 hot springs and geysers—more than anyplace else in the world. Old Faithful, the most famous geyser, erupts for about four minutes every one to two hours, shooting 3,700-8,400 gallons of hot water as high as 185 feet. Other geysers include the Giant, which shoots a column of hot water 200 feet high, and the Giantess, which erupts for over four hours at a time, but only about two times per year. There are grizzly bears, wolves, elk, moose, buffalo, deer, beavers, coyotes, antelopes, and 300 species of birds. The use of snowmobiles in the park has been a big controversy. Some people want to ban them because of noise and air pollution; others disagree. They are allowed now, but their use is somewhat limited.

UNITED STATES

Which amendment gave women the right to vote? → page 257

FACTS & FIGURES

AREA	50 states and Washington, D.C.
LAND	3,531,822 square miles
WATER	264,129 square miles
TOTAL	3,795,951 square miles

POPULATION (2010 CENSUS): 308,745,538

CAPITAL: WASHINGTON, D.C.

LARGEST, HIGHEST, and OTHER STATISTICS

Largest state:	Alaska (663,267 square miles)
Smallest state:	Rhode Island (1,545 square miles)
Northernmost city:	Barrow, Alaska (71°17′ north latitude)
Southernmost city:	Hilo, Hawaii (19°44′ north latitude)
Easternmost city:	Eastport, Maine (66°59′ west longitude)
Westernmost city:	Atka, Alaska (174°12′ west longitude)
Highest settlement:	Climax, Colorado (11,360 feet)
Lowest settlement:	Calipatria, California (184 feet below sea level)
Oldest national park:	Yellowstone National Park (Idaho, Montana, Wyoming), 2,219,791 acres, established 1872
Largest national park:	Wrangell-St. Elias, Alaska (8,323,148 acres)
Longest river system:	Mississippi-Missouri-Red Rock (3,710 miles)
Deepest lake:	Crater Lake, Oregon (1,932 feet)
Highest mountain:	Mount McKinley, Alaska (20,320 feet)
Lowest point:	Death Valley, California (282 feet below sea level)
Tallest building:	Willis Tower, Chicago, Illinois (1,450 feet)
Tallest structure:	TV tower, Blanchard, North Dakota (2,063 feet)
Longest bridge span:	Verrazano-Narrows Bridge, New York (4,260 feet)
Highest bridge:	Royal Gorge, Colorado (1,053 feet above water)

Willis Tower

did you Know?

There is only one place in the United States where you can stand in four states at the same time. The Four Corners monument marks the spot where Utah, Colorado, Arizona, and New Mexico meet.

SYMBOLS OF THE UNITED STATES

The Great Seal

The Great Seal of the United States shows an American bald eagle with a ribbon in its mouth bearing the Latin words *e pluribus unum* (out of many, one). In its talons are the arrows of war and an olive branch of peace. On the back of the Great Seal is an unfinished pyramid with an eye (the eye of Providence) above it. The seal was approved by Congress on June 20, 1782.

The Flag

The flag of the United States has 50 stars (one for each state) and 13 stripes (one for each of the original 13 states). It is unofficially called the "Stars and Stripes."

1777

The first U.S. flag was commissioned by the Second Continental Congress in 1777 but did not exist until 1783, after the American Revolution. Historians are not certain who designed the Stars and Stripes. Many different flags are believed to have been used during the American Revolution.

1795

The flag of 1777 was used until 1795. In that year, Congress passed an act ordering that a new flag have 15 stripes, alternate red and white, and 15 stars on a blue field. In 1818, Congress directed that the flag have 13 stripes and that a new star be added for each new state of the Union. The last star was added in 1960 for the state of Hawaii.

1818

There are many customs for flying the flag and treating it with respect. For example, it should not touch the floor and no other flag should be flown above it, except for the UN flag at UN headquarters. When the flag is raised or lowered, or passes in a parade, or during the Pledge of Allegiance, people should face it and stand at attention. Those in military uniform should salute. Others should put their right hand over their heart. The flag is flown at half-staff as a sign of mourning.

Pledge of Allegiance to the Flag

"I pledge allegiance to the flag of the United States of America and to the republic for which it stands, one nation under God, indivisible, with liberty and justice for all."

The National Anthem

"The Star-Spangled Banner" was a poem written in 1814 by Francis Scott Key after he watched British ships bombard Fort McHenry, Maryland, during the War of 1812. It became the National Anthem by an act of Congress in 1931. The music to "The Star-Spangled Banner" was originally a tune called "Anacreon in Heaven."

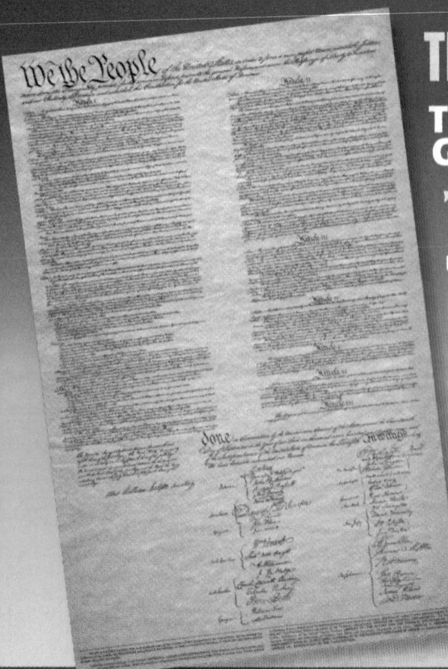

THE U.S. CONSTITUTION

The Foundation of American Government

The Constitution is the document that created the present government of the United States. It was written in 1787 and went into effect in 1789. It establishes the three branches of the U.S. government—the executive (headed by the president), the legislative (Congress), and the judicial (the Supreme Court and other federal courts). The first 10 amendments to the Constitution (the **Bill of Rights**) explain the basic rights of all American citizens.

You can find the Constitution online at: ***www.archives.gov/exhibits/charters/constitution.html.***

THE PREAMBLE TO THE CONSTITUTION

The Constitution begins with a short statement called the Preamble. The Preamble states that the government of the United States was established by the people.

"We the people of the United States, in order to form a more perfect union, establish justice, insure domestic tranquility, provide for the common defense, promote the general welfare, and secure the blessings of liberty to ourselves and our posterity, do ordain and establish this Constitution for the United States of America."

THE ARTICLES

The original Constitution contained seven articles. The first three articles of the Constitution establish the three branches of the U.S. government.

Article 1, Legislative Branch Creates the Senate and House of Representatives and describes their functions and powers.

Article 2, Executive Branch Creates the office of the President and the Electoral College and lists their powers and responsibilities.

Article 3, Judicial Branch Creates the Supreme Court and gives Congress the power to create lower courts. The powers of the courts and certain crimes are defined.

Article 4, The States Discusses the relationship of the states to one another and to the citizens. Defines the states' powers.

Article 5, Amending the Constitution Describes how the Constitution can be amended (changed).

Article 6, Federal Law Makes the Constitution the supreme law of the land over state laws and constitutions.

Article 7, Ratifying the Constitution Establishes how to ratify (approve) the Constitution.

AMENDMENTS TO THE CONSTITUTION

The writers of the Constitution understood that it might need to be amended, or changed, in the future, but they wanted to be careful and made it hard to change. Article 5 describes how the Constitution can be amended.

In order to take effect, an amendment must be approved by a two-thirds majority in both the House of Representatives and the Senate. It must then be approved (ratified) by three-fourths of the states (38 states). So far, there have been 27 amendments. One of them (the 18th, ratified in 1919) banned the manufacture or sale of liquor. It was canceled by the 21st Amendment, in 1933.

The Bill of Rights: The First Ten Amendments

The first ten amendments were adopted in 1791 and contain the basic freedoms Americans enjoy as a people. These amendments are known as the Bill of Rights.

1. Guarantees freedom of religion, speech, and the press.
2. Guarantees the right to have firearms.
3. Guarantees that soldiers cannot be lodged in private homes unless the owner agrees.
4. Protects people from being searched or having property searched or taken away by the government without reason.
5. Protects rights of people on trial for crimes.
6. Guarantees people accused of crimes the right to a speedy public trial by jury.
7. Guarantees the right to a trial by jury for other kinds of cases.
8. Prohibits "cruel and unusual punishments."
9. Says specific rights listed in the Constitution do not take away rights that may not be listed.
10. Establishes that any powers not given specifically to the federal government belong to states or the people.

Other Important Amendments

13 (1865): Ends slavery in the United States.

14 (1868): Bars states from denying rights to citizens; guarantees equal protection under the law for all citizens.

15 (1870): Guarantees that a person cannot be denied the right to vote because of race or color.

19 (1920): Gives women the right to vote.

22 (1951): Limits the president to two four-year terms of office.

24 (1964): Outlaws the poll tax (a tax people had to pay before they could vote) in federal elections. (The poll tax had been used to keep African Americans in the South from voting.)

25 (1967): Specifies presidential succession; also gives the president the power to appoint a new vice president, if one dies or leaves office in the middle of a term.

26 (1971): Lowers the voting age to 18 from 21.

THE EXECUTIVE BRANCH

The **executive branch** of the federal government is headed by the president, who enforces the laws passed by Congress and is commander in chief of the U.S. armed forces. It also includes the vice president, people who work for the president or vice president, the major departments of the government, and special agencies. The **cabinet** is made up of the vice president, heads of major departments, and other officials. It meets when the president chooses. The chart at right shows cabinet departments in the order in which they were created.

PRESIDENT

VICE PRESIDENT

CABINET DEPARTMENTS

1. State
2. Treasury
3. Defense
4. Justice
5. Interior
6. Agriculture
7. Commerce
8. Labor
9. Housing and Urban Development
10. Transportation
11. Energy
12. Education
13. Health and Human Services
14. Veterans Affairs
15. Homeland Security

Who Can Be President?

To be eligible to serve as president, a person must be a native-born U.S. citizen, must be at least 35 years old, and must have been a resident of the United States for at least 14 years.

How Long Does the President Serve?

The president serves a four-year term, starting on January 20. No president can be elected more than twice, or more than once if he or she had served two years as president filling out the term of a president who left office.

What Happens If the President Dies?

If the president dies in office or cannot complete the term, the vice president becomes president. If the president is temporarily unable to perform his or her duties, the vice president can become acting president.

The White House has a web site. It is: *www.whitehouse.gov*

You can send e-mail to the president at: *president@whitehouse.gov*

The White House, home of the U.S. president

Voter Turnout in Presidential Elections, 1968–2008

(Percent of voting age population: 18 and over in 1972 and afterward, 21 and over in 1968.)

Year	Turnout	Year	Turnout
1968	60.7%	1992	55.2%
1972	55.1%	1996	49.0%
1976	53.6%	2000	50.3%
1980	52.8%	2004	55.5%
1984	53.3%	2008	58.2%
1988	50.3%		

Source: U.S. Census Bureau

THE LEGISLATIVE BRANCH

CONGRESS

Congress is the legislative branch of the federal government. Congress's major responsibility is to pass the laws that govern the country and determine how money collected in taxes is spent. Congress consists of two parts—the Senate and the House of Representatives. ▶

THE SENATE

The Senate has 100 members, two from each state. The Constitution says that the Senate will have equal representation (the same number of representatives) from each state. Thus, small states have the same number of senators as large states. Senators are elected for six-year terms. There is no limit on the number of terms a senator can serve.

The Senate also has the responsibility of approving people the president appoints for certain jobs: for example, cabinet members and Supreme Court justices. The Senate must approve all treaties by at least a two-thirds vote. It also has the responsibility under the Constitution of putting on trial high-ranking federal officials who have been impeached (accused of wrongdoing) by the House of Representatives.

For more information, see: ***www.senate.gov***

THE HOUSE OF REPRESENTATIVES

The number of members of the House of Representatives for each state depends on its population according to a recent census. But each state has at least one representative, no matter how small its population. A term lasts two years.

The first House of Representatives in 1789 had 65 members. As the country's population grew, the number of representatives increased. Since 1911, however, the total membership has been kept at 435.

For more information, see: ***www.house.gov***

The Capitol, where Congress meets

The House of Representatives, by State

As a result of the 2010 Census, some states will gain or lose House members (or "seats"), starting in 2013, because of population changes. The table shows how many seats each state

State	Seats 2013	Seats 2003-2012	Change
Alabama	7	7	0
Alaska	1	1	0
Arizona	9	8	+1
Arkansas	4	4	0
California	53	53	0
Colorado	7	7	0
Connecticut	5	5	0
Delaware	1	1	0
Florida	27	25	+2
Georgia	14	13	+1
Hawaii	2	2	0
Idaho	2	2	0
Illinois	18	19	-1
Indiana	9	9	0
Iowa	4	5	-1
Kansas	4	4	0
Kentucky	6	6	0
Louisiana	6	7	-1
Maine	2	2	0
Maryland	8	8	0
Massachusetts	9	10	-1
Michigan	14	15	-1
Minnesota	8	8	0
Mississippi	4	4	0
Missouri	8	9	-1
Montana	1	1	0
Nebraska	3	3	0
Nevada	4	3	+1
New Hampshire	2	2	0
New Jersey	12	13	-1
New Mexico	3	3	0
New York	27	29	-2
North Carolina	13	13	0
North Dakota	1	1	0
Ohio	16	18	-2
Oklahoma	5	5	0
Oregon	5	5	0
Pennsylvania	18	19	-1
Rhode Island	2	2	0
South Carolina	7	6	+1
South Dakota	1	1	0
Tennessee	9	9	0
Texas	36	32	+4
Utah	4	3	+1
Vermont	1	1	0
Virginia	11	11	0
Washington	10	9	+1
West Virginia	3	3	0
Wisconsin	8	8	0
Wyoming	1	1	0

Washington, D.C., Puerto Rico, American Samoa, Guam, and the Virgin Islands each has one nonvoting member of the House of Representatives.

HOW A BILL BECOMES LAW

A proposed law is called a bill. To become a law, a bill must first be approved by both houses, or chambers, of Congress. Most kinds of bills can start in either chamber.

Let's assume that a bill starts in the House of Representatives. It is introduced by one or more members and then assigned to one of the many House committees, where it is studied and possibly changed. The committee may get advice from outside experts and hold public hearings, or meetings, on the proposal. Then the committee votes on the bill. If a majority of the committee members support the bill, it goes to the full House. The House will then debate the bill, perhaps make changes to it, and then vote on the bill. If a majority of the full House votes for the bill, it is approved. It then goes to the Senate, where the process is repeated.

If the two chambers approve different versions of the same bill, usually a committee made up of members from the House and the Senate tries to work out the disagreements and come up with one revised bill. If both chambers of Congress pass this new version, the bill goes to the president. The president can either sign the bill, making it a law, or veto it (turn it down). If the president vetoes the bill, it can still become law if it is passed again by a two-thirds majority in both chambers of Congress.

THE JUDICIAL BRANCH

THE SUPREME COURT

The highest court in the United States is the Supreme Court. It has nine justices who are appointed for life by the president with the approval of the Senate. Eight of the nine members are called associate justices. The ninth is the Chief Justice, who presides over the Court's meetings.

What Does the Supreme Court Do?

The Supreme Court's major responsibilities are to judge cases that involve reviewing federal laws, actions of the president, treaties of the United States, and laws passed by state governments to be sure they do not conflict with the U.S. Constitution. If the Supreme Court finds that a law or action violates the Constitution, the law is struck down or the action is reversed.

The Supreme Court's Decision Is Final.

Most cases must go through other state courts or federal courts before they reach the Supreme Court. The Supreme Court is the final court for a case, and the justices generally can decide which cases they will review. After the Supreme Court hears a case, it may agree or disagree with the decision by a lower court. Each justice has one vote, and the majority rules. When the Supreme Court makes a ruling, its decision is final, so each of the justices has a very important job.

Below are the nine justices who were on the Supreme Court in the 2010–2011 term (October 2010 to June 2011). The justices are (standing from left to right) Sonia Sotomayor, Stephen Breyer, Samuel Alito, and Elena Kagan; (seated from left to right) Clarence Thomas, Antonin Scalia, Chief Justice John Roberts, Anthony Kennedy, and Ruth Bader Ginsburg.

PRESIDENTS ★ OF THE ★ UNITED STATES

★ ★ ★ ★ ★

In November 2008, Senator Barack Obama, a Democrat, was elected president of the United States, defeating Republican Senator John McCain. Obama is counted as the 44th president. There have really been only 43 different presidents including Obama, but Grover Cleveland served two terms that were not in a row, so he is counted twice.

Obama and his running mate, Senator Joe Biden, took office as president and vice president on January 20, 2009.

President Barack Obama

Born in Honolulu, Hawaii, in 1961, Barack Obama graduated from Columbia University in 1983. He became a community organizer in Chicago, helping poor residents cope with a wave of unemployment. He then attended Harvard Law School, where he became the first African-American editor of the *Harvard Law Review*.

After graduating, Obama practiced civil-rights law, taught in law school, and served in the Illinois state senate. He gained national attention by giving a rousing keynote speech at the Democratic National Convention in 2004, and he was elected to the U.S. Senate later that year. In 2007, he began his campaign for president.

He and his wife, Michelle, have two children, Malia and Sasha.

★ ★ ★ ★ ★

Vice President Joe Biden

Joe Biden was born in 1942, in Scranton, Pennsylvania. He is a lawyer by profession. In 1972, he was elected to the U.S. Senate, representing the state of Delaware. He served in the Senate for 35 years and became known as an expert on foreign policy. In the summer of 2008, Obama chose him to be his running mate.

What Does the President Do?

According to the U.S. Constitution, the president is the chief executive, or head, of the executive branch of the government. The president has many important roles. Here are some of them:

★ Suggest laws to Congress;

★ Send Congress a budget, which recommends how the government should raise and spend money;

★ Approve or veto (reject) bills passed by Congress; ▼

★ Act as commander-in-chief of the U.S. armed forces;

★ Make treaties, or agreements, with other countries;

★ Appoint justices to the Supreme Court and judges to other federal courts.

The president must share power with the other two branches of government. They are the legislative branch, or Congress, and the judicial branch, headed by the U.S. Supreme Court.

President Obama signs a children's health and nutrition law.

The U.S. Constitution tells how each of the three branches of government checks, or limits, the powers of the other two. This system of checks and balances is intended to prevent any branch from becoming too powerful.

What Does the Vice President Do?

John Adams, the first vice president, described it as "the most insignificant office that ever the invention of man contrived or his imagination conceived." But the vice president is just a heartbeat away from the presidency.

According to the U.S. Constitution, the vice president has two major duties. First, the vice president takes over as president if the president dies, resigns, or is removed from office. Second, the vice president presides over the Senate and can cast the deciding vote in case of a tie. In modern times the vice president is often given other important duties by the president.

Vice President Biden visits U.S. troops in Afghanistan. ▶

Electing a President

Who elects the president?

The president is actually elected by a group of "electors" known as the Electoral College. Members of this group from each state meet in December in their state capitals to cast their votes.

But I thought Election Day was in November!

It is, but on Election Day voters don't directly vote for president. Instead, they vote for a group of presidential electors who have pledged to support whichever candidate wins that state's popular vote.

What's the total number of electoral votes?

There are 538 total votes. A presidential candidate must win at least 270 of those.

How many electoral votes does each state get?

Each state gets one vote for each of its senators (2) and one for each of its members in the House of Representatives. Also, Washington, D.C., has 3 electoral votes.

What if there's a tie in the end?

Then the election is in the hands of the U.S. House of Representatives. That's what happened in 1801, after Thomas Jefferson and Aaron Burr each received an equal number of electoral votes in the 1800 election. The House then voted to make Jefferson president.

Note: Of Nebraska's 5 electoral votes, John McCain received 4 electoral votes; Barack Obama received 1.

On November 4, 2008, Barack Obama won about 53 percent of the popular vote. But what really counted was the electoral votes. He picked up 365 of them, from 29 states and the District of Columbia, more than enough for a majority.

Can a candidate who didn't win the most popular votes still win a majority of electoral votes? Yes. That's what happened in 1876, 1888, and again in 2000, when George W. Bush was elected to a first term.

Who CAN Vote?

Voting rules vary from state to state, but they must agree with the Constitution. No state can deny the right to vote because of a person's race or gender, or because of age if the voter is at least 18 years old.

All voters must be U.S citizens. In all states except North Dakota, they must also register, or sign up, beforehand. However, under a 1993 federal law, states took steps to allow people to register in many different locations or by mail.

Who DOES Vote?

Voter turnout is generally highest in presidential elections, and recent presidential elections have shown some increase. But even in the 2008 election, only about 58 percent of the voting age population actually voted.

Sometimes only a few votes can make a big difference. In 2000, for example, George W. Bush defeated Al Gore in Florida by only 537 votes and became president!

LOOking Ahead

On November 6, 2012, voters will go to the polls to elect a president. Barack Obama said that he would seek the Democratic Party's nomination for a second term as president. On the Republican side, there were many possible presidential candidates.

Contenders for the nomination in each party will compete in a series of primaries and caucuses in different states, starting in January 2012. In primary elections, voters go to the polls to cast a ballot for the person they want to be their party's candidate. In caucuses, party members get together in small groups to indicate the person they prefer to be their candidate. The primaries and caucuses will continue through the spring of 2012. Winning as many of these as possible is the key to success for a person trying to become his or her party's candidate for president.

FACTS ABOUT THE PRESIDENTS

1

GEORGE WASHINGTON Federalist Party 1789–1797

Born: Feb. 22, 1732, at Wakefield, Westmoreland County, Virginia
Married: Martha Dandridge Custis (1731–1802); no children
Died: Dec. 14, 1799; buried at Mount Vernon, Fairfax County, Virginia
Vice President: John Adams (1789–1797)

2

JOHN ADAMS Federalist Party 1797–1801

Born: Oct. 30, 1735, in Braintree (now Quincy), Massachusetts
Married: Abigail Smith (1744–1818); 3 sons, 2 daughters
Died: July 4, 1826; buried in Quincy, Massachusetts
Vice President: Thomas Jefferson (1797–1801)

3

THOMAS JEFFERSON Democratic-Republican Party 1801–1809

Born: Apr. 13, 1743, at Shadwell, Albemarle County, Virginia
Married: Martha Wayles Skelton (1748–1782); 1 son, 5 daughters
Died: July 4, 1826; buried at Monticello, Albemarle County, Virginia
Vice President: Aaron Burr (1801–1805), George Clinton (1805–1809)

4

JAMES MADISON Democratic-Republican Party 1809–1817

Born: Mar. 16, 1751, at Port Conway, King George County, Virginia
Married: Dolley Payne Todd (1768–1849); no children
Died: June 28, 1836; buried at Montpelier Station, Virginia
Vice President: George Clinton (1809–1813), Elbridge Gerry (1813–1817)

5

JAMES MONROE Democratic-Republican Party 1817–1825

Born: Apr. 28, 1758, in Westmoreland County, Virginia
Married: Elizabeth Kortright (1768–1830); 1 son, 2 daughters
Died: July 4, 1831; buried in Richmond, Virginia
Vice President: Daniel D. Tompkins (1817–1825)

6

JOHN QUINCY ADAMS Democratic-Republican Party 1825–1829

Born: July 11, 1767, in Braintree (now Quincy), Massachusetts
Married: Louisa Catherine Johnson (1775–1852); 3 sons, 1 daughter
Died: Feb. 23, 1848; buried in Quincy, Massachusetts
Vice President: John C. Calhoun (1825–1829)

7 ANDREW JACKSON Democratic Party 1829–1837
Born: Mar. 15, 1767, in Waxhaw, South Carolina
Married: Rachel Donelson Robards (1767–1828); 1 son (adopted)
Died: June 8, 1845; buried in Nashville, Tennessee
Vice President: John C. Calhoun (1829–1833), Martin Van Buren (1833–1837)

8 MARTIN VAN BUREN Democratic Party 1837–1841
Born: Dec. 5, 1782, at Kinderhook, New York
Married: Hannah Hoes (1783–1819); 4 sons
Died: July 24, 1862; buried at Kinderhook, New York
Vice President: Richard M. Johnson (1837–1841)

9 WILLIAM HENRY HARRISON Whig Party 1841
Born: Feb. 9, 1773, at Berkeley, Charles City County, Virginia
Married: Anna Symmes (1775–1864); 6 sons, 4 daughters
Died: Apr. 4, 1841; buried in North Bend, Ohio
Vice President: John Tyler (1841–1845)

10 JOHN TYLER Whig Party 1841–1845
Born: Mar. 29, 1790, in Greenway, Charles City County, Virginia
Married: Letitia Christian (1790–1842); 3 sons, 5 daughters
Julia Gardiner (1820–1889); 5 sons, 2 daughters
Died: Jan. 18, 1862; buried in Richmond, Virginia
Vice President: none

11 JAMES KNOX POLK Democratic Party 1845–1849
Born: Nov. 2, 1795, in Mecklenburg County, North Carolina
Married: Sarah Childress (1803–1891); no children
Died: June 15, 1849; buried in Nashville, Tennessee
Vice President: George M. Dallas (1845–1849)

12 ZACHARY TAYLOR Whig Party 1849–1850
Born: Nov. 24, 1784, in Orange County, Virginia
Married: Margaret Smith (1788–1852); 1 son, 5 daughters
Died: July 9, 1850; buried in Louisville, Kentucky
Vice President: Millard Fillmore (1849–1850)

13 MILLARD FILLMORE Whig Party 1850–1853
Born: Jan. 7, 1800, in Cayuga County, New York
Married: Abigail Powers (1798–1853); 1 son, 1 daughter
Caroline Carmichael McIntosh (1813–1881); no children
Died: Mar. 8, 1874; buried in Buffalo, New York
Vice President: none

14 FRANKLIN PIERCE Democratic Party 1853–1857

Born: Nov. 23, 1804, in Hillsboro, New Hampshire
Married: Jane Means Appleton (1806–1863); 3 sons
Died: Oct. 8, 1869; buried in Concord, New Hampshire
Vice President: William R. King (1853–1857)

15 JAMES BUCHANAN Democratic Party 1857–1861

Born: Apr. 23, 1791, Cove Gap, near Mercersburg, Pennsylvania
Married: Never
Died: June 1, 1868, buried in Lancaster, Pennsylvania
Vice President: John C. Breckinridge (1857–1861)

16 ABRAHAM LINCOLN Republican Party 1861–1865

Born: Feb. 12, 1809, in Hardin County, Kentucky
Married: Mary Todd (1818–1882); 4 sons
Died: Apr. 15, 1865; buried in Springfield, Illinois
Vice President: Hannibal Hamlin (1861–1865),
Andrew Johnson (1865)

17 ANDREW JOHNSON Democratic Party 1865–1869

Born: Dec. 29, 1808, in Raleigh, North Carolina
Married: Eliza McCardle (1810–1876); 3 sons, 2 daughters
Died: July 31, 1875; buried in Greeneville, Tennessee
Vice President: none

18 ULYSSES S. GRANT Republican Party 1869–1877

Born: Apr. 27, 1822, in Point Pleasant, Ohio
Married: Julia Dent (1826–1902); 3 sons, 1 daughter
Died: July 23, 1885; buried in New York City
Vice President: Schuyler Colfax (1869–1873),
Henry Wilson (1873–1877)

19 RUTHERFORD B. HAYES Republican Party 1877–1881

Born: Oct. 4, 1822, in Delaware, Ohio
Married: Lucy Ware Webb (1831–1889); 7 sons, 1 daughter
Died: Jan. 17, 1893; buried in Fremont, Ohio
Vice President: William A. Wheeler (1877–1881)

20 JAMES A. GARFIELD Republican Party 1881

Born: Nov. 19, 1831, in Orange, Cuyahoga County, Ohio
Married: Lucretia Rudolph (1832–1918); 5 sons, 2 daughters
Died: Sept. 19, 1881; buried in Cleveland, Ohio
Vice President: Chester A. Arthur (1881)

21 CHESTER A. ARTHUR Republican Party 1881–1885

Born: Oct. 5, 1829, in Fairfield, Vermont
Married: Ellen Lewis Herndon (1837–1880); 2 sons, 1 daughter
Died: Nov. 18, 1886; buried in Albany, New York
Vice President: none

22 GROVER CLEVELAND Democratic Party 1885–1889

Born: Mar. 18, 1837, in Caldwell, New Jersey
Married: Frances Folsom (1864–1947); 2 sons, 3 daughters
Died: June 24, 1908; buried in Princeton, New Jersey
Vice President: Thomas A. Hendricks (1885–1889)

23 BENJAMIN HARRISON Republican Party 1889–1893

Born: Aug. 20, 1833, in North Bend, Ohio
Married: Caroline Lavinia Scott (1832–1892); 1 son, 1 daughter
Mary Scott Lord Dimmick (1858–1948); 1 daughter
Died: Mar. 13, 1901; buried in Indianapolis, Indiana
Vice President: Levi Morton (1889–1893)

24 GROVER CLEVELAND 1893–1897

See 22, above
Vice President: Adlai E. Stevenson (1893–1897)

25 WILLIAM MCKINLEY Republican Party 1897–1901

Born: Jan. 29, 1843, in Niles, Ohio
Married: Ida Saxton (1847–1907); 2 daughters
Died: Sept. 14, 1901; buried in Canton, Ohio
Vice President: Garret A. Hobart (1897–1901),
Theodore Roosevelt (1901)

26 THEODORE ROOSEVELT Republican Party 1901–1909

Born: Oct. 27, 1858, in New York City
Married: Alice Hathaway Lee (1861–1884); 1 daughter
Edith Kermit Carow (1861–1948); 4 sons, 1 daughter
Died: Jan. 6, 1919; buried in Oyster Bay, New York
Vice President: none 1901–1905, Charles W. Fairbanks (1905–1909)

27

WILLIAM HOWARD TAFT Republican Party 1909–1913

Born: Sept. 15, 1857, in Cincinnati, Ohio
Married: Helen Herron (1861–1943); 2 sons, 1 daughter
Died: Mar. 8, 1930; buried in Arlington National Cemetery, Virginia
Vice President: James S. Sherman (1909–1913)

28

WOODROW WILSON Democratic Party 1913–1921

Born: Dec. 28, 1856, in Staunton, Virginia
Married: Ellen Louise Axson (1860–1914); 3 daughters
Edith Bolling Galt (1872–1961); no children
Died: Feb. 3, 1924; buried in Washington, D.C.
Vice President: Thomas R. Marshall (1913–1921)

29

WARREN G. HARDING Republican Party 1921–1923

Born: Nov. 2, 1865, near Corsica (now Blooming Grove), Ohio
Married: Florence Kling De Wolfe (1860–1924; no children)
Died: Aug. 2, 1923; buried in Marion, Ohio
Vice President: Calvin Coolidge (1921–1923)

30

CALVIN COOLIDGE Republican Party 1923–1929

Born: July 4, 1872, in Plymouth, Vermont
Married: Grace Anna Goodhue (1879–1957); 2 sons
Died: Jan. 5, 1933; buried in Plymouth, Vermont
Vice President: none 1923–1925, Charles G. Dawes (1925–1929)

31

HERBERT C. HOOVER Republican Party 1929–1933

Born: Aug. 10, 1874, in West Branch, Iowa
Married: Lou Henry (1875–1944); 2 sons
Died: Oct. 20, 1964; buried in West Branch, Iowa
Vice President: Charles Curtis (1929–1933)

32

FRANKLIN DELANO ROOSEVELT Democratic Party 1933–1945

Born: Jan. 30, 1882, in Hyde Park, New York
Married: Anna Eleanor Roosevelt (1884–1962); 4 sons, 1 daughter
Died: Apr. 12, 1945; buried in Hyde Park, New York
Vice President: John N. Garner (1933–1941),
Henry A. Wallace (1941–1945),
Harry S. Truman (1945)

33 **HARRY S. TRUMAN** Democratic Party 1945–1953

Born: May 8, 1884, in Lamar, Missouri
Married: Elizabeth Virginia "Bess" Wallace (1885–1982); 1 daughter
Died: Dec. 26, 1972; buried in Independence, Missouri
Vice President: none from 1945–1949, Alben W. Barkley (1949–1953)

34 **DWIGHT D. EISENHOWER** Republican Party 1953–1961

Born: Oct. 14, 1890, in Denison, Texas
Married: Mary "Mamie" Geneva Doud (1896–1979); 2 sons
Died: Mar. 28, 1969; buried in Abilene, Kansas
Vice President: Richard M. Nixon (1953–1961)

35 **JOHN FITZGERALD KENNEDY** Democratic Party 1961–1963

Born: May 29, 1917, in Brookline, Massachusetts
Married: Jacqueline Lee Bouvier (1929–1994); 2 sons, 1 daughter
Died: Nov. 22, 1963; buried in Arlington National Cemetery, Virginia
Vice President: Lyndon B. Johnson (1961–1963)

36 **LYNDON BAINES JOHNSON** Democratic Party 1963–1969

Born: Aug. 27, 1908, near Stonewall, Texas
Married: Claudia "Lady Bird" Alta Taylor (1912–2007); 2 daughters
Died: Jan. 22, 1973; buried in Johnson City, Texas
Vice President: none 1963–1965, Hubert H. Humphrey (1965–1969)

37 **RICHARD MILHOUS NIXON** Republican Party 1969–1974

Born: Jan. 9, 1913, in Yorba Linda, California
Married: Thelma "Pat" Ryan (1912–1993); 2 daughters
Died: Apr. 22, 1994; buried in Yorba Linda, California
Vice President: Spiro T. Agnew (1969–1973),
Gerald R. Ford (1973–1974)

38 **GERALD R. FORD** Republican Party 1974–1977

Born: July 14, 1913, in Omaha, Nebraska
Married: Elizabeth "Betty" Bloomer (1918–2011); 3 sons, 1 daughter
Died: Dec. 26, 2006; buried in Grand Rapids, Michigan
Vice President: Nelson A. Rockefeller (1974–1977)

39 JIMMY (JAMES EARL) CARTER Democratic Party 1977–1981

Born: Oct. 1, 1924, in Plains, Georgia
Married: Rosalynn Smith (b. 1927); 3 sons, 1 daughter
Vice President: Walter F. Mondale (1977–1981)

40 RONALD REAGAN Republican Party 1981–1989

Born: Feb. 6, 1911, in Tampico, Illinois
Married: Jane Wyman (1914–2007); 1 son, 1 daughter
Nancy Davis (b. 1923); 1 son, 1 daughter
Died: June 5, 2004; buried in Simi Valley, California
Vice President: George H. W. Bush (1981–1989)

41 GEORGE H. W. BUSH Republican Party 1989–1993

Born: June 12, 1924, in Milton, Massachusetts
Married: Barbara Pierce (b. 1925); 4 sons, 2 daughters
Vice President: Dan Quayle (1989–1993)

42 BILL (WILLIAM JEFFERSON) CLINTON 1993–2001

Democratic Party
Born: Aug. 19, 1946, in Hope, Arkansas
Married: Hillary Rodham (b. 1947); 1 daughter
Vice President: Al Gore (1993–2001)

43 GEORGE W. BUSH Republican Party 2001–2009

Born: July 6, 1946, in New Haven, Connecticut
Married: Laura Welch (b. 1946); 2 daughters
Vice President: Dick Cheney (2001–2009)

44 BARACK OBAMA Democratic Party 2009–

Born: August 4, 1961, in Honolulu, Hawaii
Married: Michelle Robinson (b. 1964); 2 daughters
Vice President: Joe Biden (2009–)

Meet the First Ladies

For many years there was no title for the wife of the president. Wives of the early presidents were sometimes addressed as "Lady," "Mrs. President," "Mrs. Presidentress," or even "Queen." The term "First Lady" did not become common until after 1849. That year, President Zachary Taylor called Dolley Madison "First Lady" in a eulogy at her funeral.

Here are a few of the best-known First Ladies of the United States.

ABIGAIL ADAMS, wife of John Adams, never went to school, but she learned to read at home. She was a close adviser to her husband. She is well-known for the many letters she wrote to him when they were separated. The Adamses became the first family to move into the White House.

DOLLEY MADISON, wife of James Madison, was famous as a hostess and for saving a portrait of George Washington during the War of 1812, when the British were about to burn the White House.

MARY TODD LINCOLN, wife of Abraham Lincoln, was a well-educated Southerner who strongly opposed slavery. She suffered many tragedies in her lifetime. Her husband was assassinated, and three of her four children died young.

LUCY WEBB HAYES, wife of Rutherford B. Hayes, was the first First Lady to have graduated from college. A popular figure, she visited disabled soldiers and gave large sums of money to the poor. Because alcohol was banned at the White House for most of her time there, she got the nickname "Lemonade Lucy."

EDITH WILSON, wife of Woodrow Wilson, was one of the most powerful First Ladies in U.S. history. After her husband suffered a stroke in 1919, she played a key role, in his last 18 months in office, in deciding whom he would meet with and what papers he would see. According to some, she made decisions that normally would have been made by a president.

ELEANOR ROOSEVELT, wife of Franklin D. Roosevelt, supported the New Deal policies of her husband and was a strong advocate for civil rights. She had a lifelong career as a writer and champion of causes she believed in. After her husband's death in 1945, she served as a delegate to the United Nations.

JACQUELINE KENNEDY, wife of John F. Kennedy, met her husband while she was working as a photographer and reporter. As First Lady, she filled the White House with historic furnishings and artwork. Her elegant clothes and hairstyle were copied by millions of women.

NANCY REAGAN, wife of Ronald Reagan, met her husband when they both were Hollywood actors in the 1940s. As First Lady, she led a campaign to encourage young people to "just say no" if offered illegal drugs.

MICHELLE OBAMA, wife of Barack Obama, met her husband when they both were working as lawyers in Chicago. They were married in 1992 and have two daughters, Malia, born in 1998, and Sasha, born in 2001. One of her main projects as First Lady has been working to promote good eating habits for children.

WHITE HOUSE Pets

The Clinton family cat Socks

The White House has been home to many animals, beginning with John Adams's favorite horse, Cleopatra. John Quincy Adams had an alligator that sometimes hung out in the East Room.

The Lincolns had a variety of animals, including cats, dogs, goats, and a white rabbit.

Theodore Roosevelt's family had a badger and a macaw, along with horses, dogs, cats, snakes, guinea pigs, and even bears. When Roosevelt's son Archie was sick with measles, the family's pony Algonquin was brought up to visit him in his room.

The Coolidge family kept a small zoo that included lion cubs, a bobcat, a pygmy hippo, and a raccoon that got walked on a leash.

Millie, a springer spaniel owned by Barbara and George H. W. Bush, was the make-believe writer of a book published by the First Lady.

The Clintons had a cat named Socks and a chocolate Labrador retriever named Buddy.

The Obama family adopted Bo, a Portuguese water dog.

Other White House pets have included Franklin D. Roosevelt's Scottish terrier, Fala, and Macaroni, a pony that belonged to John F. Kennedy's daughter, Caroline.

The Obama family pet Bo

AMERICAN INDIANS

People may have arrived in the Americas more than 15,000 years ago, most likely from northeast Asia. Although the American Indian population decreased significantly through the 17th, 18th, and 19th centuries from disease and war, there are still hundreds of tribes, or nations, each with unique languages and traditions.

WHAT CAME FROM AMERICAN INDIANS

FIRST AMERICAN INDIAN WRITING SYSTEM

Sequoyah was a Cherokee scholar born in Tennessee in about 1766. After observing white people writing and reading letters, or "talking leaves," Sequoyah began creating a writing system for the Cherokee language, which he completed probably in 1821. His system of about 85 symbols represented all the sounds used in the language. Thousands of Cherokee quickly became literate as a result of Sequoyah's work. By 1828, the nation's first bilingual newspaper (in Cherokee and English), the *Cherokee Phoenix*, was in print. Sequoyah's achievement emphasized the importance of literacy in passing on knowledge. Sequoyah died in 1843. The sequoia, California's giant evergreen tree, is named in his honor.

NAVAJO (DINE) WAR CODE

The Navajo Nation spans 27,000 square miles across Arizona, New Mexico, and Utah and is America's most populated reservation, with about 175,000 residents. The Dine (dee-NAY), as they call themselves, belong to clans in which members trace descent through the mother. Many Dine still speak a highly descriptive and unique language called Athapaskan. Used as a code in World War II, it was never cracked. Code talkers from at least 16 tribes served during the war. Local radio still broadcasts sports, including New Mexico State University's football games, in Athapaskan.

World War II "code talkers" ▲

GAMES AND SPORTS

Many of today's games and sports came from early American Indian ways of life. The game of lacrosse began as an ancient Indian event called baggataway. Algonquian Indians in the northeastern U.S. used birchbark canoes for fishing and travel. The toboggan started out as an American Indian bark-and-skin runnerless sled to move heavy objects over snow or ice. In the far north, the Inuit wore snowshoes strung with caribou skin to walk on deep, soft snow. Many people today canoe, toboggan, or travel on snowshoes just for fun.

TIME LINE **NORTH AMERICAN INDIANS**

For events before 1492, see page 279.

1492	Christopher Columbus made contact with Taino tribes on the island he named Hispaniola.
c. 1600	Five tribes—the Mohawk, Oneida, Onondaga, Cayuga, and Seneca—formed the Iroquois Confederacy in the Northeast.
1637	Settlers in Connecticut defeated Pequot Indians in the Pequot War.
1754–63	Many American Indians fought as allies of either French or British troops in the French and Indian War.
1804–06	Sacagawea served as an interpreter and guide for Lewis and Clark.
1827	Cherokee tribes in what is now Georgia formed the Cherokee Nation with a constitution and elected governing officials.
1830	Congress passed the Indian Removal Act, the first law that forced tribes to move so that U.S. citizens could settle certain areas of land.
1834	Congress created the Indian Territory for tribes removed from their lands. It covered present-day Oklahoma, Kansas, and Nebraska.
1835–42	Seminoles battled U.S. troops in the Second Seminole War. They lost the conflict and their homeland in Florida.
1838–39	The U.S. government forced Cherokees to move to Indian Territory. Thousands died during the so-called Trail of Tears.
1876	Sioux and Cheyenne Indians defeated troops led by U.S. colonel George Armstrong Custer in the Battle of the Little Bighorn.
1877	After the U.S. government tried to remove his people to Idaho, Chief Joseph led a Nez Percé retreat to Canada but surrendered before reaching the border.
1890	U.S. soldiers massacred more than 200 Sioux, including unarmed women and children, in the Battle of Wounded Knee, the last major conflict between U.S. troops and American Indians.
1912	Jim Thorpe, an American Indian, won the decathalon and the pentathalon in the 1912 Olympic Games.
1924	Congress granted all American Indians U.S. citizenship.
1929	Charles Curtis, a member of the Kaw Nation, became the first American of Indian ancestry elected vice president of the U.S.
1934	Congress passed the Indian Reorganization Act to increase tribal self-government.
1968	The American Indian Movement, a civil rights organization, was founded.
1985	Wilma Mankiller became the first female chief of the Cherokee Nation.
2004	The National Museum of the American Indian opened in Washington, D.C.
2011	The U.S. Mint released the 2011 Native American dollar coin, celebrating the Wampanoag Treaty of 1621.

MAJOR CULTURAL AREAS OF NATIVE NORTH AMERICANS

Climate and geography influenced the culture of the people who lived in these regions. On the plains, for example, people depended on the great herds of buffalo for food. For Aleuts and Inuit in the far north, seals and whales were an important food source. There are more than 560 tribes officially recognized by the U.S. government today and more than 56 million acres of tribal lands. Below are some of the major cultural areas of North American Indians and other native peoples.

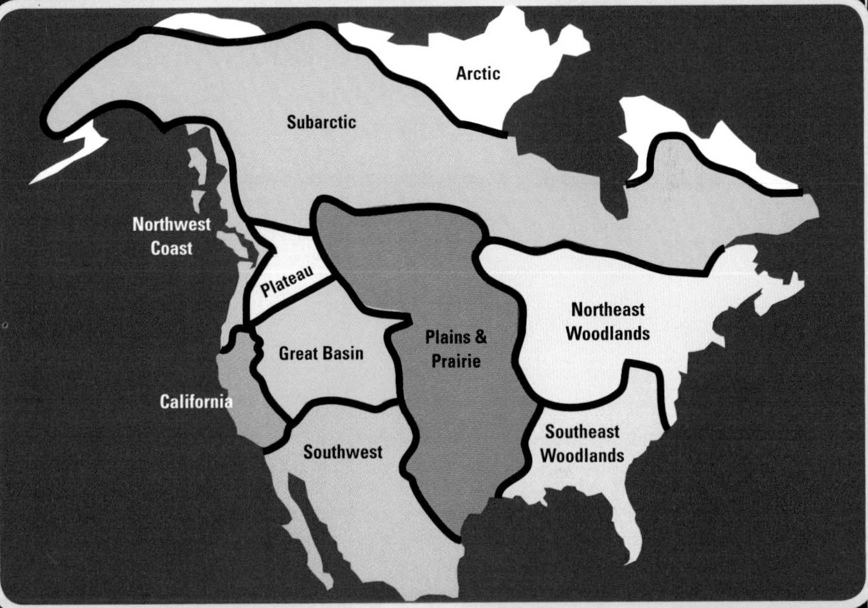

NORTHEAST WOODLANDS The Illinois, Iroquois (Mohawk, Onondaga, Cayuga, Oneida, Seneca, and Tuscarora), Lenape, Menominee, Micmac, Narragansett, Potawatomi, Shawnee

SOUTHEAST WOODLANDS The Cherokee, Chickasaw, Choctaw, Creek, Seminole

PLAINS & PRAIRIE The Arapaho, Blackfoot, Cheyenne, Comanche, Hidatsa, Kaw, Mandan, Sioux

SOUTHWEST The Apache, Navajo, Havasupai, Mojave, Pima, Pueblo (Hopi, Isleta, Laguna, Zuñi)

GREAT BASIN The Paiute, Shoshoni, Ute

CALIFORNIA The Klamath, Maidu, Miwok, Modoc, Patwin, Pomo, Wintun, Yurok

PLATEAU The Cayuse, Nez Percé, Okanagon, Salish, Spokan, Umatilla, Walla Walla, Yakima

NORTHWEST COAST The Chinook, Haida, Kwakiutl, Makah, Nootka, Salish, Tillamook, Tlingit, Tsimshian

SUBARCTIC The Beaver, Chipewyan, Chippewa, Cree, Ingalik, Kaska, Kutchin, Montagnais, Naskapi, Tanana

ARCTIC The Aleut, Inuit, and Yuit

AMERICAN INDIAN NUMBERS*

Here are some facts from the U.S. Census Bureau about the American Indian population of the U.S. today, compared to statistics for the U.S. population as a whole:

	American Indians	Total U.S. Population
Median age	31 years	36.8 years
Average number of people in a family	3.7	3.2
Percentage of people 5 years and older who speak only English at home	71%	80%
Percentage of households owning their own home	55%	66%

*2009 U.S. Census Bureau estimates (American Community Survey). Figures refer to the American Indian population who reported only one race.

American Indian and Alaska Native Populations by State*

Alabama	28,218
Alaska	104,871
Arizona	296,529
Arkansas	22,248
California	362,801
Colorado	56,010
Connecticut	11,256
Delaware	4,181
Florida	71,458
Georgia	32,151
Hawaii	4,164
Idaho	21,441
Illinois	43,963
Indiana	18,462
Iowa	11,084
Kansas	28,150
Kentucky	10,120
Louisiana	30,579
Maine	8,568
Maryland	20,420
Massachusetts	18,850
Michigan	62,007
Minnesota	60,916
Mississippi	15,030
Missouri	27,376
Montana	62,555
Nebraska	18,427
Nevada	32,062
New Hampshire	3,150
New Jersey	29,026
New Mexico	193,222
New York	106,906
North Carolina	122,110
North Dakota	36,591
Ohio	25,292
Oklahoma	321,687
Oregon	53,203
Pennsylvania	26,843
Rhode Island	6,058
South Carolina	19,524
South Dakota	71,817
Tennessee	19,994
Texas	170,972
Utah	32,927
Vermont	2,207
Virginia	29,225
Washington	103,869
West Virginia	3,787
Wisconsin	54,526
Wyoming	13,336
Wash., DC	2,079
U.S. TOTAL	2,932,248

*U.S. Census Bureau, 2010 Census. Figures do not include people who reported belonging to additional ethnic groups.

TOTEM POLES

Northwest Coast Indians carve totem poles with painted images of animals and human faces. The poles, often carved from tree trunks, serve as memorials, gravemarkers, and welcome signs in front of homes. The tallest totem pole, erected in 1994 and dismantled in 1997, was located in Victoria, British Columbia, Canada. It was 180 feet, 3 inches tall.

United States History

Before 13,000 B.C.
First people (called **Paleo-Indians**) cross from Siberia to Alaska and begin to move into North America.

Before 11,000 B.C.
Paleo-Indians use stone points attached to spears to hunt big **mammoths** in northern parts of North America.

11,000 B.C.
Big mammoths disappear and Paleo-Indians begin to gather **plants** for food.

9500 B.C.–1000 B.C.
North American Indians begin using **stone** to grind food and to hunt bison and smaller animals.

1000 B.C.–A.D. 500
Woodland Indians, who lived east of the Mississippi River, bury their dead under large **mounds** of earth (which can still be seen today).

After A.D. 500
The Ancestral Puebloans in the Southwestern United States live in homes on cliffs, called **cliff dwellings**. These people's pottery and dishes are known for their beautiful patterns.

After A.D. 700
Mississippian Indian people in the Southeastern United States **develop farms** and build burial mounds.

700–1492
Many **different Indian cultures** develop throughout North America.

Colonial America and the American Revolution: 1492-1783

1492 Christopher **Columbus** sails across the Atlantic Ocean and reaches an island in the Bahamas in the Caribbean Sea.

1513 Juan **Ponce de León** explores the Florida coast.

1524 Giovanni da **Verrazano** explores the coast from Carolina north to Nova Scotia, enters New York harbor.

1540 Francisco Vásquez de **Coronado** explores the Southwest.

1565 St. Augustine, Florida, the ***first* town** established by Europeans in the United States, is founded by the Spanish. Later burned by the English in 1586.

BENJAMIN FRANKLIN (1706–1790) was a great American leader, printer, scientist, and writer. In 1732, he began publishing a magazine called ***Poor Richard's Almanack***. Poor Richard was a make-believe person who gave advice about common sense and honesty. Many of Poor Richard's sayings are still known today. Among the most famous are "God helps them that help themselves" and "Early to bed, early to rise, makes a man healthy, wealthy, and wise."

1634 **Maryland** is founded as a Catholic colony, with religious freedom for all granted in 1649.

1664 The English seize **New Amsterdam** from the Dutch. The city is renamed New York.

1699 **French settlers** move into Mississippi and Louisiana.

1732 Benjamin Franklin begins publishing ***Poor Richard's Almanack***.

1754–1763 **French and Indian War** between Great Britain and France. The French lose their lands in Canada and the Midwest.

1764–1766 Britain places taxes on sugar that comes from its North American colonies. Britain also requires colonists to buy stamps to help pay for royal troops. Colonists protest, and the **Stamp Act** is repealed in 1766.

1607
Jamestown, Virginia, the first permanent English settlement in North America, is founded by Captain John Smith.

1609
Henry Hudson sails into **New York Harbor**, explores the Hudson River. Spaniards settle Santa Fe, New Mexico.

1619
The first African **slaves** are brought to Jamestown. (Slavery is made legal in 1650.)

1620
Pilgrims from England arrive at Plymouth, Massachusetts, on the *Mayflower*.

1626
Peter Minuit buys **Manhattan** island for the Dutch from Manahata Indians for goods worth $24. The island is renamed New Amsterdam.

1630
Boston is founded by Massachusetts colonists led by John Winthrop.

FAMOUS WORDS FROM THE DECLARATION OF INDEPENDENCE, JULY 4, 1776

"We hold these truths to be self-evident, that all men are created equal, that they are endowed by their Creator with certain unalienable rights, that among these are life, liberty, and the pursuit of happiness."

1770
Boston Massacre: Demonstrators against British taxes throw rocks at British troops. The troops open fire, killing 7.

1773
Boston Tea Party: British tea is thrown into the harbor to protest a tax on tea.

1775
Fighting at **Lexington and Concord,** Massachusetts, marks the beginning of the American Revolution.

1776
The Declaration of Independence is approved July 4 by the Continental Congress (made up of representatives from the American colonies).

1781
British General **Charles Cornwallis** surrenders to the Americans at Yorktown, Virginia, ending major fighting in the Revolutionary War.

The New Nation 1784-1900

1784
The first successful daily **newspaper** in the U.S., the *Pennsylvania Packet & General Advertiser*, is published.

1787
The **Constitutional Convention** meets to write a Constitution for the U.S.

1789
The new **Constitution** is approved by the states. George Washington is chosen as the first president.

1800
The federal government moves from Philadelphia to a new capital, **Washington, D.C.**

1803
The U.S. makes the **Louisiana Purchase** ▶ from France. The Purchase doubles the area of the U.S.

WHO ATTENDED THE CONVENTION?

The **Constitutional Convention** met in Philadelphia in the hot summer of 1787. Most of the great founders of America attended. Among those present were George Washington, James Madison, and John Adams. They met to form a new government that would be strong and, at the same time, protect the liberties that were fought for in the American Revolution. The Constitution they created is still the law of the United States.

1836
Texans fighting for independence from Mexico are defeated at the **Alamo**.

1838
Cherokee Indians are forced to move to Oklahoma, along "The **Trail of Tears**." On the long march, thousands die because of disease and the cold weather.

1844
The **first telegraph** line connects Washington, D.C., and Baltimore.

1846–1848
U.S. war with Mexico: Mexico is defeated, and the United States takes control of the Republic of Texas and of Mexican territories in the West.

1848
The discovery of **gold** in California leads to a "rush" of 80,000 people to the West in search of gold.

1852
Uncle Tom's Cabin Harriet Beecher Stowe's novel about the suffering of slaves, is published.

1804
Lewis and Clark, with their guide Sacagawea, explore what is now the northwestern United States.

1812–1815
War of 1812 with Great Britain: British forces burn the Capitol and White House. Francis Scott Key writes the words to "The Star-Spangled Banner."

1820
The **Missouri Compromise** bans slavery west of the Mississippi River and north of 36°30′ latitude, except in Missouri.

1823
The **Monroe Doctrine** warns European countries not to interfere in the Americas.

1825
The **Erie Canal** opens, linking New York City with the Great Lakes.

1831
The Liberator, a newspaper opposing slavery, is published in Boston.

1869
The **first railroad** connecting the East and West coasts is completed.

1898
Spanish-American War: The U.S. defeats Spain, gains control of the Philippines, Puerto Rico, and Guam.

1858
Abraham Lincoln and Stephen Douglas **debate about slavery** during their Senate campaign in Illinois.

1860
Abraham **Lincoln** is elected president.

1861
The **Civil War** begins.

1863
President Lincoln issues the **Emancipation Proclamation**, freeing most slaves.

1865
The **Civil War** ends as the South surrenders. President Lincoln is assassinated.

1890
Battle of Wounded Knee is fought in South Dakota—the last major battle between Indians and U.S. troops.

CIVIL WAR DEAD AND WOUNDED

The U.S. **Civil War** between the North and South lasted four years (1861–1865) and resulted in the death or wounding of more than 600,000 people. Little was known at the time about infections and the spread of diseases. As a result, many soldiers died from illnesses such as influenza and measles. Many also died from infections from battle wounds.

United States Since 1900

1903
The United States begins digging the **Panama Canal**. The canal opens in 1914, connecting the Atlantic and Pacific oceans.

1908
Henry Ford introduces the **Model T** car, priced at $850.

1916
Jeannette Rankin of Montana becomes the first woman elected to Congress.

1917–1918
The United States joins **World War I** on the side of the Allies against Germany.

1927
Charles A. **Lindbergh** becomes the first person to fly alone nonstop across the Atlantic Ocean.

1929
A stock market crash marks the beginning of the **Great Depression**.

WORLD WAR I

In **World War I** the United States fought with Great Britain, France, and Russia (the Allies) against Germany and Austria-Hungary. The Allies won the war in 1918.

1954
The U.S. Supreme Court **forbids racial segregration** in public schools.

SCHOOL SEGREGATION

The U.S. Supreme Court ruled that **separate schools** for black students and white students were **not equal**. The Court said such schools were in violation of the U.S. Constitution.

1963
President John **Kennedy** is assassinated.

1964
Congress passes the **Civil Rights Act**, which outlaws discrimination in voting and jobs.

1965
The United States sends first soldiers to fight in the **Vietnam War**.

1968
Civil rights leader **Martin Luther King Jr.** is assassinated in Memphis. Senator **Robert F. Kennedy** is assassinated in Los Angeles.

1969
U.S. astronaut Neil Armstrong becomes the **first person** to walk **on the moon**.

1973
U.S. participation in the **Vietnam War ends**.

THE GREAT DEPRESSION

The stock market crash of October 1929 led to a period of severe hardship for the American people—the **Great Depression**. As many as 25 percent of all workers could not find jobs. The Depression lasted until the early 1940s. The Depression also led to a great change in politics. In 1932, Franklin D. Roosevelt, a Democrat, was elected president. He served as president for 12 years, longer than any other president.

1933 President Franklin D. Roosevelt's **New Deal** increases government help to people hurt by the Depression.

1941 Japan attacks **Pearl Harbor**, Hawaii. The United States enters World War II.

1945 Germany surrenders in May. The U.S. drops atomic bombs on **Hiroshima** and Nagasaki in August, leading to Japan's surrender and the end of **World War II**.

1947 Jackie Robinson becomes the **first black baseball player** in the major leagues when he joins the Brooklyn Dodgers.

1950–1953 U.S. armed forces fight in the **Korean War**.

WORLD WAR II

From 1941 to 1945 the United States, joining Britain, the Soviet Union, and other Allied powers, fought the Axis powers, led by Germany, Italy, and Japan, in the deadliest conflict in human history.

2008 **Barack Obama** defeats **John McCain** to become the first African-American president.

2011 The U.S. and allies support rebels in **Libya** trying to overthrow Muammar al-Qaddafi.

1974 President Richard **Nixon resigns** because of the **Watergate** scandal.

1979 U.S. **hostages** are taken **in Iran**, beginning a 444-day crisis that ends with their release in 1981.

1981 Sandra Day O'Connor becomes the **first woman** on the U.S. Supreme Court.

1991 **The Persian Gulf War**: The United States and its allies defeat Iraq.

2001 Hijacked jets crash into the **World Trade Center** and the **Pentagon**, September 11, killing about 3,000 people.

2003 U.S.-led forces invade Iraq and remove dictator **Saddam Hussein**.

2011 U.S. forces kill **Osama bin Laden**, mastermind of the September 11, 2001, terrorist attacks.

African Americans: A Time Line

From the era of slavery to the present, African Americans have struggled to obtain freedom and equal opportunity. The timeline below pinpoints many of the key events and personalities that helped shape this long struggle. *Thurgood Marshall* ▶

1619	**First slaves** from Africa are brought to Virginia.
1831	Nat Turner starts a **slave revolt** in Virginia that is unsuccessful.
1856–57	**Dred Scott**, a slave, sues to be freed because he had left slave territory, but the Supreme Court denies his claim.
1861–65	The North defeats the South in the brutal Civil War; the **13th Amendment** ends nearly 250 years of slavery. The Ku Klux Klan is founded.
1865–77	Southern blacks play leadership roles in government under **Reconstruction**; the 15th Amendment (1870) gives black men the right to vote.
1896	Supreme Court rules in a case called *Plessy v. Ferguson* that racial segregation is legal when facilities are **"separate but equal."** Discrimination and violence against blacks increase.
1910	W. E. B. Du Bois (1868–1963) founds National Association for the Advancement of Colored People (**NAACP**), fighting for equality for blacks.
1920s	African American culture (jazz music, dance, literature) flourishes during the **Harlem Renaissance**.
1954	Supreme Court rules in a case called ***Brown v. Board of Education*** *of Topeka* that school segregation is unconstitutional.
1957	Black students, backed by federal troops, enter recently desegregated Central High School in **Little Rock**, Arkansas.
1955–65	**Malcolm X** (1925–1965) emerges as key spokesperson for black nationalism.
1963	**Rev. Dr. Martin Luther King, Jr.** (1929–1968) gives his "I Have a Dream" speech at a march that inspires more than 200,000 people in Washington, D.C.—and many others throughout the nation.
1964	Sweeping **civil rights bill** banning racial discrimination is signed by President Lyndon Johnson.
1965	Martin Luther King leads protest march in **Selma**, Alabama. Blacks riot in **Watts** section of Los Angeles.
1967	Gary, Indiana, and Cleveland, Ohio, are first major U.S. cities to elect black mayors. **Thurgood Marshall** (1908–1993) becomes first African American on the Supreme Court.
2001	**Colin Powell** becomes first African American secretary of state.
2005	**Condoleezza Rice** becomes first African American woman secretary of state.
2008	Barack Obama becomes the **first African American elected president** of the United States.

THEY MADE HISTORY

People of many different backgrounds have played important roles in the history of the United States.

FREDERICK DOUGLASS (1818–1895) escaped from slavery at age 20. In the decades before the Civil War (1861–1865), he had a major influence on the anti-slavery movement through his lectures and writings. He became a friend and adviser to President Abraham Lincoln and encouraged him to issue the Emancipation Proclamation (1863), which declared free all slaves in Confederate-controlled territory in the South.

CRAZY HORSE (1840s–1877) led the Oglala Sioux Indians in battles with the U.S. Army over land, including in the Black Hills of what is now South Dakota. He helped defeat General George Armstrong Custer at the Battle of the Little Bighorn in Montana. He later surrendered to the Army and was killed in a scuffle with troops at a military outpost.

DALIP SINGH SAUND (1899–1973) was the first Asian-American member of Congress. Born in India, Saund immigrated to California, where he became a farmer, businessman, and judge. Elected to the House of Representatives in 1956, he worked hard to aid farmers and to uphold the rights of immigrants.

ROSA PARKS (1913–2005) refused to give up her bus seat to a white man one day in 1955. Spurred on by her brave action, blacks in Montgomery, Alabama, started a boycott of the bus system. It led to desegregation of the city's buses, a key event in the history of the civil rights movement.

MALCOLM X (1925–1965) was a Nation of Islam (Black Muslim) leader who spoke out against injustices toward African Americans and believed they should live and develop separately from white people. After leaving the Nation of Islam, he was assassinated by rivals. His life story, *The Autobiography of Malcolm X*, published after he died, became a best-seller and helped make him a hero to many.

CESAR CHAVEZ (1927–1993), a Mexican American who was raised in migrant worker camps, started the union known as the United Farm Workers of America in 1966. Along with UFW cofounder **DOLORES HUERTA** (born 1930), he organized boycotts that eventually made growers agree to better conditions for field workers.

REV. DR. MARTIN LUTHER KING, JR. (1929–1968) was the most influential leader of the civil rights movement from the mid-1950s to his assassination in 1968. A believer in peaceful protest, he received the Nobel Peace Prize in 1964. The federal government and all 50 states now have a holiday in his honor. His wife, **CORETTA SCOTT KING** (1927–2006), helped carry on his work.

STEVEN CHU (born 1948), a prominent Chinese-American scientist, won a 1997 Nobel Prize in physics for his nuclear research. More recently, his work focused on studying and promoting the use of alternative fuels. Chu became U.S. secretary of energy in 2009.

SONIA SOTOMAYOR (born 1954), who grew up in a public housing project in New York City, went on to graduate from Princeton University and Yale Law School. Experienced as a prosecutor and a judge, she was named to the U.S. Supreme Court in 2009, becoming the court's first Hispanic justice.

BARACK OBAMA (born 1961), is the son of an American mother and a Kenyan father. After serving in the Illinois Senate for eight years, he was elected to the U.S. Senate in 2004. From there he launched a successful campaign to become president of the U.S. Inaugurated in 2009, he worked to help resolve the nation's economic problems. He won passage of legislation to reform health care and to tighten regulation of financial institutions.

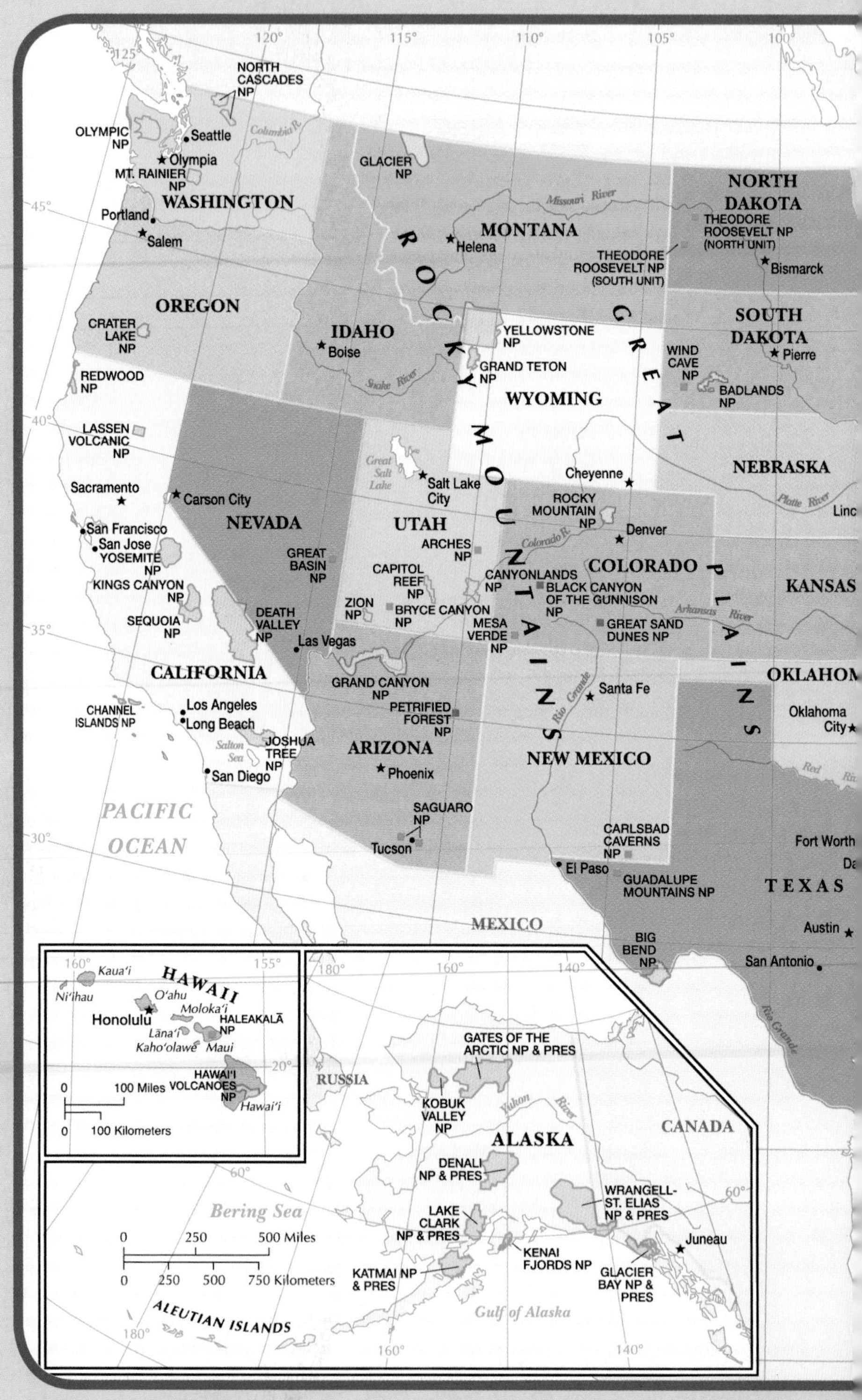

NORTH CASCADES NP
OLYMPIC NP
Seattle
Olympia
MT. RAINIER NP
WASHINGTON
Portland
Salem
Columbia R.
GLACIER NP
Missouri River
MONTANA
Helena
NORTH DAKOTA
THEODORE ROOSEVELT NP (NORTH UNIT)
THEODORE ROOSEVELT NP (SOUTH UNIT)
Bismarck
OREGON
CRATER LAKE NP
IDAHO
Boise
Snake River
YELLOWSTONE NP
GRAND TETON NP
SOUTH DAKOTA
Pierre
WIND CAVE NP
BADLANDS NP
REDWOOD NP
WYOMING
ROCKY MOUNTAINS
GREAT PLAINS
LASSEN VOLCANIC NP
Great Salt Lake
Salt Lake City
Cheyenne
NEBRASKA
Platte River
Sacramento
Carson City
NEVADA
UTAH
ROCKY MOUNTAIN NP
Denver
San Francisco
San Jose
YOSEMITE NP
GREAT BASIN NP
ARCHES NP
Colorado R.
COLORADO
KANSAS
KINGS CANYON NP
CAPITOL REEF NP
CANYONLANDS NP
BLACK CANYON OF THE GUNNISON NP
SEQUOIA NP
DEATH VALLEY NP
ZION NP
BRYCE CANYON NP
MESA VERDE NP
Arkansas River
GREAT SAND DUNES NP
Las Vegas
CALIFORNIA
GRAND CANYON NP
Rio Grande
Santa Fe
OKLAHOMA
CHANNEL ISLANDS NP
Los Angeles
Long Beach
PETRIFIED FOREST NP
Oklahoma City
Salton Sea
JOSHUA TREE NP
ARIZONA
NEW MEXICO
San Diego
Phoenix
Red
PACIFIC OCEAN
SAGUARO NP
Tucson
CARLSBAD CAVERNS NP
Fort Worth
El Paso
GUADALUPE MOUNTAINS NP
TEXAS
MEXICO
Austin
BIG BEND NP
San Antonio
Rio Grande
HAWAII
Kaua'i
Ni'ihau
O'ahu
Honolulu
Moloka'i
HALEAKALĀ NP
Lāna'i
Kaho'olawe
Maui
HAWAI'I VOLCANOES NP
Hawai'i
0 100 Miles
0 100 Kilometers
RUSSIA
GATES OF THE ARCTIC NP & PRES
KOBUK VALLEY NP
Yukon River
ALASKA
CANADA
DENALI NP & PRES
Bering Sea
WRANGELL-ST. ELIAS NP & PRES
LAKE CLARK NP & PRES
KENAI FJORDS NP
Juneau
0 250 500 Miles
0 250 500 750 Kilometers
KATMAI NP & PRES
GLACIER BAY NP & PRES
Gulf of Alaska
ALEUTIAN ISLANDS

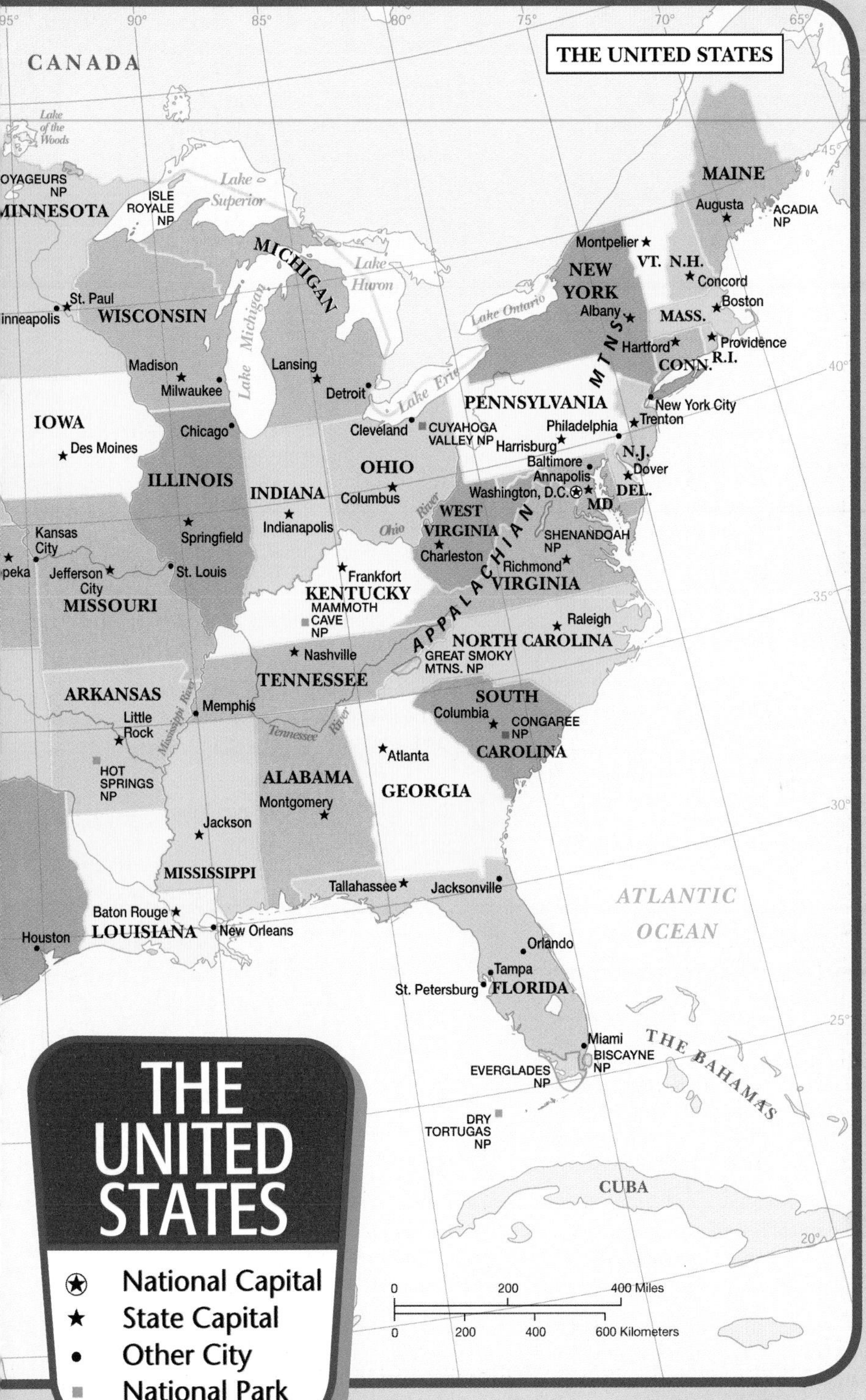
THE UNITED STATES
CANADA
MINNESOTA
WISCONSIN
MICHIGAN
IOWA
ILLINOIS
INDIANA
OHIO
PENNSYLVANIA
NEW YORK
MAINE
VT.
N.H.
MASS.
CONN.
R.I.
N.J.
DEL.
MD
WEST VIRGINIA
VIRGINIA
KENTUCKY
MISSOURI
TENNESSEE
NORTH CAROLINA
SOUTH CAROLINA
GEORGIA
ALABAMA
MISSISSIPPI
ARKANSAS
LOUISIANA
FLORIDA
APPALACHIAN MTNS.
Lake Superior
Lake Michigan
Lake Huron
Lake Ontario
Lake Erie
Lake of the Woods
Ohio River
Mississippi River
Tennessee River
ATLANTIC OCEAN
THE BAHAMAS
CUBA
VOYAGEURS NP
ISLE ROYALE NP
ACADIA NP
CUYAHOGA VALLEY NP
SHENANDOAH NP
MAMMOTH CAVE NP
GREAT SMOKY MTNS. NP
CONGAREE NP
HOT SPRINGS NP
EVERGLADES NP
BISCAYNE NP
DRY TORTUGAS NP
St. Paul
Minneapolis
Madison
Milwaukee
Lansing
Detroit
Chicago
Des Moines
Springfield
Indianapolis
Columbus
Cleveland
Kansas City
Topeka
Jefferson City
St. Louis
Frankfort
Nashville
Memphis
Little Rock
Jackson
Montgomery
Atlanta
Columbia
Raleigh
Charleston
Richmond
Washington, D.C.
Annapolis
Baltimore
Dover
Philadelphia
Harrisburg
Trenton
New York City
Hartford
Providence
Boston
Concord
Albany
Montpelier
Augusta
Tallahassee
Jacksonville
Orlando
Tampa
St. Petersburg
Miami
Baton Rouge
New Orleans
Houston
95°
90°
85°
80°
75°
70°
65°
45°
40°
35°
30°
25°
20°
0
200
400 Miles
0
200
400
600 Kilometers
THE UNITED STATES
National Capital
State Capital
Other City
National Park

How the States

ALABAMA comes from the name of an Indian tribe, which may mean "gathering thick vegetation."

ALASKA comes from *alakshak*, an Aleut word meaning "peninsula" or "land that is not an island."

ARIZONA comes from a Pima Indian word meaning "little spring place" or the Aztec word *arizuma,* meaning "silver-bearing."

ARKANSAS is a variation of Quapaw, the name of an Indian tribe. Quapaw means "south wind."

California

CALIFORNIA is the name of an imaginary island in a Spanish story. It was named by Spanish explorers of Baja California, a part of Mexico.

COLORADO comes from a Spanish word meaning "red." It was first given to the Colorado River because of its reddish color.

CONNECTICUT comes from an Algonquin Indian word meaning "long river place."

DELAWARE is named after Lord De La Warr, the English governor of Virginia in colonial times.

Florida

FLORIDA, which means "flowery" in Spanish, was named by the explorer Ponce de León, who landed there during Easter.

GEORGIA was named after King George II of England, who granted the right to create a colony there in 1732.

HAWAII probably comes from *Hawaiki,* or *Owhyhee,* the native Polynesian word for "homeland."

IDAHO's name is of uncertain origin, but it may come from a Kiowa Apache name for the Comanche Indians.

ILLINOIS is the French version of *Illini,* an Algonquin Indian word meaning "men" or "warriors."

INDIANA means "land of the Indians."

IOWA comes from the name of an American Indian tribe that once lived in the region.

KANSAS comes from a Sioux Indian word that possibly meant "people of the south wind."

KENTUCKY comes from an Iroquois Indian word, possibly meaning "meadowland."

LOUISIANA, which was first settled by French explorers, was named after King Louis XIV of France.

MAINE means "the mainland." English explorers called it that to distinguish it from islands nearby.

MARYLAND was named after Queen Henrietta Maria, wife of King Charles I of England, who granted the right to establish an English colony there.

MASSACHUSETTS comes from an Indian word meaning "large hill place."

Michigan

MICHIGAN comes from the Chippewa Indian words *mici gama*, meaning "great water" (referring to Lake Michigan).

MINNESOTA got its name from a Dakota Sioux Indian word meaning "cloudy water" or "sky-tinted water."

MISSISSIPPI is probably from Chippewa Indian words meaning "great river" or "gathering of all the waters," or from an Algonquin word, *messipi.*

MISSOURI comes from an Algonquin Indian term meaning "river of the big canoes."

Got Their Names

MONTANA comes from a Latin or Spanish word meaning "mountainous."

NEBRASKA comes from an Omaha or Otos Indian word meaning "flat river" or "broad water"; the word was used to refer to the Platte River.

NEVADA means "snow-clad" in Spanish. Spanish explorers gave the name to the Sierra Nevada Mountains.

NEW HAMPSHIRE was named by an early settler after his home county of Hampshire, in England.

NEW JERSEY was named for the English Channel island of Jersey.

NEW MEXICO was given its name by 16th-century Spaniards in Mexico.

NEW YORK, first called New Netherland, was renamed for the Duke of York after the English took it from Dutch settlers.

NORTH CAROLINA, the northern part of the English colony of Carolana, was named for King Charles I.

NORTH DAKOTA comes from a Sioux Indian word meaning "friend" or "ally."

OHIO is the Iroquois Indian word for "good river."

OKLAHOMA comes from a Choctaw Indian word meaning "red man."

Oregon

OREGON may have come from *Ouaricon-sint,* a name on an old French map that was once given to what is now called the Columbia River. That river runs between Oregon and Washington.

PENNSYLVANIA meaning "Penn's woods," was the name given to the colony founded by William Penn.

RHODE ISLAND may have come from the Dutch *Roode Eylandt* ("red island") or may have been named after the Greek island of Rhodes.

SOUTH CAROLINA, the southern part of the English colony of Carolana, was named for King Charles I.

South Dakota

SOUTH DAKOTA comes from a Sioux Indian word meaning "friend" or "ally."

TENNESSEE comes from *Tanasi*, the name of Cherokee Indian villages on what is now the Little Tennessee River.

TEXAS comes from a word meaning "friends" or "allies," used by the Spanish to describe some of the American Indians living there.

UTAH comes from a Navajo word meaning "upper" or "higher up."

VERMONT comes from two French words, *vert* meaning "green" and *mont* meaning "mountain."

VIRGINIA was named in honor of Queen Elizabeth I of England, who was known as the Virgin Queen because she was never married.

WASHINGTON was named after George Washington, the first president of the United States. It is the only state named after a president.

WEST VIRGINIA got its name from the people of western Virginia, who formed their own government during the Civil War.

WISCONSIN comes from a Chippewa name that is believed to mean "grassy place." It was once spelled *Ouisconsin* and *Mesconsing.*

WYOMING comes from Algonquin Indian words that are said to mean "at the big plains," "large prairie place," or "on the great plain."

Facts About the States

After every state name is the postal abbreviation. The Area includes both land and water; it is given in square miles (sq mi) and square kilometers (sq km). Numbers in parentheses after Population, Area, and Entered Union show the state's rank compared with other states. All population figures are from the 2010 U.S. Census.

ALABAMA

(AL) Heart of Dixie, Camellia State

POPULATION: 4,779,736 (23rd) **AREA:** 52,420 sq mi (30th) (135,768 sq km) Camellia Yellowhammer Southern longleaf pine "Alabama" **ENTERED UNION:** December 14, 1819 (22nd) Montgomery **LARGEST CITIES (WITH POP.):** Birmingham, 212,237; Montgomery, 205,764; Mobile, 195,111; Huntsville, 180,105 motor vehicles, metal products, chemicals, paper, food products, clothing, lumber, coal, oil, natural gas, chickens, livestock, peanuts, cotton

did you know? *About 9,000 years ago Indians came to live in Russell Cave, in northern Alabama. They hunted, fished, and gathered nuts and other foods from plants. The cave is part of a national monument today.*

ALASKA

(AK) The Last Frontier State

POPULATION: 710,231 (47th) **AREA:** 664,988 sq mi (1st) (1,722,319 sq km) Forget-me-not Willow ptarmigan Sitka spruce "Alaska's Flag" **ENTERED UNION:** January 3, 1959 (49th) Juneau **LARGEST CITIES (WITH POP.):** Anchorage, 291,826; Fairbanks, 31,535; Juneau, 31,275 oil, natural gas, fish, food products, lumber and wood products, nursery and greenhouse products, hay, fur

did you know? *Barrow, AK, is the northernmost city in North America. For more than two months each year, starting in late November, the sun does not rise there. Then, in late spring and early summer, there is light or twilight for 24 hours a day.*

ARIZONA

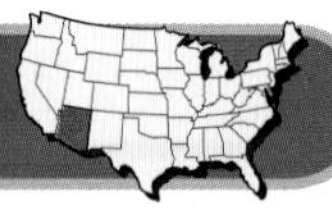

(AZ) Grand Canyon State

POPULATION: 6,392,017 (16th) **AREA:** 113,990 sq mi (6th) (295,235 sq km) Blossom of the Saguaro cactus Cactus wren Paloverde "Arizona" **ENTERED UNION:** February 14, 1912 (48th) Phoenix **LARGEST CITIES (WITH POP.):** Phoenix, 1,445,632; Tucson, 520,116; Mesa, 439,041; Chandler, 236,123; Glendale, 226,721; Scottsdale, 217,385; Gilbert, 208,453 electronic equipment, transportation and industrial equipment, aerospace products, copper and other minerals

did you know? *At the Petrified Forest National Park, in northeast Arizona, you can see remains of trees that lived more than 200 million years ago and have turned into colorful rock.*

ARKANSAS (AR) Natural State, Razorback State

POPULATION: 2,915,918 (32nd) **AREA:** 53,178 sq mi (29th) (137,732 sq km) Apple blossom Mockingbird Pine "Arkansas" **ENTERED UNION:** June 15, 1836 (25th) Little Rock **LARGEST CITIES (WITH POP.):** Little Rock, 193,524; Fort Smith, 86,209; Fayetteville, 73,580; Springdale, 69,797; Jonesboro, 67,263 food products, transportation and industrial equipment, paper, metal products, lumber and wood products, chickens, soybeans, rice, cotton, natural gas

Little Rock

did you know? *Wal-Mart, now the world's biggest retail company and the biggest private employer in the U.S., started from a single discount store that opened in Rogers, AR, in 1962.*

CALIFORNIA (CA) Golden State

POPULATION: 37,253,956 (1st) **AREA:** 163,694 sq mi (3rd) (423,967 sq km) Golden poppy California valley quail California redwood "I Love You, California" **ENTERED UNION:** September 9, 1850 (31st) Sacramento **LARGEST CITIES (WITH POP.):** Los Angeles, 3,792,621; San Diego, 1,307,402; San Jose, 945,942; San Francisco, 805,235; Fresno, 494,665; Sacramento, 466,488; Long Beach, 462,257; Oakland, 390,724; Bakersfield, 347,483; Anaheim, 336,265. electronic equipment, oil, transportation and industrial equipment, motion pictures, printed materials, wine, food products, milk, cattle, fruit, vegetables

Sacramento
San Francisco
Los Angeles
San Diego

did you know? *San Francisco is said to be the second-hilliest city in the world, after La Paz, Bolivia. Some of the hills are very high and steep, with great views of the city and surrounding area.*

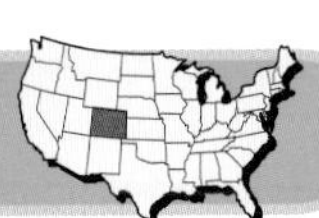

COLORADO (CO) Centennial State

POPULATION: 5,029,196 (22nd) **AREA:** 104,094 sq mi (8th) (269,604 sq km) Rocky Mountain columbine Lark bunting Colorado blue spruce "Where the Columbines Grow" **ENTERED UNION:** August 1, 1876 (38th) Denver **LARGEST CITIES (WITH POP.):** Denver, 600,158; Colorado Springs, 416,427; Aurora, 325,078; Fort Collins, 143,986; Lakewood, 142,980 electronic equipment, instruments and industrial machinery, food products, metal products, oil, natural gas, coal, cattle

Denver
Colorado Springs

did you know? *The small town of Dinosaur, CO, is located near Dinosaur National Monument. Street names in the town include Brontosaurus Boulevard, Stegosaurus Freeway, and Triceratops Terrace.*

Key:      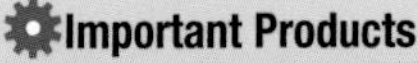

CONNECTICUT (CT) Constitution State, Nutmeg State

POPULATION: 3,574,097 (29th) **AREA:** 5,544 sq mi (48th) (14,358 sq km) Mountain laurel American robin White oak "Yankee Doodle" **ENTERED UNION:** January 9, 1788 (5th) Hartford **LARGEST CITIES (WITH POP.):** Bridgeport, 144,229; New Haven, 129,779; Hartford, 124,775; Stamford, 122,643; Waterbury, 110,366; Norwalk, 85,603; Danbury, 80,893 aircraft parts, helicopters, metals and metal products, electronic equipment, medical instruments, chemicals, greenhouse and nursery products, dairy products, stone

did you know? ***Mystic Seaport, on the Connecticut shore, contains a re-creation of a 19th-century seafaring village, along with many historic ships and other exhibits. The Mystic Aquarium nearby has a wide variety of sea creatures—and even a bat cave.***

DELAWARE (DE) First State, Diamond State

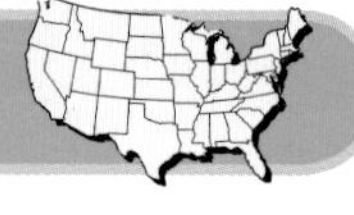

Dover

POPULATION: 900,877 (45th) **AREA:** 2,489 sq mi (49th) (6,445 sq km) Peach blossom Blue hen chicken American holly "Our Delaware" **ENTERED UNION:** December 7, 1787 (1st) Dover **LARGEST CITIES (WITH POP.):** Wilmington, 70,851; Dover, 36,047; Newark, 31,454 chemicals, drugs, transportation equipment, food products, chickens

did you know? ***People from Sweden first settled at Fort Christina (later Wilmington) in 1636. In 1787, Delaware became the first state to ratify the U.S. Constitution.***

FLORIDA (FL) Sunshine State

Tallahassee
Jacksonville
Miami

POPULATION: 18,801,310 (4th) **AREA:** 65,758 sq mi (22nd) (170,312 sq km) Orange blossom Mockingbird Sabal palmetto palm "Old Folks at Home" **ENTERED UNION:** March 3, 1845 (27th) Tallahassee **LARGEST CITIES (WITH POP.):** Jacksonville, 821,764; Miami, 399,457; Tampa, 335,709; St. Petersburg, 244,769; Orlando, 238,300; Hialeah, 224,669; Tallahassee, 181,376; Ft. Lauderdale, 165,521; Port St. Lucie, 164,603 electronic and transportation equipment, instruments, printed materials, food products, nursery plants, oranges and other citrus fruits, vegetables, phosphates, fish

did you know? ***Jacksonville is the biggest city in the lower 48 U.S. states—if you go by area. It's about the size of New York City and Los Angeles combined. The city is named after Andrew Jackson, who was military governor of Florida before it became a state.***

GEORGIA

(GA) Empire State of the South, Peach State

POPULATION: 9,687,653 (9th) **AREA:** 59,425 sq mi (24th) (153,911 sq km) Cherokee rose Brown thrasher Live oak "Georgia on My Mind" **ENTERED UNION:** January 2, 1788 (4th) Atlanta **LARGEST CITIES (WITH POP.):** Atlanta, 420,003; Augusta, 195,844; Columbus, 189,885; Savannah, 136,296; Athens, 115,452 clothing and textiles, carpets, transportation equipment, food products, paper, chickens, eggs, cotton, peanuts, peaches, clay

Atlanta

did you know? ***At the Okefenokee National Wildlife Refuge in southern Georgia, visitors can explore forests, marshes, and prairies and see many kinds of animals, including alligators, sandhill cranes, and red-cockaded woodpeckers.***

HAWAII

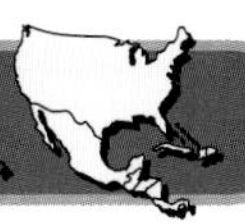

(HI) Aloha State

POPULATION: 1,360,301 (40th) **AREA:** 10,926 sq mi (43rd) (28,300 sq km) Yellow hibiscus Hawaiian goose Kukui "Hawaii Ponoi" **ENTERED UNION:** August 21, 1959 (50th) Honolulu **LARGEST CITIES (WITH POP.):** Honolulu, 337,256; East Honolulu, 49,914; Pearl 47,698; Hilo, 43,263; Kailua, 38,635; Waipahu, 38,216; Kaneohe, 34,597 food products, pineapples, nursery and greenhouse products, sugar, concrete, printing and publishing, fish

Honolulu

did you know? ***President Barack Obama was born in Honolulu and spent many years living in Hawaii. He used to body surf at a beach on Oahu and once worked at a Baskin Robbins ice cream store that still exists today.***

IDAHO

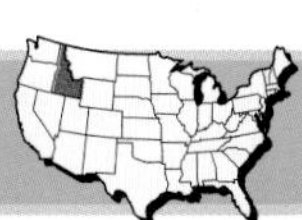

(ID) Gem State

POPULATION: 1,567,582 (39th) **AREA:** 83,568 sq mi (14th) (216,442 sq km) Syringa Mountain bluebird White pine "Here We Have Idaho" **ENTERED UNION:** July 3, 1890 (43rd) Boise **LARGEST CITIES (WITH POP.):** Boise, 205,871; Nampa, 81,557; Meridian, 75,092; Idaho Falls, 56,813; Pocatello, 54,255 electronic products, lumber and wood products, cattle, dairy products, food products, potatoes, sugar beets, hay, wheat

Boise

did you know? ***Craters of the Moon National Monument, in southern Idaho, has an unusual, almost unearthly landscape, with its lava flows, craters, and cinder cones. They are left over from volcanic eruptions, the last of which came about 1,600 years ago.***

Key: 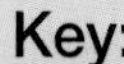  Flower  Bird  Tree  Song  Capital 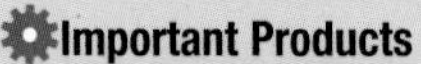 Important Products

ILLINOIS

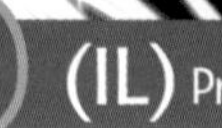

(IL) Prairie State

POPULATION: 12,830,632 (5th) **AREA:** 57,916 sq mi (25th) (150,002 sq km) Native violet Cardinal White oak "Illinois" **ENTERED UNION:** December 3, 1818 (21st) Springfield **LARGEST CITIES (WITH POP.):** Chicago, 2,695,598; Aurora, 197,899; Rockford, 152,871; Joliet, 147,433; Naperville, 141,853; Springfield, 116,250; Peoria, 115,007; Elgin, 108,188 industrial machinery, metals and metal products, coal, electronic equipment, food products, corn, soybeans, hogs

did you know? ***The world's first skyscraper was built in Chicago, in 1885, and the city's Willis Tower (formerly the Sears Tower) is the tallest U.S. building. Presidents Abraham Lincoln, Ulysses S. Grant, and Barack Obama lived in Illinois, and President Ronald Reagan was born there.***

INDIANA

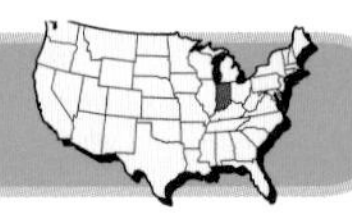

(IN) Hoosier State

POPULATION: 6,483,802 (15th) **AREA:** 36,417 sq mi (38th) (94,321 sq km) Peony Cardinal Tulip poplar "On the Banks of the Wabash, Far Away" **ENTERED UNION:** December 11, 1816 (19th) Indianapolis **LARGEST CITIES (WITH POP.):** Indianapolis, 820,445; Fort Wayne, 253,691; Evansville, 117,429; South Bend, 101,168; Hammond, 80,830; Bloomington, 80,405; Gary, 80,294 motor vehicles and parts, electronic equipment, iron and steel, coal, metal products, drugs, corn, soybeans, hogs, coal

did you know? ***Two main routes of the Underground Railroad, a movement that helped free black slaves, went through Indiana. From 1827 to 1847, the Coffin family ran a stop, in Newport (now Fountain City). They helped more than 2,000 runaway slaves escape.***

IOWA

(IA) Hawkeye State

POPULATION: 3,046,355 (30th) **AREA:** 56,273 sq mi (26th) (145,746 sq km) Wild rose Eastern goldfinch Oak "The Song of Iowa" **ENTERED UNION:** December 28, 1846 (29th) Des Moines **LARGEST CITIES (WITH POP.):** Des Moines, 203,433; Cedar Rapids, 126,326; Davenport, 99,685; Sioux City, 82,684 corn, soybeans, hogs, cattle, food products, industrial machinery

did you know? ***Famous people born in Iowa include "Buffalo Bill" Cody (born in 1846), baseball player/manager "Cap" Anson (1851), President Herbert Hoover (1874), and actors John Wayne (1907) and Elijah Wood (1981).***

KANSAS

(KS) Sunflower State

POPULATION: 2,853,118 (33rd) **AREA:** 82,278 sq mi (15th) (213,101 sq km) Native sunflower Western meadowlark Cottonwood "Home on the Range" **ENTERED UNION:** January 29, 1861 (34th) Topeka **LARGEST CITIES (WITH POP.):** Wichita, 382,368; Overland Park, 173,372; Kansas City, 145,786; Topeka, 127,473; Olathe, 125,872 cattle, aircraft and other transportation equipment, industrial machinery, food products, wheat, corn, soybeans, hay, oil, natural gas

Topeka

Wichita

did you know? ***In October 2005, Steven Arnold discovered a 1,400-pound meteorite—a piece of rock from outer space—on farmland in Kansas. He found it by searching with a metal detector and then digging into the ground at a likely spot.***

KENTUCKY

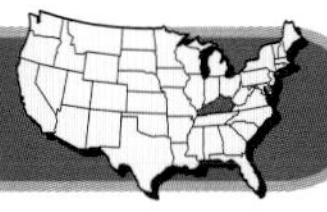

(KY) Bluegrass State

POPULATION: 4,339,367 (26th) **AREA:** 40,411 sq mi (37th) (104,665 sq km) Goldenrod Cardinal Tulip poplar "My Old Kentucky Home" **ENTERED UNION:** June 1, 1792 (15th) Frankfort **LARGEST CITIES (WITH POP.):** Louisville, 597,337; Lexington-Fayette, 295,803; Bowling Green, 58,067; Owensboro, 57,265 coal, industrial machinery, electronic equipment, transportation equipment, metals, tobacco, horses, cattle

Frankfort

Louisville

did you know? ***More than 360 miles of natural caves and underground passageways have been mapped under Mammoth Cave National Park. It's the largest network of natural tunnels in the world and extends up to 1,000 miles.***

LOUISIANA

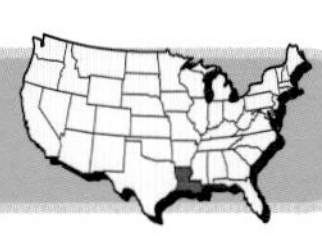

(LA) Pelican State

POPULATION: 4,533,372 (25th) **AREA:** 51,988 sq mi (31st) (134,649 sq km) Magnolia Eastern brown pelican Cypress "Give Me Louisiana" **ENTERED UNION:** April 30, 1812 (18th) Baton Rouge **LARGEST CITIES (WITH POP.):** New Orleans, 343,829; Baton Rouge, 229,493; Shreveport, 199,311; Metaire, 138,481; Lafayette, 120,623 natural gas, oil, chemicals, transportation equipment, paper, food products, sugar, cotton, cattle, fish

Baton Rouge

New Orleans

did you know? ***Hurricane Katrina struck the Gulf coast in August 2005, flooding four-fifths of the city of New Orleans. While many residents were able to return and resume their lives, the population in 2010 was still about 25 percent lower than it had been before Katrina.***

Key: Flower Bird Tree Song Capital Important Products

MAINE

(ME) Pine Tree State

POPULATION: 1,328,361 (41st) **AREA:** 35,384 sq mi (39th) (91,644 sq km) White pine cone and tassel Chickadee Eastern white pine "State of Maine Song" **ENTERED UNION:** March 15, 1820 (23rd) Augusta **LARGEST CITIES (WITH POP.):** Portland, 66,194; Lewiston, 36,592; Bangor, 33,039 paper, ships and boats, plastics, wood and wood products, food products, potatoes, blueberries, milk, eggs, fish, shellfish

Augusta

did you know? ***In 1948, Maine elected its first female U.S. senator, Margaret Chase Smith; she served for 24 years, a record for a woman senator. Since the mid-1990s, both of Maine's senators have been women: Olympia Snowe and Susan Collins.***

MARYLAND

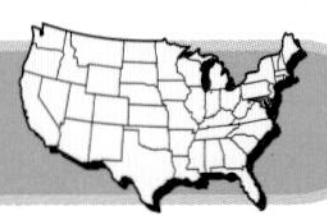

(MD) Old Line State, Free State

Baltimore

Annapolis

POPULATION: 5,773,552 (19th) **AREA:** 12,406 sq mi (42nd) (32,131 sq km) Black-eyed susan Baltimore oriole White oak "Maryland, My Maryland" **ENTERED UNION:** April 28, 1788 (7th) Annapolis **LARGEST CITIES (WITH POP.):** Baltimore, 620,961; Columbia, 99,615; Germantown, 86,395; Silver Spring, 71,452; Waldorf, 67,752; Glen Burnie, 67,639 food products, electronic equipment, chemicals, instruments, drugs, chickens, soybeans, corn, stone

did you know? ***Maryland's official state sport is jousting. Competitors on horseback ride through a course and use their lances to collect rings. Competitors are called either "knights" or "maids."***

MASSACHUSETTS

(MA) Bay State, Old Colony

POPULATION: 6,547,629 (14th) **AREA:** 10,554 sq mi (44th) (27,336 sq km) Mayflower Chickadee American elm "All Hail to Massachusetts" **ENTERED UNION:** February 6, 1788 (6th) Boston **LARGEST CITIES (WITH POP.):** Boston, 617,594; Worcester, 181,045; Springfield, 153,060; Lowell, 106,519; Cambridge, 105,162 electronic equipment, instruments, chemicals, drugs, metal products, fish, flowers, shrubs, cranberries

did you know? ***The first shots of the American Revolution were fired on the village green in Lexington on April 19, 1775. Massachusetts residents remember the events of that day with a state holiday, called Patriots' Day, now celebrated each year on the third Monday in April. The Boston Marathon is held on that day.***

MICHIGAN

(MI) Great Lakes State, Wolverine State

POPULATION: 9,883,640 (8th) **AREA:** 96,713 sq mi (11th) (250,486 sq km) Apple blossom Robin White pine "Michigan, My Michigan" **ENTERED UNION:** January 26, 1837 (26th) Lansing **LARGEST CITIES (WITH POP.):** Detroit, 713,777; Grand Rapids, 188,040; Warren, 134,056; Sterling Heights, 129,699; Ann Arbor, 113,934; Lansing, 109,565; Flint, 102,434 automobiles, chemicals, industrial machinery, metal products, furniture, plastic products, iron ore, food products, milk, corn, blueberries

Lansing

Detroit

did you know? ***Michigan was the only state to lose population between 2000 and 2010, according to the 2010 U.S. Census. The city of Detroit lost one-fourth of its population in those ten years.***

MINNESOTA

(MN) North Star State, Gopher State

POPULATION: 5,303,925 (21st) **AREA:** 86,935 sq mi (12th) (225,163 sq km) Pink and white lady slipper Common loon Red pine "Hail! Minnesota" **ENTERED UNION:** May 11, 1858 (32nd) St. Paul **LARGEST CITIES (WITH POP.):** Minneapolis, 382,578; St. Paul, 285,068; Rochester, 106,769; Duluth, 86,265; Bloomington, 82,893 food products, electronic products, petroleum and asphalt, scientific and medical instruments, iron ore, paper, milk, turkeys, hogs, cattle, corn, soybeans

did you know? ***The city of St. Paul grew from a tiny settlement first known as Pig's Eye Landing. It got its new name from a log cabin chapel built there by a Catholic missionary priest. In the 1920s and 1930s, St. Paul was a safe haven for gangsters fleeing from the law in other Midwestern cities.***

MISSISSIPPI

(MS) Magnolia State

POPULATION: 2,967,297 (31st) **AREA:** 48,432 sq mi (32nd) (125,438 sq km) Magnolia Mockingbird Magnolia "Go, Mississippi!" **ENTERED UNION:** December 10, 1817 (20th) Jackson **LARGEST CITIES (WITH POP.):** Jackson, 173,514; Gulfport, 67,793; Hattiesburg, 48,982; Biloxi, 45,989 transportation equipment, chemicals, furniture, electrical machinery, lumber and wood products, cotton, soybeans, rice, chickens, cattle

did you know? ***In 1902, President Theodore "Teddy" Roosevelt went bear hunting in Mississippi. He refused to shoot a bear that had been tied to a tree by his companions. The story inspired some toy makers to create a stuffed toy bear, which they called "Teddy's Bear." That's how the teddy bear was born.***

Key:  Flower  Bird  Tree  Song 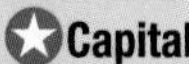 Capital 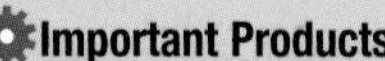 Important Products

MISSOURI

(MO) Show Me State

POPULATION: 5,988,927 (18th) **AREA:** 69,702 sq mi (21st) (180,529 sq km) Hawthorn Bluebird Dogwood "Missouri Waltz" **ENTERED UNION:** August 10, 1821 (24th) Jefferson City **LARGEST CITIES (WITH POP.):** Kansas City, 459,787; St. Louis, 319,294; Springfield, 159,498; Independence, 116,830; Columbia, 108,500 motor vehicles, aerospace equipment, chemicals, electrical and electronic equipment, food products, cattle, hogs, milk, soybeans, corn, hay, lead

did you know? *The stainless steel Gateway Arch (630 feet high), in St. Louis, is the state's most famous landmark. The state's most famous citizen is probably President Harry S. Truman, who was born and lived most of his life in Missouri.*

MONTANA

(MT) Treasure State

POPULATION: 989,415 (44th) **AREA:** 147,039 sq mi (4th) (380,831 sq km) Bitterroot Western meadowlark Ponderosa pine "Montana" **ENTERED UNION:** November 8, 1889 (41st) Helena **LARGEST CITIES (WITH POP.):** Billings, 104,170; Missoula, 66,788; Great Falls, 58,505; Bozeman, 37,280 cattle, copper, gold, coal, petroleum products, food products, wheat, barley, wood and paper products

did you know? *The Little Bighorn National Monument, in southeastern Montana, commemorates "Custer's last stand." U.S. Army cavalry troops, under Lt. Col. George Armstrong Custer, were outnumbered and crushed by Sioux and Northern Cheyenne Indians, in a famous 1876 battle on that site.*

NEBRASKA

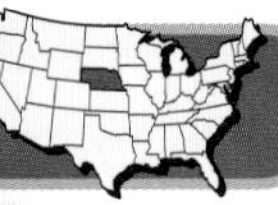

(NE) Cornhusker State

POPULATION: 1,826,341 (38th) **AREA:** 77,349 sq mi (16th) (200,334 sq km) Goldenrod Western meadowlark Cottonwood "Beautiful Nebraska" **ENTERED UNION:** March 1, 1867 (37th) Lincoln **LARGEST CITIES (WITH POP.):** Omaha, 408,958; Lincoln, 258,379; Bellevue, 50,137; Grand Island, 48,520 cattle, hogs, milk, corn, soybeans, hay, sorghum, food products, chemicals, industrial machinery

did you know? *Nebraska has the only unicameral (one-house) state legislature in the U.S. It is called the Nebraska Unicameral. The members are called senators, and they serve four-year terms. The leader of the legislature is called the Speaker.*

NEVADA (NV) Sagebrush State, Battle Born State, Silver State

POPULATION: 2,700,551 (35th) **AREA:** 110,572 sq mi (7th) (286,382 sq km) Sagebrush Mountain bluebird Single-leaf piñon, bristlecone pine "Home Means Nevada" **ENTERED UNION:** October 31, 1864 (36th) Carson City **LARGEST CITIES (WITH POP.):** Las Vegas, 583,756; Henderson, 257,729; North Las Vegas, 216,961; Reno, 225,221; Paradise, 223,107 gold, silver, cattle, hay, food products, plastics, cement, chemicals

Carson City
Las Vegas

did you know? ***The state's population grew by 35% between 2000 and 2010, according to the 2010 U.S. Census, making Nevada the fastest-growing U.S. state.***

NEW HAMPSHIRE (NH) Granite State

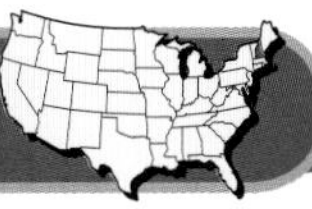

POPULATION: 1,316,470 (42nd) **AREA:** 9,348 sq mi (46th) (24,210 sq km) Purple lilac Purple finch White birch "Old New Hampshire" **ENTERED UNION:** June 21, 1788 (9th) Concord **LARGEST CITIES (WITH POP.):** Manchester, 109,565; Nashua, 86,494; Concord, 42,695 electric and electronic equipment, machinery, metal products, plastic products, greenhouse and dairy products, apples, maple syrup and maple sugar

Concord

did you know? ***Mount Washington, in New Hampshire, is the highest mountain in the northeastern United States. Visitors can ride to the top on a cog railway. But it's windy up there! A weather observatory on the mountain once reported a record wind speed of 231 miles an hour.***

NEW JERSEY (NJ) Garden State

POPULATION: 8,791,894 (11th) **AREA:** 8,723 sq mi (47th) (22,592 sq km) Purple violet Eastern goldfinch Red oak none **ENTERED UNION:** December 18, 1787 (3rd) Trenton **LARGEST CITIES (WITH POP.):** Newark, 277,140; Jersey City, 247,597; Paterson, 146,199; Elizabeth, 124,969; Edison, 99,967; Woodbridge, 99,585 chemicals, drugs and medical equipment, electronic equipment, petroleum products, nursery and greenhouse products, food products, tomatoes, blueberries, peaches

Newark
Trenton

did you know? ***New Jersey has parks, meadows, farms, and beaches, but it is still the most crowded U.S. state, with an average of around 1,200 people per square mile.***

Key: Flower     Important Products

NEW MEXICO

(NM) Land of Enchantment

POPULATION: 2,059,179 (36th) **AREA:** 121,590 sq mi (5th) (314,919 sq km) Yucca Roadrunner Piñon "O, Fair New Mexico" **ENTERED UNION:** January 6, 1912 (47th) Santa Fe **LARGEST CITIES (WITH POP.):** Albuquerque, 545,852; Las Cruces, 97,618; Rio Rancho, 87,521; Santa Fe, 67,947 electronic equipment, medical equipment, aircraft, natural gas, oil, copper, potash, uranium, cattle, hay, onions, chilies

did you know? ***Every summer, hundreds of thousands of bats come to stay and give birth to their young at the Bat Cave in Carlsbad Caverns National Park. Adult bats fly out at night in huge swarms to search for insects, their main food source. During the day, bat families rest, hanging from the ceiling of the dark cave.***

NEW YORK

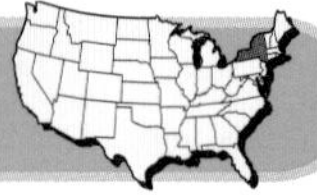

(NY) Empire State

POPULATION: 19,378,102 (3rd) **AREA:** 54,555 sq mi (27th) (141,298 sq km) Rose Bluebird Sugar maple "I Love New York" **ENTERED UNION:** July 26, 1788 (11th) Albany **LARGEST CITIES (WITH POP.):** New York, 8,175,133; Buffalo, 261,310; Rochester, 210,565; Yonkers, 195,976; Syracuse, 145,170 chemicals, drugs, automobile and aircraft parts, electronic equipment, machinery, metal products, books and magazines, milk, cattle, hay, nursery and greenhouse products apples, salt, stone

did you know? ***In January 1892, Annie Moore, a 15-year-old Irish girl, became the first of some 12 million immigrants to enter the United States through Ellis Island in New York Harbor.***

NORTH CAROLINA

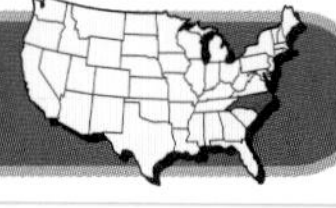

(NC) Tar Heel State, Old North State

POPULATION: 9,535,483 (10th) **AREA:** 53,819 sq mi (28th) (139,391 sq km) Dogwood Cardinal Pine "The Old North State" **ENTERED UNION:** November 21, 1789 (12th) Raleigh **LARGEST CITIES (WITH POP.):** Charlotte, 731,424; Raleigh, 403,892; Greensboro, 269,666; Winston-Salem, 229,617; Durham, 228,330; Fayetteville, 200,564 tobacco and tobacco products, chemicals, drugs, electronic equipment, clothing and textiles, furniture, chickens, hogs, nursery and greenhouse products, sweet potatoes, cotton, soybeans, peanuts

did you know? ***The Outer Banks, a line of offshore sandy islands, were full of pirates and smugglers in the early 1700s. The most notorious, Blackbeard, terrorized sailors along the coast before the crews of two British ships sent him to his watery grave there in 1718.***

NORTH DAKOTA

(ND) Peace Garden State

POPULATION: 672,591 (48th) **AREA:** 70,698 sq mi (19th) (183,109 sq km) Wild prairie rose Western meadowlark American elm "North Dakota Hymn" **ENTERED UNION:** November 2, 1889 (39th) Bismarck **LARGEST CITIES (WITH POP.):** Fargo, 105,549; Bismarck, 61,272; Grand Forks, 52,838; Minot, 40,888 wheat, soybeans, barley, hay, sunflowers, sugar beets, cattle, oil, food products, farm equipment, transportation equipment, metal products

Bismarck

did you know? ***During their expedition, Lewis and Clark spent the winter of 1804–05 in North Dakota. They named their fort after the Mandan tribe that lived nearby. They met Sacagawea, who gave birth to her son at Fort Mandan.***

OHIO

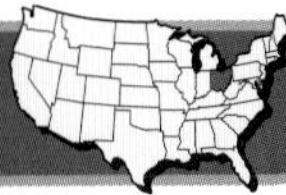

(OH) Buckeye State

POPULATION: 11,536,504 (7th) **AREA:** 44,825 sq mi (34th) (116,097 sq km) Scarlet carnation Cardinal Buckeye "Beautiful Ohio" **ENTERED UNION:** March 1, 1803 (17th) Columbus **LARGEST CITIES (WITH POP.):** Columbus, 787,033; Cleveland, 396,815; Cincinnati, 296,943; Toledo, 287,288; Akron, 199,110; Dayton, 141,527 metals and metal products, transportation equipment, chemicals, machinery, rubber and plastic products, electronic equipment, food products, corn, soybeans, livestock, milk

Cleveland
Columbus
Cincinnati

did you know? ***Wilbur and Orville Wright, the famous brothers who made the world's first plane flight, grew up mostly in Dayton, OH. They became interested in aviation when their father gave them a toy helicopter powered by a rubber band.***

OKLAHOMA

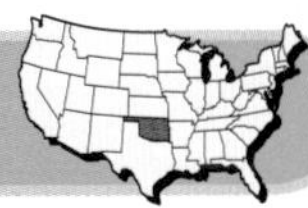

(OK) Sooner State

POPULATION: 3,751,351 (28th) **AREA:** 69,899 sq mi (20th) (181,038 sq km) Mistletoe Scissor-tailed flycatcher Redbud "Oklahoma!" **ENTERED UNION:** November 16, 1907 (46th) Oklahoma City **LARGEST CITIES (WITH POP.):** Oklahoma City, 579,999; Tulsa, 391,906; Norman, 110,925; Broken Arrow, 98,850; Lawton, 96,867 natural gas, oil, machinery, transportation equipment, metal products, food products, cattle, hogs, wheat, hay

Tulsa
Oklahoma City

did you know? ***The American Indian nations called the Five Civilized Tribes (Cherokee, Chickasaw, Choctaw, Creek, and Seminole) were resettled from the Southeast to Oklahoma by the federal government between 1817 and 1842.***

Key:

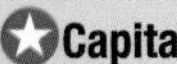

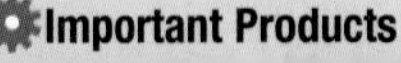

OREGON

(OR) Beaver State

POPULATION: 3,831,074 (27th) **AREA:** 98,379 sq mi (9th) (254,801 sq km) Oregon grape Western meadowlark Douglas fir "Oregon, My Oregon" **ENTERED UNION:** February 14, 1859 (33rd) Salem **LARGEST CITIES (WITH POP.):** Portland, 583,776; Eugene, 156,185; Salem, 154,637; Gresham, 105,594; Hillsboro, 91,611; Beaverton, 89,803 electronic products and semiconductors, lumber and wood products, cattle, dairy products, hay, fruits and vegetables

did you know? ***Crater Lake, in southern Oregon, is almost 2,000 feet deep. It is the deepest lake in the United States and seventh deepest in the world. The lake occupies the crater of a huge volcano that erupted thousands of years ago.***

PENNSYLVANIA

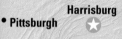

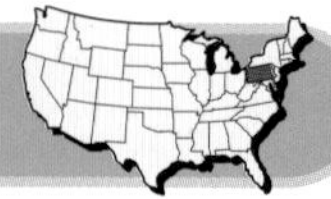

(PA) Keystone State

Harrisburg
Pittsburgh
Philadelphia

POPULATION: 12,702,379 (6th) **AREA:** 46,055 sq mi (33rd) (119,281 sq km) Mountain laurel Ruffed grouse Hemlock "Pennsylvania" **ENTERED UNION:** December 12, 1787 (2nd) Harrisburg **LARGEST CITIES (WITH POP.):** Philadelphia, 1,526,006; Pittsburgh, 305,704; Allentown, 118,032; Erie, 101,786; Reading, 88,082; Upper Darby, 82,795; Scranton, 76,089 food products, iron and steel, coal, petroleum products, metal products, drugs, machinery, transportation equipment, stone and glass products, nursery plants, mushrooms

did you know? ***Philadelphia was the capital of Pennsylvania for many years in the 1600s and 1700s and capital of the U.S. from 1790 to 1800. Independence Hall, perhaps the city's most famous building, is where the Declaration of Independence was approved in 1776 and the U.S. Constitution was written in 1787.***

RHODE ISLAND

(RI) Little Rhody, Ocean State

Providence

POPULATION: 1,052,567 (43rd) **AREA:** 1,545 sq mi (50th) (4,001 sq km) Violet Rhode Island red Red maple "Rhode Island" **ENTERED UNION:** May 29, 1790 (13th) Providence **LARGEST CITIES (WITH POP.):** Providence, 178,042; Warwick, 82,672; Cranston, 80,387; Pawtucket, 71,148 metal products, plastics, chemicals, costume jewelry, electronic equipment, nursery and greenhouse products, corn, fish

did you know? ***Newport is known for its huge mansions, many built during the "Gilded Age" of the late 19th century. Years before then, the city was a major whaling port—and even earlier, a haven for pirates.***

SOUTH CAROLINA

(SC) Palmetto State

POPULATION: 4,625,364 (24th) **AREA:** 32,021 sq mi (40th) (82,934 sq km) Yellow jessamine Carolina wren Palmetto "Carolina" **ENTERED UNION:** May 23, 1788 (8th) Columbia **LARGEST CITIES (WITH POP.):** Columbia, 129,272; Charleston, 120,083; North Charleston, 97,471; Mount Pleasant, 67,843; Rock Hill, 66,154 chemicals, motor vehicles, plastics, machinery, metal products, chickens, nursery and greenhouse products, tobacco, cement

Columbia

did you know? ***On January 12, 2011, Nikki Haley, whose parents were immigrants from India, became the state's first nonwhite and first woman governor. At age 38 she was also the youngest governor in the nation.***

SOUTH DAKOTA

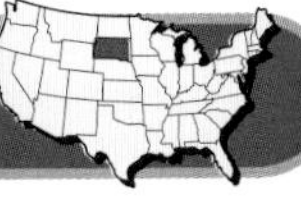

(SD) Mt. Rushmore State, Coyote State

POPULATION: 814,180 (46th) **AREA:** 77,116 sq mi (17th) (199,730 sq km) Pasqueflower Chinese ring-necked pheasant Black Hills spruce "Hail, South Dakota" **ENTERED UNION:** November 2, 1889 (40th) Pierre **LARGEST CITIES (WITH POP.):** Sioux Falls, 153,888; Rapid City, 67,956; Aberdeen, 26,091 food products, chemicals, machinery, electrical and electronic equipment, corn, soybeans, oats

did you know? ***The four presidents whose faces are carved on South Dakota's famous Mount Rushmore are George Washington, Thomas Jefferson, Abraham Lincoln, and Theodore Roosevelt. Each head is 50 to 70 feet high.***

TENNESSEE

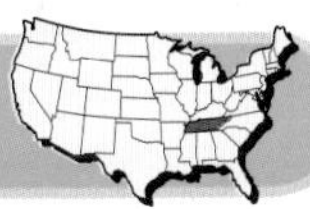

(TN) Volunteer State

Nashville

Memphis

POPULATION: 6,346,105 (17th) **AREA:** 42,144 sq mi (36th) (109,154 sq km) Iris Mockingbird Tulip poplar "My Homeland, Tennessee"; "When It's Iris Time in Tennessee"; "My Tennessee"; "Tennessee Waltz"; "Rocky Top" **ENTERED UNION:** June 1, 1796 (16th) Nashville **LARGEST CITIES (WITH POP.):** Memphis, 646,899; Nashville-Davidson, 601,222; Knoxville, 178,874; Chattanooga, 167,674; Clarksville, 132,929; Murfreesboro, 108,755 motor vehicles, chemicals, machinery, metal products, electronic equipment, rubber and plastic products, food products, cattle, chickens, nursery and greenhouse products, tobacco

did you know? ***Great Smoky Mountains National Park, along the Tennessee–North Carolina border, has more than 10,000 kinds of plants and animals. It is the most visited national park in the United States.***

Key:  Flower  Bird  Tree  Song  Capital 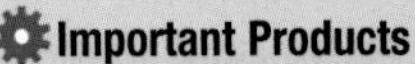 Important Products

TEXAS

(TX) Lone Star State

Dallas
El Paso
Austin
Houston
San Antonio

POPULATION: 25,145,561 (2nd) **AREA:** 268,597 sq mi (2nd) (695,666 sq km) Bluebonnet Mockingbird Pecan "Texas, Our Texas" **ENTERED UNION:** December 29, 1845 (28th) Austin **LARGEST CITIES (WITH POP.):** Houston, 2,099,451; San Antonio, 1,327,407; Dallas, 1,197,816; Austin, 790,390; Fort Worth, 741,206; El Paso, 649,121; Arlington, 365,438; Corpus Christi, 305,215; Plano, 259,841; Laredo, 236,091 oil, natural gas, coal, cattle, chemicals and resins, aerospace products, machinery, electrical and electronic equipment, cotton, corn, wheat, dairy products, nursery and greenhouse products, fish

did you know? *In March 1836, during Texas's war for independence, several thousand troops under the Mexican commander Santa Anna captured the Alamo in San Antonio after a long siege. Some 200 men tried to defend the fortress. Nearly all of them were killed, either in fierce hand-to-hand fighting or by execution.*

UTAH

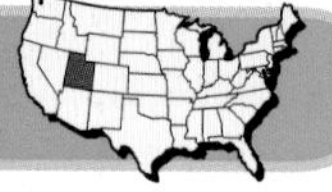

(UT) Beehive State

POPULATION: 2,763,885 (34th) **AREA:** 84,897 sq mi (13th) (219,883 sq km) Sego lily Seagull Blue spruce "Utah, This is the Place" **ENTERED UNION:** January 4, 1896 (45th) Salt Lake City **LARGEST CITIES (WITH POP.):** Salt Lake City, 186,440; West Valley City, 129,480; Provo, 112,488; West Jordan, 103,712; Orem, 88,328; Sandy, 87,461; Ogden, 82,825 food products, petroleum products, transportation equipment, medical instruments, electronic equipment, metal products, sporting goods, copper, cattle, hogs, dairy products, hay, wheat

did you know? *The Great Salt Lake, in northwest Utah, is the biggest lake in the U.S. outside of the Great Lakes, and is the world's saltiest lake except for the Dead Sea. It holds 6 billion tons of dissolved salts, mostly common table salt.*

VERMONT

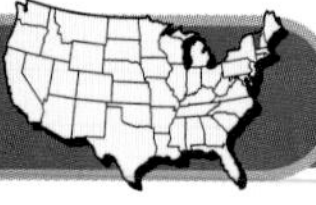

(VT) Green Mountain State

Montpelier

POPULATION: 625,741 (49th) **AREA:** 9,616 sq mi (45th) (24,906 sq km) Red clover Hermit thrush Sugar maple "These Green Mountains" **ENTERED UNION:** March 4, 1791 (14th) Montpelier **LARGEST CITIES (WITH POP.):** Burlington, 42,417; South Burlington, 17,904; Rutland, 16,495 computers and electronic equipment, machinery, furniture, books, dairy products, cattle, apples, maple syrup

did you know? *Places for kids to visit in Vermont include the Vermont Teddy Bear Factory, in Shelburne, and the factory in Waterbury where Ben & Jerry's ice cream is whipped up. Kids may also enjoy a scenic ride on the Green Mountain Railroad, which runs along three different routes in the state.*

VIRGINIA

(VA) Old Dominion

POPULATION: 8,001,024 (12th) **AREA:** 42,775 sq mi (35th) (110,787 sq km) Flower: Dogwood Bird: Cardinal Tree: Dogwood Song: none **ENTERED UNION:** June 25, 1788 (10th) Capital: Richmond **LARGEST CITIES (WITH POP.):** Virginia Beach, 437,994; Norfolk, 242,803; Chesapeake, 222,209; Arlington, 207,627; Richmond, 204,214; Newport News, 180,719 Important Products: food products, transportation equipment, chemicals, machinery, electronic equipment, coal, chickens, cattle, hogs, dairy products, tobacco, hay, wood products, furniture

Alexandria
Richmond
Virginia Beach

did you know? ***The world's biggest candy company has its headquarters in McLean, VA. Mars Incorporated makes Snickers, M&Ms, Milky Way, Twix, Mars bars, and many other candies, along with some other products such as Uncle Ben's rice and Pedigree dog food.***

WASHINGTON

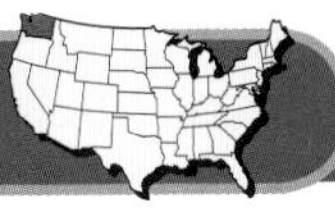

(WA) Evergreen State

POPULATION: 6,724,540 (13th) **AREA:** 71,298 sq mi (18th) (184,661 sq km) Flower: Western rhododendron Bird: Willow goldfinch Tree: Western hemlock Song: "Washington, My Home" **ENTERED UNION:** November 11, 1889 (42nd) Capital: Olympia **LARGEST CITIES (WITH POP.):** Seattle, 608,660; Spokane, 208,916; Tacoma, 198,397; Vancouver, 161,791; Bellevue, 122,363; Everett, 103,019 Important Products: aircraft, electronic products and computer software, lumber and wood products, machinery, metal products, food products, wheat, apples, potatoes, fish

Seattle
Olympia

did you know? ***The Seattle suburb of Redmond is the home of the computer software giant Microsoft, founded in the 1970s by Seattle native Bill Gates. Seattle also helped give birth to Starbucks coffee and Amazon.com.***

WEST VIRGINIA

(WV) Mountain State

POPULATION: 1,852,994 (37th) **AREA:** 24,230 sq mi (41st) (62,755 sq km) Flower: Big rhododendron Bird: Cardinal Tree: Sugar maple Song: "The West Virginia Hills"; "This Is My West Virginia"; "West Virginia, My Home Sweet Home" **ENTERED UNION:** June 20, 1863 (35th) Capital: Charleston **LARGEST CITIES (WITH POP.):** Charleston, 51,400; Huntington, 49,138; Parkersburg, 31,492; Morgantown, 29,660; Wheeling, 28,486 Important Products: chemicals, automobile parts, metal products, coal, aluminum, chickens, cattle, eggs, hay, apples, peaches, tobacco

Charleston

did you know? ***When Virginia seceded from the Union in 1861 and joined the Confederacy, people in the northwestern counties got together and agreed to split off from the rest of Virginia. "West Virginia" was admitted to the Union in June 1863. It became the 35th state.***

Key:     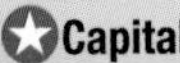 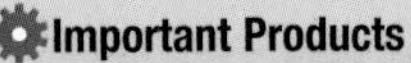

WISCONSIN (WI) Badger State

Madison
Milwaukee

POPULATION: 5,686,986 (20th) **AREA:** 65,496 sq mi (23rd) (169,636 sq km) Wood violet Robin Sugar maple "On, Wisconsin!" **ENTERED UNION:** May 29, 1848 (30th) Madison **LARGEST CITIES (WITH POP.):** Milwaukee, 594,833; Madison, 233,209; Green Bay, 104,057; Kenosha, 99,218; Racine, 78,860 food products, milk, butter, cheese, machinery, transportation equipment, lumber and wood products, electrical and electronic products, plastics, cattle, corn, hay, vegetables

did you know? *Architect Frank Lloyd Wright, artist Georgia O'Keeffe, and* Little House on the Prairie *author Laura Ingalls Wilder were all born in Wisconsin.*

WYOMING 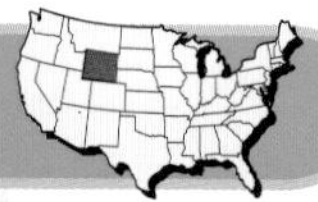 (WY) Cowboy State

Cheyenne

POPULATION: 563,626 (50th) **AREA:** 97,812 sq mi (10th) (253,334 sq km) Indian paintbrush Western meadowlark Plains cottonwood "Wyoming" **ENTERED UNION:** July 10, 1890 (44th) Cheyenne **LARGEST CITIES (WITH POP.):** Cheyenne, 59,466; Casper, 55,316; Laramie, 30,816; Gillette, 29,087 oil, natural gas, coal, petroleum and coal products, chemicals, cattle, hay, wheat, sugar beets

did you know? *Wyoming has plenty of wide open spaces. With an average of only 5.8 people per square mile, it is the least crowded of the 50 states.*

COMMONWEALTH OF PUERTO RICO  (PR)

HISTORY: Christopher Columbus landed in Puerto Rico in 1493. Puerto Rico was a Spanish colony for centuries, then was ceded (given) to the United States in 1898 after the Spanish-American War. In 1952, still associated with the United States, Puerto Rico became a commonwealth with its own constitution. **POPULATION (2009):** 3,725,789 **AREA:** 5,325 sq mi (13,791 sq km) Maga Reinita Ceiba **NATIONAL ANTHEM:** "La Borinqueña" San Juan **LARGEST CITIES (WITH POP.):** San Juan, 395,326; Bayamon, 208,116; Carolina, 176,762; Ponce, 166,327; Caguas, 142,893 drugs, medical equipment, electronic equipment, clothing and textiles, dairy products, chickens, cattle, coffee, fruit

did you know? *The El Yunque National Forest, in the east, is the only tropical rain forest in the U.S. National Forest system. Only 44 square miles in area, it is home to many exotic plants and animals, including Puerto Rico's tiny coqui frogs and the rare Puerto Rican parrot.*

Washington, D.C.

The Capital of the UNITED STATES

AREA: 68 sq mi (177 sq km) **POPULATION (2010):** 601,723
FLOWER: American beauty rose **BIRD:** Wood thrush
For more information, see: *www.dc.gov • www.washington.org*

HISTORY The District of Columbia, or Washington, D.C., became the capital of the United States in 1800, when the federal government moved there from Philadelphia. The city of Washington was designed and built to be the capital. It was named after George Washington. Many of the city's major sights are on the ▼ **Mall**, an open grassy area that runs from the Capitol to the Potomac River.

CAPITOL, which houses the U.S. Congress, is at the east end of the Mall on Capitol Hill. Its dome can be seen from far away.

JEFFERSON MEMORIAL, a circular marble building located near the Potomac River, is partly based on a design by Thomas Jefferson for the University of Virginia.

LIBRARY OF CONGRESS, research library for Congress and the largest library in the world, is on Independence Avenue across the street from the Capitol.

LINCOLN MEMORIAL, at the west end of the Mall, is built of white marble and styled like a Greek temple. Inside is a large, seated statue of Abraham Lincoln. His Gettysburg Address is carved on a nearby wall.

NATIONAL ARCHIVES, on Constitution Avenue, holds the Declaration of Independence, Constitution, and Bill of Rights.

NATIONAL WORLD WAR II MEMORIAL, located between the Lincoln Memorial and the Washington Monument at the Mall, honors the 16 million Americans who served during the war.

SMITHSONIAN ▶ INSTITUTION has 18 museums, including the National Air and Space Museum and the Museum of Natural History.

U.S. HOLOCAUST MEMORIAL MUSEUM presents the history of the Nazis' murder of more than six million Jews and millions of other people from 1933 to 1945.

VIETNAM VETERANS MEMORIAL includes a wall with the names of those killed or missing in action during the conflict.

WASHINGTON MONUMENT is a white marble pillar, or obelisk, standing on the Mall and rising to more than 555 feet. From the top there are wonderful views of the city.

WHITE HOUSE, at 1600 Pennsylvania Avenue, has been the home of every U.S. president except George Washington.

WOMEN IN MILITARY SERVICE FOR AMERICA MEMORIAL, near Arlington National Cemetery in Virginia, honors women who have served in the U.S. armed forces.

VOLUNTEERING

What is Drinking Water for India? page 311

Environmental threats, poverty, natural disasters... sometimes the problems of the world seem so large that it's hard to imagine how we can help. But just one person really can make a difference. And people who help others also help themselves! Studies have shown that kids who volunteer perform better in school, are happier, and feel more positive about themselves. Does this win-win situation have you ready to take action? Here's how to get started.

RESEARCH Pick an area that interests you, and research different ways you can help. The web site ***www.dosomething.org*** features a great search tool to get you started. First pick a cause—such as the environment, animal welfare, or disaster relief. Then decide whom you want to work with (alone? with your family? with friends?), where you want to help, and how much time you have to volunteer. The search generates a list of action guides that fit your needs.

ASK AROUND There's a good chance that different groups in your community already have projects under way—and would welcome another helping hand. Many people volunteer through their **religious community**. Churches, synagogues, and mosques often organize ways to help the needy. Many **schools** also offer opportunities for their students to volunteer. Schools may sponsor plant sales to raise money for a worthy cause or ask students to visit elderly people in a nursing home. Girl Scout councils, county 4-H organizations, American Red Cross chapters, and other **community groups** participate in volunteering projects such as cleaning up a local park or organizing a car wash to raise money for a cause.

MAKE A CHOICE Do you want to provide direct services or raise money for your cause? For example, you can read to patients in a children's hospital or hold a bake sale and buy an acre of rain forest with the money you raise.

Volunteering All-Stars

Something Sweet from Home

When Glennita Williams learned that a friend's father serving in Iraq had a craving for Twinkies, she thought, "All the soldiers must be craving something sweet from home." She asked for donations and, 10 days later, sent 1,000 snack cakes overseas. In the past four years, this eighth grader from South Holland, Illinois, has collected food and personal care items worth more than $14,000 for U.S. troops in Iraq and Afghanistan. "Once, to show me how thankful they were for a shipment, a unit sent me a very large U.S. flag that was attached to a C-12 aircraft for a combat mission on September 11, 2009," Glennita explains. "The flag was flown in my honor!"

River Cleanup

Christian Hanna, 12, lives along the Waccamaw River in Conway, South Carolina. "It is so pretty, but I hate to see trash floating down the river and stuck on the bank," she says. In 2008, when a local group organized a cleanup day, Christian and her family took part. But they didn't stop there. Now Christian, with help from her parents and sister, regularly takes a boat out to collect garbage. "I have a good time and I feel good about helping," Christian says. "I would encourage other people to volunteer to do something they like because even if you are a kid, you can do a lot to help."

One Well at a Time

On a family trip to India, Rujul Zaparde, age 16, visited a village with no fresh water. "The villagers had to walk a few kilometers each way to reach the nearest water source—and that water wasn't even clean," he explains. Back home in Plainsboro, New Jersey, Rujul and a friend decided to raise $1,000 for a well for the village. They organized bake sales, car washes, and door-to-door fund-raising. Then, Rujul returned to India and built the well. "I realized then that we could do even more," he said. "We could build more wells, and help more villagers." So Rujul founded the student-led charity Drinking Water for India. Now, more than 30 villages in India have new wells.

AND THE WINNER IS...

Are you or is someone you know a volunteer all-star? The Prudential Spirit of Community Awards honor young people for outstanding volunteer community service. To find out more, visit ***spirit.prudential.com***

WEATHER

What is a blizzard? → page 312

Weather Forecasting

Rain or shine? Weather scientists called **meteorologists** help forecast the weather for tomorrow or even the week ahead. They are able to do this by studying winds, temperature, and changes in the atmosphere. For example, an area of high pressure usually means dry, calm weather, while an area of low pressure often brings rain, clouds, and wind.

A front is a sharp change in air temperature. Storms usually come before a cold front. As a cold front passes through an area, the temperature drops. Light rain might bring a warm front. As a warm front moves in, the air gets warmer.

Around the world, meteorologists use the same set of symbols to show weather conditions. These common symbols let them share weather data.

Selected Weather Symbols

Sky Cover	Fronts	Weather
○ Clear	▲▲ Cold front	▪ Rain = Fog
◔ Scattered	●●● Warm front	* Snow ∞ Haze
● Overcast	Stationary front	Thunderstorm
Wind: ◎ Calm	— 1-2 knots (1-2 mph)	3-7 knots (3-8 mph)
L Low Pressure Center	**H** High Pressure Center	

WILD WEATHER FACTS

- A lightning bolt can be as hot as 55,000 degrees Fahrenheit. That's about five times hotter than the surface of the sun!
- The largest hailstone known to have fallen in the United States was found in Aurora, Nebraska, on June 22, 2003. It was about seven inches wide, almost as big as a soccer ball.
- A blizzard is a severe snowstorm with winds of 35 miles per hour or higher and enough falling or blowing snow to reduce visibility below a quarter-mile for at least three hours.

did you Know?

Many cities experienced record-setting snowstorms during the winter of 2010–2011. Syracuse, New York, had its snowiest December ever in 2010 with 72.8 inches. So did Minneapolis/St. Paul with 33.6 inches. Hartford, Connecticut, recorded its snowiest month ever in January 2011 with 54.3 inches.

RECORD TEMPERATURES BY STATE (Through May 2011)

Coldest Temperature

Hottest Temperature

STATE	Lowest °F	Lowest Latest date	Highest °F	Highest Latest date
Alabama	–27	Jan. 30, 1966	112	Sept. 5, 1925
Alaska	–80	Jan. 23, 1971	100	June 27, 1915
Arizona	–40	Jan. 7, 1971	128	July 5, 2007
Arkansas	–29	Feb. 13, 1905	120	Aug. 10, 1936
California	–45	Jan. 20, 1937	134	July 10, 1913
Colorado	–61	Feb. 1, 1985	118	July 11, 1888
Connecticut	–32	Jan. 22, 1961	106	July 15, 1995
Delaware	–17	Jan. 17, 1893	110	July 21, 1930
Florida	–2	Feb. 13, 1899	109	June 29, 1931
Georgia	–17	Jan. 27, 1940	112	Aug. 20, 1983
Hawaii	12	May 17, 1979	100	Apr. 27, 1931
Idaho	–60	Jan. 18, 1943	118	July 28, 1934
Illinois	–36	Jan. 5, 1999	117	July 14, 1954
Indiana	–36	Jan. 19, 1994	116	July 14, 1936
Iowa	–47	Feb. 3, 1996	118	July 20, 1934
Kansas	–40	Feb. 13, 1905	121	July 24, 1936
Kentucky	–37	Jan. 19, 1994	114	July 28, 1930
Louisiana	–16	Feb. 13, 1899	114	Aug. 10, 1936
Maine	–50	Jan. 16, 2009	105	July 10, 1911
Maryland	–40	Jan. 13, 1912	109	July 10, 1936
Massachusetts	–35	Jan. 12, 1981	107	Aug. 2, 1975
Michigan	–51	Feb. 9, 1934	112	July 13, 1936
Minnesota	–60	Feb. 2, 1996	114	July 6, 1936
Mississippi	–19	Jan. 30, 1966	115	July 29, 1930
Missouri	–40	Feb. 13, 1905	118	July 14, 1954
Montana	–70	Jan. 20, 1954	117	July 5, 1937
Nebraska	–47	Dec. 22, 1989	118	July 24, 1936
Nevada	–50	Jan. 8, 1937	125	June 29, 1994
New Hampshire	–47	Jan. 29, 1934	106	July 4, 1911
New Jersey	–34	Jan. 5, 1904	110	July 10, 1936
New Mexico	–50	Feb. 1, 1951	122	June 27, 1994
New York	–52	Feb. 18, 1979	108	July 22, 1926
North Carolina	–34	Jan. 21, 1985	110	Aug. 21, 1983
North Dakota	–60	Feb. 15, 1936	121	July 6, 1936
Ohio	–39	Feb. 10, 1899	113	July 21, 1934
Oklahoma	–31	Feb. 10, 2011	120	June 27, 1994
Oregon	–54	Feb. 10, 1933	119	Aug. 10, 1898
Pennsylvania	–42	Jan. 5, 1904	111	July 10, 1936
Rhode Island	–25	Feb. 5, 1996	104	Aug. 2, 1975
South Carolina	–19	Jan. 21, 1985	111	June 28, 1954
South Dakota	–58	Feb. 17, 1936	120	July 15, 2006
Tennessee	–32	Dec. 30, 1917	113	Aug. 9, 1930
Texas	–23	Feb. 8, 1933	120	June 28, 1994
Utah	–69	Feb. 1, 1985	117	July 5, 1985
Vermont	–50	Dec. 30, 1933	105	July 4, 1911
Virginia	–30	Jan. 22, 1985	110	July 15, 1954
Washington	–48	Dec. 30, 1968	118	Aug. 5, 1961
West Virginia	–37	Dec. 30, 1917	112	July 10, 1936
Wisconsin	–55	Feb. 4, 1996	114	July 13, 1936
Wyoming	–66	Feb. 9, 1933	115	Aug. 8, 1983

Record temperatures may have occurred on earlier dates. Dates listed here are for most recent occurrence of a record temperature.

WEIGHTS & MEASURES

Why are 12 inches called a foot? → page 314

Metrology isn't the study of weather. (That's meteorology.) It is the science of measurement. Almost everything you use (or eat or drink) is measured—either when it is made or when it's sold. Materials for buildings and parts for machines must be measured carefully so they will fit together. Clothes have sizes so you'll know which to wear. Many items sold in a supermarket are priced by weight or by volume.

EARLIEST MEASUREMENTS

The human body was the first "ruler." An "inch" was the width of a thumb; a "hand" was five fingers wide; a "foot" was—you guessed it—the length of a foot! A "cubit" ran from the elbow to the tip of the middle finger (about 20 inches), and a "yard" was roughly the length of a whole arm.

Later, measurements came from daily activities, like plowing a field. A "furlong" was the distance a pair of oxen could plow before stopping to rest (now we say it is about 220 yards). The trouble with these units is that they vary from person to person, place to place, and ox to ox.

MEASUREMENTS WE USE TODAY

The official system in the U.S. is the customary system (sometimes called the imperial or English system). Scientists and most other countries use the International System of Units (SI, or the metric system). The Weights and Measures Division of the U.S. National Institute of Standards and Technology (NIST) makes sure that a gallon of milk is the same in every state. When the NIST was founded in 1901, the U.S. had as many as eight different "standard" gallons, and there were four different legal measures of a "foot" in Brooklyn, New York, alone.

ANCIENT MEASURE

1 foot = length of a person's foot

1 yard = from nose to fingertip

1 acre = land a pair of oxen could plow in a day

MODERN MEASURE

12 inches

3 feet or 36 inches

4,840 square yards

TAKING TEMPERATURES

There are two main systems for measuring temperature. One is **Fahrenheit** (abbreviated F). The other is **Celsius** (abbreviated C). Another word for Celsius is Centigrade.

Zero degrees (0°) Celsius is equal to 32 degrees (32°) Fahrenheit.

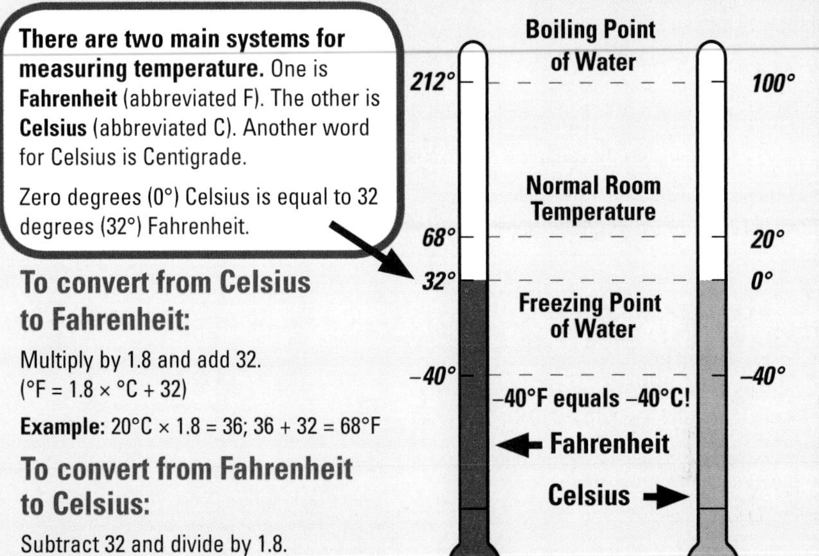

To convert from Celsius to Fahrenheit:

Multiply by 1.8 and add 32.
(°F = 1.8 × °C + 32)

Example: 20°C × 1.8 = 36; 36 + 32 = 68°F

To convert from Fahrenheit to Celsius:

Subtract 32 and divide by 1.8.

Example: 68°F – 32 = 36; 36 ÷ 1.8 = 20°C

HOTTEST and COLDEST Places in the World

Continent	Highest Temperature	Lowest Temperature
AFRICA	El Azizia, Libya, 136°F (58°C)	Ifrane, Morocco, –11°F (–24°C)
ANTARCTICA	Vanda Station, 59°F (15°C)	Vostok, –129°F (–89°C)
ASIA	Tirat Tsvi, Israel, 129°F (54°C)	Verkhoyansk, Russia, and Oimekon, Russia, –90°F (–68°C)
AUSTRALIA	Cloncurry, Queensland, 128°F (53°C)	Charlotte Pass, New South Wales, –9°F (–23°C)
EUROPE	Seville, Spain, 122°F (50°C)	Ust'Shchugor, Russia, –67°F (–55°C)
NORTH AMERICA	Death Valley, California, U.S.A., 134°F (57°C)	Snag, Yukon Territory, Canada, –81°F (–63°C)
SOUTH AMERICA	Rivadavia, Argentina, 120°F (49°C)	Sarmiento, Argentina, –27°F (–33°C)

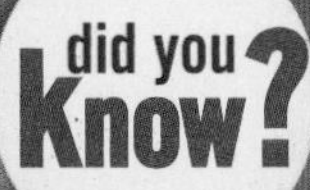

The coldest official temperature in the United States was recorded on January 23, 1971. It was –80°F (–62°C) at Prospect Creek Camp in northern Alaska. The only state that has never recorded a temperature below 0°F (–18°C) is Hawaii.

LENGTH

The basic unit of **length** in the U.S. system is the **inch**. Length, width, and thickness all use the inch or larger related units.

1 foot (ft) = 12 inches (in)
1 yard (yd) = 3 feet = 36 inches
1 rod (rd) = 5½ yards
1 furlong (fur) = 40 rods = 220 yards = 660 feet
1 mile (mi) (also called statute mile) = 8 furlongs = 1,760 yards = 5,280 feet
1 nautical mile = 6,076 feet = 1.15 statute miles
1 league = 3 miles

CAPACITY

Units of **capacity** measure how much of something will fit into a container. **Liquid measure** is used to measure liquids such as water or gasoline. **Dry measure** is used with large amounts of solid materials such as grain or fruit. Although both liquid and dry measures use the terms "pint" and "quart," they mean different amounts and should not be confused.

Dry Measure

1 quart (qt) = 2 pints (pt)
1 peck (pk) = 8 quarts
1 bushel (bu) = 4 pecks

Liquid Measure

1 gill = 4 fluid ounces (fl oz)
1 pint (pt) = 4 gills = 16 ounces (oz)
1 quart (qt) = 2 pints = 32 ounces
1 gallon (gal) = 4 quarts = 128 ounces

For measuring most U.S. liquids, 1 barrel (bbl) = 31½ gallons

For measuring oil, 1 barrel = 42 gallons

Cooking Measurements

The measurements in cooking are based on the **fluid ounce**.
1 teaspoon (tsp) = ⅙ fluid ounce (fl oz)
1 tablespoon (tbsp) = 3 teaspoons = ½ fluid ounce
1 cup = 16 tablespoons = 8 fluid ounces
1 pint = 2 cups
1 quart (qt) = 2 pints (pt)
1 gallon (gal) = 4 quarts

AREA

Area measures a section of a two-dimensional surface like a floor or a piece of paper. Most area measurements are given in **square units**. Land is measured in **acres**.

1 square foot (sq ft) = 144 square inches (sq in)
1 square yard (sq yd) = 9 square feet = 1,296 square inches
1 square rod (sq rd) = 30¼ square yards
1 acre = 160 square rods = 4,840 square yards = 43,560 square feet
1 square mile (sq mi) = 640 acres

VOLUME

The amount of space taken up by a three-dimensional object (or the amount of space available within an object) is measured in **volume**. Volume is usually expressed in **cubic units**.

1 cubic foot (cu ft) = 12 inches x 12 inches x 12 inches = 1,728 cubic inches (cu in)
1 cubic yard (cu yd) = 27 cubic feet

DEPTH

Some measurements of length measure ocean depth and distance.

1 fathom = 6 feet (ft)
1 cable = 120 fathoms = 720 feet

WEIGHT

Although 1 cubic foot of popcorn and 1 cubic foot of rock take up the same amount of space, lifting them isn't the same. We measure heaviness as **weight**. Most objects are measured in **avoirdupois weight** (pronounced a-ver-de-POIZ):

1 dram (dr) = 27.344 grains (gr)
1 ounce (oz) = 16 drams = 437.5 grains
1 pound (lb) = 16 ounces
1 hundredweight (cwt) = 100 pounds
1 (short) ton = 2,000 pounds

THE METRIC SYSTEM

The metric system was created in France in 1795. Standardized in 1960, the International System of Units is now used in most countries and in scientific works. The system is based on 10, like the decimal counting system. The basic unit for length is the **meter**. The **liter** is a basic unit of volume or capacity, and the **gram** is a basic unit of mass. Related units are made by adding a prefix to the basic unit. The prefixes and their meanings are:

milli- = $\frac{1}{1,000}$

centi- = $\frac{1}{100}$

deci- = $\frac{1}{10}$

deka- = 10

hecto- = 100

kilo- = **1,000**

For Example

millimeter (mm) = $\frac{1}{1,000}$ of a meter

kilometer (km) = 1,000 meters

milligram (mg) = $\frac{1}{1,000}$ of a gram

kilogram (kg) = 1,000 grams

To get a rough idea of measurements in the metric system, it helps to know that a **liter** is a little more than a quart. A **meter** is a little more than a yard. A **kilogram** is a little more than 2 pounds. And a **kilometer** is just over half a mile.

HOMEWORK TIP

Converting Measurements

If you have:	Multiply by:	To get:	If you have:	Multiply by:	To get:
inches	*2.54*	centimeters	**centimeters**	*0.3937*	inches
inches	*0.0254*	meters	**centimeters**	*0.0328*	feet
feet	*30.48*	centimeters	**meters**	*39.3701*	inches
feet	*0.3048*	meters	**meters**	*3.2808*	feet
yards	*0.9144*	meters	**meters**	*1.0936*	yards
miles	*1.6093*	kilometers	**kilometers**	*0.621*	miles
square inches	*6.4516*	square centimeters	**square centimeters**	*0.155*	square inches
square feet	*0.0929*	square meters	**square meters**	*10.7639*	square feet
square yards	*0.8361*	square meters	**square meters**	*1.196*	square yards
acres	*0.4047*	hectares	**hectares**	*2.471*	acres
cubic inches	*16.3871*	cubic centimeters	**cubic centimeters**	*0.061*	cubic inches
cubic feet	*0.0283*	cubic meters	**cubic meters**	*35.3147*	cubic feet
cubic yards	*0.7646*	cubic meters	**cubic meters**	*1.308*	cubic yards
quarts (liquid)	*0.9464*	liters	**liters**	*1.0567*	quarts (liquid)
ounces	*28.3495*	grams	**grams**	*0.0353*	ounces
pounds	*0.4536*	kilograms	**kilograms**	*2.2046*	pounds

WORLD HISTORY

When was Julius Caesar assassinated? → page 325

Each of the five sections in this chapter tells the history of a major region of the world: the Middle East, Africa, Asia, Europe, or the Americas. Major events from ancient times to the present are described under the headings for each region.

THE ANCIENT MIDDLE EAST

◀ *hieroglyphics*

▲ *The pyramids at Giza*

4000–3000 B.C. The world's first cities are built by the Sumerian peoples in Mesopotamia, now southern Iraq. Sumerians develop a kind of writing called **cuneiform**. Egyptians develop a kind of writing called **hieroglyphics**.

2700 B.C. Egyptians begin building the great pyramids in the desert.

1792 B.C. Some of the first written laws are created in Babylonia. They are called the **Code of Hammurabi**.

1200 B.C. Hebrew people settle in Canaan in Palestine after escaping from slavery in Egypt. They are led by the prophet Moses.

1000 B.C. King David unites the Hebrews.

ANCIENT PALESTINE Palestine is invaded by many different peoples after 1000 B.C., including the Babylonians, Egyptians, Persians, and Romans.

336 B.C. Alexander the Great, King of Macedonia, builds an empire from Egypt to India. ▶

ISLAM: A RELIGION GROWS IN THE MIDDLE EAST A.D. 610–632 Around 610, the prophet Muhammad starts to proclaim and teach Islam. This religion spreads from Arabia to all the neighboring regions in the Middle East and North Africa. Its followers are called Muslims.

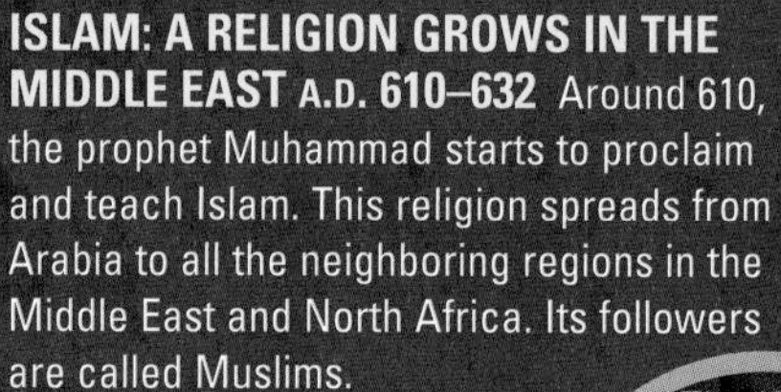

The Koran

THE KORAN
The holy book of Islam is the Koran. It was related by Muhammad beginning in 611.

THE SPREAD OF ISLAM
The Arab armies that move across North Africa bring great change:

- The people who live there are converted to Islam.
- The Arabic language replaces many local languages as an official language. North Africa is still an Arabic-speaking region today, and Islam is the major faith.

63 B.C. Romans conquer Palestine and make it part of their empire.

Around 4 B.C. Jesus Christ, the founder of the Christian religion, is born in Bethlehem. He is crucified about A.D. 29.

A.D. 632 Muhammad dies. By now, Islam is accepted in Arabia as a religion.

641 Arab Muslims conquer the Persians.

Late 600s Islam begins to spread to the west into Africa and Spain.

THE MIDDLE EAST

THE UMAYYAD AND ABBASID DYNASTIES The Umayyads (661–750) and the Abbasids (750–1256) are the first two Muslim-led dynasties. Both empires stretch across northern Africa and the Middle East into Asia.

711–732 Umayyads invade Europe but are defeated by Frankish leader Charles Martel in France. This defeat halts the spread of Islam into Western Europe.

1071 Muslim Turks conquer Jerusalem.

1095–1291 Europeans try to take back Jerusalem and other parts of the Middle East for Christians during the Crusades.

1300–1900s The Ottoman Turks, who are Muslims, create a huge empire, covering the Middle East, North Africa, and part of Eastern Europe. European countries take over portions of it beginning in the 1800s.

1914–1918 World War I begins in 1914. Most of the Middle East falls under British or French control.

1921 Two new Arab kingdoms are created: Transjordan and Iraq. The French take control of Syria and Lebanon.

1922 Egypt becomes independent from Great Britain.

JEWS MIGRATE TO PALESTINE Jews begin migrating to Palestine in the 1880s. In 1945, after World War II, many Jews who survived the Holocaust migrate to Palestine.

1948 The state of Israel is created.

THE ARAB-ISRAELI WARS Arab countries near Israel (Egypt, Iraq, Jordan, Lebanon, and Syria) attack the new country in 1948 but fail to destroy it. Israel and its neighbors fight wars again in 1956, 1967, and 1973. Israel wins each war. In the 1967 war, Israel captures the Sinai Peninsula and Gaza from Egypt, the Golan Heights from Syria, and the West Bank from Jordan.

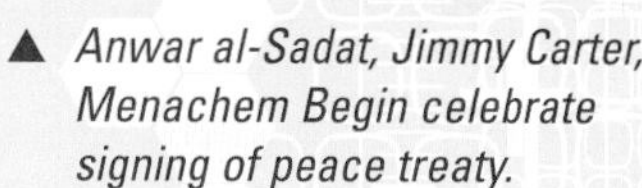

▲ *Anwar al-Sadat, Jimmy Carter, Menachem Begin celebrate signing of peace treaty.*

1979 Egypt and Israel sign a peace treaty. Israel returns the Sinai to Egypt.

THE MIDDLE EAST AND OIL Many countries rely on oil imports from the region, which has more than half the world's crude oil reserves.

1991 The U.S. and its allies go to war with Iraq after Iraq invades Kuwait. Iraq is defeated but is accused of violating the peace treaty.

2003–2010 The U.S. and its allies invade Iraq and remove the regime of dictator Saddam Hussein. Iraqis hold elections in 2005 and again in March 2010. The U.S. removes all combat troops in 2010.

2011 Huge demonstrations against repressive governments break out across the region, including in Syria, Lebanon, Egypt, Bahrain, and Yemen. Longtime Egyptian dictator Hosni Mubarak is overthrown in February.

Dome of the Rock and the Western Wall, Jerusalem ▶

ANCIENT AFRICA

▲Camel train moving across the Sahara

ANCIENT AFRICA In ancient times, northern Africa was dominated by the Egyptians, Greeks, and Romans. Ancient Africans south of the Sahara Desert did not have written languages. What we learn about them comes from weapons, tools, and other items from their civilization.

2000 B.C. The Nubian Kingdom of Kush, rich with gold, ivory, and jewels, arises south of Egypt. It is a major center of art, learning, and trade until around A.D. 350.

1000 B.C. Bantu-speaking people around Cameroon begin an 1,800-year expansion into much of eastern and southern Africa.

500 B.C. Carthage, an empire centered in Tunisia, becomes rich and powerful through trading. Its ports span the African coast of the Mediterranean. Rome defeats Carthage and ▼Hannibal, its most famous leader, during the second Punic War (218–201 B.C.).

• The Nok in Nigeria are the earliest users of iron for tools and weapons south of the Sahara Desert. They are also known for their terracotta sculptures.

• The Christian Kingdom of Aksum in northern Ethiopia becomes a wealthy trading center on the Red Sea.

By A.D. 700 Ghana, the first known empire south of the Sahara Desert, takes power through trade around the upper Senegal and Niger Rivers. Its Mande people control the trade in gold from nearby mines to Arabs in the north.

By 900 Arab Muslim merchants bring Islam to the Bantu speakers along the east coast of Africa, creating the Swahili language and culture. Traders in Kenya and Tanzania export ivory, slaves, perfumes, and gold to Asia.

1054–1145 Islamic Berbers unite into the Almoravid Kingdom centered at Marrakech, Morocco. They spread into Ghana and southern Spain.

1230–1400s A Mande prince named Sundiata (the "Lion King") forms the Mali Kingdom where Ghana once stood. Timbuktu becomes its main city.

TIMBUKTU Located on the trade routes between North Africa and West Africa, Timbuktu was one of the wealthiest cities in Africa in the 1300s, as well as a center for scholarship. Gold, ivory, cloth, salt, and slaves were all traded in Timbuktu.

1250–1400s Great Zimbabwe becomes the largest settlement (12,000–20,000 Bantu-speaking people) in southern Africa.

1464–1591 As Mali loses power, Songhai rises to become the third and final great empire of western Africa.

1481 Portugal sets up the first permanent European trading post south of the Sahara Desert at Elmina, Ghana. Slaves, in addition to gold and ivory, are soon exported.

1483–1665 Kongo, the most powerful kingdom on central Africa's west coast, provides thousands of slaves each year for Portugal. Portugal's colony Angola overtakes the Kongo in 1665.

AFRICA

1650–1810 Slave trading peaks across the "Slave Coast" from eastern Ghana to western Nigeria as African states sell tens of thousands of captured foes each year to European traders.

THE AFRICAN SLAVE TRADE

African slaves are taken to the Caribbean to harvest sugar on European plantations and then taken to South America and the United States. The ships from Africa are overcrowded and diseased. About 20% of the slaves die during the long journey.

1652 The Dutch East India Company sets up a supply camp in southern Africa at the Cape of Good Hope (later Cape Town). Dutch settlers and French Protestants (Huguenots) establish Cape Colony. Their descendants are known as the Boers or Afrikaners.

1792 Freed slaves, mostly from Britain and the Americas, found Freetown in Sierra Leone.

1803 Denmark is the first European country to ban slave trading. Britain follows in 1807, the U.S. in 1808. Most European nations ban the trade by 1820, but illegal trading continues for decades.

1814 Britain purchases the Dutch South African colony at Cape Town. British colonists arrive after 1820.

1835–43 The "Great Trek" (march) of the Boers away from British Cape Town takes place.

1884–85 European nations meet in Berlin and agree to divide control of Africa. The "Scramble for Africa" lasts until World War I.

1899–1902 Great Britain and the Boers fight in South Africa in the Boer War. The Boers accept British rule but are allowed a role in government.

1948 The white Afrikaner-dominated South African government creates the policy of apartheid ("apartness"), the total separation of races. Blacks are banned from many public places.

1957 Ghana gains independence from Britain, becoming the first territory in Africa below the Sahara to regain freedom from European rule. Over the next 20 years, the rest of Africa gains independence.

1990–94 South Africa abolishes apartheid. In 1994, Nelson Mandela becomes South Africa's first black president. ▶

1994 Members of Rwanda's Hutu majority launch a genocide against the country's Tutsi minority, killing about 800,000 people.

1998–2004 Fighting in the Democratic Republic of the Congo involves 9 nations. About 4 million die, mostly from starvation and disease.

2006 Ellen Johnson-Sirleaf becomes president of Liberia, and Africa's first elected female leader. ▶

2011 Conflict that began in 2003 and that many call a genocide continues in the Darfur region of Sudan, despite a truce. After a referendum, the new nation of South Sudan, which does not include Darfur, is scheduled to become independent on July 9. In January, protestors in Tunisia overthrow that country's longtime dictator. In Libya, rebels helped by Western governments attempt to overthrow dictator Muammar al-Qaddafi.

A savanna in Kenya

ANCIENT ASIA

▲The Great Wall

3500 B.C. People settle in the Indus River Valley of India and Pakistan and the Yellow River Valley of China.

Around 1523 B.C. Shang peoples in China build walled towns and use a kind of writing based on pictures. This writing develops into the writing Chinese people use today.

Around 1050 B.C. Zhou peoples in China overthrow the Shang and control large territories.

563 B.C. Siddhartha Gautama is born in India. He becomes known as the Buddha—the "Enlightened One"—and is the founder of the Buddhist religion (Buddhism). ▶

551 B.C. The Chinese philosopher Confucius is born. His teachings—especially rules about how people should treat each other—spread ▼ throughout China and are still followed.

320–232 B.C.

- Northern India is united under the emperor Chandragupta Maurya.
- Asoka, emperor of India, sends Buddhist missionaries throughout southern Asia to spread the Buddhist religion.

221 B.C. The Chinese begin building the Great Wall. Its main section is more than 2,000 miles long and is meant to keep invading peoples out.

202 B.C. The Han people of China win control of all of China.

A.D. 320 The Gupta Empire controls northern India. The Guptas, who are Hindus, drive the Buddhist religion out of India. They are well known for their many advances in mathematics and medicine.

618 The Tang dynasty begins in China. The Tang dynasty is well known for music, poetry, and painting. They export silk and porcelains as far away as Africa.

THE SILK ROAD Around 100 B.C., only the Chinese know how to make silk. To get this light, comfortable material, Europeans send fortunes in glass, gold, jade, and other items to China. The exchanges between Europeans and Chinese create one of the greatest trading routes in history—the Silk Road. Chinese inventions such as paper and gunpowder are also spread via the Silk Road. Europeans find out how to make silk around A.D. 500, but trade continues until about 1400.

960 The Northern Sung dynasty in China makes advances in banking and paper money. China's population of 50 million doubles over 200 years, thanks to improved ways of farming that lead to greater food production.

ASIA

1000 The Samurai, a warrior people, become powerful in Japan. They live by a code of honor known as *Bushido*.

1180 The Khmer Empire in Cambodia becomes widely known for its beautiful temples.

1206 The Mongol leader Genghis Khan creates an empire that stretches from China to India, Russia, and Eastern Europe. ▶

1264 Kublai Khan, grandson of Genghis Khan, rules China as emperor from his new capital at Beijing.

1368 The Ming dynasty comes to power in China and drives out the Mongols.

1526 The Mughal Empire in India begins under Babur. The Mughals are Muslims who invade and conquer India.

1644 The Ming dynasty in China is overthrown by the Manchu peoples.

1839 The Opium War takes place in China between the Chinese and the British. The British and other Western powers want to control trade in Asia. The Chinese want the British to stop selling opium to the Chinese. Britain wins the war in 1842.

1858 The French begin to take control of Indochina (Southeast Asia).

1868 In Japan, Emperor Meiji comes to power. Western ideas begin to influence the Japanese.

THE JAPANESE IN ASIA In the 1930s, Japan begins to invade some of its neighbors. In 1941, the United States and Japan go to war after Japan attacks the U.S. Navy base at Pearl Harbor, Hawaii.

◀ *Statues from Angkor Wat temple, Cambodia*

1945 Japan is defeated in World War II after the U.S. drops atomic bombs on the Japanese cities of Hiroshima and Nagasaki.

1947 India and Pakistan become independent from Great Britain.

1949 China comes under the rule of the Communists led by Mao Zedong, who abolishes private property and businesses. ▶

1950–1953 THE KOREAN WAR Communist North Korea invades South Korea. The U.S. and allies fight the invasion. China sides with North Korea. The fighting ends in a truce in 1953.

1954–1975 THE VIETNAM WAR The French are defeated in Indochina in 1954 by Vietnamese nationalists. The U.S. sends troops in 1965 to help South Vietnam fight against the Communists in the North. The U.S. withdraws in 1973. In 1975, South Vietnam is taken over by North Vietnam.

1989 Chinese students protest for democracy, but the protests are crushed by the army in Beijing's Tiananmen Square.

1997 Britain returns Hong Kong to China.

2004 A powerful earthquake in the Indian Ocean in December sets off huge waves (tsunamis) that kill more than 225,000 people in Indonesia, Sri Lanka, and other countries.

THE U.S. IN AFGHANISTAN U.S.-led military action overthrows the Taliban regime in Afghanistan in 2001 and seeks to root out terrorists there. In 2009 and 2010, the United States sends additional troops to Afghanistan to fight the Taliban, which had regained strength. The U.S. announces plans to start withdrawing troops in 2011.

2011 A massive earthquake and tsunami in March cause widespread destruction and thousands of deaths in northeastern Japan. A damaged nuclear power plant releases radiation into the air and ground.

ANCIENT EUROPE

▲Stonehenge

4000 B.C. People in Europe start building monuments out of large stones called megaliths, such as Stonehenge in England.

2500 B.C. –1200 B.C.
The Minoans and the Mycenaeans
- People on the island of Crete (Minoans) in the Mediterranean Sea build great palaces and become sailors and traders.
- People from Mycenae invade Crete and destroy the power of the Minoans.

THE TROJAN WAR
The Trojan War is a conflict between invading Greeks and the people of Troas (Troy) in Southwestern Turkey around 1200 B.C. Although little is known today about the real war, according to legend, a group of Greek soldiers hides inside a huge wooden horse. The horse is pulled into the city of Troy. Then the soldiers jump out and conquer Troy.

900–600 B.C. Celtic peoples in Northern Europe settle on farms and in villages and learn to mine for iron ore.

600 B.C. Etruscan peoples take over most of Italy. They build many cities and become traders.

SOME ACHIEVEMENTS OF THE GREEKS
The early Greeks are responsible for:
- the first governments that were elected by the people,
- great poets such as Homer, who composed the *Iliad* and the *Odyssey*,
- great thinkers such as Socrates, Plato, and Aristotle,
- great architecture, like the Parthenon and the Temple of Athena Nike on the Acropolis in Athens.

▲ Aristotle

431 B.C. The Peloponnesian Wars begin between the Greek cities of Athens and Sparta. The wars end in 404 B.C. when Sparta wins.

338 B.C. King Philip II of Macedonia in northern Greece conquers all of Greece.

336 B.C. Philip's son Alexander the Great becomes king. He makes an empire from the Mediterranean Sea to India. For the next 300 years, Greek culture dominates this vast area.

264 B.C. – A.D. 476 **THE ROMAN EMPIRE**
The city of Rome in Italy begins to expand and capture surrounding lands. The Romans gradually build a great empire and control all of the Mediterranean region. At its height, the Roman Empire includes Western Europe, Greece, Egypt, and much of the Middle East. It lasts until A.D. 476.

ROMAN ACHIEVEMENTS

- Roman law; many of our laws are based on Roman law.
- Great roads to connect their huge empire; the Appian Way, south of Rome, is a Roman road that is still in use today.
- Aqueducts to bring water to large cities.
- Great sculpture; Roman statues can still be seen in Europe.
- Great architecture; the Colosseum, which still stands in Rome today, is an example.
- Great writers, such as the poet Virgil, who wrote the *Aeneid*.

49 B.C. A civil war breaks out that destroys Rome's republican form of government.

45 B.C. Julius Caesar becomes the sole ruler of Rome but is murdered one year later by rivals.

▲ *Julius Caesar*

27 B.C. Octavian becomes the first emperor of Rome. He takes the name Augustus.

THE CHRISTIAN FAITH Christians believe that Jesus Christ is the Son of God. The history and beliefs of Christianity are found in the New Testament of the Bible. Christianity spreads slowly throughout the Roman Empire. The Romans try to stop the new religion, and they persecute Christians. Over time, however, more and more Romans become Christian.

▼ *The Colosseum, Rome*

THE BYZANTINE EMPIRE, centered in modern-day Turkey, is the eastern half of the old Roman Empire. Byzantine rulers extend their power into western Europe. Constantinople (now Istanbul, Turkey) becomes the capital of the Byzantine Empire in A.D. 330.

A.D. 313 The Roman Emperor Constantine gives full rights to Christians. He eventually becomes a Christian himself.

▲ *Constantine*

410 The Visigoths and other barbarian tribes from northern Europe invade the Roman Empire and begin to take over its lands.

476 The last Roman emperor, Romulus Augustus, is overthrown.

768 Charlemagne becomes king of the Franks in northern Europe. He rules a kingdom that includes parts of France, Germany, and northern Italy.

800 Feudalism becomes important in Europe. Feudalism means that poor farmers are allowed to farm a lord's land in return for certain services to the lord.

896 Magyar peoples found Hungary.

800s–900s Viking warriors and traders from Scandinavia begin to move into the British Isles, France, and parts of the Mediterranean.

989 The Russian state of Kiev becomes Christian.

EUROPE

◀ *Arc de Triomphe, Paris*

1066 William of Normandy, a Frenchman, successfully invades England and makes himself king. He is known as William the Conqueror.

1096–1291 **THE CRUSADES** Beginning in 1096, Christian leaders send a series of armies to try to capture Jerusalem from the Muslims. In the end, the Christians do not succeed. However, trade increases greatly between the Middle East and Europe.

▲ *King John*

1215 The Magna Carta is a document agreed to by King John of England and the English nobility. The English king agrees that he does not have absolute power and has to obey the laws of the land. The Magna Carta is an important step toward democracy.

1290 The Ottoman Empire begins. It is controlled by Turkish Muslims who conquer lands in the eastern Mediterranean and the Middle East.

1337 The Hundred Years' War begins in Europe between France and England. The war lasts until 1453 when France wins.

1348 The bubonic plague (Black Death) begins in Europe. As much as one-third of the whole population of Europe dies from this disease, caused by the bite of infected fleas.

1453 The Ottoman Turks capture the city of Constantinople and rename it Istanbul.

1517 **THE REFORMATION** The Protestant Reformation splits European Christians apart. It starts when German priest Martin Luther breaks away from the Roman Catholic pope.

▲ *Martin Luther*

1534 King Henry VIII of England breaks away from the Roman Catholic church. He names himself head of the English (Anglican) church.

1558 The reign of King Henry's daughter Elizabeth I begins in England.

1588 The Spanish Armada (fleet of warships) is defeated by the English Navy as Spain tries to invade England.

1600s The Ottoman Turks expand their empire through most of eastern and central Europe.

1618 Much of Europe is destroyed in the Thirty Years' War, which ends in 1648.

1642 The English Civil War begins. King Charles I fights against the forces of the Parliament. The king is defeated, and executed in 1649. His son, Charles II, returns as king in 1660.

1789 **THE FRENCH REVOLUTION** The French Revolution ends the rule of kings in France and leads to democracy there. At first, however, there are wars and times when dictators take control. Many people are executed. King Louis XVI and Queen Marie Antoinette are overthrown in the Revolution, and both are executed in 1793.

1762 Catherine the Great becomes Empress of Russia. She extends the Russian Empire.

1799 Napoleon Bonaparte, an army officer, becomes dictator of France. Under his rule, France conquers most of Europe by 1812.

1815 Napoleon's forces are defeated by the British and German armies at Waterloo (in Belgium). Napoleon is exiled to a remote island and dies there in 1821.

1848 Revolutions break out in countries of Europe. People force their rulers to make more democratic changes.

1914–1918 **WORLD WAR I IN EUROPE** At the start of World War I in Europe, Germany, Austria-Hungary, and the Ottoman Empire oppose Britain, France, Russia—later joined by the U.S. (the Allies). The Allies win in 1918.

▼*Tsar Nicholas II*

1917 The Tsar is overthrown in the Russian Revolution. The Bolsheviks (Communists) under Vladimir Lenin take control. Millions are starved, sent to labor camps, or executed under Joseph Stalin (1929–1953).

THE RISE OF HITLER

Adolf Hitler becomes dictator of Germany in 1933. He joins forces with rulers in Italy and Japan to form the Axis powers. In World War II (1939–1945), the Axis powers are defeated by the Allies—Great Britain, the Soviet Union, the U.S., and others. During his rule, Hitler's Nazis kill millions of Jews and other people in the Holocaust.

▲ *Italian leader Benito Mussolini and Adolf Hitler*

The 1990s Communist governments in Eastern Europe are replaced by democratic ones. Divided Germany is reunited, and the Soviet Union breaks up. The European Union (EU) forms. The North Atlantic Treaty Organization (NATO) bombs Yugoslavia to protect ethnic Albanians who are being driven out of the Kosovo region.

2009 Europe suffers through major economic recession, and unemployment surges.

2010–2011 Some countries' economies begin to improve, but others remain very weak. Ireland, Greece, and Portugal all receive financial aid from the European Union to help them pay their debts.

All About AUSTRALIA

Aborigines (native peoples) have lived there for more than 60,000 years. In the 17th century, Portuguese, Dutch, and Spanish expeditions explored Australian coasts. In the 1770s, Capt. James Cook of Britain made three voyages to the continent, cementing Britain's claims of ownership. On May 13, 1787, Capt. Arthur Phillip brought 11 ships from Britain, carrying convicts and guards. Although the first communities were prison colonies, other immigrants settled around the continent over the 19th century. Wool and mining were major industries. Australia was established as a commonwealth of Great Britain on January 1, 1901. Today, it is a country of almost 22 million people. It is famous for such animals as kangaroos and koalas. The Sydney Opera House is a world-famous landmark.

Sydney Opera House ▶

THE AMERICAS

Chac Mool, Mayan Figure ▶

10,000–8000 B.C. People in North and South America gather plants for food and hunt animals using stone-pointed spears.

Around 3000 B.C. People in Central America begin farming, growing corn and beans for food.

1500 B.C. Mayan people in Central America begin to live in small villages.

500 B.C. People in North America begin to hunt buffalo to use for meat and for clothing.

100 B.C. The city of Teotihuacán is founded in Mexico. It becomes the center of a huge empire extending from central Mexico to Guatemala. Teotihuacán contains many large pyramids and temples.

A.D. 150 Mayan people in Guatemala build many centers for religious ceremonies. They create a calendar and learn mathematics and astronomy.

900 Toltec warriors in Mexico begin to invade lands of Mayan people. Mayans leave their old cities and move to the Yucatan Peninsula of Mexico.

1000 Native Americans in the southwestern United States begin to live in settlements called pueblos. They learn to farm.

1325 Mexican Indians known as Aztecs create the huge city of Tenochtitlán and rule a large empire in Mexico. They are warriors who practice human sacrifice.

1492 Christopher Columbus sails from Europe across the Atlantic Ocean and lands in the Bahamas, in the Caribbean Sea. This marks the first step toward the founding of European settlements in the Americas.

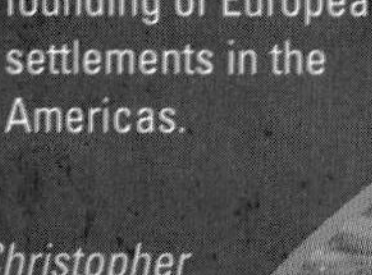

Christopher Columbus ▶

1500 Portuguese explorers reach Brazil and claim it for Portugal.

1519 Spanish conqueror Hernán Cortés travels into the Aztec Empire in search of gold. The Aztecs are defeated in 1521, and Spain takes control of Mexico. ▶

WHY DID THE SPANISH WIN? How did the Spanish defeat the powerful Aztec Empire? One reason is that the Spanish had better weapons. Another is that many Aztecs died from diseases brought to the New World by the Spanish. Also, many neighboring Indians hated the Aztecs as conquerors and helped the Spanish.

1534 Jacques Cartier of France explores Canada.

1583 The first English colony in Canada is set up in Newfoundland.

1607 English colonists led by Captain John Smith settle in Jamestown, Virginia. Virginia becomes the oldest of the thirteen colonies that will form the United States.

1619 First African slaves arrive in English-controlled America.

1682 The French explorer René-Robert Cavelier, sieur de La Salle, sails down the Mississippi River. The area is named Louisiana after the French King Louis XIV.

THE AMERICAS

EUROPEAN COLONIES By 1700, most of the Americas are under the control of Europeans.

Spain: Florida, southwestern United States, Mexico, Central America, western South America

Portugal: eastern South America

France: central United States, parts of Canada

England: eastern U.S., parts of Canada

Holland: West Indies, eastern South America

1700s European colonies in North and South America grow in population and wealth.

1775–1783 **AMERICAN REVOLUTION** The American Revolution begins in 1775 when the first shot is fired in Lexington, Massachusetts. The thirteen British colonies that become the United States officially gain independence in 1783.

SIMÓN BOLÍVAR: LIBERATOR OF SOUTH AMERICA

In 1810, Simón Bolívar begins a revolt against Spain. He becomes president of the independent country of Greater Colombia in 1824. As a result of his leadership, nine South American countries gain their independence from Spain by 1830.

1846–1848 **MEXICAN-AMERICAN WAR** In 1846, Mexico and the United States go to war. Mexico loses parts of the Southwest and California to the U.S.

1911 A revolution in Mexico that began in 1910 overthrows Porfirio Díaz. ▼

Becoming Independent

Most countries of Latin America gained independence from Spain in the early 1800s. Others weren't liberated until much later.

COUNTRY	YEAR OF INDEPENDENCE
Argentina	1816
Bolivia	1825
Brazil	1822[1]
Chile	1818
Colombia	1819
Ecuador	1822
Guyana	1966[2]
Mexico	1821
Paraguay	1811
Peru	1824
Suriname	1975[3]
Uruguay	1825
Venezuela	1821

(1) From Portugal. (2) From Britain. (3) From the Netherlands.

1867 The Canadian provinces are united as the Dominion of Canada.

1898 **SPANISH-AMERICAN WAR** Spain and the U.S. fight a brief war in 1898. Spain loses its colonies Cuba, Puerto Rico, and the Philippines.

1959 Fidel Castro becomes president of Cuba, which becomes a Communist country allied with the Soviet Union.

1962 U.S. President John F. Kennedy forces the Soviet Union to withdraw missiles it had installed in Cuba.

1994 The North American Free Trade Agreement (NAFTA) increases trade between the U.S., Canada, and Mexico.

2001 On 9/11, Muslim terrorists crash planes into U.S. targets, killing about 3,000 people; the U.S. launches a "war on terrorism."

2009 Barack Obama becomes the first African American president of the U.S.

2010 About 230,000 people are killed in a devastating earthquake in Haiti.

2011 U.S. Navy Seals enter a compound in Pakistan and kill Osama bin Laden, who was behind the 9/11 terrorist attack on the U.S.

THEN & NOW 2012

10 Years Ago—2002

Then: The 2002 Winter Olympics are held in Salt Lake City, Utah.

Now: London, U.K., prepares to host the 2012 Summer Olympics.

U.S. figure skater Sarah Hughes at the 2002 Winter Olympics

Then: Euro notes and coins replace all other currency in 12 European Union countries.

Now: The euro is now the currency in 17 European Union nations and 6 other countries as well. More than 325 million people use this currency every day.

50 Years Ago—1962

Then: Nelson Mandela, leader of the opposition to white-minority rule in South Africa, is jailed by the South African government.

Now: Mandela is awarded the 1993 Nobel Peace Prize, and he serves as South Africa's first black president from 1994 to 1999. He continues to speak out for human rights.

Then: During the Cold War, the Cuban missile crisis takes place after the U.S. discovers that the Soviet Union has installed missiles in Cuba. Experts say it was the closest the world ever came to nuclear war.

Now: After the collapse of Communism in Eastern Europe, the Soviet Union officially dissolves in 1991. Cuba remains one of the world's few Communist nations.

100 Years Ago—1912

Ship's bell from the Titanic

Then: New Mexico and Arizona are admitted as the 47th and 48th U.S. states.

Now: Arizona is the country's second-fastest-growing state, after Nevada. New Mexico's population has more than doubled in the past 50 years.

Then: The British ocean liner RMS *Titanic* strikes an iceberg and sinks. More than 1,500 people lose their lives.

Now: In 1985, underwater explorers find the wreck of the *Titanic*. An exhibition of artifacts from the ship travels the world. James Cameron's blockbuster movie *Titanic* is set to release in a 3-D version.

500 Years Ago—1512

The Italian sculptor and painter Michelangelo completes work on the Sistine Chapel ceiling in Rome's Vatican Palace. These religious paintings are considered among the greatest in the world. Today, millions of tourists visit the site every year.

THEN & NOW 2013

10 Years Ago—2003

Then: An invasion of Iraq, led by the U.S. and Britain, topples Saddam Hussein's government in three weeks.

Now: About 47,000 U.S. troops, in Iraq to help maintain security, prepare to withdraw from the war-torn country.

Then: The space shuttle *Columbia* explodes, killing all seven crew members.

Now: NASA, citing the high operation costs, plans to retire the 30-year-old space shuttle program.

50 Years Ago—1963

Then: Civil rights leader Martin Luther King Jr. helps organize the March on Washington. At the event, attended by some 250,000 people, he gives his famous "I Have a Dream" speech (right) about the goal of equal treatment and opportunity.

Now: On the 48th anniversary of the March on Washington, the Martin Luther King Jr. National Memorial, including a 30-foot statue of King, is officially dedicated in Washington, D.C.

Then: John F. Kennedy, the 35th U.S. president, is shot and killed by an assassin in Dallas, Texas.

Now: The JFK Library and Museum in Boston, Massachusetts, unveils the nation's largest online presidential archives, 50 years after Kennedy's inauguration.

100 Years Ago—1913

Then: Henry Ford develops his moving assembly line (right), which produces the popular Model T car. More than 15 million of the so-called Tin Lizzies are sold before their production ends in 1927.

Now: Based on vehicle sales, the Ford Motor Company is the fifth-largest automaker in the world.

Then: The 16th and 17th amendments to the U.S. Constitution are ratified. The 16th amendment allows the U.S. government to collect income tax, and the 17th amendment requires the popular election of U.S. senators.

Now: The Constitution has a total of 27 amendments, including those guaranteeing women the right to vote and lowering the voting age to 18.

500 Years Ago—1513

Explorer Juan Ponce de León sails from Puerto Rico in search of gold and a "fountain of youth." He lands near today's Saint Augustine and claims what is now Florida for Spain. In honor of the 500th anniversary of his landing, the Spain-Florida Foundation announces an annual Juan Ponce de León Award for promoting understanding of the Hispanic community in the United States.

WOMEN in History

The following women played important roles in shaping history and made major contributions to human knowledge and culture.

CLEOPATRA (69–30 B.C.), queen of Egypt who used her association with Roman leaders Julius Caesar and Mark Antony to increase her power. After her father's death, Cleopatra, at the age of about 17, and her 12-year-old brother Ptolemy jointly ruled. By custom, they were forced to marry each other. A few years later, she was sent away but came back to rule when Caesar defeated her enemies. For a time, she lived with Caesar in Rome until his assassination in 44 B.C. She later went back to Egypt, where she met and married Antony.

QUEEN ELIZABETH I (1533–1603), one of the greatest rulers of England. She was the daughter of King Henry VIII and his second wife, Anne Boleyn. Elizabeth became queen at the age of 25 in 1558 and ruled for 45 years, until her death. She built England into a world power, especially after her navy's victory in 1588 over the Spanish Armada, an invasion force sent by Spain's king, Philip II. Elizabeth never married, and she used the possibility of marriage to play off her many suitors against each other, increasing her political power. During Elizabeth's reign, the arts flourished, and some of England's greatest works of literature, including the plays of William Shakespeare, were created.

CATHERINE THE GREAT (1729–1796), empress of Russia (1762–1796). Catherine made Russia a European power and greatly expanded the territory of the Russian Empire. She raised the status of the nobles by granting them privileges such as freedom from military service and legal control over their serfs. She promoted culture, as well as the education of women and religious tolerance.

JANE AUSTEN (1775–1817), English author whose works remain as popular today as when they were written 200 years ago. Her six novels focus on the daily lives of families in small, rural villages and gently mock social conventions. Austen began writing stories as a young child. As an adult, she traveled very little and disliked large cities. Four of her books, including her most famous, *Pride and Prejudice*, were published in her lifetime (without her name on them, since it was not acceptable for a woman to be an author). All her books have been made into movies, some many times.

SOJOURNER TRUTH (c. 1797–1883), abolitionist and women's rights activist (born Isabella Baumfree). She was raised as a slave on an estate in upstate New York. She escaped in 1826. In 1843, she became a traveling preacher and took the name Sojourner Truth. She traveled widely, speaking out against slavery and for women's rights. Her famous speech, "Ain't I a Woman?" was about how women were as smart and strong as men.

ELIZABETH BLACKWELL (1821–1910), first woman to receive a degree from a medical school in the United States. At first she couldn't find a medical school that would accept her, but finally she did—and she graduated first in her class. She later trained nurses during the Civil War and founded the New York Infirmary for Women and Children. She also started a medical school for women. Blackwell eventually moved back to England, where she had been born.

RACHEL CARSON

(1907–1964), scientist and author. She is often credited with launching the modern environmental movement with the publication of her book *Silent Spring* (1962), about the dangers of pesticides. She grew up in rural Pennsylvania and came to love nature at an early age. Carson worked for many years as a scientist with the U.S. Fish and Wildlife Service. After *Silent Spring* appeared, she was a target of much criticism from the chemical industry and some politicians, but she never wavered in her conviction that protecting the environment was essential.

ANNE FRANK

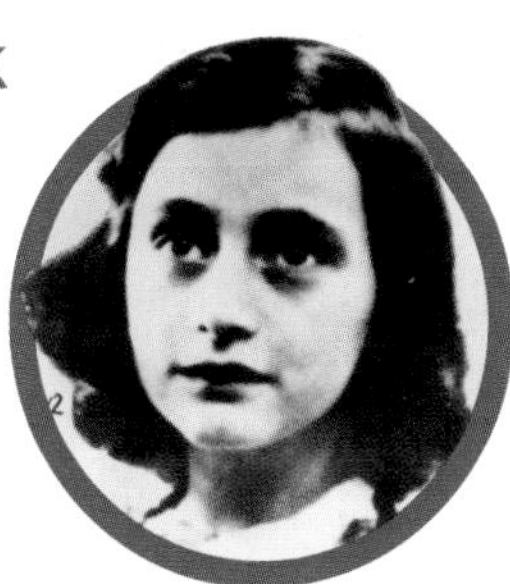

(1929–1945), German-born Jewish girl. Her diary of her family's two years in hiding—in the back rooms of an Amsterdam office building—during the German occupation of the Netherlands in World War II became a worldwide classic in literature. The Gestapo arrested the occupants of the secret annex after acting on a tip. Frank died in the Bergen-Belsen concentration camp in 1945. Her diary was saved by office worker Miep Gies. Published in 1947 as *Het Achterhuis* (The House Behind), it appeared in the U.S. in 1952 as *Anne Frank: The Diary of a Young Girl.*

TONI MORRISON (born 1931), distinguished writer, editor, teacher, and critic. She has won the National Book Critics Award, the Pulitzer Prize for fiction (for the novel *Beloved*), the American Book Award, and the Nobel Prize for literature. Morrison's books focus on the brutality of African-American slavery, the lives of black women, and the emotional ties that bind families together.

VALENTINA TERESHKOVA

(born 1937), Russian cosmonaut and the first woman in space. During her 3-day spaceflight in June 1963 aboard the *Vostok 6,* she orbited Earth 48 times. Five months later, she married cosmonaut Andrian Nikolayev. In 1964, she gave birth to a daughter, the first child born to parents who had both flown in space.

BILLIE JEAN KING

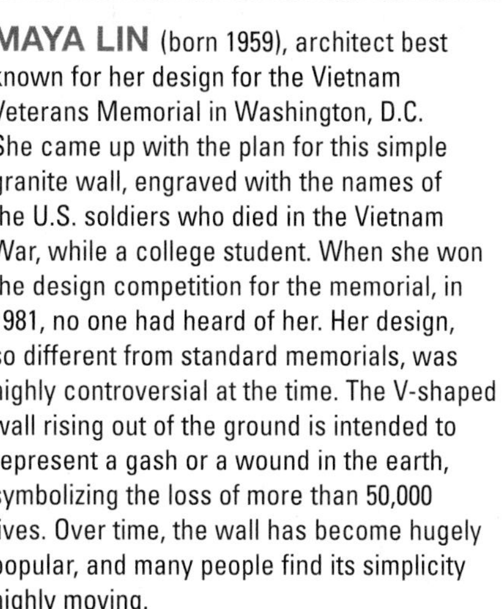

(born 1943), tennis player who became a symbol for women's equality. King won 12 Grand Slam singles titles. But her most famous victory may have been in the 1973 "Battle of the Sexes" match, when she beat male player Bobby Riggs in three straight sets. King helped start the first women's pro tennis tour in 1970. In 1971, she became the first woman athlete to win more than $100,000 in one season.

MAYA LIN (born 1959), architect best known for her design for the Vietnam Veterans Memorial in Washington, D.C. She came up with the plan for this simple granite wall, engraved with the names of the U.S. soldiers who died in the Vietnam War, while a college student. When she won the design competition for the memorial, in 1981, no one had heard of her. Her design, so different from standard memorials, was highly controversial at the time. The V-shaped wall rising out of the ground is intended to represent a gash or a wound in the earth, symbolizing the loss of more than 50,000 lives. Over time, the wall has become hugely popular, and many people find its simplicity highly moving.

ANSWERS

Animals Word Scramble p. 31

snow leopard
manatee
black rhino
orangutan
Siberian tiger
Komodo dragon

Celebrity Crossword Puzzle p. 43

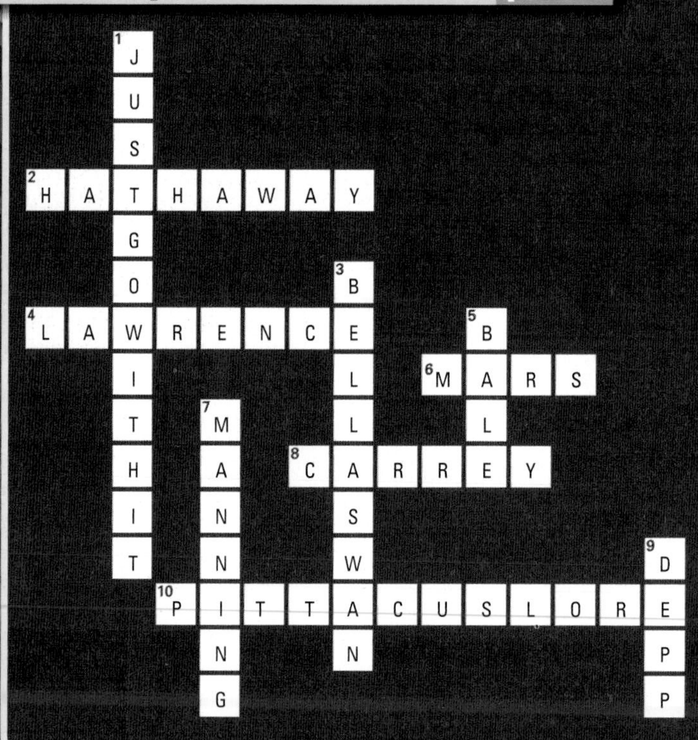

Building Quiz p. 54

Guggenheim Museum	Building shaped like a ship
30 St. Mary Axe	Building that looks like a pickle
Burj Khalifa	**Tallest building in the world**
El Castillo	Ancient pyramid that served as a calendar

Movies & TV Word Search p. 131

T	A	V	S	O	Z	X	X	X	O	R	D	V	K	S
A	U	U	X	G	W	I	Q	K	S	B	U	A	E	I
M	R	O	H	S	K	R	K	H	F	V	Z	N	H	I
E	A	E	E	A	T	E	L	A	T	A	V	F	S	N
R	T	K	P	P	R	O	M	E	S	P	I	L	C	E
I	A	E	H	H	I	I	Q	O	D	W	V	M	D	T
C	V	W	S	M	L	W	U	V	R	G	G	N	N	G
A	A	Z	I	Y	L	Q	T	P	B	V	E	L	L	Z
N	B	F	G	J	B	K	R	T	S	I	E	H	C	Q
I	I	U	M	X	C	T	X	I	L	Q	M	P	M	P
D	Y	I	W	J	D	R	L	C	W	G	L	E	E	Z
O	F	D	E	I	Z	V	E	A	F	D	M	Y	Y	B
L	R	N	X	J	L	M	O	R	L	G	F	L	V	A
H	B	O	N	F	Q	F	L	L	C	B	P	N	O	I
Z	C	N	O	K	W	O	P	Y	S	A	L	A	O	G

Roman Numerals p. 179

Super Bowl XLV was the 45th Super Bowl.

2011 = MMXI

Super Bowl XI (11) was played in 1977.

Homework Tip: Decimals to Fractions p. 180

0.4 = 2/5 0.75 = 3/4 0.9 = 9/10

Go Figure p. 181

			1 S	E	V	E	N	2 T	E	3 E	N	
4 N	I	N	E					W		I		
			V					5 E	I	G	H	6 T
7 F	I	V	E					N		H		W
			N		8 F	I	F	T	Y	T	W	O
								Y		Y		
9 F		10 F					11 T			O		
I		O		12 E		13 S	E	V	E	N	T	Y
F		U		L			N			E		
14 T	H	R	E	E								
E				V				15 Z	E	R	16 O	
E				E							N	
N			17 O	N	E	H	U	N	D	R	E	D

Sports Star Spiral p. 239

The answers are:

1. Johnson, 2. Newton, 3. Nadal, 4. Lincecum, 5. Mirra, 6. Adams, 7. Sedin, 8. Nicklaus, 9. Sanders

1 J	O	H	N	S	O	2 N
I	R	R	6 A	D	A	E
5 M	A	U	9 S	A	M	W
U	L	S		N	7 S	T
C	K	R	E	D	E	O
E	C	I	8 N	I	D	3 N
C	N	I	4 L	A	D	A

Championship Word Search p. 239

S	E	I	G	U	S	K	I	E	S
S	I	J	O	Q	D	Z	V	B	T
E	H	U	S	K	I	E	S	O	E
I	O	Y	E	R	P	L	E	C	G
G	I	A	N	F	A	M	S	K	G
G	O	L	D	P	R	I	D	E	I
A	W	P	K	O	R	P	A	R	E
I	A	C	T	I	G	E	R	S	S
R	A	S	T	N	A	I	G	U	X
P	S	R	E	K	C	A	P	S	H

INDEX

Note: Words in **boldface** refer to key content sections. Page numbers in **boldface** refer to maps.

O

P

T

U

V

W

Z

PHOTO CREDITS

FRONT COVER: AP Images: Charles Sykes (Greyson Chance); Getty Images: Victor Decolongon (Marta); Rick Diamond (Taylor Swift); Newscom: imago stock@people (iPhone); se4/ZUMA Press (Ryan Sheckler). **BACK COVER:** Newscom: Ron Asadorian/Splash News (Glee); Louis Lopez/Cal Sport Media (Kevin Durant); WUF/Splash News (royal wedding). **INTERIOR: Courtesy of Simon Alexander,** 33. **Courtesy of Apple Inc.**: 3, 112 (iPhone). **AP Images:** 22 (hippo & tortoise), 65 (Ponzi), 331 (King), 333 (Frank); Jim Mone, 3, 35 (Oldenburg); Cody Duty, 4, 186 (new citizens); Sipa, 6 (Egypt), 41 (Smith); Time Magazine, 7 (Bin Laden cover); Charles Dharapak, 8 (Boehner); Charlie Riedel, 9 (Joplin), 20 (Rowe); Frank Micelotta/Fox/PictureGroup, 10 (*American Idol*); Mark Davis/PictureGroup, 17 (Lady Antebellum); Tom DiPace, 18 (Rodgers); The Canadian Press, Darryl Dyck, 19 (Tim Thomas), 233 (Sedin brothers); David J. Phillip, 21 (Nowitzki); Evan Agostini, 40 (Tisdale); Gregg DeGuire/PictureGroup, 88 (Wasikowska); Michelle McLoughlin, 95 (Ballard); Kevin P. Casey, 124 (Gates); Imaginechina, 124 (Yang); Douglas C. Pizac, 124 (Brin); Mark J. Terrill, 128 (Academy Awards); Ray Mickshaw/Fox/PictureGroup, 132 (McCreery); Peter Kramer/NBCUniversal, Inc., 133 (Adele); Sayyid Azim, 139 (Sudanese voters); Jacquelyn Martin, 184 (census); Kyodo, 188 (Liu), 224 (2010 World Series), 234 (2010 World Cup); Frank Micelotta/Fox/PictureGroup, 189 (Black, Vonn); Frank Gunn, CP, 221 (Vonn); Terry Renna, 223 (Johnson); Darron Cummings, 223 (Wheldon); Alan Diaz, 225 (Expos); Elaine Thompson, 227 (Jackson); Eric Gay, 228 (Walker); Jessica Hill, 228 (Moore); Chris Carlson, 229 (Byrum); David Drapkin, 230 (Brady); Jason DeCrow, 231 (Newton); Sakchai Lalit, 232 (Tseng); Matt Dunham, 232 (Uchimura); Tony Gutierrez, 235 (Ferreira); Press Association, 237 (Williams sisters); Marcy Nighswander, 274 (Socks); ITAR-TASS, 333 (Tereshkova); Harry Harris, 333 (King). **The Bridgeman Art Library International:** *The Lady with the Ermine* (Cecilia Gallerani), 1496 (oil on walnut panel), Vinci, Leonardo da (1452–1519)/© Czartoryski Museum, Cracow, Poland, 35; *White Nenuphars,* 1899, Monet, Claude (1840–1926)/Pushkin Museum, Moscow, Russia, 35. **Timothy Bryk:** 314 (1 yard). **Jimmy Carter Library and Museum:** 319 (1979 peace treaty). **© 2009 The Children's Museum of Indianapolis, Inc.:** 251, (Egypt). **EA Mobile:** 90 (Tetris); 91 (Madden NFL 2012). **Gregg M. Erickson,** 73 (Coulee). **Courtesy of Meredith Evans:** 89. **Courtesy of the Everett Collection:** Peter Mountain/©Walt Disney Pictures, 3, 15 (*Pirates of the Caribbean: On Stranger Tides*); Adam Rose/© Fox, 11 (*Glee*); Bob Mahoney/© The CW, 11 (*The Vampire Diaries*); Francois Duhamel/©Warner Bros. Pictures, 12 (*Green Lantern*); Jaap Buitendjik/©Warner Bros. Pictures, 12, 131 (*Harry Potter and the Deathly Hallows Part 2*); Diyah Pera/TM and ©copyright Twentieth Century Fox Film Corporation. All rights reserved, 13 (*Diary of a Wimpy Kid: Rodrick Rules*); Industrial Light & Magic/©Paramount Pictures, 13 (*Rango*); ©Walt Disney Studios Motion Pictures, 14 (*Gnomeo & Juliet*); Mario Perez/©TriStar Pictures, 14 (*Soul Surfer*); Tracy Bennett/©Columbia Pictures, 15 (*Just Go With It*); Giovanni Rufino/© The CW, 87 (*Gossip Girl*); ©Warner Bros, 129 (*The Dark Knight*); 20th Century Fox, 130 (*Mr. Popper's Penguins*); John Bramley/©Walt Disney Pictures, 130 (*I Am Number Four*). **Getty Images:** Cavan Images, 3, 49 (man reading e-book); *The New York Daily News,* 3, 64 (crime scene); Fairfax Media, 3, 66 (New Zealand earthquake); Frank A. Cezus, 3, 87 (disco dancers); Dennis Hallinan/Archive Photos, 3, 91 (*PacMan*); Hans Neleman, 4, 134 (dancers); PAUL ELLIS/AFP, 7 (royal wedding); Richard Ellis, 9 (Civil War); Karen Neal/ABC, 10 (*Modern Family*); Michael Caulfield/WireImage, 16

(Perry); Danny Martindale/FilmMagic, 16 (Lady Gaga); Marc Grimwade/WireImage, 17 (Bieber); Michael Heiman, 18 (Jeter); Getty Images Sports, 19 (Adams); Al Bello, 20 (Clijsters); Patrick Farrell/Miami Herald/MCT, 21 (Johnson); Peter Macdiarmid, 22 (Komodo dragon); Joseph Van Os, 31 (rhino); Andy Lyons, 38 (Manning); Ferdaus Shamim/WireImage, 39 (Lewis); Larry Busacca/Getty Images for GLAAD, 39 (Fey); Michael Ochs Archives, 40 (Charles); FilmMagic, 45 (Meyers); Gandee Vasan, 49 (girl reading e-book); Eugene Gologursky/WireImage, 65 (Abagnale); JIJI PRESS/AFP, 67 (Japan tsunami); David McNew, 78 (bags); Gustavo Caballero/WireImage, 88 (Klein); Justin Sullivan, 124 (Zuckerberg); Jordan Strauss/FilmMagic, 130 (Twilight cast); Jeff Kravitz/FilmMagic, 132 (Eminem); Kevin Mazur/WireImage, 133 (Mars); Adam Taylor/Disney ABC, 134 (*Dancing With the Stars*); Alvis Upitis, 135 (orchestra); Kevin C. Cox, 179 (Super Bowl), 232 (sledge hockey); Bryan Bedder, 205 (Tyson); GIANLUIGI GUERCIA/AFP, 217 (cricket); XINHUA/Gamma-Rapho, 218 (stadium); Mark Dadswell, 219 (Youth Olympics); AFP PHOTO/JAVIER SORIANO , 220 (Bjørgen); Cameron Spencer, 221 (White); Joe Robbins, 224 (Fenway); Mike Ehrmann, 226 (Nowitzki); Michael Zagaris, 230 (Rodgers); Nelson Antoine/FotoArena/LatinContent, 235 (Marta); Julian Finney, 236 (Nadal); Doug Pensinger, 238 (Jacobellis); Jeff Gross, 238 (Mirra); Chip Somodevilla, 250 (Saturn V), 261 (Supreme Court); Nikki Kahn/The Washington Post, 263 (Obama); Jeff Swenson, 265 (voters); Cynthia Johnson/Time & Life Pictures, 286 (Marshall); NICOLAS ASFOURI/AFP, 330 (*Titanic*); Hulton Archive, 331 (Model T); The Bridgeman Art Library, 332 (Elizabeth I); Alfred Eisenstaedt/Time Life Pictures, 333 (Carson). **Courtesy of Jenifer Glynn:** 205 (Franklin). **Courtesy of Christian Hanna:** 311. **HarperCollins**: *Justin Bieber: First Step 2 Forever–My Story,* 47. **HarperCollins Children's Books:** *Gettysburg: The Graphic Novel,* by C. M. Butzer, 47. **Houghton Mifflin Harcourt:** *The Day of the Pelican,* by Katherine Paterson, Clarion Books, 46. **Courtesy of Infobase Publishing:** *World Almanac for Kids 2012,* 47. **International Astronomical Union:** Martin Kornmesser, 206 (star and planets). **Dusso Janladde:** 249 (Kingda Ka). **The Kansas City Public Library:** Mike Sinclair, 52 (Kansas City library). **John F. Kennedy Library:** 274 (Kennedy). **Russell Knightly Media:** 203 (mimivirus). **Library of Congress:** 269-272 (U.S. presidents, Washington–Clinton); LOC LC-DIG-ppmsc-01269, 38 (King); LC-DIG-ppmsca-19301, 38 (Lincoln); LC-USZ61-452, 41 (Alcott); LC-USZ62-108565, 41 (Barton); LC-USZ62-69629, 51 (early skyscraper); POS-TH-STO, no. 8, 86 (Edwardian clothing); LC-USZ62-71723, 86 (flapper); LC-USW361-109, 86 (woman working on bomber); LC-USZ62-17372, 94 (Lewis & Clark); LC-USZC4-7503, 95 (Henson); LC-USZC4-2737, 120 (Revolution); LC-USZC4-6893, 120 (War of 1812); LC-B8184-10086, 120 (Civil War); LC-USZC4-3933, 120 (Spanish-American War); LC-USZC4-3859, 121 (World War I); LC-USZC4-3266, 245 (stagecoach); LC-USZ62-43058, 245 (balloon); LC-D4-22602, 245 (Fulton steamboat); LC-USZ62-6166A, 246 (Wright plane); LC-USZ62-56782, 273 (Adams); LC-DIG-hec-00962, 273 (Madison); LC-USZ62-15325, 273 (Lincoln); LC-USZ62-25792, 273 (Hayes); LC-G432-0932, 273 (Wilson); LOC LC-DIG-pga-02388, 280 (Columbus); LOC LC-USZC2-2004, 280 (Franklin); LOC LC-USZC4-12217, 280 (New Amsterdam); LC-H8-CT-C01-063-E, 281 (Declaration of Independence); LC-USZC4-6127, 282 (Buena Vista); LC-USZC2-3796, 283 (War of 1812); LC-DIG-stereo-1s00612, 283 (train); LC-DIG-pga-02502, 283 (Emancipation); LC-USZ62-86846, 285 (O'Connor); LC-USZ62-109426, 287 (Parks); LC-USZC4-6895, 326 (Luther); LC-DIG-hec-04921, 327 (Nicholas); LC-DIG-pga-00710, 328 (Columbus); LC-USZ62-47764, 328 (Cortes); LC-USZ62-100275, 329 (Diaz). **Naismith Basketball Hall of Fame:** 226. **NASA:** 40 (Armstrong), 112 (Goddard), 207 (Sun), 214 (X-37B), 284 (man on Moon); NRDC, 81 (ice cap); GSFC, 81 (solar rays); JPL/GSFC/Ames, 207 (Saturn rings); JPL, 211 (Moon); Johns Hopkins University Applied Physics Laboratory/Southwest Research Institute, 212 (New Horizon); JPL-Caltech/University of Arizona, 212 (Phoenix Lander); JPL-Caltech, 214 (Mars Rover), 215 (Siding Spring comet); Space Telescope Science Institute, 215 (M100); JSC, 247 (shuttle). **National Archives:** 256 (Constitution), 275 (code talkers), 282 (Constitutional Convention), 284 (segregation); Army Signal Corps Collection, 121 (D-Day); Collection of Foreign Records Seized, 327 (Hitler & Mussolini). **NOAA:** 70 (tornado). **Naval Air Engineering Station, Lakehurst:** 71 (*Hindenburg*). **Newscom:** Tim Sloan/AFP/Getty Images, 3, 100 (Obama); Mark Ralston/AFP/Getty Images, 4, 217 (Griffin); UPI/David Banks, 8 (Wisconsin); Photo Take Medical, 25 (tapeworm), 32 (tubeworm); dbcstock, 32 (fangtooth); Random House, 45 (Paolini); WENN, 45

(Rowling); Chris Martinez/La Opinion, 64 (forensics); Richard B. Levine, 79 (phone collection); Ahmad Elatab–Saleem Elatab/Splash News, 88 (Jay-Z); Staff/MCT, 219 (Olympic logo); Robin Alam/Icon SMI 164, 234 (Wambach); Stock Connection, 250 (*T-rex*); OE Rimkus Jr./MIAMI HERALD, 330 (Hughes). **Jerry Newton Photography–Reno, NV:** 191 (wool). **Nuclear Regulatory Commission:** 74 (nuclear plant). **Oakland Museum of California:** Andrew J. Russell Collection, 246 (Model T). **Penguin Books:** *The House With the Clock in Its Walls* by John Bellairs, illustrated by Edward Gorey. Used courtesy of Penguin Books for Young Readers, 46. **Photofest:** © ABC Photographer: Jeff Samaripa, 129 (*Wipeout*); **Random House, Inc.:** "Book Cover," copyright © 2010 by Delacorte Kids, from MOON OVER MANIFEST by Clare Vanderpool. Used by permission of Delacorte Press, an imprint of Random House Children's Books, a division of Random House, Inc., 44; "Book Cover," copyright © 2010 by Random House Children's Books, from TURTLE IN PARADISE by Jennifer L. Holm. Used by permission of Random House Children's Books, a division of Random House, Inc., 44; "Book Cover," copyright © 2010 by Knopf Children, from HOOT by Carl Hiassen. Used by permission of Knopf Children, an imprint of Random House Children's Books, a division of Random House, Inc., 46. **Ronald Reagan Presidential Library:** 274 (Reagan). **Courtesy of Chris Robley:** 243. **Franklin D. Roosevelt Library:** 273 (Roosevelt). **Martin Rowe:** 188 (Maathai). **Courtesy of Dan Sabia:** 77. **David Shankbone:** 51 (Chrysler Building). **Scholastic, Inc.:** *The Hunger Games,* by Suzanne Collins, 46. **ShurTech Brands, LLC:** 191 (duct tape). **Edward A. Thomas:** 318 (Hieroglyphics). **Tuskegee University Archives/ Museum:** 205 (Carver). **UN Photo/Mark Garten:** 321 (Johnson-Sirleaf). **U.S. Air Force:** 4, 121 (A-10A); Airman 1st Class Laura Goodgame, 122 (Afghanistan); Senior Airman Perry Aston (Iraq); Senior Airman Joshua Stran, 204 (aurora). **U.S. Army:** Staff Sgt. Helen Miller, 263 (Biden). **USDA:** 101 (food plate). **U.S. Department of Energy:** 287 (Chu). **U.S. Marine Corps:** Cpl. Erin Kirk-Cuomo, 262 (Obama). **U.S. Mint:** 4 (Vicksburg quarter), 125 (presidential dollar coins, state quarters). **U.S. Navy:** Chief Petty Officer Daniel Sanfo, 6 (Japan earthquake); Mass Communication Specialist 2nd Class Aaron M. Pineda, 123 (Japan relief); Photographer's Mate 2nd Class Jim Watson, 285 (9/11); Mass Communication Specialist 3rd Class Jonathan Sunderman, 285 (Libya). **© 2008 The United States Treasury Bureau of Engraving and Printing:** 126 (dollar bill). **University of Oklahoma Libraries:** courtesy of History of Science Collections, 203 (van Leeuwenhoek). **Visuals Unlimited, Inc.:** Wim van Egmond, 203 (amoebas). **Courtesy of Michael Waters:** 197 (Buttermilk Creek dig). **Courtesy of Tammy West:** 37. **The White House:** 262 (Biden), 272 (G. W. Bush), 272 (Obama), 274 (Obama); Pete Souza, 7 (cabinet); Lawrence Jackson, 259 (Congress); Chuck Kennedy, 274 (Bo). **Courtesy of Glennita Williams:** 311. **Courtesy of Rujul Zaparde:** 311.

THE WORLD ALMANAC FOR KIDS 2012

#1 for Facts and Fun

Amazing facts fill every page of *The World Almanac for Kids*. Here are just a few...

Which animal can run faster, a rabbit or a giraffe? see page 26

About how many people in the world speak Spanish? see page 114

Who was named the NBA Rookie of the Year in 2011? see page 217

Which U.S. president's family kept a pygmy hippo as a pet? see page 274

How many of the country's ten largest cities are in Texas? see page 185

What TV show is the most watched among kids? see page 129

What month is Cell Phone Courtesy Month? see page 60

What famous baseball stadium celebrates its 100th birthday in 2012? see page 224

When did San Francisco's famous cable cars begin running? see page 246

What's the coldest temperature ever recorded in the United States? see page 313